OTHER BOOKS BY JIM BERKENSTADT

NEVERMIND NIRVANA

by Jim Berkenstadt and Charles R. Cross

BLACK MARKET BEATLES: THE STORY BEHIND THEIR LOST RECORDINGS

by Jim Berkenstadt and Belmo

THE BEATLES DIGEST

by J.G. Schuberk (aka Jim Berkenstadt) and others

JOHN, PAUL & ME BEFORE THE BEATLES

by Len Garry

Edited by Jim Berkenstadt

SCOTTY MOORE: THE GUITAR THAT ROCKED THE WORLD

by Scotty Moore, Jim Berkenstadt and Ron Lovely

TBA

THE BEATLE WHO VANISHED

Jim Berkenstadt

**ROCK AND ROLL DETECTIVE® PUBLISHING,
A DIVISION OF ROCK AND ROLL DETECTIVE, LLC.
Madison, WI.**

Requests to the Publisher for permission and for information regarding special discounts for bulk purchases please contact:

Rock And Roll Detective® Publishing, a division of Rock And Roll Detective®, LLC.

4230 E. Towne Blvd., No. 254

Madison, WI. 53704

(608) 250-2627

Email: info@thebeatlewhovanished.com

All photos in this book are the copyright of respective copyright holders.

Library of Congress Cataloging-in-Publication Data is available upon request

LCCN: 2012911439

ISBN# 978-0-9856677-0-2 Paperback book

ISBN# 978-09856677-1-9 Hardback book

ISBN# 978-0-9856677-2-6 eBook

The Beatle Who Vanished / Jim Berkenstadt - First Edition

Manufactured in the USA.

DEDICATION

To Holly, Becca and Brad

THE BEATLE WHO VANISHED

Acknowledgements

In writing any book, one incurs debts that can never be repaid. Literally hundreds of individuals have helped me with research and interviews, and I thank them all. The following are just some of the people who helped in this project. To those I've missed, I extend sincere apologies.

Editor in Chief: Gary Schumacher

Interior Layout Design: Jen Moulios

Book Cover Design: Elizabeth Neely

Director of Videography: Jay Olsen (Directed and produced the video promos for the book)

Cover Layout Photography: Brian Ebner, http://www.opticnervephoto.com

Additional Videos: Rebecca Berkenstadt

Production Advisor: Brad Berkenstadt

Foreword: Chas Newby, (bass player) The Beatles, 1960

Web Site Design and Creation: Daniel Hornung and Rebecca Berkenstadt
www.thebeatlewhovanished.com and www.youtube/thebeatlewhovanished.com

Social Media Marketing and SEO Director: Rebecca Berkenstadt

Translations: Marcus Cederstrom, Christopher Ray Bishop, Ariette Hennemann-Hartzema, Yukiko Sato, Jorgen Billing, Rebecca Berkenstadt, and Brad Berkenstadt

Director of Drum History and Analysis: David Stanoch

Additional Proofing: Nancy Turman

Research Assistance & Artifact Loans:
Mark Lewisohn, Belmo, Andy Babiuk, Koop Geersing, René van Haarlem (special thanks for the 1984 Jimmie Nicol Holland interview and photos), Beatles Unlimited, Ton Vandraanen, Renato Facconi, Vince Medina Sanna, Brendon Pearce, Patricia Convery- Curator of Arts Centre, Melbourne, Performing Arts Collection, Kenn Brodziak Beatles' Australian Tour Collection, The Spotnicks, Frank Caiazzo, Wayne Rodgers, Professor Gordon Thompson; Piet Muys; Marlene Matalon, Marco Matalon; Broadway International; Peggy Lescrenier; Eamonn Walsh, BBC-TV Panorama, Roy Hodkinson, Jeffrey Kruger, MBE, Azing Moltmaker, Paolo Hewit, Ray Kelley, Jim Cox, Henk Looijestijn, www.storyofindorock.com , Roy Tull, Miss Judy, Jorgen Billing, www.beathouse.dk, Blair Foster, Hanalei Perez-Lopez, Misha Hasfeld & The Clarks, Phil Chamberlain, Butch Vig and Beth Halper, Charles Cross and Sandy Maris.

Interviewees, Musicians, Friends of Jimmie Nicol and Special Assistance:

Sir Jeffrey Kruger, MBE, (founder of The Flamingo club), Greg Tesser; Pete Best, Sir George Martin CBE; Neil Aspinall, Derek Taylor, Tony Bramwell, Sam Leach, Jonathan Clyde, Allen J. Wiener, Matt Hurwitz, Jim Brandmeier, Peter Winsnes, Bo Winberg, Bob Starander, Roland Ferneborg, Inga Lill Ferneborg, The Spotnicks, Lars Akerström, Hans Sidén, Julia Maria Villaseñor, Ricardo Toral, Bill Harry, John Hodkinson, Johnny Harris, Dave Quincy, the Shubdubs; Vince Eager, the Quiet Three; Joe Brown; John Taylor; Rick Hardy; Mike O'Neil; Colin Hicks & His Cabin Boys; Bob Hunter; Max Lobkowitz; Herb Reed & The Platters; Tony Newman of Sounds Incorporated; Johnny Chester; Peter (Asher) & Gordon (Waller); Torben Sardorf & The Hitmakers, Misha Hasfeld; David Matalon, Colin Green; Tex Makins, Dave Clark & the Dave Clark Five; Graham Nash, The Hollies, Corrina "Cree" Miller, Esq., Johnny Gentle; Georgie Fame, Ben Sidran, Noel Wallis, Federico Rubli, Raye Du-Val, Tony Sheridan, Andy White, Klaus Voormann, Jim & Cynthia Keltner, Will McClain, Ray Kelley, Albert Lee, Oscar Rexhauser and The Hot Jumpers, Joe Johnson, Don E. Gee, Beatle Brunch, Rachel Cooper and indirectly Olivia, Yoko, John, Paul, George, Jimmie, Brian, & Ringo.

Family:

Very special thanks to my wife Holly, who listened to all of my daily Jimmie Nicol discoveries along the way with the book.

Our kids: Becca & Brad Berkenstadt, who helped in so many ways!

Gene and Laurie Berkenstadt

Joy and Jack Charney

Bonnie Laviron

Scott Cremer and Ellen Whitman

Very special thanks to my parents: Ed and Lois Berkenstadt who are no longer with us.

The Legal Team: Dan Black, Greenburg Traurig LLP, Dan Hardy, Axley Brynelson LLP

The Medical Team: Dr. John Wilson, Dr. Thomas Zdeblick, Dr. Mark Linzer

Helpful Friends and Gangs:

The Fiji's, The Hack 'N Slash gang, The Smart gang, The Genna's gang, Team Fab Four, The Pergola Gang, The Lola's Gang, The Prairie Dogs Gang, Riffmaster & The Rockme Foundation, The Practical Theater Gang, Garbage- Butch, Duke, Steve and Shirley and Billy Bush, The KIAB's, Scott & Lynne Faulkner &The Edgewater, Kris Warren, Ken LaBarre & Roll It Take It, Breakfast with The Beatles, Chris Carter, Mike Spound, Jim Shaw, Bob Weber, Brad Hall, Rob Wolken, John Tomko, Rain Management, Jenna Adler, CAA, Sylvie Rabineau, J Sikura, Roy Elkins & Broadjam, and Widen Enterprises.

FOREWORD BY FORMER BEATLE

Chas Newby

Jimmie Nicol and I are both members of a relatively small group of people who have played live with The Beatles on stage. Our appearances with the greatest band in the history of popular music were for the same reason; we were substituting for a member of The Beatles on a short term basis. However, the timing and consequences of being part of the band were very different.

In December 1960, The Beatles had just completed their first visit to Hamburg. At that time the band comprised John, Paul and George, plus Pete Best on drums and bass player Stuart Sutcliffe. During their stay, Stuart met Astrid Kirchherr and was invited to spend the Christmas break with the Kirchherr family while the rest of the band returned home to Liverpool. Once back on home soil, the band were looking for gigs to play and a bass player to fill in for Stuart until he returned in the New Year. I had no aspirations to be a professional musician; I was studying chemistry at college and was back home for the Christmas vacation. I had known Pete Best from school and we had played together in the Blackjacks before Pete joined The Beatles for their trip to Hamburg. I was familiar with the repertoire they played at that time and so for four nights at the end of 1960, I played bass with The Beatles. I went back to college early January and Stuart came home to resume his role with the band.

In 1964, the situation was very different. The Beatles were famous on both sides of the Atlantic. They had played in Paris during January. In February, they had made their first tour to America, and a world tour to The Netherlands, Far East, and Down Under during June had been confirmed. Ringo became ill with tonsillitis and was rushed to a hospital the day before the tour was due to start. Jimmie Nicol took the seat behind the skins with The Beatles up until the time that Ringo was well enough to rejoin the band. Jimmie, an experienced professional drummer, joined the Beatles 4 June for gigs in Denmark, Holland, Hong Kong and then Australia. Ringo recovered to meet up with the Beatles in Melbourne, Australia on 15 June and Jimmie flew back to England on his own.

After graduation, I got married and my wife and I moved away from Liverpool to rural Warwickshire. I am now retired and spend my days playing golf and spoiling my four beautiful grandchildren. I play bass with a local oldies band called the Racketts. At the end of August each year I go "back home" to the Casbah Club in Liverpool for the annual Beatles weekend and meet up with Pete Best and his two brothers, Rory and Roag, play a few tunes and relive old times.

And what happened to Jimmie after his brief and exciting time with The Beatles? To find out you have to read this remarkable book. Jim Berkenstadt has used his renowned literary and investigative skills to piece together the story of *The Beatle Who Vanished*. This is a significant addition to the bibliography of that most exciting period of music and social history. Read and enjoy.

Chas. Newby

Alcester, May 2012

CONTENTS

INTRODUCTION

Jimmie Nicol* died alone and nearly penniless in 1988, or that is what the world has been led to believe. But did he die? Only one outsider played with The Beatles onstage at the height of their Beatlemania fame. Jimmie Nicol had this good fortune. But was this brief episode of fame a stroke of good fortune or a curse that would haunt him the rest of his life?

The life and career of Jimmie Nicol is like an incomplete puzzle with pieces missing - not easily explained or understood. For a brief 13 days in June of 1964, Jimmie Nicol was asked to do the impossible - fill in as a substitute drummer for the hospitalized Ringo Starr. The Beatles - perhaps at the height of their global notoriety - were just 24 hours away from launching their first ever world tour. Suddenly, a session player - known to fellow musicians in London at the time, but otherwise completely invisible to the public - became the most desired understudy in the history of music. How he came to be chosen, and why he was the *only* possible candidate destined for the job, and his life after The Beatles is an extraordinary story of fleeting fame and creative tenacity.

When Ringo Starr returned to the band two weeks after his hospitalization, Nicol was flying high with The Beatles in Melbourne, Australia; and he very graciously stepped out of The Beatles' limelight. This soft-spoken "Everyman" - teased with having the world at his feet for a short, sweet time - now sat alone in an airport bound for London with a few souvenirs – a gold watch, a Beatles flight bag, and a week's wages – pondering where he had been and where his life was now headed.

Jimmie Nicol eventually recorded and toured the world again with other bands. In the 1970s, he walked away from the music business and the world stage forever. It was almost as if he had stepped out the door of his home for a stroll and never returned, as if he had vanished from the face of the earth. After this, however, the trail goes cold. Over the years, there have been rumors about Jimmie living in different countries around the world – playing jazz in Australia, Bossa nova in Brazil, opening a nightclub in Mexico, or working a construction job in London. A more recent rumor, believed by many of the musicians who played with him in the 1950s and 1960s, is that Nicol died at age 49 in 1988.

If he had been a bigger star in his own right, we would know more about this Everyman. If he had written a book about his adventures, we would know what became of his life. Sadly, more than forty years after his brief brush with fame, most have stopped wondering about Jimmie Nicol – except as a point of Beatles-related trivia. This is unfortunate, for in the words of Gary Schumacher, noted Beatles aficionado, "Jimmie Nicol is perhaps the classiest footnote in Beatles' history"; a footnote that until now only yielded a one or two sentence mention in Beatles books.

Nicol may be a classy footnote, but he is also an *obscure* footnote in music history. He recorded anonymously on radio shows, on records, and he composed film soundtracks that most of the world never heard. There is little-to-no mention of him in general music histories and no mention of a career playing behind many well-known, popular bands. His life is a study of his brief public persona and musical output, and little has been known of the private life of Jimmie Nicol *until now*.

Thousands of books on The Beatles have been written by every ex-maid, former assistant, Apple scruff, horoscope reader, and limo driver. Unlike countless Beatle "wannabes" who weren't in the band or part of the lads' inner circle, Jimmie Nicol actually played onstage and on TV with The Beatles. He was also an extremely talented composer, band leader, arranger, producer and versatile drummer. This is a sideman's journey of 50 years ago.

He is truly an enigma. None of Jimmie's fellow band mates have seen or spoken to him in over 40 years. Countless questions have been asked about him. Why has Jimmie Nicol always intrigued fans of The Beatles? How did The Beatles choose him? Did Jimmie almost permanently replace Ringo Starr in the group? Was Nicol's moment of musical immortality a blessing or a curse? And most importantly, whatever became of *The Beatle Who Vanished*? Jimmie Nicol catapulted from respected session man and band member in several popular groups, to the "Toppermost of the Poppermost". This book investigates and reveals much about the man that is…or was… Jimmie Nicol, *The Beatle Who Vanished*.

Jim Berkenstadt

June, 2012

* "Jimmie" has been spelled incorrectly by record labels, the media, and Beatles scholars for over forty years as "Jimmy". His last name has been misspelled as Nicols, Nichol and Nichols. Visual evidence from Jimmie's bass drum heads and autographs demonstrate the correct spelling of his name as Jimmie Nicol. His birth certificate lists his proper name as James George Nicol.

Chapter One

The Call

The call, it took only the routine ring of the telephone to turn Jimmie Nicol's world upside down. It came out of the blue, born of immense urgency. It was neither a fluke nor a "lucky break" as some have described that fateful day of Wednesday, June 3, 1964. The call had meaning on many levels. It came out of desperation, yet it was also a reward, a once-in-a-lifetime opportunity that sprang from years of hard work, determination, fate, and musical dues-paying. For Jimmie Nicol, becoming one of the "go-to" drummers in London meant moving up from one band to the next, one recording session to another. He had mastered different musical styles from Rock and Big Band, to Ska and Trad Jazz. He had played every ballroom gig, radio show, and recording session offered to him since the late 1950s. Even Jimmie's hair played a role, as he had recently started growing it in the famous "mop top" style. Nicol even had the right "look" to sit behind the most famous drum kit in the world.

"Hello, is Jimmie Nicol in please? This is George Martin calling." At first, it did not seem these introductory words would have much impact on his life or everyday routine. Martin, The Beatles' producer, had found Nicol hanging around his Barnes, West London home in the late morning with a friend. But why was he calling Nicol today? Certainly it couldn't be about The Beatles, since Nicol was well aware of their permanent drummer, Ringo Starr. Aside from The Beatles, George Martin had begun to produce some of the other bands in manager Brian Epstein's stable of artists at the time. These included: Gerry and the Pacemakers, Cilla Black, and Billy J. Kramer. Nicol likely assumed Martin wanted to hire him to play drums on one of Epstein's other artists' recording sessions. Nicol's work as a session drummer on Pye and Decca recordings was well known in London music circles at the time. Perhaps Martin wanted Jimmie to join one of Epstein's groups? Nicol recalled seeing music impresario and Beatles' manager Brian Epstein at the last Tommy Quickly recording session at Pye in March of that year. Perhaps he had impressed him with his drumming? Or maybe Epstein had signed a new band that needed a good rock and roll drummer?

Meanwhile, nearby in Nicol's own neighborhood, Beatles manager Brian Epstein was facing the most serious crisis of The Beatles' exploding career. He had a problem so monumental that it threatened to economically devastate the band, dilute its fan base, and destroy his master plan to take The Beatles worldwide. The schedule for June 3, 1964 originally called for the group to pose for photos in the morning, followed by an afternoon and evening recording session at EMI Studios. The following day, June 4, the group would fly off on their first ever world tour, one that would feature them playing live in Denmark, The Netherlands, Hong Kong, Australia, and New Zealand.

This was not just any tour, but one that had been carefully planned for months, planned with the preparation and detail of a military campaign. Epstein believed that touring was the most difficult part of his job, and it occupied most of his time and concern. "I think traveling around and going around the world, making the arrangements for moving around, is the most difficult thing in managing the group, because you don't know what's going to happen,"[1] said Epstein in an interview that seemed to foreshadow the looming problem. The Beatles had already conquered the United Kingdom and the eastern seaboard of the United States by June of 1964. They had the top five chart positions simultaneously on the U.S. Billboard Hot 100 Singles Chart with their songs, *I Want To Hold Your Hand; She Loves You; Please Please Me; Can't Buy Me Love;* and *Twist and Shout.* Despite this success, Epstein was driven more by his fear of failure than his will to succeed. This apprehension in The Beatles' climb to fame was weighing heavily as the clock ticked down to the world tour launch of the next day. "I hold myself responsible. It isn't the money that worries me," he recalled. "It is the failure; partly because of my youth; partly because of my background; and partly because of my provincial origin."[2] Their ambitious manager wanted to prove to himself he could be the first to have his pop group conquer no less than the entire world.

The contracts for the shows were all signed; hotels, security and transportation were reserved;

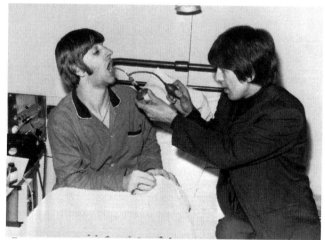

Ringo Starr in the Hospital with George Harrison, 1964.
Topham/© The Image Works.

records, concert programs and merchandise were stocked; and the tickets were already selling out. There was no turning back. The media was ready to cover their every move, and now it seemed as if all of Epstein's plans were about to implode like the demolition of a large skyscraper.

The Beatles were posing for photographs at Prospect Studios in Barnes for a *Saturday Evening Post* session with photographer John Launois, when suddenly Ringo Starr collapsed to the floor.[3] Beatles' road manager Neil Aspinall witnessed the event and recalls, "Ringo has never been particularly strong. He collapsed during the photo session… I was with them when it happened and I got quite a fright when I saw Ringo sink to his knees."[4] This event instantly threw The Beatles' world tour into serious doubt and panic, and their recording schedule that day into turmoil. Ringo was discreetly deposited into the private patients' wing of Middlesex University College Hospital. The diagnosis was tonsillitis and pharyingitis. Starr recalls that day, "I was desperately ill. (laughs)."[5]

Thinking quickly on his feet, Epstein knew he needed to find a replacement for Ringo Starr. He also knew he had to convince the other three Beatles to go along with the plan; and he needed to fulfill the multiple media, legal, and financial obligations of the world tour. Faced with the greatest crisis of his career thus far, Epstein had only a few hours to find a suitable replacement, or risk losing hundreds of thousands of dollars in concert fees, merchandise, publishing, and record revenues for his remarkable group. His challenge was daunting. Epstein had to find a drummer who "looked like a Beatle"; knew Ringo's parts to all the songs; fit into Ringo's stage suits (no time for a tailor); and could comport himself in a way that would not start rumors of a new Beatles' drummer. This was a tall order on such short notice!

In 1964, concert contracts were usually no more than one or two pages in length, containing the mere skeletal deal points of artist, price, location, and performance. They did not include cancellation or "out clauses" due to illness of a band member (standard in today's entertainment agreements). In other words, "the show must go on!" Furthermore, Epstein realized the risk to the band's reputation, image, and future popularity, due to cancellation. This was a time when pop stars had a very brief and unstable shelf life.

Aside from the job of replacing Ringo with another drummer who could play the arrangements and *looked* the part of a Beatle, Epstein faced a more daunting task, one in which a greater showdown emerged. He knew his decision would affect the other members of the band. The Beatles, more than any of his other artists, were like four very close brothers. This was an issue of business vs. loyalty, and success vs. friendship.

Within The Beatles' camp, there was a deep emotional split over Epstein's insistence on finding a substitute for Starr. Lead guitarist George Harrison had drawn a line in the sand; he flat out told Epstein that without Ringo, there would be no Beatles' tour. He would not participate. Harrison was The Beatle who, more often than not, took on the role as the group's "moral compass". George Martin recalls the showdown and comments, "George is a very loyal person. And he said, 'If Ringo's not part of the group, it's not The Beatles. And I don't see why we should do it. I'm not going to go'."[6] Paul McCartney remembers, "For some reason, we couldn't really cancel it. So, the idea came up, we'll get a stand-in drummer."[7]

In the end, it took all of Brian Epstein's and George Martin's powers of persuasion to convince Harrison that if he didn't go along with the idea, he would be letting everybody down. George finally relented and the showdown was averted, but not without some lingering bad feelings. "Well of course we shouldn't have done it," said Harrison in an interview decades later. "I mean, with all respect to Jimmie who came with us. It was silly. I couldn't understand it. But its 'How many Beatles does it take to change a light bulb?' See? Four![8] "Jimmie was actually quite a lovely guy. But, imagine The Beatles without Ringo!" said George."[9]

With the argument resolved, Epstein began his search for a drummer to deputize for Ringo. Many fans have wondered if The Beatles might have looked back to their previous drummer Pete Best. However, the wounds of that parting two years prior were likely still fresh, for years later when asked if Epstein had offered him the substitute job, Best's reply was an emphatic, "No!"[10]

At the time of *The Call,* Jimmie Nicol – a drummer known within the London musical community, but unknown to the public – was relaxing on the couch of his flat with a friend. A few weeks earlier, Georgie Fame had hired Jimmie to join his rhythm and blues combo. Georgie Fame & the Blue Flames were packing people in during an extended residency at the Flamingo club. Everybody who was anybody was checking out the band at The Flamingo. It was *the* prime live gig in London, and Jimmie filled the back seat of the band with his flashy, but controlled, rhythm and blues style drumming.

Landing the gig with Georgie Fame & the Blue Flames was yet another big step up the ladder for drummer Jimmie Nicol. His professional career began with jams at the 2 I's Coffee Bar. Nicol continued his upward rise, serving successful stints first generation rock bands and last generation big bands. He had climbed even further by doing frequent session work for Pye and Decca Records and the Top Six label. However, no amount of experience could completely prepare Jimmie for his next gig.

Jimmie Nicol's life was about to change forever. Before he received *The Call,* his phone rang in the flat. It was his bandleader Georgie Fame. "Hey Jimmie," said Fame. "Have you got a passport?" Jimmie was still tired from the previous night and was confused by the question. "No," replied Nicol. "Well," said Fame with a big smile as he spoke, "Get yourself down to the Post Office tomorrow morning."[11]

Singer and good friend, John Hodkinson, was staying with Jimmie and his wife Patricia and son Howie when the telephone started ringing on that momentous day. They had been partying when Georgie Fame called earlier. "The phone rang," says Hodkinson. "We had been drinking and listening to music and stuff. Someone had first phoned Georgie Fame asking about Jimmie's availability. Georgie called and asked Jimmie about it. He was on the phone maybe ten minutes."[12]

Later that morning, another call interrupted the two friends' reverie. *The Call.* This time it was George Martin on the phone, calling to change Jimmie Nicol's life forever. However history recalls this moment, it was anything but routine. Decades later, Nicol remembered *The Call* coming from Martin. "I was playing around in a small band and in the studio wherever I was needed," he says. "I was actually making money as a drummer, something not many were doing… It was George Martin... He asked, 'What are you doing for the next four days? Ringo is ill, and we want you take his place on The Beatles' tour. Would you mind going to Australia?'" A ridiculous question, thought the amazed Mr. Nicol. "Be at Abbey Road Studios at 3:00 pm," Martin continued. "The Beatles want to run through some numbers with you."[13]

After hanging up the phone, Jimmie turned the radio back on and resumed his drinking with Hodkinson without a word about *The Call*. Jimmie was deep in thought processing the shock of what had just taken place. Some time passed before the initial surprise of *The Call* finally sank in. Jimmie turned to his pal and said, "Do you want to guess what that phone call was about?" Hodkinson recalls, "I didn't know who it was." Jimmie said, "Guess what? The Beatles want me to play drums with them. Ringo is sick and I'm leaving to go on tour with them."[14]

Interestingly, Nicol was already thinking past the audition of that day. He knew why he had been chosen. He was perhaps the only drummer at that time who knew the drum arrangements for practically every Beatles hit song. He had the musical knowledge, experience, maturity, and even the haircut to fill the bill. To Jimmie Nicol, the biggest gig of his life was already a done deal.

Hodkinson's reaction was one of shock. "I just couldn't believe it." Jimmie, smiling from ear to ear, asked John, "Do you think I should do it?" "I just sort of jumped through the ceiling," says Hodkinson laughing. "Jimmie didn't even own a suitcase, so he had to borrow my red suitcase for the trip."[15]

Prior to heading over to the studio, Jimmie called his good friend, producer/arranger Johnny Harris, excitedly exclaiming, "Guess what John, they've asked me to go audition for… The Beatles!" Harris replied, "Yeah? I heard the news that Ringo is in the hospital with tonsillitis." Jimmie was confident in his ability to pass the audition. "You know, the thing is John, I think I'm going to get it," he said. Harris congratulated Jimmie on his good fortune and told him, "Let me know what happens. This is great!"[16]

Jimmie Nicol could not help thinking about what this gig would mean to his musical career, in terms of the boost in fame and the financial rewards for his family. Surely, he could quit his part time work at Boosey & Hawkes music store and his occasional carpentry work. Perhaps, he even wondered to himself, he could possibly take over permanently for Ringo Starr! After all, Ringo had replaced Pete Best less than two years earlier. Was destiny going to make Nicol a Beatle? Or should he start his own band? The wheels were turning and fate was dealing the cards. He was philosophical, reflecting, "I happened to be the right person, in the right place at the right time, with the right tools."[17]

As he set down the telephone with Johnny Harris and prepared to head over to Abbey Road studios, he would surely have reflected on the progress he had made since the late 1950s and the musical path that had led him from music classes as a school boy, to jamming as a teen at the 2 I's Coffee Club, to the very top of the musical entertainment world. But how had it all started?

Chapter Two

The Early Years - Battersea

Little is known about the formative years of James George Nicol who was born on August 3, 1939 at the St. James' Hospital, Battersea, in the borough of Wandsworth, England. Perhaps this is by design of Jimmie Nicol himself. In the few interviews he conducted in his career, none ever seemed to touch on his youth and upbringing. As such, only documents and the occasional comment have given us any clues into his early life.

His mother Edith Louise Isabel Nicol was a homemaker and his father, George Ford Nicol worked for the government at the Messenger Inland Revenue Service after serving in the British army. He was a "Taxman". Their home was a simple red brick two-story walk-up, one of many identical row houses along Silverthorne Road.

The Battersea district is part of south London's inner-city on the south bank of the River Thames. As Jimmie Nicol came into the world at the end of the 1930s, Battersea was clearing slums and starting to build modern homes equipped with gas and electricity. This made housework and cooking for home-makers easier, and many families, including the Nicols, had bathrooms inside their home.

In the 1940's, the Nicol family found their entertainment by attending the cinema, dancing in the public halls, and trips to the seaside. No doubt Jimmie got his first exposure to music from being taken to the dance halls. Life was not easy in the early 1940's as World War II had been declared in September, 1939, just one month after Nicol's birth. The local Battersea council spent many months preparing for air raids. Volunteer rescue teams were formed, and stockpiles of gas masks and other supplies were readied,

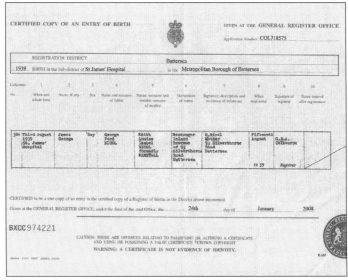

Jimmie Nicol's birth certificate. Photo Credit: Courtesy of Author.

as were the iron fallout shelters. Those Brits who did not go off to fight were enlisted to help with munitions, fire-fighting, fundraising, and volunteering other assistance. Women played a vital role at home in Battersea. They helped with first aid and rationing of food, clothing, and other essential needs. Iron railings, paper and other materials were collected for recycling during the war to help the effort.

Enduring an infancy of Nazi air raids, rationing, and hiding in shelters, Nicol was only five years old when World War II came to an end in May of 1945. Things were still difficult for the Nicol family and their Battersea neighbors at the end of the war. Daily life was affected for years afterward with shortages of food and other essential supplies, not to mention the necessary repair of buildings destroyed by the War. However, the dawn of the 1950s envisioned a new landscape in Battersea, as new rebuilding schemes of homes and high rises began to change the look of their local district.

In 1946 Jimmie Nicol was enrolled at Honeywell Junior School in Battersea. This was a school with a mission and vision. Their policy statement reads, "Our expectations are that all pupils achieve the highest personal standards of excellence in learning, behaviour and understanding of themselves and others, through a caring, supportive and secure environment, where every child is valued as important as the next."[1] This school would be a perfect place for Nicol's early years, for it emphasized and valued creativity and imagination. The arts, especially music, played an important role in Nicol's curriculum.

Jimmie was unconventional from the start. He did not conform to the norm. According to one report, he began tying his shoes backward from the top down. He would make the knot and bow at the bottom instead of the top. It was his protest against conformity, a theme that would continue throughout his life.[2] He was known as a sincere lad, but one happy to be a contrarian. It was his way to protest against conventional society. He did not shy away from giving his opinions, regardless of the consequence.[3]

Jimmie Nicol's birthplace home. Photo Credit: © 2011 Jim Berkenstadt

At home, Nicol began playing the piano, which was his first instrument.[4] While at Honeywell, Nicol's first real exposure to music outside the home came as a member of the Boy's choir group.[5] He started to form casual musical associations with other students at his school. One report has Jimmie playing drums in a school band with one saxophone player and two trumpets.[6]

It appears that Jimmie Nicol would not be the only famous musician to develop from the Battersea area. The district was also home to other young men and women of Nicol's generation who would achieve fame in popular music beginning in the 1950's and beyond. These included Sir Bob Geldof (Boom Town Rats and Live Aid founder); Danni Minogue; Rick Parfitt (Status Quo); and Simon Le Bon

(Duran Duran). One other interesting rock reference to Nicol's birthplace is the Battersea Power Station. Construction began in 1929 and was completed the year of Jimmie's birth. This mammoth structure would later provide the ominous background to the cover of Pink Floyd's famous *Animals* album.

In the early 1950s, Jimmie Nicol signed up for The Army Cadet Force (ACF), Britain's oldest youth organization, having been founded in 1860. The ACF is somewhat similar in mission to the Boy Scouts of America. They help young boys aged 12 to 18 develop confidence, discipline, initiative, loyalty, and a sense of service to other people. These character building traits would serve Nicol well in the challenging future he would face as a professional musician. The ACF was famous for its military marching and concert band. As a drummer/ percussionist in the ACF band, Jimmie learned musical theory, how to read music, and diverse drumming and performance skills. Perhaps most importantly, he learned the skill of playing in an ensemble with other players of different and varied abilities. He also learned to play under many different conditions – at parade grounds, churches, concert venues, and everywhere else bands are called upon to perform.

Battersea Power Station.

Nicol thrived as a drummer and enjoyed the enthusiastic response of the audiences to the band's live performances. The rigorous training included rehearsals twice during weekdays, plus each weekend and a two week summer stint all while balancing his school work, chores, and other activities.

At the age of 14, Jimmie Nicol obtained his first drum at a pawn shop. This allowed him to practice at home, much to the chagrin of nearby neighbors attached to the Nicol building on both sides. He began to listen to jazz music on the radio and loved it. He was initially inspired by jazz drummer Gene Krupa. "I like Brubeck," said Nicol, "but I think my own particular favorites are Cannonball Adderley, Duke Ellington and (Count) Basie of course."[7]

But the moment that changed his life forever as a teenager was when he heard a Chuck Berry Rock and Roll song. Nicol recalls, "Chuck let the drummer cut loose on a particular song." The drummer took off on his own carrying the song with his own style of rocking beats. The impact on Jimmie Nicol was powerful and immediate. "Man that was it for me. I loved it."[8] That was all it took for Jimmie Nicol to decide what he wanted to do for the rest of his life: play the drums and make music for a living!

At the age of sixteen, Nicol took his O-level exams and passed them, which conferred upon him Britain's General Certificate of Education. It also meant that he was no longer required to attend school when he reached his seventeenth birthday. He decided he wanted to explore the city of London with the hope of somehow getting into music as a career. His dad apparently had other plans for his son. Jimmie's mom, however, did not protest when he told her, "I'm thinking about quitting my job and becoming a professional drummer."[9]

Little did he know the road to success would take a route of many hills, peaks, ruts and curves. Life for young Mr. Nicol would soon be traveling at a rapid steady beat in the Soho coffee clubs of London.

Chapter Three

Post-War London and the 2 I's Coffee Bar

Culture, politics, and economics often play a powerful role in the development of artists, musicians, and their audiences. Post-World War II Great Britain faced a complex series of problems that lasted well into the 1950s. There was the task of rebuilding homes, businesses, factories, schools, and hospitals that had been bombed by Nazi Germany. Additionally, Britain faced high unemployment, rationing, long-term debt, and the related problem of inflation. Much of Britain's infrastructure that had survived the war needed updating. Factors such as high unemployment, the national debt, and the collapse of the British Empire in the post-war years left a new generation of young people unemployed and directionless. Typically many of these young men would have been conscripted into the Army or employed in factories, but now they were seemingly adrift, left to find their own direction to adulthood.

What lay ahead was a rebellious and creative course. This new social order gave rise to a unique identity created by these youths labeled "Teddy Boys."[1] Teddy Boys were really the first group of teenagers in England to identify and differentiate themselves by their actions and dress. Some groups of Teddy Boys or "Teds" gained infamy by forming gangs that often clashed with rival gangs. The British media tended to exaggerate this "social problem" among the youth. Laughable by today's standards, these "wild youth" were terrifying to the proper English adult mind set.

The heyday of the Teddy Boy occurred during the mid 1950s, and "Ted" was followed closely by the American-born "rocker". James Dean and Marlon Brando provided the "look" (tight-legged blue jeans, tee shirts, and leather jackets) and Elvis Presley, Buddy Holly and others provided the soundtrack in the form of early Rock and Roll. British Baby Boomers were quick to model themselves after these new American icons. The mantra of this new working class youth was to "live fast and die young."

Central to this new era of youth culture in Britain was live music and the pursuit of late-night wild abandon. There were no "mums" around, and these new rockers were drawn to coffee bars in the West End Soho area of London to live the Rock and Roll dream all night long and forget their daily drudgery. "Enter the cosmopolitan mix of Soho and you've tapped into a defining spirit of tolerance; a den of artists, writers and worldly souls. There's an openness and acceptance of different ways and no pressure to conform."[2] It was the perfect environment for a free-spirited, nonconformist drummer to begin his career.

The 2 I's Coffee Bar

The Soho section of London exploded with the music of Jazz, Skiffle, New Orleans "Dixieland", and Britain's own version of Rock and Roll in the 1950s. Teens from around the city were drawn to the many coffee bars lining Soho's Old Compton Street like moths to a flame. The invention

The 2 I's Coffee Bar 1950s.

of the espresso machine by Achille Gaggia in Milan in 1946 gave rise to the mania of coffee bars that hit London with enormous impact in the 1950s.[3] The chrome, art-deco coffeemaker was often the dominant visual element in many coffee houses. As the number of coffee bars increased, competition among bar owners helped create new novelties such as jukeboxes, expanded menus, and eventually live music. Lunch time music sessions, as well as evening coffee sets, were packed to the rafters with teens seeking their daily fix of this fiery new music scene. However, no coffee bar was more packed, hotter, and more jiving than the 2 I's Coffee Bar located at 59 Old Compton Street.

The 2 I's Coffee Bar opened in the spring of 1956. Paul Lincoln, a former world middleweight wrestler – nicknamed "The President" standing behind the Formica bar serving frothy coffees – owned the 2 I's. His partner was an Australian named Ray Hunter. One could easily credit these two men with the birth of the modern British music scene, for without their supplying teens with gallons of caffeine and a hassle-free home to play and listen to new music, the scene might well have blossomed in another city or even another country. Lincoln and Hunter quickly expanded their business from serving coffee to music promotion and management, as talented young musicians flocked to play at their club.

In April 1956, the 2 I's business had not yet begun to thrive. However, within a short time, the new owners began to feature guitarists and singers. The early clientele consisted of Soho artists, unemployed layabouts, and Rock and Roll dreamers. With live music, word-of-mouth began to spread as more bohemians floated in for their all-night espresso fix and music. The musical melting pot of Country, Ska, Jazz, Skiffle, and Rock was an irresistible minestrone of new sounds.

Standing outside 59 Old Compton Street in the mid-to-late 1950s, one would have heard the muffled sounds of Rock and Roll escaping from its basement. On the outside, it looked quite innocent with its rectangular sign that simply read "2 I's Coffee Bar, Home to the Stars." Hundreds of people would pass the coffee house each day, without a clue that a cultural revolution was going on inside. But behind its doors, the 2 I's served as a breeding ground for Britain's first generation of Rock stars, including Tommy Steele; Joe Brown; Johnny Gentle; Billy Fury; Marty Wilde; Georgie Fame; Vince Eager; Colin Hicks; and ultimately, a young drummer named Jimmie Nicol.

Upon entering the 2 I's, you initially passed the American jukebox straight ahead between the service counter with its coffee machine, juice dispenser, and sandwich selection on the left. The Formica shelf to the right was built to rest your coffee cup and saucer. At the end of the room was the narrow "stairway to heaven" that led down (rather than up) to the world-famous basement where the coffee bar's music was performed. If you were lucky enough to get to the bottom of the stairs, you would run into a wall of humanity. Musician Ian Samwell described the scene aptly, "Rock and Roll sardines all packed in neatly and all facing the same direction; about fifty or sixty of them, the crème de la crème of London teendom."[4]

Singer Vince Eager fondly recalls the basement of the 2 I's. "It was an amazing place. You wouldn't believe how small it was. In width, it was about twice the width of my arms extended and half again. The length of the 2 I's would be only about 25-30 feet."[5] The sound system was quite primitive even by 1950's standards. "It was awful and very archaic," recalls Eager. "You really didn't need a sound system because it was such a small place people could hear you. The stage was at the opposite end of the stairs, in which you came down. So, when the place was packed and a band had to get onstage, they'd have to carry and pack all of their equipment over the heads of the audience. It was manic. The 2 I's was a fascinating place. It was around long before the Cavern in Liverpool and it really was the birthplace of British Rock and Roll!"[6] The 2 I's was the place to be discovered.

In 1957, Bill Haley & His Comets took America and England by storm with their hit *Rock Around The Clock*. Elvis Presley's *Heartbreak Hotel* was another non-stop jukebox staple in all of the coffee bars. New bands and combinations of artists started to drift down to the 2 I's, as the coffee bar's reputation began to spread throughout England.

Not far from the 2 I's, Jimmie Nicol found a job repairing and maintaining drums at the Boosey & Hawkes musical equipment store. His days were full and he was making a decent wage. At the time, Boosey & Hawkes was one of the leading music publishers and manufacturers of musical instruments. Picking up more valuable techniques at Boosey & Hawkes, Nicol came to realize it was easier to play melodies in several ways on the drums than to jump on the piano at home.[7] His job was not very glamorous, but at least it was related to his instrument, and it taught him how to be his own drum tech. Working at Boosey & Hawkes, also provided networking opportunities with other bands and musicians via word-of-mouth. Jimmie often heard about band tryouts and jam sessions needing drummers before any of the competition, thanks to his position at Boosey & Hawkes.

Nicol followed the beat of the music to the 2 I's. He was developing the chops to sit in with any musician in need of a drummer. This talent would serve him well as he began his descent down the steps of the 2 I's basement and his ascent up the British music industry ladder. Nicol had developed a raw, energetic style that could swing from the rafters with his full, muscular, arms-flying approach to drumming.

The music scene for drummers began to change in the mid-1950s. Many big bands were beginning to lose favor with this new generation of teens who wanted their own music. Jazz and swing-band percussion players formed smaller groups to twist their sound into Rock and Roll combos. Bill Haley's "Rock Around The Clock" was a guiding force to Brit drummers listening for Rock music's new percussive patterns, and it set them free to experiment with their own kits.

Apprenticeship

Tony Crombie, a drummer who backed up singer Wee Willie Harris, was mining the rhythm and blues sounds of the 1940s to develop a new sound in England. In 1956, Crombie left Wee Willie Harris to start up his own Rock combo modeled after Bill Haley.

Wee Willie's loss of drummer Crombie was Jimmie Nicol's gain, for Nicol briefly filled in behind Wee Willie on the drum kit.[8] In the second half of the 1950s, Wee Willie served his apprenticeship at the 2 I's coffee bar as its resident piano player. Harris loved American Rock and Roll and performed with great energy to rile up the crowds. He would go on to record the song, *Rocking at the Two I's* that would immortalize the club and an era. Jimmie Nicol learned a valuable lesson in showmanship from his brief stint with Harris that would serve him well with future bands.

During his day offs, Nicol would spend his time hanging out with other drummers. Brian Bennett, a drummer who would end up playing with Cliff Richard and the Shadows, recalls, "Three other drummers and myself used to have some great workouts together. They were Red Reece, Jimmy [sic] Nicol and Clem Cattini." He says they all used to get advice from veteran drummer Crombie.

"Tony Crombie, a really fine player, lived above one of these coffee houses and often came in to give us words of advice and encouragement, which meant a great deal to us all."[9]

Drummers in the 1950s used a standard dance band drum set that included a bass drum and pedal, with a small tom-tom mounted on the bass drum. Off to the drummer's right hand laid the floor tom, with a snare drum tucked between the legs. On the left side, the hi-hat cymbals faced each other like clapping hands and were controlled by the left foot pedal that could bring them together on an offbeat pattern to accompany the snare drum. Two larger cymbals were used respectively for the sudden "crash" sound and the continuous time-keeping play of the "ride".

Nicol's first kit at the 2 I's lacked the mounted tom-tom and a crash cymbal. However, he more than compensated for his smaller kit with his hard hitting enthusiasm and precision. Nicol's white bass drumhead featured a nondescript blank white face, for he had not yet come up with a name or logo to display.

Jimmie continued paying his dues at the 2 I's and other coffee houses in Soho by sitting in for any band or singer who needed a drummer. This gave him the opportunity to listen, learn, and practice. Word began to spread that Jimmie Nicol could *really* play the drums. For a brief time, Rory Blackwell took Jimmie under his wing and provided him with an informal apprenticeship.[10] Blackwell, who is considered Britain's first true Rock and Roller, was exciting teens with his wild performances in the 1950's. With his group, the Blackjacks, Blackwell was a regular performer in the London pubs, dance halls, and especially at the 2 I's coffee club. Occasionally, when the cockney singer came out front to sing his wild, new Rock music, he would let his trainee Jimmie Nicol slide in behind his drum kit to quarterback the Blackjacks' rhythm section. Despite his love of drumming, Blackwell was happy to share the spotlight with his young up-and-coming protégé Mr. Nicol.

Guitarist Rick Hardy recalled working with Jimmie Nicol in 1958. "I first met Jimmie Nicol in the 2 I's Coffee Bar. Most Rock musicians at the time would 'pop' in to mix and get up and play. Jimmie was so good when he arrived on the scene that he MUST have had previous experience, but I don't know what it was."[11] Rick Hardy had recently started as a guest singer at the 2 I's Coffee

London's Soho District, late 1950s

12

Bar. Soon afterwards he was asked to join the resident house band – "The Worried Men". "I was the resident singer at the 2 I's from March 1958 until May 1959. During that time, I made over 300 appearances there and when that happened I was the only singer to get paid! I can remember Jimmie Nicol sitting in quite a few times."[12] The Worried Men were impressed with Nicol's work behind the kit. "He swung like the clappers, as we used to say," says Hardy. "Jimmie was as good as anybody and better than most. And he was very professional in his manner."[13]

Nicol had mastered Rock and Roll drumming very quickly and had developed the necessary hand and foot mechanics, accurate time keeping, and his own swinging groove to attract the interest of several up and coming bands. All he needed now was a steady, full-time, paying gig with a band, and he would be on his way. A steady gig would have to wait, however, for two men to come along who would turn the loose fraternal musicianship of the 2 I's into Britain's first wave of Rock stars. Their names were John Kennedy and Larry Parnes. They would become Britain's first Rock and Roll managers.

The Men behind the Curtain and Britain's Elvis

As the music of the 2 I's washed out of the cellar onto the street like water breaching a levy, the waves of backbeats washed over John Kennedy. Kennedy, a Heathrow freelance photographer, was invited by the club's owner on this particular night to check out The Vipers skiffle group. It was a hot, sticky fall night in September 1956.

Curious at the loud music pouring onto Old Compton Street, Kennedy decided to investigate. After squeezing through the crowded entrance and down the steps to the basement's swinging masses of humanity, he witnessed what many say was the moment Rock and Roll was born in England.[14] Kennedy was no music producer, nor did he have perfect pitch to evaluate the young man singing up on stage that night. However, what Kennedy lacked in a musical ear, he more than made up for in his astute observations of the singer's style and the crowd's reaction. "The music bounced back and forth off the walls, flooded through the crowd and hit you in the ears like a tidal wave," he recalls.[15] What he saw was a revelation. Waves of young men and women were smoking cigarettes and drinking their coffee, with eyes fixed on a blond youth singing, strumming, and dancing about on the stage. The cheeky lad had strolled casually up onto the stage during a break in The Vipers' set. Kennedy was witnessing modern day idolatry and "layer after layer of adulation."[16] The young man was singing a new Elvis Presley song, *Heartbreak Hotel*, normally reserved for the jukebox. But this singer performed the song live and raw for an adoring audience.

The moment was an epiphany to Kennedy. He realized this young man could be the catalyst to transform his own career from news photographer into show business manager. He could not wait for the young rocker to finish. Describing the songs performed, Kennedy noted, "They were just hypnotic. I knew that for the first time in my life I was watching reaction to a performer that was getting close to hysteria."[17] The singer ended his set and began to step down from the tiny stage as John Kennedy made his move to talk to him before the girls could stampede in. He overheard others talking about the singer and heard his name – Tommy Hicks.

Hicks was a quick study, and he picked up many different styles of music as he visited various seaports. "I came to Rock music from country music. Hank Williams and Red Foley and Tennessee Ernie (Ford),"says Hicks. "I was singing Country songs which had this emphasized 2nd and 4th beat in the bar, which became Rock."[18]

On August 7, 1956, Tommy Hicks walked off the gangplank of the *RMS Mauretania* for another shore leave. On his way out, he spotted his teenage brother Colin coming up the gangplank heading out to sea, the younger brother following in his big brother's footsteps as a sailor. Tommy stopped his brother and told him, "Keep my bunk warm."[19] Ironically, this would not be the last time that Tommy's younger brother Colin would follow his older brother's lead. However, unbeknownst to Tommy Hicks at the time, he was walking off his last gangplank and last tour of duty at sea. His future "tours" would be in a radically different setting - on land and onstage.

By mid-September, Tommy had stopped in to sing at the 2 I's when John Kennedy first caught his act. Tommy Hicks still recalls what that fateful night felt like. "It was fabulous. You were surrounded. Especially when you were a young man… Probably 90% of the crowds around you were girls all drinking coffee and listening to you. And it was lovely, kids dancing amongst the little coffee tables and chairs."[20]

After his impressive set, Kennedy cornered Tommy. With little introduction Kennedy asked him point blank, "Do you want to go into serious show business? If you do, I can make you a star."[21] Tommy's reaction was cool and calm to the abrupt question. After thinking to himself for a minute, he responded, "All right Johnny mate. I'll tell you what I'll do. I'm going back to sea in a fortnight. I'll do what you tell me until then. If we get anywhere I'll stay on. If we don't, then you've had me mate."[22]

Kennedy and Hicks both got to work quickly. Kennedy secured an audition for Tommy with Decca Records. By the end of September 1956, Cunard set sail *without* Tommy Hicks, who was now in Decca Records' red brick studio at Broadhurst Gardens cutting his first hit single.

As Kennedy wheeled-and-dealed for his new protégé, he began to entertain offers for Hicks to appear on TV, radio, and live in concert. Kennedy quickly realized that he would need the advice, as well as financial strength of an experienced business partner, if he were to take Tommy Hicks to the top of the entertainment world in England. He chose a man who had been a passing acquaintance when Kennedy served as his publicist for a play in 1955. This man would become known as the pop world's first manager of a stable of music artists. His name was Larry Parnes.

In the fall of 1956, John Kennedy ran into Parnes at The Sabrina coffee bar in Soho. While there, Kennedy took the opportunity to tell Parnes about his new discovery. "I told Parnes about Tommy Hicks," recalled Kennedy.[23] Parnes liked what he saw of the talented blond haired singer

Larry Parnes, England's first pop manager

who had the style and moves of Elvis Presley. After the show, Kennedy and Parnes agreed to co-manage Tommy Hicks. Hicks was impressed with Parnes and readily agreed to the new arrangement.

The first order of business was to create a stage name for Tommy that would both sound good and play well up on the marquees of the clubs and music halls. Tommy suggested his Scandinavian paternal grandfather's sir name, Tommy Stil-Hicks (pronounced "Steel"). The e's were added by Parnes, and "Tommy Steele" was born.[24] "With the Rock and Roll, I think that Larry Parnes was to be what I suppose you'd call the first Svengali of the Rock scene,"[25] says Steele. Parnes immediately set out to make Tommy Steele an all-around entertainer.

Larry Parnes began to troll the coffee bars of London looking for more talent. Others would follow into Parnes' stable, including Dickie Pride, Roy Taylor (aka Vince Eager) and Joe Brown (who steadfastly refused to change his name to the suggested "Elmer Twitch"). According to journalist John Edwards, "The first six pop singers in that anybody can remember in this country [England] were all his [Parnes'] artists."[26] Parnes wanted to collect and groom attractive young people to entertain their teen peers. Like rows of corn, Parnes continued to harvest even more young artists such as Johnny Gentle (formerly John Askew) and Duffy Power (formally Ray Howard).

John Kennedy continued to look for talent around the coffee clubs. He observed Jimmie Nicol sitting in on drums at the 2 I's with various groups, as well as a young piano player who was always pinch-hitting with bands. He went by the name Clive Powell. The musical lives of Nicol and Powell would intersect on more than one occasion as both of them worked hard to latch onto a regular band with a future.

Powell's recollection illustrates what both back-up musicians endured to be discovered. "At first, I was always hanging around with the musicians. I was always playing for all the other guys. I was over-awed by this whole thing. I was working with all of Britain's top Rock and Rollers playing piano behind them. I used to stand in the wings most nights watching all these people. If anybody sort of missed their cue or turned up late, I'd sort of run on stage and cover for them."[27]

Jimmie Nicol's hard work playing around the coffee clubs would soon pay off, and his "ship" was about to come in when Tommy Steele's younger brother Colin returned from his extended Cunard cruise in the late fall of 1957. Upon disembarking, Colin discovered that his big brother was now a national celebrity. Like his older brother, Colin had been singing and performing for his fellow shipmates. Seeing the swooning girls and the money his brother Tommy was attracting, Colin Hicks once again followed his brother's lead, this time into the entertainment business as a Rock and Roll singer. As they were for his brother, the "men behind the curtain" would also be there for Colin – watching him perform and helping him start a band, a hard-rocking band that lacked only a flashy and sure-handed drummer…

Chapter Four
Colin Hicks & His Cabin Boys

Upon his return from working the high seas as a cabin boy, Colin Hicks decided to trade his life as a merchant seaman in favor of a career as a "beat" merchant. He never looked back. The sixteen year old immediately began plying his new talent as a Rock and Roll singer in the Soho coffee club scene. Colin had gained a bit of performing experience in a South African nightclub for laughs while his ship was docked there.[1] It didn't hurt that his older brother Tommy Steele was already established as a top pop singer with hits on the radio, the jukebox, and TV. There is no doubt that Tommy put in a good word to his managers, John Kennedy and Larry Parnes, to catch his younger brother's act down at the coffee bars.

Musician Rick Hardy recalls seeing Colin Hicks at the 2 I's with his famous brother. "I only met Colin a few times," he says, "He didn't come into the 2 I's very often and I never got to see him sing. I saw him with his brother Tommy there, drinking coffee."[2] One thing is for sure, Colin had every bit as much singing ability as his brother, and people were beginning to take notice. Things began to move quickly for Colin in the fall of 1957. Steele's manager John Kennedy was sufficiently impressed with the younger brother's talent and signed Hicks to sing in a nightclub in London's posh Mayfair district.

It is interesting that Larry Parnes allowed Colin Hicks to keep his own name, perhaps to distance Colin's career from his brother Tommy. On November 4, 1957, Larry Parnes accompanied Colin to his first British TV appearance. The TV singing spots attracted Pye Records which were interested in Hicks. Pye was hoping, with Colin Hicks, to duplicate the great record sales that his older brother Tommy Steele enjoyed on the competitor's Decca Records label. Pye took a chance and signed Colin Hicks in late 1957 to a three single (six song) contract.

In December 1957, an audition was arranged to form a backing group for Colin Hicks to be used for upcoming tours. Someone at the 2 I's arranged for Jimmie Nicol to audition as the drummer for Colin's new backing group, "The Cabin Boys". Jimmie passed with flying colors and would soon be on his way to a steady paycheck as an official band member. His flashy rocking style was a perfect fit for the swinging, hi-stepping Colin Hicks. The name Cabin Boys for the backing band had its origin with Colin's brother Tommy Steele. Cabin Boys' piano player Mike O'Neil explains, "Tommy Steele was a cabin boy. A cabin boy is like a gopher on the ship. So that is where Colin got the idea for the name from Tommy who had had that job. At least," says O'Neil, "we never had to wear cabin boy outfits on stage (laughing)."[3] Colin Hicks & His Cabin Boys made a splash debut in December, 1957 as co-headliners along with Marty Wilde at the Old Finsbury Park Empire.[4]

Colin Hicks 1957
Photo Credit: Nixa Record Co.

Colin Hicks & His Cabin Boys with Jimmie Nicol holding the drum. Credit: © Broadway Records.

The original Cabin Boys consisted of Colin Hicks on vocals; Rod 'Boots' Slade on bass guitar; Dave 'Zom' Tick on lead guitar; Mike O'Neil on piano; Mike Elliott on tenor saxophone; and, of course, Jimmie Nicol on drums. Confident that steady work was in his future as a musician; Jimmie Nicol - at only 18 years of age - took the plunge and married his girlfriend Patricia. Jimmie's personal life and career were beginning to fall into place for the young drummer as 1958 dawned.

Once the band was assembled for live shows, Colin Hicks set about recording his first single, *Empty Arm Blues*, backed with *Wild Eyes and Tender Lips*. Neither Nicol, nor any of the other Cabin Boys participated in these first recordings. Pye organized these sessions with known session regulars, not wanting to waste valuable time with young coffee club Rock musicians. Strangely, Hicks' first single is credited to "Colin Hicks & His Cabin Boys".

However, despite the fine performance and production value, Colin Hicks struck out with his first single in 1957. Sales were disappointing and the record was a flop. Undeterred, Colin Hicks and the boys would press on, looking for success onstage in the coming year.

From touring and TV, it was back to the studio as Colin Hicks returned to Pye to make more records, again without the assistance of his backing group. Unfortunately, the Hicks group was a bona fide Rock band that was unable to get its true sound or potential realized on record at Pye.

All was not lost, however. On February 28, 1958, Colin Hicks & His Cabin Boys caught a break - akin to coming off the bench - getting a starting spot on a big-time tour. Singer Terry Dene was another alumnus singer from the 2 I's coffee bar. He was performing at a Gloucester cinema one night when he ran afoul of the law and the media. He was charged with causing willful and malicious damage and of being drunk and disorderly. As a result, the newspapers roasted Mr. Dene, which (along with his newly earned legal problems) took him off the touring circuit for a while. Dene's loss was Colin Hicks' gain. The ABC Theatre chain that was presenting the tour replaced Dene with Colin Hicks & His Cabin Boys and put them on the same bill with the highly popular

Marty Wilde. Colin and the boys responded with a rollicking and rocking show that resulted in some notoriety and landed them on TV for their first group debut performance featuring the song *Giddy-Up-A Ding Dong*.

A US group, Freddy Bell and the Bellboys, had made the song *Giddy-Up-A Ding Dong* a hit in Europe, and they toured with their signature song in 1957, supporting Colin's older brother Tommy Steele. No doubt Tommy suggested to Colin & His Cabin Boys that they would benefit from working on their own rocked-up cover version of this song. A surviving TV clip shows the band in a small club filled with dancing teenagers. Colin starts in on the herky-jerky novelty song and twitches along with his fellow guitarists during each halting verse. Jimmie is prominently featured behind a small drum kit with no logo on the bass drum and a single snare with two cymbals. Nicol's concentration is evident with his jaw open wide as he stares hard at each of Colin's Elvis-like moves, hitting every halting beat perfectly. Hicks proceeds to work himself into a frenzy of Elvis and James Brown moves as he repeatedly sings the chorus *Giddy-Up-A Ding Dong*. Piano player Mike O'Neil jumps on top of the piano and reaches down to play the keyboard solo with one hand. Meanwhile, the crowds of dancers perfect their jitterbug moves. The couple in front performs a series of tap step, tap step, and ball changes, followed by the male dancer lifting his girlfriend into the air and tossing her around his body. The excitement generated by the band is quite amazing for a one-song performance, though the song really did not tax Jimmie Nicol in his role as timekeeper. Jimmie and the group play their hearts out to the sweaty teenagers who seem to be truly enjoying themselves.

Nicol was grateful to be in a band that was now setting out on another tour, this time as the headliner. Undeterred by the loss of Hicks' record deal, the band hit the road throughout the United Kingdom to pay its dues and grow their fan base. Colin & His Cabin Boys began an extended series of shows; it was welcome work and steady pay for their newlywed drummer.

In April, 1958, the band was on top-of-the-bill to play two one-night stands at The Boys Brigade Hall, in the town of Wick, Scotland. The band was 600 miles away from its home in London. It may have been part of the United Kingdom, but to Colin Hicks it seemed like a foreign land. When the doors opened at 9:00 pm there was no stampede of fans. A local band, Jimmy Wilson and the Melotones, kicked off the show as the warm up act. Bob Hunter, a guitarist in the Melotones, recalls his band supporting Colin Hicks & His Cabin Boys throughout the Scotland leg of their tour. "We were the local support band. We played mostly Skiffle," he says. "Colin was sort of enjoying himself as the younger brother of Tommy Steele. He was very impressed with being top-of-the-bill. He was acting sort of high-minded. Trouble is, *he* wasn't as good as he thought he was."[5] Hunter recalls that his band usually would go off in search of a drink after its set, but someone in the Cabin Boys caught his eye and impressed him, the drummer. "I noticed their drummer, Jimmie Nicol; a very nice chap. And he was a dammed good drummer. But we still felt we were better than Colin Hicks."[6]

Local witnesses recall, "They found barely a dozen girls jiving half-heartedly to Colin Hicks & His Cabin Boys."[7] The review of the evening focused not on the band's playing, but rather on its alleged misbehavior. It read, "Worse, these newcomers proved somewhat disrespectful to their distinguished guests, jeering, scoffing and dishing out a selection of ribald sarcasms."[8] Though the slim audience did not respond well to Hicks' sarcasm, the band dutifully finished its set and left, anxious to return home to London. The evening must have remained on Hicks' mind as an article in a national magazine came out shortly thereafter, with a quote from an "unnamed rocker" who advised other musicians, "to avoid, at all costs, a miserable placed called Thurso, where the locals were utterly ignorant of what constituted good music."[9]

Sybil Richardson was a singer who had started with the Vernon Girls group in the mid-1950s. The Vernon Girls had emerged from Liverpool originally as a choir put together as part of the social activities of Vernon Pools, the Liverpool based football betting pool company. There were sixteen girls in all with one or two as understudies. The group was a great success on TV. Television exposure led to more work for the all-girl group as studio and concert tour backup singers.

Richardson had been sent to serve as a backup singer to Colin Hicks on the national tour. She recalls, "It was very poorly put together. The whole thing just collapsed, financially I think. The halls weren't full. People weren't interested. They wanted to see Tommy (Steele) not Colin."[10] Colin's apparent bad attitude didn't help matters and actually caused strife with audiences, as well as within the traveling musical troupe. "He (Colin) could be rude to people and I didn't appreciate that. From my point of view the whole thing was a complete disaster," recalls Richardson. "I was so young and green that I just went to pieces."[11]

THE NIGHT LIFE OF EUROPE COMES TO TOWN
...in this great color spectacular!

"FABULOUS ... QUITE A SHOW"
—San Francisco Examiner

Join the after-dark-to-dawn cabaret whirl and thrill to some of the world's brightest entertainers!

EUROPEAN NIGHTS

EASTMANCOLOR

Carmen Sevilla • Domenico Modugno • The Platters • Channing Pollock • Henri Salvador
Coccinelle • Robert Lamouret • The Rastellis • Colin Hicks • Candid Comment—Henry Morgan
Presented by JOSEPH BURSTYN RELEASING

Film Poster from "European Nights"

Back home in London, Colin Hicks & His Cabin Boys were regrouping for more shows when they suddenly got a break that might lift the giant shadow cast over them by Tommy Steele, albeit in an unexpected way. Word from Colin's manager came that an Italian film director, Alessandro Blassetti, was making a film about European pop culture, and he wanted Colin Hicks & His Cabin Boys to represent British Rock and Roll in the film. Hicks, Nicol, and the rest of the band were ecstatic with the idea of making a film. Colin had come to realize, his career dilemma was his similarity in looks and style to his more famous brother Tommy. His poor behavior on tour was at least partially a reflection of his frustration over performing in his brother's shadow. He needed something to set him apart from his brother's career, and perhaps a film appearance would do just the trick.

Italian Director Alessandro Blasetti was considered one of the most consequential, eclectic and diverse directors in the history of Italian cinema.[12] Blasetti was a trendsetter in different genres of Italian cinema, from neo-realism to Italian sitcoms.[13] In 1958, he decided to direct a sexy documentary that would provide the audience with a continental mondo crash-course, displaying "some of the greatest stars of European show business caught in the act - in night clubs, circuses, music halls and theatres all over Europe."[14] The film would be called "Europa di Notte" or "European Nights".

The "mondo" style of filmmaking got its start in Italy, using a formula that contained sexy and shocking vignettes in a documentary format. No plot was necessary as the director searched the European Continent for voluptuous strippers, magicians, hedonist rockers and more. "The mondo film usually attracted a mostly male audience anxious to view the forbidden nude images offered within. They were equally willing to accept the staginess and artificiality of product that still managed to excite the sense," according to film historian Ellie Castiel.[15]

Jimmie Nicol was excited to be filming a Rock performance with Colin Hicks and the band. This was a milestone in his blossoming career. It was an opportunity in which he planned to go all out to get noticed. The filming for this Italian "epic" was to take place at a music hall in London. This time, Jimmie graduated to a full Gretsch drum kit all decked out in white pearl. Given the cost of such a kit, it is highly likely that Jimmie borrowed the kit as a loaner from his daytime employer, Boosey & Hawkes, just for this film performance. Also, for the first time, his own name "Jimmie Nicol" was proudly printed onto the bass drum head. This was a bold statement, for Nicol put his name and his name alone - out front during the filmed performance. At this point, there was no imprint of Colin Hicks and no mention of the Cabin Boys. The band got outfitted with tuxedos for their film debut. Colin chose a brown sparkled tux, while the Cabin Boys all went with traditional black. All had black bow ties and white folded handkerchiefs in their breast pockets. Jimmie's hair had a pound of grease in it, with curls quaffed high on his forehead like Elvis Presley.

The theatre was packed with teenagers bursting with energy. The scene which would serve as the rousing closer of the film's musical segment starts with a voice-over by humorist Henry Morgan who sets the stage, "Even the European nights grow late. The only action left is in London, where Colin Hicks is inexhaustible. The British may forgive us [Americans] Bunker Hill and the Tea Party in Boston, but they may hold Rock and Roll against us forever. And they'll be so right!"[16] As the narrator fades out, we hear the band in mid-song, with a highly charged Colin singing, *Baby I love You*. While Colin wiggles about the stage singing to the adoring teen extras, Jimmie is seen manically rocking his kit. His left arm is swinging in a circular windmill that would predate Pete Townsend on guitar by several years, hitting double speed cymbal shots in time with the band as Mike Elliott belts out a blistering sax solo from his knees. A young man in the audience is seen jumping uncontrollably out of his seat while the girls around him scream. When Colin wails the last of the lyrics, "Baby, I love you sooooo", the crowd in the first four rows jumps to its feet and moves to the edge of the stage, ecstatic with the band's performance.

Jitterbug dancing breaks out in front of the stage as Colin and the boys immediately start into Eddie Cochran's hit, *Twenty Flight Rock*, a sure-bet crowd pleaser. The song leads in with a brief drum solo by Jimmie as Colin Hicks starts singing the now-familiar lyrics. Hicks' frenetic dancing appears to combine the moves of Chuck Berry with the dramatic knee crashing-to-the-stage move of James Brown. Certainly Hicks' moves were a precursor to Mick Jagger's, who wouldn't hit the stage for several more years.

Now it was Jimmie's time to shine, and he takes center stage with an unforgettable extended drum solo. The melody of "Twenty Flight Rock" drifts through Nicol's mind as he plays the solo-lost in his own polyrhythmic bliss. His jaw is wide open as he pushes himself further, dangerously rocking the entire kit as if he is hitting every drum and cymbal simultaneously. His solo moves smoothly from Rock tempo into free form jazz, as Jimmie appears in a crazed zone - a precursor to The Who's Keith Moon in the Sixties. After holding the attention of his own band mates who have jumped up on the drum riser to watch, Jimmie gives a demonstration that would set the trend for future Rock drummers like Moon and Ginger Baker. Nicol blazes along, changing his role as time-keeper to crazy soloist. His improvisation of the song is more like a guitar player or horn player. Three steady beats on the tom toms signal the band to dramatically leap off the riser in unison and finish the song with a flurry – sending the fans into a rabid frenzy of screams and applause.

Suddenly, Colin Hicks & His Cabin Boys had turned a corner. With their amazing performance in "Europa di Notte", Colin, Jimmie, and the boys were about to gain special notice, though they didn't realize it at the time. Nor did they realize that they would have to travel overseas from their home country of England in order to taste the fruits of fame and success.

In early May of 1958, Jimmie got a call from Colin Hicks with great news. Hicks told him the band had been invited to tour Italy as a result of its well-received performance in the Italian film, "Europa di Notte". Jimmie was ecstatic and asked if he could bring his wife, and Hicks agreed.

With the regular income anticipated from the Cabin Boy's upcoming tour of Italy, Jimmie was ready to purchase his first new drum kit. He was influenced by London drummer Phil Seaman, his role model, who played a Trixon drum set in the late 1950s. This fact - coupled with the Trixon kit's modern shape and big, booming sound - likely influenced Jimmie's decision to purchase a Trixon drum set for the upcoming tour.[17] The new band rehearsed for two weeks and then set off for a new adventure as Italy's favorite new Rock band.

Chapter Five
Touring Italy and Searching for Elvis

Italy is famous for its rich culture comprised of historic buildings; ancient statues; priceless paintings; and, most importantly, a rich and wonderful cuisine. Tourists from around the world have enjoyed visiting Italy for its perfect blend of past and present. For Colin Hicks & His Cabin Boys, Italy meant different things to each of its band members. To Hicks, it meant escaping the shadow of his famous brother, Tommy Steele, and seducing beautiful female fans in every city they visited. To Jimmie Nicol, Italy meant a chance to improve his skills as a touring drummer and honeymoon with his wife. To yet other members of the Cabin Boys, it meant the chance to take a road trip to Germany in hopes of meeting "The King", Elvis Presley, who was currently stationed there, courtesy of the U.S. Army. The tour of an overseas country represented yet another notch on Jimmie Nicol's musical belt; although the so-called "tour" was more a series of disjointed one-night stands spread around the country than an organized tour in today's terms. Hicks would earn the princely sum of £300 per week for the tour.[1] The Cabin Boys would have made quite a bit less as sidemen. As was the case in the late 1950s and early 1960s, these types of tours typically ended with musicians having little money left after paying for their own living expenses, instruments, stage clothing and transportation, and other costs skimmed off by agents and promoters. Nevertheless, it was a real overseas tour, and the band was excited by the prospects of playing in a foreign land.

Although he was not the bandleader, it may well have been Nicol's show-stealing drum solo in the film "Europa di Notte" that had earned them this tour in a foreign country. Colin Hicks relished the chance to lead his band in a faraway place, where he would not have to worry about comparisons to his pop star brother, Tommy Steele.

Max Lobkowitz was a young boy of 16 when he saw the film "Europa di Notte" in Italy. His early years provided Max with a liberal upbringing which permitted attendance at films with nudity and Rock and Roll as he grew up in Italy. He was even permitted to hang out in adult nightclubs. Lobkowitz became infatuated with the performance of Colin Hicks & His Cabin Boys in the film. His dream to see the band perform live came true in a very short time. He recalls, "I was thrilled when Colin and his band were booked at the Lido in the summer of 1958. My family was members there and back before Walt Disney invented childhood; I was able to get into nightclubs. It was a golden age for kids; a time and place when any kid could go to a club and we learned to drink responsibly."[2] The Lido was one of Italy's most beautiful complexes for well-heeled Italians. The club at Lido was called La Grota ("the Cave"). And although post-war Italy was economically poor, Genoa was a very rich industrial port. As a result, all of the rich kids would flock to The Lido.

The journey literally started out with a bang! The band was en-route from Paris to Milan for the start of their tour supporting the Platters. Band manager John Edwards was accompanying Colin Hicks & His Cabin Boys on the drive which began on May 11, 1958. Their rented car was in France, making its way to Italy, when smoke started to billow from the engine under the hood. Either the car had run out of oil or did not have sufficient water for cooling. The clouds of smoke got so thick as to make driving unsafe. Suddenly the engine blew up! Edwards, Nicol, and his band mates all quickly piled out of the car to safety. Luckily no one was hurt. A new car was quickly obtained to get the band back on their way and fortunately, the car problem did not serve as foreshadow of what would otherwise be a successful trip.[3]

When Colin Hicks & His Cabin Boys arrived in Genoa, their biggest fan Lobkowitz was there to greet them. He immediately latched onto Colin Hicks. "I was very close with Colin," recalls Max. "I basically took care of him. He was quite temperamental and excitable. The band was part of it. I knew them too, but they were peripheral. I was focused on Colin."[4] So, Lobkowitz settled in as the unofficial "roadie" and translator. The band set up in Genoa for a series of shows before moving on through Italy.

Keyboard player Mike O'Neil grew closer to Jimmie during the musical trip. He recalls the band did not need to rehearse much. "They were pretty simple, straightforward Rock and Roll songs."[5] The two musicians began to share a mutual passion in Jazz music, though their live shows were limited to Rock and Roll. "I remember Jimmie had this one Modern Jazz Quartet album called *Fontessa*. He was more interested in that type of music than anything else. Jimmie and this album was the thing that really turned me on to Jazz. I found myself walking down the street, whistling some phrase and I didn't know where I had got it from."[6] O'Neil would later turn keyboardist Georgie Fame onto Jazz. Fame, in turn, would play an important role in Nicol's career in 1964. O'Neil and Nicol's friendship in Italy also allowed O'Neal to observe Jimmie's less than perfect newlywed status. According to O'Neil, "She [Patty Nicol] was a bit of harridan. He brought her to Italy and she did nothing buy complain about everything. Unfortunately, she was on his back about everything."[7] However, Nicol did not let his wife interfere with his desire to improve his musicianship or to gain the touring experience that would serve him well in the future.

The band traveled through Italy as part of a caravan that included headlining vocal act The Platters and American Ramblin' Jack Elliott. Founding Platters member Herb Reed recalls the bands toured many different places in Italy, but cannot remember where or how long they were all there. "On many occasions the Italian promoters put us on a hot train or sometimes in a car, but we traveled separately from the others on the tour", recalls Reed.[8] The Platters, as top of the bill, even had an audience with the Pope when the tour hit Rome, and felt greatly honored just to have an audience with His Holiness. No such luck for the Cabin Boys, however, who were fortunate enough just to reach each city in one piece for their performance.

O'Neil recalls Colin and the band initially had to fit five Cabin Boys into a four-seater car. "We went on very long journeys to reach our gigs," he recalls. "The management was in a car around the bend and I remember coming around the bend one time and the management's car was on its head, upside down. No one was seriously injured." At times, the band would use Milan as a home base and venture out to play around the country. "One time we played Sicily and then the next gig we had to play was near Venice; with a very short amount of time to get there. We went to Bologna, Florence, and Genoa and all along the Adriatic coast," recalls O'Neil.[9]

O'Neil would play whatever piano was available at the hall or club. Nicol had the toughest job of lugging his drum equipment everywhere the band went. "Half of his kit was strapped to the roof of our car and some of it went into the trunk with guitars and things." Their poor bass player, Boots Slade, didn't even have an amplifier. "He would just find a speaker that someone would roll on stage," recalls O'Neil.[10]

The long and sometimes treacherous drives were not the only obstacles facing Hicks and his crew. Roadie Max Lobkowitz was enlisted as the band's translator, not just with promoters, but especially with female fans. "I was chasing the band everywhere and basically trying to help the guys keep out of mischief."[11] That is, all the guys except Jimmie who was not running around - what with his wife in tow. Hidden away in their hotel room one night, Lobkowitz recalls his introduction to smoking marijuana coming via the Cabin Boys. "It was great, better than alcohol and it made the music sound great too."[12]

Max recalls one of the funnier moments involving Hicks and another band member when they got caught in the ladies room of a nightclub. "They were always trying to get in there to make it with the girls," recalls Lobkowitz. "They got into trouble. They had gone into the girl's room after a show. When the Police came, I had to tell them, 'They can't understand Italian. You couldn't read the word on the door, right Colin?' It was funny. I had to translate and help them out of this bind. They were of course trying to make time with the girls. They were always up to something."[13]

To Max, the music was the most important thing. "I knew Jimmie Nicol and all of the Cabin Boys. I was only sixteen, but a very grown up sixteen. The band was made up of all wonderfully crazy English people. Colin was a very great singer and Jimmie was an amazing and clever drummer."[14] The band was well-received and was loved all over Italy. From the Lido, where the band had an extended stay, Max traveled with the band to Milan, Bologna, and Rome. "We did quite a few cities and one-night stands."[15]

Each night during the performance, one of Colin's trademarked moves was a big kick high up into the air, synched perfectly with the well-timed rim shot of Jimmie Nicol. Today a move like this one would appear quite tame, but in the late 1950s, music fans were used to handsome crooners standing dead still behind a microphone. Hicks & His Cabin Boys were used to falling on the ground and jumping up on Nicol's drum rostrum, all while playing their instruments. O'Neil liked to jump up onto the top of the piano and play with one hand hanging down. All of these innovative moves were clearly aimed at stirring the fans into frenzy. "When they got onstage, it was amazing. Colin was like electricity," recalls Lobkowitz. "They were all full of energy and never stopped. These guys should have been the biggest things in England. I've never really understood that. When Colin and the guys were rockin' The Lido, everybody went nuts."[16]

A review from the Roman newspaper *Il Messaggero* confirmed Max's assessment. The review of Colin Hicks & His Cabin Boys focused on their two shows with The Platters at the Sistina Theatre in Rome. The translated review revealed, "He who received total personal success was the 'English Elvis Presley', the young blond singer, Colin Hicks, who, accompanied by his Cabin Boys, has almost surpassed his American model in exhibiting frenetic movement both in the Rock and Roll and in Calypso areas of music. His voice was especially suited for the screaming style. The syncopated endings of his songs were always greeted by waves of applause."[17] This was high praise indeed from the local Roman media, a highly favorable comparison to Elvis Presley, and significantly, no mention of Hicks' famous brother, Tommy Steele. It is interesting that the reviewer also favorably noted Jimmie Nicol's "syncopated endings", though not mentioning him by name.

In Search of Elvis Presley

Although Rome considered Colin Hicks & His Cabin Boys as bigger than Elvis Presley, the band members themselves still held Elvis in the highest esteem. They so revered Elvis, that, when the band had a few extra days off, they decided to take a road trip to Munich for their private audience with the King himself- Sgt. Elvis Presley; who was reportedly there on Leave. "We had heard that Elvis Presley was in Germany during his National Service. And we had a few days off and had just gotten a hold of this Studebaker because we wanted a bigger car to travel around in," recalls O'Neil. "So with the time off, we decided to travel from Milan to Munich to hopefully meet Elvis!"[18] Of course, the best-laid plans of fun-loving young guys don't always go as planned.

A strange accident intervened on the road to see the King. After hours of driving, a deer jumped out in front of the Studebaker and was hit and killed by the Cabin Boys. The band all got out of the car and stared at the deer in the road, wondering what to do about it. Another car came along at this time and saw what had happened. "We tried to translate what the other driver was telling us," recalls the keyboard player. "I think basically he said he would take the deer off our hands. We said, 'Great!' And he put it into his boot [trunk] and drove off."[19] The band carried on with its trip and decided to stop at a hotel several miles up the road for a drink. Much to their surprise after sitting down, the chef came out of the kitchen. O'Neil explains, "He was going around the restaurant asking if anyone would like any fresh venison for dinner (laughing). It was him… the other driver. They were cooking up our dead deer!"[20]

The band passed up the venison delicacy and forged on to see Elvis, the holy grail of their trip to Germany. When they arrived, it was in the middle of a beer festival. One beer led to another... and another. "So, we just joined in the celebrations and forgot all about trying to get hold of Elvis," recalls O'Neil laughing. "We never got anywhere near him at the end. When that was done, we just turned around and came back to Italy and didn't eat anymore steaks."[21] Though not upset about their failed quest to meet the King, the band got some very positive news upon their return to Italy.

Arriving back in Milan around the first of June 1958, Colin Hicks & His Cabin Boys were asked to meet with David Matalon, founder of the Broadway International record label. Matalon was an Italian impresario who had a long and successful career in record production, management, and music publishing. "In about 1948, at the end of the second World War, I was living in Egypt where I started as an impresario," recalls Matalon. "I managed the French Comedy Companies of Louis Jouvet and Jean Louis Barrault. Then I booked tours in the Middle East for big name French singers such as Yves Montand and Edith Piaf and Italian stars like Teddy Reno, Luciano Tajoli and Murolo."[22] In 1953, the political situation in Egypt became quite tenuous, so Matalon decided to move to Italy, where he began a long and successful career producing records. In 1956 David Matalon started the Broadway International record label, which remained active well into the 1960s.

Matalon had enjoyed the live performances he had seen of Colin Hicks & His Cabin Boys as well as their film performance in "European Nights." He recalls, "My connection with Colin Hicks and his band was to sign them up to a contract to record several songs for my Broadway label while they were touring around Italy with The Platters." Matalon was especially interested in Colin Hicks. "He was recommended to me from London because he was Tommy Steele's brother," say Matalon.[23] Unlike his British producer counterparts of that era, Matalon planned to use all of the Cabin Boys on the recording session. He was suitably impressed with the Cabin Boys' live performances and wanted to capture their raw excitement on record. For Jimmie Nicol, this was a welcome experience that would serve him well in the coming years. He was eager to learn the many tricks-of-the-trade of performing in the controlled recording environment of a professional studio.

Having signed up the band, Matalon set about recording their cover songs of famous Rock hits in the summer of 1958. Broadway International tended to specialize mostly in covers of inter-

Colin Hicks and His Cabin Boys–First EP. Photo Credit: Broadway International.

national hits. "I recall us making quite a few singles in Italy," says keyboard player Mike O'Neil. "I wrote some of the later songs we recorded as well. But at first, we did make quite a few cover songs like *Mabellene*, *Tutti Frutti* and *Johnny B. Good*,"[24] The first EP of four songs recorded by the group for Broadway included: *Johnny Be Good* / *Mean Woman Blues* / *Tutti Frutti* / and *Whole Lotta Shaking*. Roadie Max Lobkowitz attended the sessions mostly to help out where needed. Besides helping lug the equipment in and out of Broadway International, Max found himself helping keep Hicks under control for his singing. "He was quite temperamental and excitable," recalls Lobkowitz.[25]

In preparation for the first EP cover, Colin Hicks used his stage suit, a two-toned blue and gray outfit with light beige socks and black leather shoes. He posed clapping his hands and smoking a cigarette with one foot up on Nicol's bass drumhead which proudly read "Colin Hicks" at the top, "Jimmie Nicol" in the middle, "and his Cabin Boys" at the bottom. The Cabin Boys all wore matching blue-purple V-neck sweaters with white shirts and wide-open pointy collars. All five members presented glazed-over expressions, as if they had never been photographed before; a stare that resembled a certain deer in the headlights of their Studebaker.

For Nicol, this was a great chance to see how recording sessions worked. Jimmie studied the producer Matalon as he set up microphones around the instruments in the studio. He watched how the session was run, and he relished the opportunity to hear the playback in the control room of his band and his drum playing. This was a new and creative experience that preserved Nicol's early career drumming and gave him a newfound interest in playing as a studio session man in the future, a skill that would have far-reaching benefits aside from the obvious financial remuneration. For the rest of the Cabin Boys, it was exciting to hear themselves on record and to see themselves on the cover of an extended play record that featured their band.

Throughout the early summer, Colin Hicks and the band continued to stay headquartered in Milan while driving out and back to more hotel and nightclub one-nighters. As the first record was prepared for release, Matalon called the group back into the studio to begin work on another EP batch of four songs in late June. This session would feature songs to help exploit the band's appearance in "Europa Di Notte". The songs included *Iea Iea* / *Oh Boy* / *Book of Love* and *20 Flight Rock*.

20 Flight Rock had been featured in the film and is the highlight of the EP. When Eddie Cochrane originally recorded *20 Flight Rock* in 1957, it was performed in a Rockabilly style. Colin Hicks & His Cabin Boys would drive this arrangement in a bigger, hotter fashion. Here, the Cabin Boys' sound is much closer in concept to a group like Louis Jordan and his Tympani Five, with a more R&B and Big Band - influenced sound.

At this point in the long day's recording schedule, the producer must have finally realized how much talent he was wasting behind the drum kit. The explosion of rhythm flies off the record as Jimmie hits every part of his kit. The song is in 2/4 time, moving almost too fast for Hicks' vocals to keep up, and the band seems to move ahead of its leader. Mike Elliott's tenor sax solo is sexy and cool, but all too brief. Then after one more verse, the spotlight falls onto the band's real star, drummer Jimmie Nicol.

Nicol takes off on a drum solo that lasts for a whopping 0:55 seconds, unheard of for a Rock song in 1958. Though not a perfect performance, it is very good, not an easy feat when playing completely alone with all eyes in the room on you, hoping that this will be the take that makes it to the finished record. To Jimmie's credit, he lets himself get "out there" in the moment, trying to keep it interesting and exciting, and he succeeds in creating a memorable record with his Cabin Boys.

The cover photo shoot for the "Europa Di Notte" EP was set up in front of an ancient Italian building in Rome. Colin Hicks is dressed in a

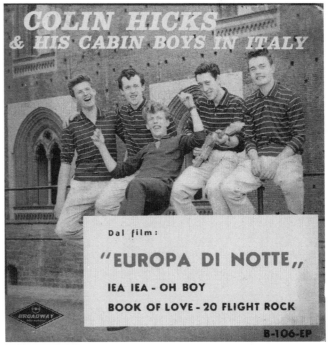

Europa Di Notte EP. Photo Credit: Broadway International

green shirt and tan slacks to stand out from his Cabin Boys who were dressed in matching maroon and white striped shirts with white slacks. "On the EP we recorded, they posed us sitting outside some old Roman building. We all sat on this metal fence and Colin stood in front kicking his foot out. Jimmie is sitting on the far right," say O'Neil.[26] Colin has his arms raised, looking like he had just won a championship-boxing match. Jimmie Nicol is seen, hands in his lap, calmly smiling at the camera with a look of pride in the recording work they had just concluded. The back cover of the EP bragged that Colin Hicks & His Cabin Boys were the "best attraction" in "Europe By Night", an accurate statement by most accounts. All in all, it was quite a thrill for the 19 year-old drummer. The band scored a number of Italian hits with its covers of American Rock and Roll records; and the success kept Colin Hicks & His Cabin Boys busy for a while with plenty of one-night gigs.

Things were looking up for Nicol and the band. Colin and the boys continued to tour Italy through the end of the summer. As the fall of 1958 dawned, Jimmie, his wife, Dave Tick, and Boots all went back to England. They were ready to go back home. Hicks and piano player O'Neil decided to stay on in Italy and launch a major tour. "I stayed on and went on tour with an Italian band called Il Solitore as a backing band for Colin. And when Colin later sent for a drummer, Jimmie didn't come back," says O'Neil. "Colin Hicks & His Cabin Boys sort of drifted apart because this big tour was coming along. And I think to save money; Colin just kept me to play with the Italian group so he wouldn't have to pay the rest of the Cabin Boys. I think we all just got fed up doing the same thing with Colin Hicks and the others wanted to do something new... Yeah, I think it was an economic thing mainly."[27]

So, with his Italian adventure at an end, Jimmie Nicol hung up his Cabin Boy outfit and headed home. Another surprise was in store for Nicol, as his wife Patty informed him that she was pregnant with their first child.

For the remainder of the year, Nicol would latch on to various Larry Parnes' acts as their drummer, doing one-nighters; and there were always gigs at the 2 I's and his occasional daytime hours repairing drums at Boosey & Hawkes. Nicol accepted another short-term gig in late 1958, drumming in the pit band of the Lionel Bart musical, *Fings Ain't Wot They Used to Be*, which had opened at The Theater Royal in East London.

With the birth of his son, Howard Nicol, came further responsibility as both a husband and a father. Jimmie Nicol was more determined than ever to create financial stability from his musical career for his family, and that meant joining a band of talented rockers who were in steady demand throughout England. His wait would not take long, for Larry Parnes was putting together another crack band to go out on the road.

Chapter Six

Vince Eager & The Quiet Three

Vince Eager is not his real name, but his easy-going presence, and powerful voice has made him a legend of early British Rock and Roll, despite a career that did not include radio hits or big record sales. In the early days of British pop, few performers were able to survive on stage work alone. However, Eager proved the exception to this rule, earning recognition for his stage career, without the hits that normally drive the music entertainment machine.

Born Roy Taylor in Grantham, Lincolnshire England on June 4, 1940, he showed an early interest in entertaining others. Soon his interests led him to the up-and-coming world of pop music. In 1955 Taylor joined together with a couple of buddies and formed a vocal trio. "I started my career playing Skiffle music in a group called the Vagabonds," recalls Eager. "We were on a show called 'Come Dancing' on BBC-TV, which put on the World Skiffle Championships in 1957."[1] It took the Vagabonds ten weeks to get to the finals. "Basically it was cheap entertainment for the Ballroom Corporation."[2] The competition was not unlike today's "American Idol" TV format, yet focused solely on Skiffle music, a blend of Jazz, Blues, Folk and Roots music.

Although the Vagabonds did not win the competition, the gig led to their 1958 residency at the popular 2 I's Coffee Bar where many musicians could be "discovered". Larry Parnes first saw Eager perform with the Vagabonds on a Sunday concert in Coventry also starring Marty Wilde and Colin Hicks. Eager got his first look at Jimmie Nicol playing drums in Colin Hicks & His Cabin Boys at this early point in his career. Parnes was suitably impressed with Eager to sign him up as a solo act.

"It was Parnes' idea to change my name from Roy Taylor to Vince Eager, within about 18 hours of meeting me," recalls Eager. "I met him on a Sunday at six o'clock in the evening, and by twelve o'clock lunch time the next day, he had changed my name to Vince Eager."[3] In fact, the stage name was the result of contributions from both Eager and Parnes. Eager says, "He'd [Parnes] chosen Eager because he thought I was eager to get on with my career. He was the guy who had picked the names Tommy Steele and Marty Wilde. He would pick those types of names to depict a type of character or the characteristics of the performer. I selected Vince because I was a big Gene Vincent fan."[4]

Eager got the chance to record a handful of songs for Decca records in 1958. The tracks would be produced by Decca's A & R man, Dick Rowe, whom history recalls as the man who turned down The Beatles' recording audition in January, 1962. Unfortunately, just as the songs were released, Eager's meddling manager Parnes pulled Vince off the Decca label in order to start his own record label. The Parnes short-lived company was called Elempi (which had the same pronunciation as its founder's initials LMP). "Of course the 'I' in Elempi was for *idiot*," says Eager.[5] As soon as Parnes pulled Eager out of the Decca deal, Decca let the records flounder without any promotion, including one song that was destined for a high profile movie soundtrack. As a result, Eager's Decca recordings faded into obscurity, along with Parnes' record label which could never get its records pressed or labels printed.

This did not deter Parnes or Eager from pursuing a live stage career. When asked by *Melody Maker* whether he could still build an artist's career without a hit record, Parnes replied matter-of-factly, "Yes. Definitely, Vince Eager is a good example."[6] Aside from upscale nightclubs, Parnes placed Eager on British television's pop showcases "6.5 Special" and ITV's "Oh Boy!" These shows helped Eager gain national recognition and sell tickets for his live shows. From the success of TV came his first national tour of theaters and ballrooms in September, 1958 as support for Parnes' big star, Marty Wilde. At the end of 1958, Eager decided he needed a change from his Skiffle-sounding Vagabonds. "I didn't really keep the Vagabonds after that," he recalls.[7] Eager knew that he wanted to get into pop music that rocked a little bit harder and to take greater advantage of his powerful voice. In order to make best use of his distinctive voice, Eager chose to form a new band.

Eager moved quickly to snap up some of the more talented rockers in the London scene, including journeyman drummer Jimmie Nicol. He came up with the name Vince Eager & The Quiet Three. "The Quiet Three with Jimmie Nicol came onto the scene in about early 1959," says Eager. "They [The Quiet Three] used to work on the same bill as me with the various groups on the theater and ballroom circuits so I knew they were talented."[8] In fact, Eager snatched Jimmie Nicol away from a band the young drummer had just joined in January of 1959.

That promising group turned out to be Tony Sheridan & The Wreckers. Seventeen year-old Tony Sheridan, had "ranked first" as the new "British recording hope" in early 1959.[9] The Wreckers had just gotten started and were rehearsing songs such as *I Like Love* and *When The Saints (Go Marching In)*. Sheridan recalls having Nicol in his band, "It was impossible not to like him. He had a warm personality and he was bright and had great depth, too."[10] Regarding how Sheridan happened to snare Nicol as his drummer, he says, "Jimmie was an exemplary drummer – one of those drummers appreciated by all other musicians, though they might not admit it! It was one of those things really," says Sheridan, "Right time, right place, right chemistry…"[11]

Just as the highly anticipated Wreckers were about to hit the ballroom circuit, Eager's manager, Larry Parnes, moved Nicol out of The Wreckers and into The Quiet Three, as if he was moving a piece on the chess board. Tony Sheridan would eventually go on to fame in Hamburg, Germany where, in 1961 he enlisted the help of The Beatles to record several songs together as Tony Sheridan & the Beat Brothers. Sheridan was realistic about losing his prized drummer. He understood where many of the Soho musicians' bread was buttered at the time as he recalls, "If Jimmy needed a long-term job and Parnes offered it to him, well, that's probably how it was."[12] Indeed, with a young wife and baby, Nicol was in need of a secure long term gig.

Thus, the original Quiet Three was born, with Vince Eager (vocals), Colin Green (lead guitar and rhythm), Tex Makins (bass guitar) and Jimmie Nicol. "I recall that Colin Hicks & His Cabin Boys came back from Italy to London. Jimmie was their drummer. I don't think Hicks' career was working out too good so the Cabin Boys disbanded. I think Larry Parnes gave me Jimmie Nicol for The Quiet Three," says Eager.[13] Tex Makins had already met Eager and had played with him at Churchill's night club. "I think I first met Colin Green at the 2 I's Coffee bar," says Eager.[14] "I was the lead guitarist in Vince Eager & The Quiet Three," says Colin Green. "I think I just got a call to be in the band. Vince put the band together. There were no other guitarists in the band. We were a trio of musicians with a big sound."[15] Green had remembered Jimmie Nicol from his own unsuccessful tryout with Colin Hicks & His Cabin Boys, and as a guitarist backing Billy Fury in the clubs and on theater tours.

Noel Wallis served as a road manager to Eager & The Quiet Three, as well as drum tech to Jimmie Nicol. "Jimmie Nicol was a very good drummer. He played with so many talented bands," says Wallis.[16] As road manager, Wallis took care of various details for touring, travel, transporting equipment and getting the band to the shows on time. "I was actually staying at Jimmie's home around the time of The Quiet Three. He was married at the time to a lady called Pat and they had a young son named Howard. He was very young at the time. Howie was the diamond in their family and to all the boys in the band. We all got on tremendously."[17]

Eager's move to assemble a trio of rockers was clearly for the purpose of doing live shows.

30

"Jimmie never recorded with me. He only played live with The Quiet Three and me. We had one of the best live sets," says Eager. Touring would not be easy without having recognizable hits to play. "I wasn't getting number one hits and all this. When we did the tours I was up against guys on the concert bill who had gotten the one hit or more. I had always been a stage performer, so I concentrated on my stage act," says Eager.[18]

However, before Vince Eager & The Quiet Three could take to the road, their drummer James George Nicol had to face up to a crisis that could have derailed the band and Jimmie's career dead in its tracks. At the conclusion of World War II, there were substantial demands placed upon the British Government to contribute troops to occupational duties in Germany; to the maintenance of security within its Empire, and to reestablishing a British influence in the Middle East. To accommodate this continuing requirement for young male soldiers, the Labour Government established a national service system in 1946. The Act, which continued its intake of young men into the early 1960s, initially required a period of one year to be served in the Armed Forces followed by a possible five years in the Reserve. The demands of Britain's involvement in the Korean Conflict led to the length of service being extended to two years. This rule applied universally to all "able-bodied" men.

Within a couple of weeks of forming The Quiet Three, "conscript" James George Nicol received a notice in the mail to attend a medical examination to ensure that he was "fit for military service." At this point, Eager and his trio had done a bit of rehearsing and were preparing for a tour in 1959 when the draft notice showed up in Jimmie's mailbox. Colin Green recalls Nicol's determination to continue with his music career and not to let the military derail his goal. "Very simply, he was going to dodge the draft. He stayed up the night before he had to go for the medical call. He got completely blind drunk, didn't sleep and just turned up for the physical and got turned down (laughing)."[19] Nicol understood that he needed to appear quite "unfit" and not at all "able-bodied" in order to fool the military and get back to drumming. "I was around with him and I remember he came back the following day and he was laughing his head off. He came back saying, 'I bloody missed it! I got out of it!' He wanted to go in looking as ragged as possible and it worked."[20] Green was too young at the time to be called in, so he didn't have to worry about the military. "I have no knowledge of anyone else trying what Jimmie tried, but it certainly worked and we got him back so we could tour (laughing)."[21]

Eager knew he needed an edge on the concert bill with his competitors, lacking a hit song, so his goal was to separate his performance from the hit makers on tour. The stage act created by the group was strong in appearance, variety and musical expertise. "I used to do gimmicky stuff and used to do a lot of variety; like a vaudeville review. I would play the piano like Fats Domino and sing *Blueberry Hill* or *I Want To Take You Home*. And we did stuff like Jimmy Rodgers' *Honeycomb*, *Your Kiss Is Sweeter Than Wine* and *Lollypop*. So we did stuff that was totally different from any other band on the circuit. All the other bands were just doing straight out Rock and Roll like Elvis and Bill Haley. But we mixed it up. All the guys before me [on the bill] had all the hit records, but it didn't make a difference because I had the strongest set and the best band. My band got the crowd more excited, which is what the promoters wanted."[22]

Excitement, surprises and first class showmanship are what Eager, Nicol and company gave their audiences in the summer of 1959. One example featured the band performing the song *San Miguel*. On this song, drummer Nicol strolled out front and center to play bongos to accompany Eager's singing. What the audience did not know was that Jimmie had rigged each bongo with a different colored light bulb, red in one and blue in the other. As Eager began to sing, Jimmie began to strike the bongo skins and the audience went wild as the colored lights appeared synchronized to his beats, playing along to *San Miguel*. Eager continues, "That's not all. I had Tex outline his bass in ultra violet paint. Colin would also paint an outline around his guitar. And it would all stand out in the black light we turned on. The crowd got quite excited," particularly in the late 1950's because there was nothing like it. "It was real theater," recalls Eager proudly.[23]

Jimmie Nicol played a major role in the glittering stage act of The Quiet Three on tour, and it was not all behind the drum kit where he excelled. One comedy bit involved Eager and Nicol getting into a mock argument over the way Nicol had played his drum part on the last song. Eager recalls, "I bought a Smith & Wesson 38 pistol with blanks that had to be registered with the police in every town, which was a real pain in the ass. Jimmie used to do *something wrong* we had planned. I would tell him to get off the stage and would yell, 'You're fired'. As he walked off the stage, I would get the gun from out of my piano and shoot him. Jimmie would play his part by yelling, 'Oh my leg'".[24]

"It was just a gag," says Eager reminiscing. "I used Jimmie for that because he loved the acting part as well as the music. He was really up for it. We used to do a lot of comedy and Jimmie played an integral part of everything we did on stage."[25]

Throughout the summer of 1959, Vince & The Quiet Three played virtually everywhere. They performed at dance halls, ballrooms, theaters and stayed weeks in some resorts. Wallis fondly recalls the summer session of 1959. "There were seaside resorts and theaters that we used to play for many weeks. People would go there with their families and we would put on the entertainment at night. We actually did the summer season for 20 or so weeks." It was great fun."[26]

"We played everything by ear. No charts. All of us in the Q3 were capable of reading charts, but that wasn't what the music was about," recalls guitarist Green. "Jimmie was a very exciting player. Very dynamic! Technically, he was very capable. He was a dangerous drummer," says his guitarist. "The thing about him was that he was a good showman, but he had the technique to back it up. He had the musical ability. He wasn't dancing around with something he wasn't sure of. He was very sure and very capable."[27] In Colin Green's mind, Jimmie Nicol's drumming was the thing that gave The Quiet Three its edge and made the band so outstanding. He says, "Not only was his playing exciting, but it was also very skillful. Jimmie had the ability to play different types of music, from Jazz to Big Band to Rock and Roll."[28] This variety in style was perfect for Vince Eager's mixture of Rock, pop, and vaudeville-esque performances.

Program for "A Fast Moving Anglo American Beat Show"

As summer faded into the fall, Larry Parnes assembled yet another barnstorming tour that would take his stable of artists around the country for a decade-ending hurrah. The tour concluded in January of 1960. Nicol would check in with his young family for a brief visit between tours. "He continued to work at Boosey & Hawkes in their drum department to supplement his income for the family, between tours," says Green.[29] Then, when the call came, Nicol would dutifully kiss his wife and young son goodbye and head back out onto the musical road to earn his living.

The Gene Vincent and Eddie Cochran Tour

The next tour in 1960 would grow out of the late 1959 tour, when Larry Parnes triumphantly presented American Rock star, Gene Vincent. Agents were called and on January 10, 1960, Gene Vincent and Eddie Cochran showed up ready to mount a major UK tour along with Parnes' stable of British stars. The innovative packaged tour of both American and British rockers was dubbed, "A Fast Moving Anglo American Beat Show". Through his connections to Britain's media machine, Parnes made sure that his protégés would be seen arm in arm in the company of these major American Rock stars. No one in England had ever thought of the idea of combining British and American pop stars into one major tour. It was a package guaranteed to fill the seats of every venue along the way.

Before Eddie Cochran came over to start the tour of England, Parnes set up a mini-tour for Vincent with several of his British musicians across the greater London area Granada theaters. Gene Vincent got to watch Vince Eager & The Quiet Three from the wings of the stage and was impressed, notably with Jimmie Nicol's drumming. He told one British journalist, "They have plenty of rhythm and they all seem excellent showmen. What's most important, the fans seem to love them."[30]

After the Vincent & Company tour ended on January 17, 1960, the groups all went into rehearsal for the upcoming Anglo American Beat Show tour. Jack Good, who had created many of Britain's top teen pop television shows, was enlisted to produce the show and whip it into shape. "I rehearsed all the singers as though they were actors. They knew what they wanted to do and I tried to give them a look, to help them do it in the most effective way," said Good.[31] Eddie Cochran rehearsed with his new backing group, borrowing them from Marty Wilde's Wildcats; and Gene Vincent worked out with a Parnes backing band called The Beat Boys. It was around this time that Colin Green, guitarist in The Quiet Three, was moved into the Beat Boys to help out Gene Vincent. Kenny Packwood replaced him in the group. "As soon as Vince heard Colin was leaving, he snapped up Packwood right away," says roadie Wallis. "Packwood was a great guitarist of course. And he and Jimmie got on as great friends right away."[32]

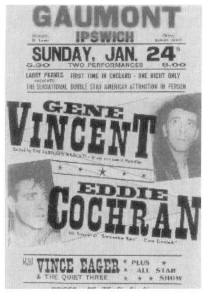

Gaumont Ipswich Poster January 24, 1960.

The historic Vincent/Cochran tour commenced at the Gaumont Ipswich Theatre on January 24, 1960. At the time, music tours were nothing like today's extravaganzas featuring 50 trucks, moving stages, digital equipment, laptops, and laser lights. None of the fancy dressing room amenities (like Cristal Champaign, caviar, etc.) demanded by today's pop stars in their contract "riders" existed in 1960. For the traveling tour, late night meals after shows were difficult to come by. Travel was mostly by trains that did not go directly to each destination, but rather, required train changes. Hotels were only for the very top stars, such as Gene Vincent and Eddie Cochran, while the other traveling minstrels were relegated to boarding houses.

Jimmie Nicol was thrilled to be a part of this big-time packaged expedition. He would be part of the lead British band in support of the headliners for a significant part of the tour. He and the other support musicians were paid around £7 pounds per week. At the time, this was a handsome fee for a young man with a wife and baby. Although, Vince Eager had an automobile he used for touring, at least part of the time; Nicol often had to lug his drum cases with him onto the British rail.

Over the course of the tour, Parnes rotated his various stable bands in and out of the line up to make sure his artists all received the huge exposure offered by the tour. More importantly, Parnes had figured out he could make more money creating two different supporting bills for Vincent and Cochran. One Vincent/Cochran package went out for one-night stands, using Vince Eager & The Quiet Three and other lower level Parnes groups. This twice-nightly, one-day visit to a city would usually sell out at 4,000 customers. The other package supporting the Vincent/Cochran tour featured support from Parnes' "A-Team" of Billy Fury and Joe Brown for weekly stays. This package was attracting 25,000 fans per week. Regardless of the package team, the tour was a sellout wherever it went.[33] It was quite a heady experience for young drummer Jimmie Nicol. He was witness to the crazy and frenetic adulation of girls screaming for the headliners in a mania that would prepare him well for a future gig a few years down the road.

Eager recalls watching Eddie Cochran for the first time, "He had his back to the audience and opened up with Ray Charles' *What'd I Say*. He knocked me out. He sounded so great and looked so cool. I actually changed my opening song after that."[34] Eager had a big ballad that all the fans loved called, *It's Only Make*

Vince Eager, Gene Vincent & Eddie Cochran on tour.
Courtesy of Vince Eager.

Believe. After the show, Eddie Cochran came to Eager's dressing room to tell him how he had enjoyed the set of Vince Eager & The Quiet Three! The two singers complimented each other and quickly became fast friends. Eager sometimes drove Vincent and Cochran to their gigs, saving them from the dreaded train system, creating more time for their growing friendship.

Some of the venues on tour were not built for Rock and Roll music. Many had long flat hard walls in the back. When Nicol and other drummers hit their bass drums, the sound would echo back to the stage on a delay of one or two seconds at the same volume. This aggravation, along with pre-concert drinking and marijuana smoking, generally made things difficult to keep time. The band didn't know whether to follow the first beat or the echo. There were few rehearsal soundchecks. "Soundchecks for us was seeing if there was sound. If we got that at all, that would be it. It was fairly acceptable at the time to have a drink or smoke a little something before you got onstage to loosen up," says Green.[35] Fortunately, the cheering teens didn't seem to notice or care how polished or rough the bands sounded. It did upset some of the more staid reviewers of the day, as one commented, "From start to finish, there seemed nothing but nerve-shattering electric guitars and pounding drums."[36]

Tragedy

Along the way Eager recalls, "Eddie [Cochran] told me that when the tour ended, we would fly back to Los Angeles together and he was going to cut an album with me."[37] This meant a great deal to Eager who had recorded a number of tracks over the years, only to see them make little or no headway on the charts or radio. But fate had other plans.

As the tour churned to an end on April 16, 1960, the artists all made arrangements to head home. Around midnight, the car carrying Vincent and Cochran veered off the road and crashed on its way to London. The young cab driver was driving too fast, braked hard, lost control of the vehicle, and it smashed into a concrete lamppost. All of the car's inhabitants were taken to the hospital. Fate had indeed intervened in the life and career of Vince Eager.

"I found out from Parnes how serious the situation was," recalls Eager, who was at the airport waiting for the group to arrive to fly back to the US. "But I was first told it was Gene that was seriously injured, and not Eddie. I went down to the hospital and found out it was really Eddie that was badly hurt. The surgeon told me if Eddie lived, he would have the mind of a child of four."[38] Eddie Cochran ultimately died at the hospital at the age of 21 from his injuries. Outside the hospital, a shocked Eager watched as Larry Parnes, surrounded by others in the "stable" addressed the press. "I was there when Parnes said to the press, 'Oh, the irony is, that Eddie Cochran's new single is *Three Steps to Heaven*." Eager was bowled over. "I was gutted by this accident as I had just lost a great friend and talented musician. But fat little Larry was making mileage out of this."[39] It was a cruel lesson learned by Vince Eager and his band: musicians were merely a bankable and disposable commodity to entertainment moguls. Eager never got over the loss of his friend or the crass commercial play by Parnes to sell records off the dead body of a great American Rock star. His anger with Parnes would

At St. Martin's Hospital:
L-R, Norm Riley, Billy Fury, Larry Parnes, Vince Eager & Dickie Pride

soon fester and cause serious consequences for Vince, Jimmie and the band.

In looking back, Eager says, "The sad part was that Eddie had died. The other sad part was that Eddie was probably the one person who had so much faith in me. He was determined to do something for me record-wise, to produce a great record for me. Who knows how music history might have changed? But it wasn't to be, so… it did affect me a lot."[40]

The Silver Beatles

On May 10, 1960, up in Liverpool, Larry Parnes auditioned young bands to see who could serve as back up for his singers, Billy Fury and Johnny Gentle, on one of his planned tours of Scotland. Ultimately, The Silver Beatles (comprised of John Lennon, Paul McCartney, George Harrison, Stuart Sutcliff on bass and Tommy Moore on drums) were chosen for the job backing Gentle. Amazingly, even though Parnes selected The Beatles, who were then known as "The Silver Beatles", he never thought they were good enough to sign to his own stable.

At the same time, Parnes had also set up Vince Eager & The Quiet Three to tour Scotland as part of The Beat Ballad Show tour. The tour ran from approximately May 20 to May 28. Vince Eager recalls, "We did this big ballroom circuit in Scotland. The Beatles were out with Johnny Gentle and we were also covering Scotland at the same time. Jimmie and I were really popular up there in Scotland."[41]

Interestingly, the fate that would one day intertwine the lives of Jimmie Nicol and The Beatles did not coalesce at this time, for the paths of these two bands did not cross on the Scotland tour.

Vince Eager & The Quiet Three, Scotland 1959, onboard an aircraft carrier, L-R, Tex, Vince, Jimmie and Kenny.
Photo Credit: Courtesy of Vince Eager.

Johnny Gentle recalls, "I knew Jimmie. He was a great drummer and a very likeable guy. He was playing with Vince up in Scotland when I was there with The Beatles, but he did occasionally back me on gigs in London."[42] According to Johnny Gentle, Parnes paid the "stars" about £15-20 pounds per week.[43] For all of his drumming and crisscrossing the Scottish Highlands carrying his drum kit over hundreds of miles of country, Nicol would split £20 with his Quiet Three band mates each week. Nicol and the others also had to pay their expenses for bed, breakfast, and drinks out of their earnings. This did not leave much money left over to bring home at the end of the tour.

"We really performed well on that tour," recalls Eager. "And the fans really responded. Unfortunately, there is no video or audio of us playing together. But Jimmie was just awesome on his playing and our stage act."[44] Fortunately, some photos survive of the Scotland tour, showing young Jimmie Nicol with Vince Eager & The Quiet Three playing on an aircraft carrier in Dingwall near Inverness. Some sailors had come to one of the ballroom shows and loved it. After sharing some post show drinks with the sailors, one of the guys said to Eager, "Would you come and do a gig for us?" The Quiet Three and their leader eagerly said, "Yea, we'd love to". So the following day, the sailors came and picked up the band and promptly deposited them on an aircraft carrier to play an informal gig for the military. Two or three photos of that day preserve the only visual evidence of Jimmie Nicol with Vince Eager & The Quiet Three. At the time, NATO forces were in the region for military exercises. As a result, Vince and the band ended up playing the gig for all of the NATO forces. The reception for the band was greatly appreciated by the military who gave the band rousing applause.[45]

Upon their return to London, Vince Eager & The Quiet Three had a brief touring hiatus in June, 1960 before they would mount yet another tour in July. However, Eager was getting more frustrated with his manager Larry Parnes. "I was on Drumbeat [TV Series] for six months and during that time, Larry didn't find me one decent song [to record and release]."[46] The frustration of not having a hit record - combined with Eager's disgust with Parnes for using the death of Eddie Cochran to promote his artists - really caused friction. The relationship was deteriorating quickly between manager and artist.

Despite the icy relations between Parnes and Eager, another tour was scheduled to exploit the summer vacationers of England. This time, Jimmie brought his wife Pat and son Howie along, since the show would be a multi-week engagement in one location. "Jimmie and I had become very good friends. In fact, when our group did the season in 1960, starting July 24, with Billy Fury at the Britannia Theatre in Great Yarmouth, Jimmie, Pat, Howard and I shared a big trailer together," says Eager.[47]

Great Yarmouth's seafront resort attracted thousands of visitors each year to its sandy beaches. Along the waterfront is the famous Britannia Pier which housed the Britannia Theatre. It was in this theatre that Larry Parnes set up shop in the summer of 1960, to provide the summer season's entertainment and rake in another truck load of money.

The show was deceivingly named, "Meet The Beat – Larry Parnes Presents The First Ever Anglo American Summer Show"; and ran it through the rest of the summer. Parnes had of course, already presented the first ever Anglo-American tour at the start of the year with Eddie Cochran and Gene Vincent topping the bill for his British acts. But this was no matter for concern, since seaside holiday families would likely have no knowledge of the previous tours. The concert bill was topped by Billy Fury, followed by Vince Eager & The Quiet Three; Johnny Gentle (minus The Beatles); and others. A review of the summer show in *New Musical Express* called it the "first live Rock and Roll show in the town of Great Yarmouth… ever."[48] Perhaps as a sign of things to come, Larry Parnes took his feud with Vince Eager to the *NME*, as it reported, "Backing [for the show] provided by *Jimmie Nicol and his group, Vince Eager's Quiet Three*, and the Beat Boys."[49] This slight to Eager as the bandleader was no accident, and it foreshadowed Eager's problems with his manager, and Nicol's elevation in the Parnes stable.

The season at Yarmouth was mostly uneventful and relaxing for Nicol, his family and his band. Eager was rightfully proud of his Quiet Three as he remembers, "They were just a phenomenal trio. When you find that they eventually became the nucleus of Georgie Fame & the Blue Flames, it just goes to show you what good musicians they were."[50]

Unfortunately for Nicol & company, this summer session with Vince Eager would be their last together. In September of 1960, the *New Musical Express* announced that Vince Eager had breached his management agreement with Larry Parnes. Eager had had it with Parnes' exploitation of Cochran's death and the lack of a hit record. "It was a major turning point for me," says Eager. "I just told him to get fucked basically. What happened then was, I couldn't work for two years. Parnes said, I could work, but I would have to pay him 50 percent. So I couldn't work for anybody else without paying him, so I didn't work for two years."[51] Eager had been blacklisted. "Larry made it very difficult for Vince to get gigs after that," recalls Road Manager Noel Wallis. "So Vince and The Quiet Three broke up and Jimmie went on his way. Larry sort of put out a major threat on Vince that he could not play cinemas or major clubs or dance halls. I was able to get a few bookings for them."[52] This was Nicol's first experience with blacklisting in the entertainment business. It was a moment that weighed heavily on the young drummer and one which would foreshadow his own concerns in years to come.

Obviously, this issue would pose an economic hardship for Jimmie who had to have regular work to support his family. "For me," says Eager, "that was an extreme hardship. The Quiet Three just sort of broke up. We played a gig or two, took a short break and then just never got back together again."[53]

As it had before, the disbanding of one of Jimmie Nicol's bands would lead to even greater opportunities and good fortune. Unbeknownst to Jimmie Nicol, Larry Parnes had been very impressed with the young drummer whom he would move around to various groups like a handy chess piece; he was always on time and *in* time. Nicol had the talent and the work ethic that Parnes needed for his next big idea, an idea that would launch the young drummer into his first starring role.

Chapter 7

The Big Band Years

At the conclusion of the summer season at Great Yarmouth, Jimmie Nicol returned with his family to London. He was well aware of Vince Eager's inability to keep The Quiet Three together. The two were close friends and Eager had explained the problems with his manager to his prized drummer. The dilemma for Nicol was to find work, and he did not have to wait long for his situation to change. One day while relaxing at his home, Nicol was duly summoned to Larry Parnes' office to hear about his next packaged tour. Opportunity was knocking for Jimmie Nicol, and the energetic drummer was ready to grab it. Jimmy Nicol was about to find out how his fortunes had changed for the better as he entered the offices of Larry Parnes.

In late August of 1960, TV and stage producer Jack Good and his pal Larry Parnes had gotten together to discuss yet another package tour for England. With the death of Eddie Cochran and the unreliability of Gene Vincent, the idea for another big Anglo-American tour seemed unrealistic. The two promoters had to find a fresh approach to basically recycle and re-present Larry Parnes' same stable of artists. Good had been very busy with musical TV productions such as the *Six-Five Special* and *Oh Boy!* However, he was itching to return to stage production, and producing Parnes' next tour for the fall was exactly what he wanted to accomplish.

The innovative team of Parnes and Good came up with an idea to present a show that combined the best of Rock and Roll, as well as adding "Trad Jazz" to the bill. Trad Jazz was short for Traditional Jazz, a genre of music that contained elements of both New Orleans traditional jazz and ragtime music. In England, this musical form was popular from post-World War II into the early 1960s. The concert posters would boast "*Billy Fury* And His Company Of 50". Parnes decided that he would present a 13 to 15-piece Big Band of players as backing for his stable of singers, as well as turning the Big Band itself into a headliner; and he knew just the man to fill the job of the new Big Band leader.

Rock and Trad Join Forces

Upon walking into the Parnes lair, Jimmie Nicol was surprised to learn of his first-ever starring role. He was thrilled with his good fortune upon hearing the news. Larry Parnes had chosen him to lead the Rock 'n Trad Jazz Big Band for the upcoming tour, which was to be aptly named, "Rock 'n Trad Spectacular – The New Noise of 1960". Only now, the concert program would feature Jimmie Nicol's name in it for the first time, and as the bandleader! The band was duly christened "Jimmie Nicol and his 15 New Orleans Rockers". Clearly Parnes was rewarding the young drummer for remaining loyal to the "stable". In reality, Nicol's loyalty remained with Eager; however, he knew he could not make money playing with Eager who had been blacklisted by Parnes, leaving little or

LARRY PARNES presents

JIMMIE NICHOL and the
15 NEW ORLEANS ROCKERS
          starring RED PRICE

JOHNNY GOODE
    Great new singing discovery

BILLY RAYMOND
    Britains top singing-compere

GEORGIE FAME
    Singing pianist sensation

DUFFY POWER
    Fontana recording artiste

JOHNNY GENTLE
    Philips young singer-composer

DAVE SAMPSON
    Star of TV and records

PETER WYNNE
    The golden voice of the 1960's

THE VERNONS GIRLS
    From TV's Oh, Boy, Boy Meets Girl and Wham

DICKIE PRIDE
    Dynamic star of TV, radio, stage and records

NELSON KEENE
    HMV's Hit Parade recorder of " Image of a Girl"

TOMMY BRUCE
    With his record hits "Ain't Misbehavin'"
    and " Broken Doll "

JOE BROWN
    The lovable cockney character of TV and
    recording fame

Star of TV and Decca Records
BILLY FURY
    Britain's newest teenage idol

Produced by JACK GOOD

Associate Producer LESLIE COOPER

Musical Direction SYD DALE

1960 Rock N Trad lineup.
Photo Credit: Courtesy of Author

nothing to pay his band.

Nicol shared the good fortune with his family and almost immediately began rehearsals to whip his new Big Band of Trad-Rockers into shape. If he needed to pinch himself to make sure he really was a band leading star, he need only open a copy of the *New Musical Express* on August 19, 1960, which proclaimed, "A big innovation for Parnes' presentation is a large band, which will be featured besides accompanying many of the artists. Consisting of at least 13 instrumentalists it will be led by drummer Jimmie Nicholls [sic]. He gets his band leading break after three years with Parnes, during which time he has been particularly connected with Vince Eager."[1] This was quite a feather in the hat of a 21-year old drummer from Battersea.

The tour was set to begin on September 25, travelling across the British Isles and lasting up through the end of November. By virtue of being a headliner, Jimmie Nicol would now receive a graduation in wages from £7 per week to approximately £20. This was a huge jump in salary for the drummer, one which demonstrated to family and friends that the young drummer could make a very handsome living as a full-time musician and bandleader.

London's *Record Retailer* magazine billed the tour as "The biggest Rock package bill ever to be staged in this country… with more than 15 stars of stage, screen, TV and discs."[2] The cast would include the Parnes stable of artists and Red Price (on tenor sax) with Jimmie Nicol and his 15 New Orleans Rockers. The show opener would be in Slough, followed by a week in Manchester and then another week in Liverpool.

Fellow co-star Joe Brown recalls the performances of Jimmie Nicol, the young bandleader as, "Good and loud. The audiences for Nicol's Rock And Trad band were very enthusiastic," recalls Brown.[3] As for the tour, Brown reminisces, "They were great times. We had fun on the road and nothing was too serious."[4]

The tour was not without its share of controversy over whether it was a Rock show or a Trad Jazz show. The September 30, 1960 issue of *New Musical Express* blared the headline: "Will Dixieland kill rock?" The article questioned whether Jazz was turning into pop music or whether Trad Jazz was killing Rock. One theory in the article wondered aloud whether the whole plot of Parnes and Good was merely to "…embrace one's enemy [Trad music] or maybe staging a calculated take-the-money-and-run operation…." Either way, the tour was selling out and receiving lots of attention, exactly as Parnes and Good had planned. The article highlighted the various singers as "pushed in front of a thundering 15-piece band led by Jimmy [sic] Nicol for an extensive trek around the British Isles under the 'Rock And Trad' banner."[5]

Jack Good tried to explain the concept to the fans and media this way, "I want the show to be fast-moving, but with a pronounced Dixieland theme…but don't get the idea that we are scrapping Rock altogether."[6] When challenged about whether the show could perform as well if it were just the same old Parnes Rock acts, Good dodged the bullet, saying only, "I can't really answer

1960 Rock N Trad Tour Program
Photo Credit: Courtesy of Author

that!" This would be his final word on the subject.[7]

In many ways, the tour and stage spectacular was a theatrical version of Good's musical variety TV shows, in which many performers were squeezed into one program, with each having their own 30 minutes under the spotlight. "There were so many people on those shows that you didn't get much time," recalls top headliner Billy Fury. "Everything was compressed into 30 minutes. But from beginning to end it was a real Rock and Roll show, with the current ballad stuck in the middle. And 'Thank you very much, Goodnight.'"[8]

It is unfortunate that no audio or video recordings survived this tour featuring the thundering band led by Jimmie Nicol. The only records left are of the original concert programs and handbills

1960 Rock N Trad Handbill–Gaumont Bournemouth.
Photo Credit: Courtesy of Author

that sell as memorabilia today and the dusty newspaper reviews of an era gone by. One such review from early in the tour was quite complimentary. *Melody Maker* reviewed a show at the Adelphi in Slough, as witnessed by 4000 rousing fans. The reporter relates, "After a run of dismal shows, featuring mediocre artists with inferior backing and absence of presentation, rock gets a new lease of life from agent Larry Parnes and producer Jack Good with something fast, fiery and imaginative."[9] The review also saw fit to acknowledge the hard work of Jimmie Nicol's debut as a band leader with great enthusiasm. "Jimmy Nichol [sic] and his New Orleans Rockers, fronted by Syd Dale and driven by torrid tenorist Red Price, provide explosive accompaniment just right for these rising recruits…"[10]

The tour came to an end in time for the holidays on November 27, 1960, with two shows at the Gaumont Theatre in Bradford. By the end of this hot-ticket tour, the advertisement for The Rock 'N' Trad Spectacular had promoted Jimmie Nicol and his 15 New Orleans Rockers up to the seventh position on the bill, ahead of "The Valentine Girls and a host of other teenage idols". The tour had been a success for Parnes & Good *and* for Jimmie Nicol. Not only had his presence been elevated with fans, but more importantly with fellow musician Georgie Fame, who would later recall how impressed he was with Nicol when his own hot band Georgie Fame & the Blue Flames was in need of a drummer. More importantly, Nicol was able to showcase his skills, front and center, as a band leader and drummer to the whole of England. This exposure did not escape the notice of one man; David Ede, leader of the Oscar Rabin Big Band, which was coincidentally, looking for a new drummer…

Oscar Rabin Band

Born in Russia in 1899, Oscar Rabin was a jolly, musical youth with a great talent. His family came to Britain while Rabin was still a young boy to start a new life and to pursue their fortunes.[11]

In his late twenties, Rabin formed a band along with singer-actor Harry Davis. Over time, the band worked its way up the British Big Band food chain to respectability through touring, traveling throughout Britain and entertaining the World War II troops.[12] In 1951, Rabin hired David Ede as the new leader for his namesake band. In June of 1958, Rabin passed away and Ede took over the band.[13]

Once Ede took over, he noticed the ever increasing popularity of Rock and Roll music in late 1950s-early 1960s Britain. Clearly wishing to keep his band relevant and to get the band onto BBC radio, Ede devised the Oscar Rabin Band's "Rock Unit". This innovation got him onto two different weekly radio BBC programs, during which the band would play cover versions of popular songs of the day. When Ede's drummer left that band in late 1960, he did not have to look far for a drummer, having seen Larry Parnes' Rock 'N Trad Spectacular. Ede knew Jimmie Nicol should be his next drummer.

"Jimmie's next move was a good one for him," recalls Vince Eager. "After me, he went with the Oscar Rabin Big Band. His drumming was brilliant, very solid and full. He was very controlled, but he wanted to play everything on his kit. Playing with the Big Bands was great experience for him. We stayed good friends after he left me," says Eager.[14] Quiet Three guitarist Colin Green concurs, "Going to Oscar Rabin's Big Band and leaving Vince's band, would have been seen very much as a step up in the world. That was a career move for Jimmie. That was a Rock and Roll musician being taken seriously." Green admits, "Everybody was rooting for him. I mean, he was a good lad... go do it."[15]

David Ede recruited Nicol for the Oscar Rabin band. The pay was steady and generous; but, the days, nights, and hours were long. The Rabin Band was performing two BBC broadcasts per week; a one-hour live show named "Go Man Go"; and a recorded show called "Saturday Club." Drummer Freddie Adamson had left the band to join another Big Band. Bass player Ron Prentice recalls, "Jimmie Nicol was brought in to replace Adamson as we were doing more and more Rock music covers. He was not a good reader at first and not so good at the swing stuff, but a very good Rock drummer."[16]

"Saturday Club" featured host Brian Matthew; and the Rabin program was recorded on Tuesday afternoons at the Playhouse Theatre, the Paris Studio, or BBC Piccadilly. The taping was then usually broadcast on Saturday mornings. "Most of the studio players were perfect sight readers and you were expected to read anything the first time without making a mistake," says bass player Ron Prentice. "Unfortunately, Jimmie really had to learn the part first before being able to play it perfectly."[17]

Nicol accepted the challenge of having to read and play brand new music each week, sight unseen for the first time. It was a valuable lesson and technique that he eventually perfected, one that would soon serve him well in the recording studio. In a Big Band, the drummer was challenged to fulfill many musical responsibilities. He needed to be able to interpret his parts with appropriate shading and expression, as well as blend his figures together with the ensemble or certain sections of the band. He also needed to be able to handle both short and long drum solos, with the ability to control the band. The drummer had to be a dominant and confident leader in the Big Band, preventing them from rushing or dragging, keeping them together, and at the same time, inspiring them by his passion and drive. Jimmie worked very hard to meet the challenges of his new band and to earn their respect.

In the early days of radio in the 1960s, playing records on the air was tightly controlled; yet teen fans expected radio to keep them informed of all the latest developments in popular music, including the latest hits. The solution the BBC came up with was to employ British bands to perform cover versions of the latest hits in the radio studio - a decision no doubt influenced by the musicians' union to employ more musicians. At the time, it was thought that playing records on the air deprived musicians from performance fees. The BBC came up with a catchy title to attract their youthful listeners – "Go Man Go". The Rabin Band regularly played live before a Friday lunchtime audience anxiously ready to swing. Fortunately, one recording of the "Go Man Go" show has survived intact, featuring Jimmie Nicol on drums, allowing a glimpse of a typical gig he played with the Oscar Rabin Band in the early part of the 1960s.

The lively show kicks off with the announcer and the band members shouting, - "Common' everybody and Go [Jimmie's drum beat] Man [drum beat] Go [drum beat]"! After the college-cheer intro, the audience hears the driving downbeat of Jimmie Nicol kicking off the band's rocking theme song, reminiscent of Jerry Lee Lewis' *Great Balls of Fire*. "Your Friday tonic, the show with the most", yells the compare Dizzy Dizley, introducing the Rabin Band and guest artists mid-song.

In addition to his weekly performances on "Go Man Go", Nicol and the Rabin Band spent

Fans lined up to see The Rabin Band with Jimmie Nicol, Wimbledon Palais.

the better part of 1962 performing live, four nights weekly for dancers at the Wimbledon Palais. The Palais was witness to the waning years of Big Band music and an era that was slowly fading away. Big Band music had provided entertainment to generations of London music fans who regularly visited their local dance hall for a much needed dose of dancing, laughter, flirting and high octane performances that would swing and Rock. Although the "mods" and "rockers" of the mid-1960s had not yet invaded the famed dance hall of Wimbledon, slight cracks in the veneer of the Big Band era were foreshadowed by Ede and the Rabin Band's commercialized cover versions of the pop hits of the day. For Nicol, however, in 1960 the Palais served as a place for gigs that kept him gainfully employed, even if he would sleep away most of the daytime between shows after staying up all night to earn his keep.

Roadie, Noel Wallis, was staying with Nicol and his family in London at the time. In exchange for the room and board, Wallis helped Jimmie get to his gigs with all of the gear that burdens a drummer. "After leaving Vince, Jimmie went to work for Oscar Rabin's band. I was staying with them when Jimmie started with Rabin," recalls Wallice. "Jimmie would be playing most nights at the Wimbledon Palais dance hall with Oscar Rabin band and he used to come home and I would say. 'Where are we going now Jimmie?' And he would say, 'We're going jamming to play the All-Niter with Georgie Fame.'"[18] Nicol played from the early evening until 6:00 in the morning, traipsing around London.

Another regular gig helped Nicol supplement his living. He occasionally played Rock and Roll in a house trio back at the 2 I's coffee bar and the Blue Gardenia. Guitarist Albert Lee recalls working with Nicol. "I was part of the house trio at the 2 I's in 1961-62 and Jimmie would sit in with us."[19] The Blue Gardenia was a late, late night club. "We would go there after the 2 I's and play until the early hours in Soho," says Lee.[20] I remember him as being a very good drummer and especially remember being poked with a drum stick when he wanted me to play a solo [laughs]; at least I think that's what he wanted."[21] Like many musicians, Lee (who went onto play with Eric Clapton, The Everly Brothers, Dave Edmunds, Jackson Browne and Bill Wyman's Rhythm Kings) regretted that he never had the opportunity to play with Nicol again after the early years.

It proved to be a very busy time for Jimmie Nicol, according to bass player Prentice who kept a diary of this time. "The first year I was in the band with Jimmie, we played 1,037 tunes during the radio broadcasts," not counting the hundreds or even thousands of tunes played live each week at the Wimbledon Palais.[22] As the Big Band era gave way to smaller Rock combos, many famous Rock and Roll bands would follow Jimmie and the Rabin Band to the Wimbledon Palais as they started their careers a couple of years later. These bands would include: The Beatles; The Rolling Stones; Pink Floyd; and David Bowie.

Cyril Stapleton Big Band

By mid-1961, another offer came to the attention of the up-and-coming Mr. Nicol. This one came with more money from a competitor. British born Cyril Stapleton got an early start in the music world playing violin at silent film theaters in the 'pit orchestras'. As a college music student, Stapleton got his first taste of fame on BBC radio broadcasts.

In the 1940s, Stapleton's band began to draw a following which led to more live remote radio appearances on the BBC's "Golden Slipper" and "Your Hit Parade". This exposure led to fame for Stapleton throughout all of England.[23]

In 1952, the BBC recognized the growing popularity of Stapleton's band to its shows and rewarded him by creating a band for him to lead called the "BBC Show Band". This band had a prestigious run, attracting famous musical guests from the US, including Frank Sinatra and Nat 'King' Cole. However, after a five-year run, the BBC abruptly cancelled the show. Stapleton, who had a large following of radio listeners, was unfazed, quickly forming a band to take his easy jazz from ballroom to theater around the greater UK during the early to mid-1960s.[24]

Stapleton was not unaware of the flashy drummer over in Oscar Rabin's band who had come from the Rock and Roll world. When his previous drummer left, Stapleton made Jimmie Nicol a generous offer to move over to the Cyril Stapleton Big Band. It was another vertical move that would again lead to steady wages; more touring; and most importantly (unbeknownst to him at the time), a connection that would give Nicol the opportunity to move into the elite club of professional recording sessions.

"I first met Jimmie when he joined the Cyril Stapleton Band as a drummer," recalls Stapleton trumpet player, Johnny Harris. "Drummers and bass players were the ones I always hung out with, and some of the trumpet players of course; but mostly bass and drums. When Jimmie joined the band, we hit it off right away."[25] Nicol described his background to Harris, having just come over from the Rabin band and playing Rock and Roll with Vince Eager and Colin Hicks on the Larry Parnes packaged tours.

Harris was intrigued by a Rock and Roll drummer who could also play Jazz and Big Band as well as read music. At the time, this was quite uncommon, for players usually picked a field of expertise and stayed within the genre they had chosen. "He was so good," says Harris of Nicol's drumming. "And he was as good at Rock and Roll as he was with the jazz music."[26] Harris does not recall any recordings made with Stapleton at this time. "No, the songs we played were live with Cyril's band. They were songs the band had recorded earlier in the 1950s. We just toured around England."[27]

By 1963, Nicol had played so many gigs on his old Trixon drum set that it was time to upgrade to a new one. With the steady earnings he was pulling in, Jimmie was comfortable springing for a new, flashier Trixon Luxus set in blue "croco". It featured a shiny blue set of drums with a crocodile skin-type design that was an instant eye-catcher. Jimmie not only wanted his playing to be the center of attention, but he also wanted the eyes of the audience on his kit![28]

An event, not easily forgotten, happened one night between Nicol and his trumpet playing pal Johnny Harris. Harris relates the story:

> I'll never forget one night we were playing at the Lyceum Ballroom
> near Covent Garden. It was November 22, 1963. The room was
> a converted movie theatre they had turned into a ballroom in those big
> band days. And it still had a back stage door. Jimmie and I walked
> out during a break in the show to have a cigarette and this stage door
> man said, 'Hey, have you heard the news?' And we said, 'No, what?'
> And he said, 'President Kennedy has been shot dead.' We just stood
> there in silence. We were dumbfounded. It was a terrible shock.
> So we just wandered around the street hardly talking to each other.
> We'd just look at each other and shrug our shoulders. It was awful.

But you know, that night we just went back and did the job and continued on. But I will never forget how we shared that moment together.[29]

The moment of sadness and regret shared by these two Big Band musicians created an even greater mutual bond that night. The tragedy in America had deeply impacted these two young British players. Many Brits and Americans at the time had high hopes that the Kennedy presidency would usher in a new era of peace and prosperity. The friendship between Harris and Nicol was solidified as they shared this trauma together, and wondered about the future. Their professional collaborations would soon become even more intertwined, for both musicians were hurtling ahead at light speed toward new career opportunities looming in 1964; a year that would prove to be Jimmie Nicol's watershed moment as a drummer.

Chapter Eight

In The Studio

Trumpeter and arranger Johnny Harris had grown weary of touring and the late night gigs in Cyril Stapleton's Big Band. He longed for a more stable career that blended with his new domestic life in the company of his wife and two young kids. "I was doing most of the arrangements for Cyril's Big Band and that is what I wanted to concentrate on," he recalls. "I didn't want to be on tour anymore. By being an arranger, I could be more settled with my family."[1] Harris' ambitions led him into a new career in the recording studio as an arranger and record producer. Towards the end of 1963 and the beginning of 1964, he started to get a few studio projects at Pye Records. Harris toiled at Pye during the day and still met his commitments of playing trumpet and arranging in Stapleton's band at night.

Tony Hatch and Johnny Harris at Pye 1964.
Photo Credit: Courtesy of Tony Hatch.

If you begin at London's famous Marble Arch and walk down Edgeware Road about 100 yards, you come to 40 Bryanston Street, home of Pye Recording Studios. During the same period Johnny Harris started working at the simple white studio, The Kinks' made their recording debut with a cover of Little Richard's hit song, *Long Tall Sally*. The record company was one of many labels that had been visited by manager Brian Epstein in the early 1960s, trying to obtain a record deal for his little known Liverpool group, The Beatles. Ironically, just like their rival Decca Records, Pye also missed the boat and rejected The Beatles, opting instead to sign The Searchers in 1962.

Top Six Record Label

Harris began to get noticed by other producers and record label executives during his day job at Pye. Among the people impressed with Harris was an Australian record executive. "This Australian guy came along. I don't remember his name, but he had formed this Top Six Record label."[2] The Aussie record boss, Bill Wellings, called Harris to set up a meeting; one that would have huge implications, not only for Harris, but also for his drummer-buddy Jimmie Nicol. At their initial meeting, the Aussie described to Harris his novel idea for releasing records that would ride the coattails of the latest hit recordings of the day. Wellings told Harris:

> I'm going to start this label and I am going to do six tracks
> on an EP vinyl. You know a double sided 45 rpm record. Three
> tracks on one side and three tracks on the other side. And we're
> going to try and guess what the top 6 songs on the pop charts
> will be. We want to try and put it out every month. And we
> want to copy the sound of the records.[3]

The concept of the "cover versions" market was Wellings' innovation. His Top Six EP concept promised to "give the people value for the money- six hits for the price of one". Never mind that these "hits" were not performed by the original bands! Initially, these EPs were sold to grocery and discount store wholesalers from the trunk of Wellings' car until he negotiated a deal with Pye Records to take over proper distribution at the start of 1964.[4]

Johnny Harris was excited by the prospect of arranging and co-producing the Top Six sessions. "When he asked me to get involved, I said sure. This was like an entrance into the recording side of arranging. We planned to cut the songs there at Pye Studios, so I had to put a band together for these regular monthly sessions for Top Six," says Harris.[5] Wellings would listen to the original "hit" record and then select a suitable session singer to copy the vocal style of the song.[6] Harris needed a small group for the Rock and Roll music; and he chose a couple of guitar players, a bass player, keyboardist, and of course, a versatile drummer who could mimic the musical hits of the day. Harris' main responsibility involved listening to each "hit" record, transcribing the musical arrangements for each player, and copying the lyrics for his singer. Most of the tracks were chosen about 10 days before recording and release in order to sell the newest "hits" on the charts.[7]

Harris' first call went out to his pal, Jimmie Nicol. He excitedly told his buddy, "Look Jimmie, this is it! This could take off!"[8] Nicol was very excited about the prospect of working on Top Six records. "That's great, count me in," was Nicol's reply.[9] Jimmie was especially thrilled for an entrée to regular session work in the studio. He had toured, played concerts, and done plenty of radio shows; but the fraternity of London studio musicians was a tough club to break into at the time. Nicol would gain access via his friend and would be able to earn a good living and see his family more often. The young drummer had once again moved up another level as a professional session musician - playing in different studios, reading the dots, and playing the lines when the red light came on. What he did not realize at the time was the significance of one group in particular that was beginning to dominate the pop charts. That group would ultimately play a significant role in his life. That group's drum parts would loom large in importance as Nicol began to get a feel for The Beatles' songs and drummer Ringo Starr's unique rhythmic style.

In January of 1964, Jimmie Nicol was an admirer of The Beatles' drummer. "I thought he was good, innovative and Ringo was making the drums an interesting instrument for aspiring musicians. He was probably the first drummer known by name." Jimmie also could not help but notice that Ringo Starr was the "… first drummer to have girls cry their eyes out, to get a touch of!"[10] Nicol started to hone in on Starr's unique style, as he listened to The Beatles' records and reviewed the dots on Johnny Harris's session arrangements. "I liked the style of his rim shots on snare, and then onto the shell… and in 'She Loves You', he used it as a lead-in to the bridge. He was different. I loved how he used to attack the hi-hat (cymbal) instead of pussyfooting about with them."[11]

"At that time, there were so many Beatles' records in the charts. Half the Top Six songs were Beatles anyway," says Harris. "This was early 1964. So I had to get studio guys who could read music. I didn't have time to bring in guys to learn the songs. They had to read it. And Jimmie was marvelous on Ringo's and the other drummer's parts. He could read of course."[12]

Singer John Hodkinson was one of the vocalists chosen to record on the Top Six sessions. He had sung on the Larry Parnes' tours, with Nicol backing him, in the early 1960's. Hodkinson used the Parnes-assigned stage name, Johnny Goode. He had come from the same town as Georgie Fame, who was presently serving a lengthy residency as the house band for the Flamingo club in London. The lines began to blur around this time, as musicians slid in and out of various bands, hustling for whatever gig that would pay. Some nights, after playing sessions all day, Jimmie would serve double duty, sitting in with Georgie Fame & the Blue Flames, with his old buddies Tex Makins and Georgie Fame.

"We were doing a lot of cover versions together of chart toppers for the Top Six record label in Pye Studios. I did vocals there for about three months in the studio. There were different Top Six songs we did every month," recalls Hodkinson.[13] One of the early EPs compiled a typical mixture of popular songs of the day, including:

John Hodkinson. Courtesey of author.

Glad All Over
I'm The One
Needles And Pins
I Want To Hold Your Hand
Twenty Four Hours From Tulsa
Hippy Hippy Shake

Hodkinson does an admirable job of copying the vocals of Lennon and McCartney on *I Want To Hold Your Hand*, except for the fact that he is harmonizing with himself on the record - quite distinguishable from the actual Lennon-McCartney harmonies. Nicol's drumming on this early Beatles cover is quite close to Ringo's part, although his drums are buried further down in the mix. Over the next months, Jimmie would record many of The Beatles' hits (that they used in their current live setlist) for Top Six. The tracks included: *Roll Over Beethoven*; *From Me To You*; *Till There Was You* (which is sung by an unknown Top Six female vocalist); *Please Mr. Postman*; *Twist And Shout*; *All My Loving*; *She Loves You*; *I Wanna Be Your Man*; *Love Me Do*; *Please Please Me* and *Money*. As fate would have it, Nicol even liked The Beatles "mop top" hairstyle and began to grow out his own "Beatles cut".

Aside from the brilliant marketing scheme to reproduce sound-alike hits and put them onto one record, the Top Six also secured a regular show slot on Radio Luxembourg, the popular predecessor to pirate radio, twice weekly. This gave the Top Six recordings further legitimacy to naïve teenage consumers. At the time of these broadcasts in the first quarter of 1964, Radio Luxembourg had a virtual monopoly in commercial radio, operating outside of the British government controlled BBC, and it was able to market its music and advertisements to the greatly expanding teen population. *The Daily Mirror* touted the consumer savings with Top Six, as declaring "Teenagers will be able to get SIX hit-parade pop numbers on a 'normal' single record." The reporter opined that Pye's Top Six concept could likely set off a price battle among record companies.[14]

The Top Six EPs sold for about $0.90 (USD) in 1964, a great savings compared to buying six different hit 45 singles, until you realized you were not buying the songs recorded by the original artists! The first big seller for Top Six rode the coattails of The Beatles. Released in late January of 1964, the EP entitled, *Beatle Mania Special*, with Nicol on drums for all tracks - sold a whopping 100,000 copies![15]
The tracks for the all-Beatles EP were as follows:

Side 1:
She Loves You
Twist and Shout
Please Please Me

Side 2:
I Wanna [sic] Hold Your Hand

From Me To You
Love Me Do

This EP split the credit for Producing between Bill Wellings on Side 1, and Music Direction to Johnny Harris on Side 2. Since the songs were published by Northern Songs (with the exception of *Love Me Do*), the recording likely came to the attention of The Beatles' song publisher, Dick James, and possibly even manager Brian Epstein. They must have marveled at their good fortune, as yet even more publishing royalties would flow to these partners and Lennon & McCartney.

"And as it happened," says Harris, "We did the first one (EP). Top Six put it out through Pye and it got into the charts! I think it actually got in at the Top 30 or something like that. So I thought, oh my goodness, we're onto a winner here. So it worked well for a few months anyway…"[16]

Top Six smartly cashed in by issuing a full-length album called *Beatlemania*. The album contained all twelve Beatles songs featuring Nicol on drums. The back cover boasted "A New Record 1st of Every Month". Amazingly, the album release got a front page reception alongside a story about the "real" Beatles.[17]

Top Six Beatlemania album. Photo Credit: Courtesy of Author.

The track listing included:

Side 1:
I Want To Hold Your Hand
Roll Over Beethoven
From Me To You
Till There Was You
Please Mr. Postman
Twist And Shout

Side 2:
All My Loving
She Loves You
I Wanna Be Your Man
Love Me Do
Please Please Me
Money

Unbeknownst to Jimmie in the first quarter of 1964, these sessions, and in particular these Beatles songs, would soon loom large in his life, his career, and musical legacy. Nicol liked his new place in the world of respected recording session work. It meant he could move away from the endless grueling tours with Cyril Stapleton and begin making regular money closer to home. Nicol's recording sessions were controlled by Charlie Katz, known to the session players as the "Fixer". Katz would call Nicol and ask about his availability for a particular session on a set date and time. Jimmie was always ready to go for a session. In some cases, Nicol was booked as a backup to drummer Phil Seamen, in case the popular veteran was unable to make it.[18] On other occasions, one player would focus on percussion while the other played drums.

The recording sessions were usually booked for a two-hour (half session) or a three-hour (full session) period. Charlie the "Fixer" was very tough and demanding. If a session musician asked the wrong question or arrived late, he could find himself on an unpaid two-week holiday. Harris made sure that Katz knew to call Nicol for his sessions. Katz soon became aware of Nicol's amazing versatility and confidence, with his knowledge of Jazz, Big Band, Blues, Ska and Rock style drumming. Jimmie earned a reputation for professionalism, being ready and able to read, play and record whatever style of music was needed in the studio.

Nicol's expertise in the studio was important, due to the fact that session musicians were brought in mainly for professional expedience and financial economy. The goal of UK producers and arrangers at the time was to finish recording four songs in a three hour session. The work was intense and there were often three-sessions per day. However, the work was financially rewarding, as the "Fixer" would come around at the end of every session with wage packets in brown envelopes for every player. Nicol was now clearing about £9 per session. Working on recording sessions and picking up late night gigs placed Jimmie Nicol among the top earning British professional musicians at the time. "Up to then, I was feeling quite happy turning over £30 to £40 a week," says Nicol.[19] This meant that Nicol was earning considerably more than the average weekly salary of a British worker (£18) in 1964!

Jimmy Nicol & the Shubdubs

In February of 1964, Nicol got the opportunity to record his own single and form a little Rock band he called, "Jimmy Nicol & the Shubdubs". Nicol signed a "singles deal" with Pye. Johnny Harris served as the arranger, trumpet player, and producer for the session. Roger Coulam, who had played with Nicol on some past sessions and in the Stapleton band, served as a musical anchor on organ. The A-side was *Humpty Dumpty*. The song was a traditional rendering of the children's story about the egg-shaped character, Humpty Dumpty, who "sat on a wall and had a great fall", yet it was interestingly set to a Ska style of music.

Ska music is a genre that developed in Jamaica in the late 1950s. Its style was a precursor to the later Jamaican genre of reggae, made popular by Bob Marley in the 1970s. Ska is a combination of different elements, including Caribbean, American Jazz, Calypso, and Rhythm and Blues. *Humpty Dumpty*, though lyrically weak, follows the musical pattern of Ska with a slow walking bass line coupled with Nicol's drum rhythms on the upbeat. The singer, an unknown Brit, uses a purposely-Jamaican vocal styling to add authenticity to the song. Perhaps most significant is Jimmie's first credit, not just as drummer or bandleader, but also in creating the studio arrangement, which lists Harris, Nicol, and (Top Six label boss) Wellings on the label.

As was often the case, the B-side of the record contained the hidden gem. *Night Train* is an instrumental masterpiece of 1960s-style, Jazz-fusion Rock. Not surprisingly, the song had Big Band origins. According to rhythm historian, Dave Stanoch, the original riff for the tune came from the saxophone of Johnny Hodges in 1940. The original recording swung in a down-and-dirty fashion to a bluesy, looping, shuffle rhythm – that is, until James Brown came along in 1962 giving the tune a face lift with a different vibe and making it into a hit. It was Brown's ingenuity to give the tune what was then called "the new beat" – a shuffle with a more pronounced backbeat, which propelled the song with a more intensive drive. Jimmie Nicol and Georgie Fame were also clearly influenced by James Brown's version in their respective covers of the song, both of which were released in 1964.

Humpty Dumpty by Jimmy Nicol & the Shubdubs.
Photo Credit: Courtesy of Author.

Though the song was a cover of a musical standard, one realizes upon first listen that this is a crack band laying down the track with the intent to make the song its own. *Night Train* jumps off the record needle with Jimmie's first crack on the tom toms. Harris' staccato trumpets set up Nicol's hard-driving backbeat and machine gun fills on snare, all while accompanied by the organ answering the trumpet melody. A blazing sax solo complements the melody. The song retains the sophisticated counterpoint of the rhythm section introduced by the James Brown band, and then, amazingly, it quickly fades out after only two minutes.[20]

If you analyze Nicol's performance on his first record through the lens of 1964's drumming standards, it stands out as being quite exceptional. Nicol drives the band forward with an easy swagger, but he is relentlessly rocking the rhythm with attitude. It is clear that Jimmie's knowledge of Jazz and Big Band drumming are in play on 'Night Train' as he sets up the band with clear and communicative fills that do not detract from the tune, but keep it chugging forward... like a train.[21]

Pye single Number 7N15623, *Humpty Dumpty/ Night Train*, would not break any sales records, but the B-side would gather steam and eventually garner a mention in *Billboard* as the 7th "Hot Pop" song highlighted in its special programming list for radio.[22] DJs, musicians and record producers took note that Jimmy Nicol & the Shubdubs was a hot little band.

The Shubdubs played a few gigs around town, trying to promote their single. According to singer John Hodkinson who did not appear on the single but would join the Shubdubs later in the year, "Jimmie was already getting a kind of group of guys together to be the Shubdubs. It was a group that would have worked with some of the Larry Parnes' stable of musicians." Hodkinson notes that the Shubdubs got an occasional gig in the clubs as the warm-up band for Georgie Fame & the Blue Flames.[23] "Jimmie was very good and had a good reputation and people wanted him."[24]

Unfortunately, for Johnny Harris and Jimmie Nicol, the Top Six project began to lose steam. Harris says, "It worked well for a few months and then it folded. It didn't work out. People started saying, 'Oh no!'"[25] Teens quickly figured out they were not getting the original artists, and sales of Top Six slowed once they were wise. Harris continues, "So I had put this band together to do all these covers, but after it didn't take off, the next two records didn't get into the charts. This foreign guy was losing money so he quit."[26] Likewise, the Shubdubs were put on hold. They had a record out, but could not get the gigs to sustain momentum as a group.

Blue Beat

1964 was a crazy year for the British music scene. Nicol was busy during the day with his recording sessions, and then racing his drum kit across town to Soho nightclubs to play live gigs with the likes of the Shubdubs, Georgie Fame & The Blue Flames, and Chris Farlowe. These gigs would continue Nicol's networking and lead to yet more work, not bad for a veteran drummer only in his mid 20s.

Blue Beat by The Beazers. Photo Credit: Courtesy of Author.

John Deighton was born in London's East End with a soulful voice beyond his years. He began to look for singing jobs in the early 1960s to ply his trade in the R&B world of smoky bars in London. Following the pattern Larry Parnes had established to rename his stars for entertainment purposes; Deighton changed his own name to Chris Farlowe. Farlowe formed a band called Chris Farlowe and The Thunderbirds and started working at the Flamingo club.[27] Around the same time, Farlowe met up with Jimmie Nicol, who would occasionally sit in and jam.

Decca Records had picked up on the new Ska music trend and wanted to exploit it. Rather than spend money importing real Jamaican singers to London, the label did some scouting and learned that Chris Farlowe could fill the bill. Decca chose Farlowe to record two songs in the Ska tradition. At the same time, Nicol's Big Band leader, Cyril Stapleton had moved away from touring, as it had become clear that small Rock combos were replacing Big Bands in both style and economy. As a result, when asked by Decca Records to start working for them, Stapleton jumped at the opportunity to serve as Decca's Artist & Repertoire Producer.

As one of his first projects, Decca assigned Stapleton the task of creating and producing a Ska single to market to the night clubbing crowd. At the end of January, Stapleton brought in his Cyril Stapleton Big Band, with Farlowe on vocals; Joe Moretti on guitar; and his former Big Band drummer Jimmie Nicol, to reproduce the authentic Ska beat. Nicol suggested old friend and bass guitarist, Tex Makins, for the session. Makins was currently playing regular gigs with Georgie Fame & the Blue Flames at the Flamingo club. Stapleton set about writing both sides of the Decca single that would be titled *Blue Beat* b/w *I Wanna Shout*.

Blue Beat featured Farlowe's soulful vocals - urging on his girl to "Shake it baby, drive me crazy, it's the blue beat…" Nicol's heavy Ska beats and cymbal crashes complement a funky Jazz saxophone solo in this crazy, sensual, song that takes advantage of a brief musical fad that continues to come and go in England. A heavy-sounding brass section reflects Stapleton's production style left over from the Big Band era.

I Wanna Shout is a throwaway tune that sounds like a Big Band 1950s pop tune, with a Ska beat thrown in as an afterthought. Stapleton was still too trapped in his Big Band genre to write a proper 1960s pop song. Nicol has little to do on the track, except repeat a snare Ska rhythm alongside the sappy lyric of a boy wanting to shout his love to his girlfriend. For good measure, Stapleton's song borrows The Beatles' "Yeah Yeah Yeah" chorus several times.

For contractual reasons that are lost to the ages, Farlowe, Nicol, Makins and the Big Band were given a one-time group name of "The Beazers" for the release. Most hipsters at the time knew that Chris Farlowe was singing on the track. London's dance clubs picked up on the A-side, "Blue Beat", and hit the floors, hi-stepping whenever DJs would play the tune. It got only the slimmest of media coverage as an example of the latest craze, "Of course, there is a disc to go with it [the craze] 'Blue Beat' by a group called the Beazers [Decca]."[28] On the all-important music charts, the single was a non-event.[29]

The Tommy Quickly Session

Meanwhile, The Beatles were back in town, fresh from a record-breaking appearance on Ed Sullivan's U.S. variety TV show and a concert in Washington, D.C. They had returned to London to begin work on their first film "A Hard Day's Night". Manager Brian Epstein was planning and executing the details of what would be The Beatles' first tour of the world. On March 13, 1964, he made a trip to The Netherlands to set up contracts and plan the initial "assault". Nothing but worldwide pop dominance was good enough for his number one group.

Epstein, however, did not want to neglect the other acts in his stable of musical stars. Thus, upon his return from the Netherlands, he went straight into the recording studio to help one of his recent signings, a young singer named Tommy Quickly, who had yet to have a hit song. Epstein recalled when he first came across the young singer, "My first solo artiste was a freckled-face boy called Quigley and his discovery was more

TOMMY QUICKLY

Tommy Quickly. Photo Credit:
Pye Records promotional photo

like the American film/musical conception of star-making than any of the other people I manage."[30] The impresario was running a concert one night backstage, when he heard a "fascinating voice over the amplification system". He watched from the wings as this young man gave it his all in the amateur spot on the bill, wowing the teenage girls. They talked that night, and after a period of weeks, Epstein agreed to represent the freckle-faced youth. Quigley agreed to change his name to Quickly and joined the Epstein stable.[31]

Epstein had negotiated a small record deal for Quickly at Pye to make three or four singles. After a couple of unsuccessful singles released in 1963, Epstein decided to get more involved in the selection of songs, hoping to get Quickly into the charts with a hit. He knew that artists at Pye usually got only a few chances for a hit before being dropped by the label. On the evening of March 24, 1964, Epstein met his young protégé at Pye's recording studio to track a new song. That same evening, coincidentally, Charlie Katz (the "Fixer") called on Jimmie Nicol to come in and play drums, along with Phil Seamen to play percussion and castanets. Over the years, many books, writers, and so-called Beatles experts" have incorrectly suggested that Beatles' producer, George Martin, produced this session and therefore learned about Jimmie Nicol by working with him in the studio. However, Martin was not involved with Quickly, for he was signed to work exclusively with Parlophone artists at EMI Studios; and he was contractually prohibited from working with a Pye recording artist or at Pye Studios. Martin had not yet worked with Nicol at this point.

Actual film footage of this recording session survives. Prior to the session, Epstein seated in the back of a limo with a BBC-TV news reporter, Epstein is asked, "Now we're going off to this recording session. Do you know that this is going to be a success?" Epstein, who typically exuded greater confidence when talking about The Beatles or Gerry and The Pacemakers, hesitates and then chooses his words carefully. He replies, "I th… I think that it has the um… ingredients of a success." Pressing him further, the reporter asks, "Before we even go there or hear it, do you know it's going to be? Are you prepared to back your reputation on it?" Epstein replies simply, "Yes."[32]

Following the limo interview, Brian is seen at Pye Studios, leaning on a piano and nodding his head to the beat of Quickly rehearsing his song. The camera pans over Brian's right shoulder to show a session guitarist in the background. In the background, the viewer sees a drum kit with a white Trixon bass drumhead that reads, "JIMMIE NICOL". Below his name is the Big Band crest showing "CS", which stands for Nicol's former Big Band, Cyril Stapleton. Jimmie is seen behind his drum kit, setting it up and playing just the kick bass drum in preparation for the recording. The next clip shows Epstein in the foreground with the arranger Brad Newman, discussing his query about the need for two drummers, as Nicol observes.

Finally, the recording session red light turns on, and we hear Tommy Quickly singing the song, *You Might As Well Forget Him* (aka *Walk The Streets*) as the recording tape rolls. Describing the session, Epstein enthuses, "The American singer Tommy Roe wrote the song and sent it to me after I'd met him in the same touring show here [in 1963]. I think this one might go."[33]

With the red light on in the studio, Jimmie drums along, using only brushes at the beginning of the track. As the song crescendos, Nicol grabs his drumsticks to add a tougher emotion to the chugging beat. Epstein is seated in the Producer's control room, Studio 2, as the camera pans through the glass window to the session in progress below. The crowded session includes two guitarists; one bass player; one piano player; three background singers; and the two drummers in the back of the studio, all accompanying Tommy Quickly. Although the arrangement is sitting on the music stand next to Nicol, it is obvious that he has already memorized the part, for he is seen playing and intently watching the other players in the room as they record the take live.

Epstein was a detail-oriented person. He had had a chance to see the experienced drummer, Jimmie Nicol, live in the studio. As for the Quickly single, *You Might As Well Forget Him* b/w *It's As Simple As That,* it was forgettable and failed to chart, despite an anemic compliment from the newspaper, stating only; "…It has chart quality."[34] Perhaps Epstein's hesitation and carefully chosen response to the BBC-TV reporter was prescient, because by 1965's end, Tommy's career in music quickly faded into obscurity.

The stars of Jimmie Nicol and The Beatles were starting to converge. Observing Nicol's performance would impact Epstein very soon and in a significant way for his number one group The Beatles. Video footage from the BBC TV Panorama recording session provides the viewer with one more glimpse of Brian looking down at Jimmie Nicol - intently watching him play his drums on the track. Nicol is dressed in a dark sport coat with a dark sweater underneath, focused very seriously on the job. Epstein would file away his favorable impressions of Jimmie Nicol for a rainy day.

Rain or shine, despite all of the money and goodwill Jimmie was earning most days at Decca and PYE, it was still fairly tedious and repetitive work. It also lacked the immediacy of jamming with a hot band. Nicol still preferred the hot, smoke- filled nightclubs and live music of London's club scene; and the band he most admired was Georgie Fame & the Blue Flames.

Chapter Nine
Fame Leads to "Fame"

Fame is considered by many to be the father of modern rhythm & blues and Jazz. The keyboardist and singer started out as Clive Powell. Rock singer, Rory Blackwell introduced Powell to the London music scene and star-maker Larry Parnes. Just as with the others in his stable, Parnes convinced Clive to change his name to Georgie Fame, and he put him to work backing up his other artists on piano. During this time Fame played on the same concert bill with Jimmie Nicol, on many of Parnes' package tours and of course, Fame toured with Jimmie Nicol and his 15 New Orleans Rockers Big Band. "I worked two years for Larry," recalls Fame, "playing behind practically every artiste on the bill. It was a case of having to, because I was the only pianist, and it wasn't too bad until a tour ended and I used to find myself out of work for two months at a time."[1] For a time, Fame was part of the headlining Parnes band, Billy Fury & the Blue Flames. However, a rift eventually developed between Fury and the Blue Flames. Fame took the Blue Flames name and set out on his own to create a separate identity, though at first, Georgie Fame & the Blues Flames were a band with a name, but a band without work!

Georgie Fame

Fame found himself out of money, out of luck and out in the cold when an old hometown friend and fellow piano player took him into his flat. Mike O'Neil was the piano player for a popular London group at the time called "Nero and the Gladiators". Coincidentally, O'Neil had also played with Jimmie Nicol in Colin Hicks & His Cabin Boys. O'Neil let Georgie stay with him in his flat on London's Old Compton Street. "Mike had a fantastic collection of Jazz records," says Fame reminiscing. "I used to spend long hours studying LPs by people like Charlie Parker, Louis Prima, Cannonball Adderley and a fabulous Jazz singer called King Pleasure who used to take Jazz solos and write his own words to them."[2] Little did he realize that it was Jimmie Nicol who had first exposed Mike O'Neil to Jazz. While staying at O'Neil's flat, Fame had an epiphany. He knew that if he could get his own band going, and perform Blues and Jazz for the public, it would catch on. He would get his chance very soon, thanks again to his fellow keyboard buddy O'Neil.

O'Neil recalls, "One day I took Georgie down to the Flamingo club, hoping to get him some work. I knew the manager there Rik."[3] Fame says, "He introduced me to Rik Gunnell, [club manager] and said, 'this is Billy Fury's piano player, blah, blah, blah'... This must have been January, 1962. A couple weeks later, we [the Blue Flames] went down there and the resident band, the Earl Watson band was going off to Birmingham to do a TV show and Rik needed a band to dep [stand in]. So we went in and stayed… for three years."[4]

The Flamingo club first opened its doors in September of 1952. From the beginning, the club began to build its reputation in London as *the* hot spot for live Jazz. The Flamingo was founded by Jeffrey Kruger, MBE, who recalls the origination for the idea. "My early aspirations were as a Jazz pianist. I soon became aware that there were others who could play better than I ever would manage, but I had flair, ambition and the courage to provide them with the means of expanding their talent and its impact. By opening the Flamingo I could work alongside these great musicians."[5]

Most nights the club with a capacity of 400, squeezed in 600 for a live session. Britain in the early 1960s was a country in transition. Political and sex scandals were rocking London; the Pill began a sexual revolution; The Beatles and others were creating a new generation of Rock and Roll; the class system was beginning to crumble; and American influences were everywhere in the form of music. Black American Blues, Jazz, and R & B were in great demand. In an era long before personal computers and digital music, the only way to access the Blues, Jazz and R & B was either via 45-rpm records or by going to see live performances. Jeffrey Kruger's Flamingo helped play an important role in satisfying London's craving for this entertainment. Wardour Street's Flamingo club was to London what the Cavern club was to Liverpool and Birdland was to New York. As Georgie Fame first took the stage, a whole new generation of music fans – lovers of R&B and Jazz - would propel the young keyboardist to a lifelong following.

Fame recalls that half of his clientele at the Flamingo were West Indian, while "the other half were black American GI's mixed up with a few gangsters and pimps and prostitutes."[6] Blue Flames bass player, Tex Makins, recalls, "All nights in the Flamingo were very stoned. It was like a party every night. The crowds - mainly American Armed Forces - were also very stoned or drunk. They went crazy over the band."[7] As Fame made friends with American soldiers, they began to share the latest Jazz and Blues records from America with him. This new music had a big impact on Fame's ever-changing set list. The song *Green Onions,* by Booker T. and the MGs, is likely to have inspired Fame to switch from keyboards to the Hammond organ. "American GI's would come to the club and bring me records," recalls Fame. "I was learning all the time. Georgie Fame & the Blue Flames were swinging like mad."[8]

The Blue Flames began their residency leading the "Friday All Niters" which went to 6 am. The All Niter was a semi-planned performance, with time reserved for extended jam sessions as well. By 1964, the Blue Flames had graduated to playing sets all over the greater London area. It was an exhausting, yet exhilarating schedule. Rik Gunnell was employed to the run the Flamingo club and to supervise the All Niter sessions, seeing that owner Jeffrey Kruger, "… had to have some sleep every now and then."[9] Gunnell could not help but notice the growing popularity of Georgie Fame and his group. Gunnell approached Fame with the idea of becoming his manager. Fame recalls, "The reason that Rik Gunnell became my manager is because he was very happy with me pack-

Fans line up for another All Niter at the Flamingo.
Photo Credit: Courtesy of Jeffery Kruger, MBE

ing out the Flamingo." Gunnell realized, "'If Georgie goes out of the club I've got no band'. So Rik went to a lawyer and my father signed the contract."[10]

During the first half of 1964, the line up of Georgie Fame & the Blue Flames included Georgie Fame on vocals and organ; Tex Makins on bass guitar; Micke Eve on saxophone; Peter Coe on saxophone; Speedy Acquaye on percussion; and Red Reece on drums. Over the spring of 1964, Jimmie Nicol occasionally subbed for Reece on drums. Fame and Makins had played with Nicol over the years, and it was a natural fit for Jimmy to fill in with the band. Given the band's exhaustive schedule and with Reece's health beginning to falter, the need for an occasional fill-in continued. Tenor Sax player Peter Coe recalls, "Red Reece was the founding member drummer who had the chair when I joined. Jimmy Nicol was one of the stand-in drummers who followed."[11]

Typically, Fame, Nicol & the Blue Flames would enter the smoke-filled bar of clinking liquor glasses and rowdy patrons while the support band was still playing. Fame and the others would just climb up on stage behind the players and start assembling their equipment for the All Niter. "We'd slap the organ on stage while they were playing, say 'Hi guys, how you doing?' Then we'd retire to the little rat-infested dressing room or go to the bar," says Fame.[12]

The first of two long All Niter sets began at 1:30 in the morning, with a break for drinks. Then Georgie and his swinging band would start up again at 4:30 for another hot set lasting until closing time at 6:00 a.m. The group would hang around the club for a bit, discussing the music and before heading off to an all-night café and back home to their flats to sleep through the day.

During the first week of May, 1964, Blue Flames drummer Red Reece became too ill to continue with the band. This left Georgie Fame with a dilemma. Who could he pick up to replace the ailing Reece behind the drum kit of the hottest Jazz and R & B band in London? It was bass player, Tex Makins, who suggested to Georgie that they should hire Jimmie Nicol on a permanent basis. Nicol knew most of their set already. "I did suggest to Georgie to hire Jim as we had both played with him many times before and really liked his drumming."[13]

Johnny Harris had begun to do studio arrangements with producer Tony Hatch (Petula Clark, David Bowie, and The Searchers) after the Top Six deal lost steam. He lost track of seeing Nicol everyday once he started working with Hatch. "Jimmie picked up studio work as he could. And he got a great gig with Georgie Fame & the Blue Flames around this time in the spring. I couldn't use Jimmie at the time with Tony, because he already had his own group of studio guys that he always used. Fame's band was a perfect fit for Nicol. He was a rough diamond. He really was a most fantastic drummer to watch."[14]

Jimmie Nicol was now a Blue Flame, the top club band in London. The money was very good and band members were pulling in several pounds per night for club gigs and more for theater shows, "a lot of money then," according to Makins.[15] Nicol recalls, "I was playing around in a small band [Georgie Fame & the Blue Flames] and in the studio wherever I was needed. I was actually making money as a drummer, something many were not doing."[16]

Nicol's contribution of controlled mayhem on drums really sparked the band anew. According to Jeffrey Kruger, other bands started showing up at the All Niters to watch the Blue Flames, including The Beatles, The Rolling Stones, and The Who.[17] The one Beatle spotted most often at the Flamingo All Niters was Paul McCartney. He had befriended Georgie Fame and really enjoyed the swinging R & B scene. McCartney, who occasionally enjoyed dabbling on the drums himself, took a keen interest in observing new Blue Flames drummer, Jimmie Nicol.

The band swung into its hot set list each night, which included many of the up-tempo Jazz and R&B songs of the era, including: *Green Onions*; *Shop Around*; *Moody's Mood for Love*; *Parkers Mood*; *Little Red Top*; *Humpty Dumpty*; *Kansas City*; *Esso Besso*; *Night Train*; *Get On The Right Track Baby*; *Yeah Yeah*; *Dr. Kitch* and many more. "We rarely did the same set two nights running," say Makins.[18] Nicol was, of course, quite comfortable playing *Humpty Dumpty*, *Night Train* and the other staples in the set. "He was a fine drummer," remembers Jeffrey Kruger, "at home playing Jazz and for Georgie's R & B moods".[19] During Nicol's brief stint with Georgie Fame, which lasted only three short weeks, the band continued to attract followers outside its circle of R & B fans, U.S. Servicemen, and friends.

Jimmie Nicol playing with Georgie Fame & the Blue Flames the night before he joined The Beatles.
Photo Credit: © Jeremy Fletcher photographer/Redferns/Getty Images.

From Fame to the Fab Four

On that fateful date of June 3, 1964, Brian Epstein and his management team were in a panic over Ringo Starr's tonsillitis and extended hospital stay, on the eve of The Beatles' first world tour. With no time to spare, Epstein sent his trusted road manager, Neil Aspinall, down to the Soho clubs in search of drummers to possibly fill the bill. He wasn't taking any chances. He needed to discreetly look for all possibilities. Epstein made it clear in discussions with his management team that the candidate must be discreet and mature; able to play the music; be fairly unknown; and not be someone who might stoke media rumors of being Ringo's permanent replacement. The first drummer asked to fill in for Ringo Starr was *not* Jimmie Nicol (in fact Nicol was the third person asked to deputize for Starr). He was in fact another excellent London drummer by the name of Raye Du-Vale.

In 1962, Raye Du-Val was the drummer in a headlining band called Emile Ford and the Checkmates. In April of 1962 The Checkmates headlined a show promoted by Sam Leach at the Tower Ballroom in Liverpool. Leach recalled, "The Beatles always observed the headliners. They wanted to be headliners and so they were quick to study the band they supported."[20] On that day, The Beatles had the chance to watch drummer Raye Du-Val play with the Checkmates. He was flashy and, at the time, was the Guinness Book of World Records holder for the longest drumming solo without a break. Du-Vale recalls a member of The Beatles management came into the London Top Ten club on June 3, 1964. "The chap asked me to fill in for Ringo who was ill," Says Du-Val. "It's not for me," Du-Val told him. "I am doing just fine with my band The Blue Notes right now." He confides, "There were so many bands like The Beatles in 1964, I thought, they are *not* going to make it (laughing)."[21]

With one strike, Epstein decided to call drummer Bobby Graham. At the time, Graham was one of the most recorded session drummers in London. He had also worked in prominent bands, including Joe Brown and the Bruvvers, and Marty Wilde's Wildcats. According to Graham's history, Epstein had previously asked the veteran drummer to replace former Beatle Pete Best in the summer of 1962.[22] Graham says, "Epstein phoned me and offered me the gig with The Beatles to Holland and Australia. But I couldn't do it because I was a session man and had so much work to do that I didn't dare not turn up for those sessions." However, Graham did suggest another drummer he knew and respected… Jimmy Nicol. "I'd seen him that day, or the day before, in one of the pubs by Denmark Street."[23] Graham was strike two, and the clock - ticking toward the next day's world tour launch - seemed to accelerate.

Brian Epstein recalled the name of Nicol and seeing him at Pye studios on Tommy Quickly's recording session in March of 1964. Though many Beatles and music history books claim George Martin was aware of Nicol's reputation as a Pye session drummer, The Beatles' producer could not recall having such knowledge at the time, especially because he had never produced a session with Nicol, since both men were contractually obligated to two different record labels.[24] It is quite likely that Paul McCartney also brought up Nicol's name as a candidate, for McCartney was friends with Georgie Fame and frequently went to the All Niter shows at The Flamingo to see his band, the Blue Flames.

On that memorable day, Georgie Fame got an unexpected call from his friend, Paul McCartney. "Hey Georgie, Ringo is ill," he told him. 'We need a drummer to tour Australia; can we take your boy Jimmie Nicol?" "Course you can," Fame replied to McCartney.[25] Jimmie Nicol's life was about to change forever. His phone rang in his Barnes flat. It was his bandleader Georgie Fame. "Hey Jimmie," said Fame. "Have you got a passport?" Jimmie was still tired from the previous night's performance and was confused by the question. "No," came Nicol's reply. "Well," said Fame with a big smile as he spoke, "Get yourself down to the Post Office tomorrow morning."[26] Nicol remembers, "Everything happened very quickly. They [The Beatles] had to move very fast."[27]

There was a gray chill in the air as Jimmie Nicol put on his best white dress shirt, buttoning the top button. He donned a dark sweater that he often used on studio sessions and was ready to go. Nicol's friend, John Hodkinson, went along with Jimmie after the call came in from producer George Martin to be at EMI Studios (later to be renamed Abbey Road) by 3:00 p.m. Hodkinson was not sure how to qualify this musical summit. "We went along to the tryout or rehearsal. I actually got into the studio with Jimmie. I knew Paul from Liverpool and he said hello and remembered me."[28] According to Nicol, "I didn't have to audition for them. It was just one rehearsal in the studio."[29] According to PR man, Greg Tesser, who was in the room, "Yes, Jimmy definitely did an audition – this I do remember."[30] The last word on the subject should go to Beatles' producer George Martin who described the scene, "Jimmie Nicol was a very good little drummer who came along and learned Ringo's parts very well. Obviously, he had to rehearse with the others. And they (Paul, John and George) worked through all the songs here [at the studio]."[31]

Meanwhile, Georgie Fame's manager had heard the news that the Blue Flames' drummer had been lent to The Beatles. His goal was to immediately summon the news media and let the world

CD cover "The Jimmy Nicol Days" features a snippet of Nicol's rehearsal with The Beatles.

know that Georgie Fame had generously lent his drummer to The Beatles. What better way to promote Fame's band than to assemble the media at EMI Studios where Jimmie Nicol was headed to play with The Beatles? At the time, eighteen-year-old Greg Tesser was working for a music public relations firm called Press Presentations, located in London's Tin Pan Alley. His job was to help create publicity for Georgie Fame, The Yardbirds and a few others. On June 3, he was contacted by Georgie Fame's manager and told that Fame was lending Jimmie Nicol to The Beatles. "My brief was to squeeze as much publicity as possible out of the Ringo situation for Georgie Fame. I had the daunting job of organizing a big press bash at the EMI studios, with the three remaining Beatles."[32] Tesser greeted Nicol upon his arrival at Abbey Road and noted, "Jimmie was overawed with the whole thing."[33] It seemed as if all of England's print, radio and TV media were shoehorned into the studio.

At first, Nicol sat behind Ringo Starr's Ludwig 20-inch diameter Bass drum set, the same set Starr had used in the recent filming of *A Hard Day's Night*.[34] John Lennon, Paul McCartney, and George Harrison squeezed into the drummer's booth, and all posed for the now famous photos that would be sensationally splashed around the world the next day in newspapers. In several of the shots, Jimmie Nicol looked the way he felt, like a deer-in-headlights and overwhelmed by the sudden change in his life from the casual obscurity of session and club work to the world famous Beatles. With the print photos out of the way, the newsreel men were allowed to film a brief clip of The Beatles with Jimmie. We see Nicol pounding out a steady beat with heavy bass drum kicks as John Lennon comes in on Jimmie's right. George Harrison comes into frame on Nicol's left and grabs Ringo's ride cymbal, then clenches his right hand into a fist and lets-fly with a thinly veiled pretend punch to Jimmie's head. Though meant as a joke, it may also have been for Ringo's benefit - to demonstrate Harrison's allegiance to The Beatles' real drummer. Clearly, Harrison's face betrays his annoyance at having to go out on tour with a deputy drummer, but he goes along with the "charade"; ever the good team player. Paul McCartney walks into frame carrying an old suitcase as Nicol finally cracks a smile. Jimmie stops playing and points at the suitcase with his drumstick. McCartney tells him (helping the press figure out the story), "We brought it for you."[35]

The media begin a session of questions and answers, during which Tesser noted, "Jimmie was on the tense side. It was true that he was playing with Georgie, and his band was on the up big-time, but to be asked to play on tour for the biggest thing since Elvis got to him a bit, I think."[36] A reporter asked John Lennon why he had not called Pete Best to replace Ringo Starr, to which Lennon replied, "He's got his own group, and it might have looked as if we were taking him back, which is not good for him."[37]

Finally, after all of the media attention, it was time to see if Jimmie Nicol could play with the biggest Rock band in the world. "I wouldn't be human if I didn't admit I was nervous," recalls Nicol as they readied themselves. "But they put me at ease straightaway. The instruments were already set up and I took my place at Ringo's drums."[38] The "new" Beatles ran through a mere six songs: *I Want To Hold Your Hand; She Loves You; I Saw Her Standing There; This Boy; Can't Buy Me Love;* and *Long Tall Sally.* None of the performances was recorded by either George Martin or the media, who had by this time been filed out of the studio. John Hodkinson, however, witnessed the run-through and still remembers it, "I basically sat in a corner and watched the three Beatles rehearse each song with Jimmie. Even though I was a fellow musician, I was excited to be in there. It was absolutely tremendous – I actually witnessed a private little show with Jimmie Nicol and The Beatles. I think they just beat around for about 15 minutes or so; just to get a feel for each other musically."[39] Unlike his other sessions in studios, Nicol was not given any sheet music to follow. However, he recalls, "That didn't matter because I already knew the numbers by heart."[40] Nicol shined in his rehearsal with The Beatles. The band, the producer, and manager Epstein were all smiles because they realized they had just found their replacement and lifesaver. Epstein had met his objective of locating someone who knew all the songs and was sufficiently unknown to the public. In Epstein's mind, a major disaster had been averted. "Jimmie was amazing that day," reflects Hodkinson.[41]

Shortly after the audition/ rehearsal, Nicol was summoned to talk to Brian Epstein in a nearby office. Jimmie was still nervous, despite having finished playing with The Beatles in the studio. He sat down in the office and the two discussed Nicol's drumming experience with Beatles' songs. Nicol talked about his work on the Top Six *Beatlemania* LP at Pye and his professional resume in Rock & Roll, Big Band, R & B, Trad Jazz, and Ska. Epstein was impressed, but made it clear to Nicol how important it was to show discretion on tour and to avoid any appearances of impropriety. Nicol understood. He will never forget what happened next: "Well, Brian had all of The Beatles – with the exception of Ringo who was already in the hospital getting the swelling down in his throat from his inflamed tonsils – in an outer office. In a passing motion, he waived them in to meet me… My mind was blown. I would have played for free as long as they needed me…They were very nice."[42]

After the greetings and small talk were over, Epstein steered the discussion back to business with the "group" all together in the office. Epstein put the issue of Jimmie's salary on the table. "When Brian talked of money in front of them," says Nicol, "I got very very nervous. They paid me £2500 per gig and a £2500 signing bonus. Now that floored me."[43] At this point, Nicol recalls John Lennon chiming in good naturedly, "Good God Brian, you'll make the chap crazy." Nicol recalls, "I thought it was over. But, no sooner had he [Lennon] said that, when he then said, 'Give him £10,000!'" Relieved, Nicol says, "Everyone laughed and I felt a hell of a lot better."[44] (Author's note: In his book, *The Beatles Live*, Mark Lewisohn states that Jimmie Nicol was actually paid £500 pounds plus expenses for the entire tour. Nicol himself in 1965 told the *Daily Mirror* his pay for the tour had been £500).[45] With the meeting concluded, Nicol, along with John Lennon, Paul McCartney and George Harrison said their goodbyes, stating they would see each other the next day for the start of the tour.

Once the business was concluded, Jimmie and his friend Hodkinson headed out on foot in St. John's Wood for a brief round-the-corner pub celebration. As Jimmie was sitting in the bar with his head spinning, suddenly a big man came up and tapped him on the shoulder. Nicol turned around, and the guy said, "My name is Mal Evans. I'm with The Beatles. Here is my card. It's got a phone number on it. Any time you need *anything,* at any time of the day or night... 24 hours, anything you want... call me"[46] Upon his arrival back home in Barnes, Nicol rang up his pal, Johnny Harris. "So he called me back," says Harris. "He was screaming on the phone, 'Johnny, I GOT IT, I GOT IT, I GOT IT!!! I'm leaving tomorrow.' Jimmie told me about playing a few numbers with The Beatles, and John Lennon said to him, 'Right then, you're in.' And that was it, I didn't hear from him again until he got back from that trip," say Harris.[47]

Now the little changes in Jimmie's life began. He recalls, "A wardrobe lady came over to my flat and a hairdresser cut my hair in a mop-top. In the mirror, I cut a mean figure as the new Beatle. I was on top of the music world, for sure."[48] It was too late to create tour suits for Nicol, so the wardrobe lady brought over Ringo Starr's stage outfits which she was barely able to alter enough to fit Nicol who was more muscular in build than the slighter Ringo Starr. In the end, it would be a tight fit, for the "husky" drummer to play with The Beatles in coming days.

With his clothes and hair finished, it was time for Jimmie to pack. Hodkinson explains, "Well, I was staying at his house in Barnes with his family at the time, and all my belongings were at Jim's house. He had to pack his clothes, so I said, 'Take this, my red suitcase.'"[49] As Nicol was packing, they learned by telephone that The Beatles management had arranged for Jimmy's passport and visa.

Meanwhile, across town at the hospital, drummer Ringo Starr sat helplessly watching. The carnival of The Beatles' first world tour was about to leave town without him. His insecurities naturally crept in, despite well wishes from his soon departing band mates. "It was very strange because I wasn't well and they'd taken Jimmie Nicol and I thought they didn't love me anymore. All that stuff went through my head."[50]

It must have been nearly impossible for Jimmie Nicol to sleep that night, knowing that the next day, he would be drumming his way into the history books with The Beatles. Playing with Georgie Fame had indeed led Nicol toward achieving his own fame. However, no one could foresee at the time that Jimmie Nicol's life would be forever transformed by this incredible experience and opportunity with The Beatles. What would this opportunity foreshadow for the young drummer?

Chapter Ten

Beatle Jimmy Nicol:
Denmark & the Netherlands

The stage was set. 1964 would be the year The Beatles conquered the world, yet only saw it from the stage, the plane, the limo, the hotel, and other assorted compartments designed to protect them from their fans. For Jimmie Nicol, 1964 was a watershed year. His resume now included big band drummer; session sideman; arranger; band leader; and a member of Georgie Fame & the Blue Flames. Destiny had intervened and was now catapulting his rise to the top of the entertainment world with The Beatles. Nicol's mind was reeling as he dressed in his best white shirt, dark slacks, and white raincoat for the journey of a lifetime.

Just to make sure all of this was really happening, Jimmie went out early in the morning to pick up a handful of newspapers. The headlines all confirmed that Jimmie Nicol was taking over for Ringo Starr in The Beatles! There was even a photo of Jimmie behind the famous Beatles' drum kit, between John Lennon, Paul McCartney, and George Harrison. The reality of the moment sunk in as Nicol scoured the big news of the day.

Jimmie said his goodbyes to the family and stepped out of his Barnes flat on a cool grey morning, into a new world – one filled with adventure, travel and unimaginable fame and adoration – all the trappings that are "Beatlemania". This would not just be another tour with another band. This journey would be one that would profoundly affect Nicol for the rest of his life, after being launched into the eye of The Beatles' hurricane. Regardless of the pressure, this was a place where Jimmie Nicol could showcase his talent and prove that he belonged in the "big leagues" of music. He had worked hard and he possessed the talent, confidence, and maturity to enter the doors of this exclusive club.

June 4, 1964, Denmark

The transformative journey began early in the morning. Nicol was picked up by Bill Corbett, The Beatles' chauffeur, in his Austin Princess; and he was greeted happily by John, Paul, George, and PR man, Derek Taylor. As they headed to the airport early to get seated ahead of the regular passengers on this flight, Nicol reflected on the sudden change in his life. "Like day and night. The day before I was a Beatle, not one girl would even look me over," he said. "The day after, when I was suited up and riding in the back of a limo with John Lennon and Paul McCartney, they were dying just to get a touch of me."[1] Nicol was just beginning to understand the magic of being a Beatle.

At the airport, there were only 50 or so fans screaming from the flight deck, standing in a misting rain, to bid their Beatles farewell. The Beatles waved from the stairs of their plane to the loyal fans. All four were smiling. Upon entering the plane, the crew immediately asked the band members for their autographs, not even realizing that Jimmie Nicol had replaced Ringo Starr. Thus,

Jimmie Nicol began to sign autographs for the next several days alongside those of John, Paul, and George. These rare autographs have become highly prized by collectors through the years. Just as

One of Jimmie's first "Beatles" autographs.
Credit: Courtesy of Author

Nicol was driven to succeed and be noticed; likewise, Jimmie's autograph was usually quite a bit larger than his band mates. His signature read simply, "Jimmie Nicol".

The flight to Copenhagen, Denmark was uneventful. Sitting on the plane he could not resist contemplating his new status. "I knew that I was the envy of every drummer in England, because I would get to experience other countries... I would be earning good money. And because I was, for a period of time, to be a real Beatle."[2]

Waiting for the group at the airport were approximately 3000 to 6000 rabid fans according to various media reports. The plane arrived with Jimmie and his Beatles - stopping first to wave from atop the stairs of the plane - to a screaming throng of teens and news media. The Beatles then made their way through the melee of hounding reporters to their car and headed for the hotel.

The scene outside the Royal Hotel in Copenhagen was chaotic amid the hundreds of teens and scores of police with dogs pushing the kids back. One report stated there were 2000 fans outside the hotel, battling the police for entry to meet The Beatles. Several were trampled when they briefly broke through the police barriers.[3] According to Beatles' Press Officer, Tony Barrow, "They were staying in the same suite of rooms as Russia's President, Mr. Krushchev, who had booked for his visit two weeks earlier."[4] Jimmy Nicol was beyond impressed with the wild reception and accommodations. He was simply in shock after only half a day of Beatlemania. But now the time had come to get down to work.

Inside Copenhagen's beautiful Tivoli Gardens there is a sports arena called KB Hallen which is owned by the local football (soccer) team. With heavy police protection, The Beatles crossed the street to begin serious rehearsals inside KB Hallen for the first of two shows that evening. John Lennon worked out a set-list for the show, as Jimmie paid close attention. Roadie Mal Evans wrote out the finished list of songs to tape onto the three guitars. Meanwhile, Road Manager Neil Aspinall wrote out the same concert setlist in red ink, for later use by Jimmie Nicol. Aspinall handed the set list to Lennon.[5] The Beatles immediately began rehearsing the songs for their upcoming concerts with Jimmie Nicol, teaching him the special timing and nuances of each tune. The set list for the first night of The Beatles' world tour included only ten songs.

Noticeably missing from the list was Ringo's standard vocal number, *I Wanna Be Your Man*. Jimmie was nervous but focused, as the rehearsals proceeded, with the other Beatles explaining when to slow down or speed up. Photographer Leslie Bryce witnessed the rehearsal and observed, "I didn't realize how difficult it was to be a Beatle until I saw a new man among them."[6] Tony Barrow concurred, "The Beatles have a special way of saying and doing things, and understandably, Jimmy [sic] found it hard to fit in, but he was obviously very excited, and very proud."[7] Up for the challenge, Nicol already knew the drum parts for six of the ten songs on the set list, thanks to his work on Top Six Records. As a result, The Beatles were at a greater advantage during the brief time allotted for rehearsal than if they had selected a different drummer for the difficult understudy position.

There would be several warm up bands preceding The Beatles onstage that night, including The Weedons, The Beethovens and The Hitmakers. When the Hitmakers' manager, Niels Wenkens had learned that Ringo Starr was sick, he had offered Hitmakers' drummer, Torben Sardorf, to replace him in Denmark. However, Epstein assured him, by telephone, that they had found a suitable replacement drummer for the tour.

Hitmakers' drummer Sardorf recalls watching Nicol and The Beatles at the afternoon soundcheck. "Jimmie was very friendly, but he seemed to be very nervous. Who wouldn't be?"[8] He noted that Jimmie was using Ringo Starr's drum kit. Nicol was playing on Starr's third Ludwig drum set with the larger 22-inch bass drum.[9] Sardorf got quite nervous himself when he noticed John Lennon watching the Hitmakers play their afternoon soundcheck. Lennon approached him. "In the afternoon after our soundcheck, John came up to me and felt my leather jacket, and said, 'Nice Jacket'. I could only mumble, 'thank you'." Sardorf was in a state of shock. He then watched as Lennon handed the Aspinall written set-list to Jimmie Nicol and wished him luck. Nicol walked over to his drum kit and laid the set-list on top of the Ludwig bass drum.[10]

After an interruption by the British Ambassador to Copenhagen and media questions from 150 photographers and journalists back at the hotel, it was time for the first of two shows to begin at six o'clock p.m. Newsreel footage shows police tussling with rowdy teenage boys as 4400 fans packed into the KB Hallen for the first show. Jimmie Nicol stood in the wings of the stage watching The Hitmakers perform their 9-song set before The Beatles. His heart was pounding hard as he realized that his big moment had come. He was minutes away from sitting behind the kit of a bass drum that read, "*THE BEATLES*" and playing with the biggest band in the world on their first-ever world tour. Failure was not an option and Nicol was a seasoned pro. He wanted to demonstrate to both The Beatles and their fans that he could drive the rhythms for the top band in the world. He knew he would be focused and he knew the butterflies would vanish after the first song started.

However, moments before The Beatles were to go onstage, a controversy erupted. The Hitmakers' live set was a big success with the audience. The fans wanted an encore. So Jimmie and The Beatles graciously waited as The Hitmakers came off stage and went back out for one more song. The only problem was they chose the same song that The Beatles planned to close with, McCartney's Little Richard rave up of *Long Tall Sally*. When The Hitmakers launched into the song, the crowd went wild and McCartney got very upset. Now The Beatles were not only cutting out Ringo's song, but they would also have to skip *Long Tall Sally* in the early evening show. McCartney had also planned to tell the 4400 strong that "Long Tall Sally" would be released in record stores the next day in Denmark.

Meanwhile, John Lennon was giving Jimmie a pep talk and encouragement. The two had begun to bond on the flight over. "I met them all backstage after our performance, but they were ready to go on stage," says Sardorf. "As Jimmie Nicol passed me by on the way out, he said, 'Good drum solo'".[11] Sardorf was flattered.

When the Hitmakers finished, The Beatles were introduced to thundering applause as they took the stage. The screaming was so loud that when Paul McCartney counted off "1, 2, 3, 4…" - the beginning of *I Saw Her Standing There,* Nicol started playing the song off the beat. He simply could not hear anything with all the fans screeching. He was craning his neck to see where the band was. Lennon, who was keeping a protective eye on Jimmie, sensed the problem immediately. It was a problem that Ringo Starr had suffered as well, ever since the screaming of Beatlemania began. Lennon came to the rescue. "Just then," explains Sardorf. "John turned towards him [Nicol] and with his rhythm guitar, showed Jimmie the 2 and 4 beats, and got him right back on the beat."[12] From that point on, Sardorf says, Nicol was "all right" through to the end of the first show. He recalls how Nicol's drumming style looked different on stage from Ringo's.[13]

An audio recording of the first concert exists on bootleg, and it confirms how difficult it was for Jimmie Nicol to hear his fellow band mates. At times, it seems that Nicol is rushing the beat, perhaps due to nervousness. There was no room for Nicol's fancy fills and solos at these shows; just keeping on the beat while watching the other three was hard enough. In the end, the recordings sound like many of the other Beatles' concerts from 1964, full of teens screaming.

On the last song of the first set, McCartney sounds slightly annoyed as he announces, "This song will have to be our last song." The song is *Twist and Shout* (not *Long Tall Sally* they *had* planned as their closer). The screaming crowd is disappointed that the show is ending so soon. Despite his annoyance at having to cut out *Long Tall Sally*, Paul makes a point to tell the crowd, "Before we go, before we go, we would like to say that we are sorry that Ringo isn't here, but we'd like you all to clap and give a really big hand for our drummer… Ring…eh… JIMMIE!" At that moment, a huge ovation of screaming rose up to wash over Jimmie Nicol for all of his efforts, a chorus of screams that lasts for a full 16 seconds. With the ovation over, the band launches into a rousing closer with

Twist and Shout.

Coming off stage, Paul McCartney made his way over to The Hitmakers' manager to complain about his band playing The Beatles' closer, *Long Tall Sally*. According to Sardorf who witnessed the exchange, "Paul McCartney tore his hair out backstage because he wanted to end their performance with *Long Tall Sally*.[14] He asked that the Hitmakers not play the song again at the late show. "We all four agreed not to play it at the second concert," says Sardorf.[15] Another "crisis" was averted.

The second show of the night went more smoothly for Jimmie for he had settled down and the butterflies mostly disappeared. The band was able to play *Long Tall Sally* as their closer; and McCartney was able to make his announcement to the second group of 4000-plus fans about the forthcoming single coming out soon in record stores.

After leaving the stage for the last set, riots ensued in the crowd when the emcee announced that The Beatles would not be coming back out for an encore appearance. One Danish youth was so upset he grabbed a potted plant of delphiniums at the front of the stage and hurled it in frustration at the emcee.[16]

Once the Beatles filed off the stage, Sardorf walked onstage to help breakdown his own drum kit. He realized he had just witnessed a piece of musical history. He casually walked over to The Beatles' drum kit and picked up The Beatles set-list Aspinall had written out and which

STANDING THERE
HOLD YOUR HAND
ALL MY LOVING
SHE LOVES YOU
TILL THERE WAS YOU
BEETHOVEN
CAN'T BOY ME LOVE
THIS BOY
TWIST + SHOUT
LONG TALL SALLY

Original handwritten Set list used by Jimmie Nicol at the first show of The Beatles' World Tour June 4, 1964. Photo Credit: Courtesy of Author.

Lennon had given to Nicol to use onstage for the first two shows of their first-ever world tour. He kept it as a souvenir for the next 42 years before ultimately selling it to a collector.

Thankfully, the reaction of the media to Jimmie Nicol's performance with The Beatles was very positive. One British reporter observed, "From what little this writer could hear, he judged that Jimmy [sic] Nicol, of Georgie Fame and the Blue Flames, was a fine temporary drummer for Ringo."[17] George Harrison commented to the press, "Playing without Ringo is like driving a car on three wheels, but Jimmy [sic] has grasped our rhythm very quickly."[18] During the show, Jimmie had had to wear Ringo's stage suit, but the pant legs were too short. So Paul sent a humorous telegram to Ringo: "Hurry up and get well Ringo, Jimmy [sic] is wearing out all your suits."[19] Meanwhile, Ringo Starr remained back in his London hospital with a 103 degree temperature.

After the concert, the newest Beatle could not sit still inside the secure hotel. He needed to take a walk outside to calm down from the excitement and tension of the first shows. As he slipped outside, in his street clothes, none of the hundreds of fans surrounding the hotel took notice of him. The crowd around the hotel after the concert was unflatteringly described by the media: "Hysterical girls screamed like moon-sick cats, cackled like hens in the spring, and whistled like punctured bicycle tires."[20] Through all of this noise, Nicol was able to stand outside, mingling amongst the fans, completely unmolested and reflecting in the moment. He watched with amusement as the throng of fans continued to scream up at the hotel, hoping for a Beatle to wave out of a window to them. Nicol looked up at the hotel and likely thought to himself after one full day on the job, "*So this is Beatlemania…*" Jimmie Nicol had been in the unique position to observe the "shock and awe" of this phenomenon from both sides of the police barricades.

The next day The Beatles headed off on a flight to Amsterdam. The plane landed around one o'clock p.m. at Schiphol Airport. As The Beatles came off the plane, they again waved to the throngs of fans and reporters. John Lennon and Jimmie Nicol are seen talking and joking around and seem to have quickly bonded in the past 24 hours, as The Beatles' founder makes sure Nicol is enjoying himself. Girls dressed in Dutch national costumes were awaiting the group. They presented The Beatles with flowers and kisses and then placed the traditional Volendammer hats on their heads.[21]

Nicol's first Beatles' Press Conference Schiphol Airport.

The arrival was broadcast like a play-by-play game live on AVRO radio. According to reporter Joop van Zijl, "It is one o'clock; the B-hour has arrived. Good Beatles listeners, here is Beatles-port Shiphol! Yeah, yeah, a safe airport for ordinary passengers, but for four unshaven lads from Liverpool the grim monster of the press awaits, with whom they had to learn to live… Several of my writing and photographing colleagues have dressed accordingly, with Beatles trousers and Beatles sideburns, with Beatles pens and Beatles notepads."[22] The media certainly seemed as giddy as the fans over The Beatles' arrival.

The Beatles were quickly herded inside the airport for a makeshift press conference by security and concert promoters. The Dutch press managed to ask the usual silly questions, leading off with, "Do you miss England?" Most importantly, the press wanted to know, when Ringo Starr would return to the line-up. This was a question that Nicol himself would wonder during the tour. What is interesting about The Beatles' answers is that Paul, George, and John each had differing answers, indicating that they really did not know the answer. Jimmie was asked how he felt playing his first two shows with The Beatles the day before, and he honestly reported, "I was very, very nervous yesterday at the first appearance in Copenhagen. Sweat was rolling off my cheeks in buckets."[23] After this brief repartee with the press, the group and their small entourage was hustled out the back service entrance into two white Cadillacs bound for the Doelen Hotel.

Next on the non-stop agenda was a taped television show at the Studio Treslong, Vosselaan, Hillegom. The group arrived in the late afternoon for a 5:30 p.m. run-through, which would follow with the show being recorded at 8:00 p.m. Nicol appreciated the opportunity to again rehearse the songs that would be performed live over the next week. The first part of the Treslong program would be a question and answer session with 150 fans, and the second part would feature a musical performance.

The TV show begins with animated images of each Beatle falling into place; George, Paul, John and then Ringo. After Ringo Starr's image is in place, we see it is quickly covered over by an animated image of Jimmie Nicol along with a facsimile of his autograph.

The producer situated The Beatles in a separate room from the fans for the Q & A session. This was to facilitate the second part of the show, in which the band moves into the performing area where the fans are already seated. As John, Paul, George, and Jimmie sat at the bar, Berend Boudewijn translated questions while The Beatles' answers were relayed back to Herman Stok, seated in the stands with the kids. All four Beatles are in their gray performance suits with black lapels, white shirts and dark ties. When asked about marriage, Nicol remains mum as John Lennon jokes about his marriage, stating that he had "bought his wife second-hand for £50 in Nairobi". This causes Jimmie to crack up and tap the counter in convulsive laughter.

Jimmie finally gets his chance to shine as the announcer asks:

Announcer: "You're on Jimmie… whether you find it difficult to take over the role of Ringo?"

Nicol: (Smiling at John and Paul) "Uh, no not really, no. (John and Paul are smiling). As far as Ringo, um, I could never make up for what Ringo is. I just try my best…"

Announcer: "How long will you be doing this?"

Nicol: "Uh, until next Thursday."

Announcer: "Next Thursday, so you are sort of his understudy?"

Nicol: (Looking very much at ease with a cigarette in one hand and what looks like a Scotch & Coke in the other): "Yes, I am (smiling proudly)."

Announcer: "Do you think it is a great break?"

Nicol: "Oh yes, excellent."

Announcer: "Are they (The Beatles) treating you good?"

Nicol: (Looking at John and Paul, smiling) "Yes, marvelous."[24]

After more small talk with The Beatles, the announcer tells them, "I will lead you into the Lion's Den". The "Lion's Den" is the concert area of the studio, filled with many fans awaiting the group's performance. As the band heads into the stage area, we see Paul giving Jimmie a pat of confidence on his back. McCartney appreciates the pressure that Nicol must feel before each performance. However, Jimmie Nicol's years of live and studio performances have prepared him well, and he seems in total control of his emotions and musical abilities as he climbs the riser up to Ringo's kit.

The musical "performance" is unfortunately misleading, as The Beatles are seen miming to a "playback" of their previously recorded records. The microphones were turned on in case The Beatles want to sing along, but no amplifiers are evident

The Beatles in Holland CD showing
Nicol and The Beatles on VARA TV.

near the stage. Paul McCartney explained the reason behind this "playback", recalling the problems the band had had with sound balance on the Ed Sullivan show. He says, "We do not trust a single sound technician in the world. And because we want a perfect sound quality – without the risk of something going wrong – we do not sing for real for the T.V., but use records for playback."[25]

The group begins their performance, pretending to play and sing to a recording of *She Loves You*, and receives a big applause. The lights go low so the TV audience will not notice if the recording and band don't begin at the same time. When starting the next song *All My Loving*, all four Beatles appear to miss the start of the song's playback. Jimmie is smartly using this artificial performance to "play-along" live on drums in preparation for his upcoming live concerts. At the end of the song, Jimmie fakes a two-handed hit on the crash and ride cymbals as he bows to the audience with the others. The irony is lost on the audience that understudy Jimmie Nicol is miming his drum part to tracks recorded by Ringo Starr.

During *Twist and Shout*, Paul and George sing live over their recorded voices, while John wisely saves his voice on this screamer for the real concerts. George Harrison then moves in to perform his song, *Roll Over Beethoven*. This tune inspires some of the fans (strangely, all males) around the stage to dance. Nicol, though missing the intro of the recording, starts really hitting skins in earnest, with swinging arms banging in wild, yet controlled, hits on his crash cymbal and tom toms. George seems preoccupied with the dancers invading the stage space, but bravely continues with his singing and playing.

Paul McCartney then launches into his cover of *Long Tall Sally*, as Jimmie really seems to warm up with his arms almost coming overhead, "chopping wood" on the kit. He seems to skip over some of Ringo's famous fills in favor of a harder rocking beat. Lennon smiles as he checks on Jimmie. Lennon notices the crowd is growing crazier and more out of control, with debris being thrown on-stage.

On the final song, *Can't Buy Me Love*, the rowdy crowd of mostly teenage males dances up, into, and around Paul, George, and John as they are trying to sing and play the song. Amazingly, the TV network has failed to provide any type of crowd control or security for The Beatles. Within a matter of seconds, The Beatles are mobbed to the point that viewers cannot see them. Worried about their safety, The Beatles' own entourage of Neil Aspinall, Derek Taylor and Mal Evans step in to protect the boys from the mob of out-of-control fans. Lennon steps out and stares at Paul, George and Jimmie, making faces at them. Nicol is banging away safely atop his drum riser, sporting a big smile on his face. George is laughing at John's antics and Paul bravely tries to continue singing along to the recording. Before the recording ends, Derek and Neil tell the boys it is time to make their escape. Paul, George, and John disappear off-stage, as Jimmie Nicol bravely continues playing alone to the bitter end of the song's playback. He then lays his sticks down on the drums and gets up to find the others as the credits roll. It was a crazy ending to another crazy day of Beatlemania. After the show, The Beatles were escorted back to their hotel under heavy police protection, where they waved to fans from the balcony.

After a hard day of work, it was time for some late-night play for the four young men. Although the legend of the "wild night in Amsterdam" is vague, some stories have emerged. The group was escorted, with help from the police, to the De Wallen Red Light District for some carousing. John Lennon recalls, "When we hit town, we hit it. There was no pissing about. There's photographs of me crawling about in Amsterdam on my knees coming out of whorehouses and things like that.

The Beatles Amsterdam canal ride.
Photo Credit: © Topham/TopFoto/The Image Works

The police escorted me to the places, because they never wanted a big scandal, you see… Suffice to say, that they [The Beatles] were 'Satyricon' on tour and that's it…"[26]

Jimmie Nicol himself was no by-stander during this long night of merriment, nor was he immune to the lure of the evening's temptations. He recalls the night vividly. "I was not even close to them when it came to mischief and carrying on. I thought I could drink and lay women with the best of them until I met up with these guys!"[27]

Original Blokker Beatles Concert Poster.
Photo Credit: Courtesy of Steve Green

The night was still young after The Beatles left De Wallen. Next stop was a visit to the Femina night club. There the band drank some more while entertained by a house orchestra called, Los Trovadores Tropicales. Nicol, comfortable with sitting in with any and every band, jumped in and played a bit of drums with them.[28] Finally, as the sun rose, The Beatles returned to their hotel for a short nap before beginning another full day of activities. Their late night carousing, however, caused them to lag behind on their busy schedule of the next day.

June 6, 1964, Amsterdam

Later that morning, The Beatles awoke, still groggy, hung-over, and behind schedule. They had to quickly board a glass-topped tourist boat to parade (and be paraded) along Amsterdam's network of canals in front of 30,000 rabid fans. One benefit of the boat tour was allowing The Beatles to be seen by their fans (who could not reach them), while still being able to take in the sites of Amsterdam. The River Police engaged four additional boats for security. Harrison and McCartney took many photos of the sites and fans, while the fans also took photos of their heroes; floating along a route that had been published earlier in the paper. The Beatles seemed amused at the rowdy fans who bravely jumped into the canals to reach the group, only to be snatched up by the River Police. The witty British newsreel narrators describe these teens as "…those who like it cool man cool… as the police pull a lot of queer fish to safety."[29] Along the way, there was a big banner hanging on a bridge. It was yet another reminder to Jimmie Nicol that his status as a Beatle was only temporary in the eyes of the fans. The banner proclaims: "Ringo Quick Recover".

The Beatles' river boat Captain, Gerrit Van Urk recalls the day. "I have guided several prominent figures around the canals," he said. "But the high point was The Beatles. It has been the greatest event in my life. The Beatles did put their autographs on my cap."[30] The trip took only two hours and then it was time to drive the group out to their afternoon concert hall in Blokker, Netherlands.

The afternoon and evening concerts were to take place at Vellinghal Op Hoop Van Zegren ("In hope of blessing"), Vellingweg, Blokker. In place of chairs, the promoter hastily set up groups of unreserved vegetable crates. These were attached together to create benched rows. But no one would be sitting down once The Beatles took the stage in a building that looked as if it was a big barn used for animal auctions. It took about an hour for

The Beatles backstage at Blokker with Oscar Rexhauser.
Photo Credit: © "Story of Indorock", Oscar Rexhauser and the Hot jumpers.

The Beatles to be transported from Amsterdam to Blokker, with Jimmie Nicol sitting in the front of a big white Cadillac, while Paul, George and John took the back seat. Hundreds of riot police were on hand to protect both The Beatles and the thousands of excited fans.

Backstage, The Beatles made friends with musician, Oscar Rexhauser. Rexhauser was the bass player in the local warm up band, The Hot Jumpers. According to Rexhauser, The Hot Jumpers played "Indo Rock" music, "a combination of Rock and Roll that comes from America; country music, Hawaiian music and also the influence of Indonesian-style music."[31] At the time, The Hot Jumpers were considered one of the best Rock bands in The Netherlands. Oscar and The Beatles mingled and talked music backstage before the performance. Just before the first show started, Oscar got up the nerve to ask each of The Beatles to sign his 1959 Hofner, violin-shaped bass guitar. John Lennon, George Harrison, and Paul McCartney each signed the bass; however, Oscar did not ask Jimmie Nicol to sign. One wonders what Nicol must have thought of this snub?

The Beatles on stage at Blokker.
Photo Credit: © Azing, Foundation Beatles Fan.

The set list for The Beatles' brief afternoon and evening concerts included the following songs:

> *I Saw Her Standing There*
> *I Want To Hold Your Hand*
> *All My Loving*
> *She Loves You*
> *Till There Was You*
> *Roll Over Beethoven*
> *Can't Buy Me Love*
> *Twist And Shout*
> *Long Tall Sally*

At 4:40 p.m., the stage announcer prepares the overly excited crowd. An explosion of screams occurs when he finally shouts, "Jimmie, John, Paul, and George...The Beatles!!!!" Again, the other Beatles made sure Nicol felt comfortable by graciously arranging to announce his name first. Only 2000 fans would see this matinee show of The Beatles, who followed over nine local warm up acts, including The Fancy Five; Wanda; Cisca Peters; and The Hot Jumpers. From newsreel footage shot of the first song, *I Saw Her Standing There*, one witnesses a few risky teens who are shown hanging above the crowd clutching steel rafters, as thousands of kids below move as one, like ocean waves swaying in the midst of a powerful tide. The newsreel cuts to a hilarious juxtaposition of images, as we witness a crazed male teen stripping off his shirt, followed by a picture of a gentleman calmly sitting on stage in front of McCartney, chewing a piece of fruit during all of the bedlam.[32]

It is fascinating to see major corporate advertisers promoting their products during the show. Hanging behind Jimmie Nicol is a huge banner with a Beatle-type animated guitarist next to "Heineken Bier (Beer)" in big letters. Behind Paul McCartney is a banner promoting "Coca Cola", and down in front of the stage is an ad for "Honda". No doubt the promoters wanted to ensure a lucrative day on top of ticket sales. It is interesting to wonder, if manager Brian Epstein had been present, would these corporate banners (which normally did not accompany Beatles' concerts) have remained up? Or would The Beatles have received a cut of the revenue from these sponsors? However, Epstein was back in London waiting for Ringo Starr to get out the hospital and rejoin the tour.

Deputy Nicol appears to finally have settled in with the group. He looks comfortable and relaxed hitting his marks. Interestingly, what stood out to Jimmie at this concert is John Lennon's condition. "His head was a balloon!" recalls Nicol. "He had drunk so much the night before; he was on stage sweating like a pig."[33]

During the concert, Jimmie is hitting the skins so hard that Ringo's kit looks like a fragile toy in his hands. Lennon also notices Nicol's ferocity as he turns to Jimmie during one song to flash him a smile of acceptance and amazement at Nicol's drumming technique. At the end of another song, roadie Mal Evans jumps onstage to offer Jimmie a new set of drum sticks concluding the original splintered ones had taken enough of a beating.

It is an interesting study to compare Nicol's drumming style at this concert to Ringo Starr's. The Beatles were a true band in every sense of musicianship. They breathe, move, and play together as one. For the band to trust an outsider to honor their overseas tour commitments was a significant event. In Jimmie Nicol, The Beatles had found someone who had not only looked the part, but could also play the part with the same level of excellence the band had established with Ringo Starr.

From the clip of Nicol and The Beatles playing *I Saw Her Standing There*, we see the song as upbeat in both tempo and spirit. It is very "on-top-of-the-beat" and driving. Jimmie captures the fire just as Ringo Starr did in making the band comfortable, and the song shines as a result. The band looks happy and the crowd goes crazy. From a technique standpoint, it is interesting to note that both drummers (Nicol and Starr) employed the matched grip versus traditional grip on the sticks. This approach to drumming was still new to drumset work in 1964. The matched grip style positions the weight of the arm over the stick, allowing the weight to assist in producing a bigger sound.

There is a clear contrast to the style of each drummer. Ringo Starr's sound is defined by his staying low to the drums and cymbals for the most part, using his strong and powerful wrists to get a beat that is clear, communicative, and which helps define and serve key sections of the song. Jimmie Nicol's sound, by contrast, is more staccato than Starr's. Nicol employs more of a whipping arm motion from a higher plane down into the drums which produces a brighter tone. His performances with The Beatles also highlight more of his Rhythm & Blues and Jazz/Big Band influences in the way he breaks away from the beat and plays strong fills to set up changes in the tune.[34]

In the clip, we see Jimmie catch more of the accents on crash cymbals and fills between song sections, which showcase more of his traditional approach to driving the band, in contrast to Ringo's stripped-down, less traditional approach. The bottom line is that each method works well! In his own way, Nicol filled the bill for The Beatles' temporary musical needs. With his skill and experience in the driver's seat, The Beatles could relax and enjoy the performance "ride". They could play to the crowd with the confidence of knowing Jimmie "had their backs", in both understanding the musical direction – playing the songs in the spirit in which they were recorded, and channeling the importance of Ringo's contribution – while also being his own man with the band in playing each tune.[35]

Between shows, the promoter offered to take The Beatles out for dinner, but they declined and stayed at Blokker. When he returned to bring them food, he found the band members asleep in the dressing room, still trying to recover from their crazy night out, the evening and morning before. Jimmie Nicol, a veteran of many years of touring, wisely slid under a dressing room table for his nap so as not to be stepped on. After they awoke and consumed their sandwiches, it was time for the evening concert.

The Beatles went on around 10:00 p.m. to a much larger crowd of 7000. Feeling more confident, Nicol was now adding his own unique fills, while locking-in with McCartney on bass. Bootleg audio of the evening show, reveals Nicol playing the songs with ease. He is in the groove. The crowd control problems seem to increase as the intensity of the concert continues to build. Girls are starting to get crushed and suffocate. Police near the front quickly step in to pull the girls to safety, lifting them over the barricade railings. Fortunately, The Beatles' brief 25-minute set ends, allowing the crowd panic to dissipate.

At the end of the show, the announcer asked the fans to give a special hand for Jimmie. As the crowd noise grew in appreciation, Nicol drummed and then clapped along to thank the fans for their support. He told one reporter following the show, "It was beautiful, playing with The Beatles, and I had no problems following them."[36] As The Beatles played their second show, stalls sold licensed Beatles merchandise to fans, including more than 1,000 concert programs; Beatles nylon stockings, glassware, pins, and postcards . In the end The Beatles walked out of Blokker with several thousand pounds, an amazing sum of money in 1964 for an hour of playing.[37]

With the shows over, it was time for the trip back to the hotel to meet up with Lennon's wife, Cynthia, who had flown in to join the touring party. The next day would be filled with travel as The Beatles would briefly fly home to London, pick up Lennon's Aunt Mimi, and then board another plane bound for Hong Kong.

Dick Van Gelder, one of The Netherland promoters, had the thankless job of getting The Beatles onto their plane back to London for the next leg of their journey to Hong Kong. "I did receive a phone call that they had to be on the plane at 10 a.m., the next day. I could not see that being possible," he noted, based upon their notorious late night celebrations. "…so, at 8:00 a.m. on Sunday, I was banging on their door, whilst they were fast asleep. It was 10:15 a.m. when they came out with their guitars in the streaming rain. We quickly hurried to the airport where the plane was waiting. I delivered them with a sigh of relief."[38]

A thunderstruck Jimmie Nicol had had his first taste of non-stop Beatlemania from inside the eye of the storm. Ringo Starr was still hospitalized, which meant for the time being that Jimmie was still a Beatle. He pondered the next trip to Hong Kong, thinking that it all seemed, "Strange and scary all at once… There is so little sanity to it all."[39] Unbeknownst to Jimmie and The Beatles, there would be a surprise guest on board the next long flight to Hong Kong; a fellow musician and friend who had played with both Nicol and the other Beatles!

Chapter Eleven

Beatle Jimmy Nicol: Hong Kong

June 7, 1964 London

The morning of June 7, 1964, took The Beatles and their drummer, Jimmie Nicol, on a long journey to Hong Kong, first backwards to London. In London, Lennon dropped off his wife, Cynthia, and picked up his Aunt Mimi. As the plane arrived in London from Amsterdam, Holland, they were greeted by 500 or so Beatles fans sporting signs that read: "Welcome Home, Don't Go Away Again!"[1]

The headlines would scream, "Hold That Jet! BOAC Wait For The Beatles". And wait they did, holding up the flight destined for Hong Kong for one hour to accommodate the Fab Four so they could process through customs and switch planes to make the connection. No doubt this special favor had been pre-arranged by manager, Brian Epstein. A Liverpool stewardess was even hand-selected to make "the boys" feel at home on their long journey to Asia. Meanwhile, Ringo Starr was still stuck in the hospital, and his mom reported to the press, "He sounded disappointed," as his band took off yet again for another exotic locale with another drummer in tow.[2]

In the 1960s, a flight from London to Hong Kong was anything but non-stop. The trip took nearly 24 hours, with stops along the way for refueling. The first stop touched down in Beirut, Lebanon, where hundreds of teens tried to reach the group's plane, only to be turned back by fire fighters hosing them down.[3] On the plane The Beatles amused each other with pillow fights, drinks, Preludin pills (intended as slimming pills, they kept one awake for hours); and games. At some point, The Beatles were surprised to discover an old friend sitting in the back coach section of the plane. An even bigger surprise to Jimmie Nicol was that *this* friend was an old friend of his too! What were the odds of the Beatles' plane to Hong Kong carrying the one person who had sang and played with The Beatles on their first professional recordings, and who had also played with Jimmie Nicol in his early 1960s band? Coincidently, this friend had also introduced The Beatles to the Preludin pills a few years earlier.

"In 1964, I had a Top 20 record in Australia ("Why Can't You Love Me Again?), and was invited to tour there. So I flew from Hamburg to London to get the BOAC flight to Darwin via Hong Kong, Karachi, Manila, etc." says the friend. "Anyway, on the plane, the stewardess came to tell me that there were some friends seated in the first class area who wanted to invite me over. I was not at first aware of anyone "special" being on the plane, anyway. I was suffering badly from smallpox and cholera jabs I'd received in Hamburg." He continues, "Well, I trundled over and there and I suddenly saw The Beatles, with Aunt Mimi, all the entourage and – Jimmie Nicol! What a nice reunion all round."[4] The friend was none other than musician Tony Sheridan!

History records, that The Beatles had served as a backing band to Tony Sheridan at the Top Ten Club in Hamburg, 1961. It is interesting to speculate if Jimmie Nicol had stayed with Tony Sheridan and the Wreckers (who later morphed into the Jets), whether he would have ended up meet-

Tony Sheridan.
Photo Credit: Courtesy of Author.

ing The Beatles years earlier by traveling with Sheridan to Hamburg. If so, could fate and The Beatles have chosen Jimmie Nicol (rather than Ringo Starr) to replace Pete Best behind the drums in August, 1962?

On board the plane, Sheridan described the reunion as "Quite a party". For all involved, it was nice to see familiar faces on such a long grueling flight. Having Tony Sheridan on board - a friend in common between The Beatles and their deputy drummer - served to knit a stronger bond between the band as they continued their tour together. Sheridan and Nicol regaled Lennon, Harrison, and McCartney with musical stories of their years together in the Larry Parnes packaged tours. The mood in first class was happy as the flight dragged onto Karachi, Pakistan for a refueling stop. Paul McCartney made one attempt to shop in the terminal, only to be chased back to the plane by screaming fans who seemingly came out of nowhere at 2:00 a.m.

June 8, 1964, Thailand & Hong Kong

Early the next morning, another refueling stop halted the journey in Bangkok, Thailand. Over one thousand teen fans greeted the sleepy group, demanding The Beatles come out of the plane. Eventually, the group carefully went to the ramp stairs of the plane to sign some autographs, while their brave drummer, Jimmie Nicol, waltzed into the terminal, oddly enough, to buy a "camel seat".[6] Perhaps Nicol was curious to try out a new type of stool for drumming?

Back in the air, Australian cameraman, Mayo Hunter captured Sydney DJ, Bob Rodgers briefly trying to interview Paul McCartney, as John Lennon threw pillows at them. Serious journalism would have to wait until the Hong Kong press conference. The party continued. For George Harrison, the flight seemed to go quickly, despite its many stops. He relates the feeling:

> I remember them saying, 'Return to your seats, we are approaching Hong Kong.' I thought, 'We can't be there already. 'We'd been sitting on the floor, drinking and taking Preludins for about 30 hours and it seemed like a 10-minute flight. On all those flights we were still on uppers; that's what helped us get through, because we'd drink a whiskey and Coke with anyone, even if he was the Devil – and charm the pants off him![7]

The reception at Hong Kong's Tai Tak Airport was anti-climatic, as The Beatles were quickly processed, sidestepping the usual customs and immigration. From there the group and its small entourage were whisked off to the safety of the President Hotel in Kowloon. For Paul, George, and John, it was time for the usual isolation up in the fifteenth floor suite. Local retailers were brought up for the boys to shop. The prices were naturally inflated, but this did not deter McCartney and road manager

The Beatles' Hong Kong Press Conference June 11, 1964.
Photo Credit:Topham/TopFoto/©The Image Works.

Neil Aspinall from negotiating better deals on suits and watches. Since Jimmie was an unknown in Kowloon, he took off in plain clothes and traveled the city freely shopping, sightseeing and even swimming.[8] "I enjoyed every minute of it, especially Hong Kong," recalls Nicol. "I found that the refugees there were very grateful to the British, and I visited one or two refugee colonies during the short time I was there."[9]

Later that evening, The Beatles - fatigued and wanting to sleep – were pressured to make an unscheduled appearance. The Miss Hong Kong Pageant was being staged in their hotel, and The Beatles' presence was strongly requested. Whenever The Beatles touched down in a city, they were the in-town celebrities, in high demand, invited to attend every event. Lennon finally agreed to make a brief appearance of hand-shaking with the beauty queens, and another PR crisis was quickly averted.

Next up on the non-stop Beatlemania train was the mandatory press conference. At the time, Hong Kong was a British dependency in eastern Asia, located on the South China Sea. The mix of Chinese, British, and Americans populating Hong Kong in 1964 was clearly evident at the press conference. The recording of this event is remarkable as a work of radio art, with excellent narration and play-by-play description provided by the commentators. We witness the band arrive: "Those haircuts are really marvelous… [The boys] are grinning and laughing and having a marvelous time of it… The boys are having a field day, the photographers are having an absolute field day… I've never seen anything like this." At one point, one of the commentators wonders out loud, "I just noticed how long their hair is, they probably can't hear themselves sing."[10]

Derek Taylor, The Beatles' press officer, does a good job of managing the photographers, newsreel filmmakers, and the radio and print media who are stacked up almost to the enormous chandelier in the middle of the conference room ceiling. The play-by-play commentator observes Nicol and states, "He is working very well on that haircut." The other DJ replies, "It's long enough to give the Sgt. Major of the Guard's Division a heart attack."[11] At one point, two beautiful Thailand film actresses, Unchuli Anantakul and Busara Narumit suddenly appear out of nowhere to have their photos taken with The Beatles. One wonders for whom is this press conference, but The Beatles are always happy to oblige beautiful women. Light bulbs are flashing everywhere.

After almost 12 minutes of general chaos, the press conference with The Beatles finally gets down to business. Taylor introduces: "John, Paul, George and Jimmie Nicol". At this point, John, Paul and George burst into loud hoots and whistles for Jimmie as he returns a smile of appreciation. It is clear that the four have become closer during the last several days of touring.

The first question out-of-the box is directed at Nicol.

> Q: "Mr. Nicol, how do you feel being rushed into this
> vast world of publicity all at once?
> Jimmie: "It's a most exciting experience."
> John & George: (Joking around) "Correct"[12]
> Commentator: "Correct… which is a Beatles pass-
> word, I think, every time a question is asked, as unan-
> imous agreement with a shout of 'correct'."

More questions follow, challenging the quality of The Beatles' musicianship and a query about the origin of the band's name. This is followed by a question about the group's rehearsal schedule, most important to its newest member, and explained by Lennon's response.

> Q: "With all this traveling about, how do you get time to rehearse?"
> Lennon: (laughing) "We don't!"
> Q: "You don't rehearse?"
> Lennon: "We do, a bit. We rehearse with Jimmie 'cuz he's new."[13]

Distinct patterns emerge as we listen to the rapid-fire barrage of questions. With razor-sharp irony, John deflects most inquiries directed his way. Paul is polite and most concerned with good public relations. George appears philosophical and patient, even with the most cynical reporter. And Jimmie, several days into this whirlwind journey, is still somewhat in awe of his situation.

Another witty repartee continues with Lennon being asked about the show performances.

> Q: "When you're standing on the stage, and you look down and see a crowd of screaming teenagers, what do you say to yourself?"
> Lennon: "Look at them, all screaming."[24]

Laughter breaks out among the entire media throng. Turning serious, Lennon suggests the journalists ask Jimmie his reaction to the screaming fans, but this suggestion is ignored as they press McCartney for his opinion.

> McCartney: "No. Actually, you get irritated when the screams go down a bit." (More laughter)[25]

After many silly questions about food and a request to pull on The Beatles' hair to see if it is real, the discussion again turns to Jimmie Nicol. The media is curious about Nicol's plans once Ringo Starr returns.

> Q: "Mr. Nicol, when Ringo Starr joins the group in Australia, what will you do?"
>
> Nicol: "Then I go back to London, and things seem to be jumping in London, so you know… I've got a couple of television shows and a band is being formed and everything. So it looks as though things might happen for me, you know."[26]

PRINCESS THEATRE JUNE 9th

THE
BEATLES
SHOW

ALSO STARRING
THE MAORI HI-FIVE
and
SOUNDS INCORPORATED
the greatest instrumental group

TICKETS STILL AVAILABLE

Beatles' Hong Kong concert poster- showing Ringo Starr instead of Jimmie Nicol.

The band, "Jimmy Nicol & the Shubdubs", and the TV shows were being carefully planned by Pye Records, which was anxious to put out another single with Nicol to take advantage of all the free, worldwide publicity generated by Nicol's playing with The Beatles. Things were indeed heating up back home, for Jimmie's triumphant return. But for now, that would have to wait, for he still had Beatles business to attend to.

Following the press conference, Nicol has a chance to sit down one-on-one with the radio journalists who are curious about Nicol and The Beatles' musical influences. Jimmie carefully sidesteps The Beatles' influences, but offers up his own.

> I like musical things that move on all the time. I like Brubeck, but I think my own particular favorite is Cannonball Adderly, Duke Ellington and [Count] Basie of course. The difference between them [The Beatles] and me is, I've played in big bands. And I've played arrangements by all these people. I have loads of tapes at home of like Adderley and good Latin-American music you know.[27]

The reporter then inquires how Jimmie was chosen to sit in for Ringo Starr. He explains:

> I'm fairly well known as a session drummer in
> England. I do quite a bit of sessions for big artists you
> know. It was just a telephone call at first. It was very
> mysterious - nobody wanted to commit themselves.
> So I had to go along to EMI and meet them all and
> just rehearsed about five numbers. And that was it.[28]

As the reporter digs deeper into Nicol's career plans, we see that despite all of the hoopla surrounding Nicol's work with The Beatles, he is clearly contemplating ways in which to use the publicity, the resume, and his experience to take himself to the next level. He reflects on the irony of his situation before The Beatles and the present circumstances.

> I've made one record in London, which didn't go up
> the charts. Two months ago, I tried to make my own
> band happen like everybody does. You know, the
> chance to get a recording contract. I had the band, but
> I didn't have any work. But now it looks as though
> I've got the work, but I don't have any band.[29]

The reporter wants to know what Nicol plans to do to rectify the situation in order to take advantage of the new work coming his way. It is obvious that Jimmie has been in touch with his record label and others back in London during this tour, as he replies: "Well that's being arranged. People are taking it on. Now, my manager is sorting it out [getting a band together], but obviously I want to supervise it, naturally, you know."[20] After 42 minutes of this verbal fencing, Beatles press officer, Derek Taylor calls an end to the press conference and the group heads upstairs for a well deserved sleep in preparation for two concerts the next day at Hong Kong's Princess Theatre.

June 9, 1964, the Hong Kong Concerts

Shortly before the group arrived in town, the Chinese promoter for the two Beatles' performances had decided to raise the ticket prices for seats. This mistake would cause the theatre to have a number of empty seats when the group arrived to play. The least expensive ticket was £2 at a time when low wage earners and kids could barely afford such a luxury. The higher end tickets at £7 each represented the average weekly wage of a Hong Kong worker. According to Hong Kong DJ, Ray Cordeiro, "The promoter who brought them to Hong Kong lost money… Of course the kids couldn't afford it. And the parents didn't even know who The Beatles were. So they had an empty hall. They started to give tickets away free of charge to fill the hall!"[21] Apparently, numerous military families were the recipients of many giveaway tickets.

The Princess Theatre first opened in 1952 on the corner of Nathan and Kimberly Roads. It was a venue that could hold 1,726 patrons. The first warm-up act for The Beatles was the "Maori Hi Fives", a New Zealand show band that played a mixture of dance, Country music, Maori songs, and comedy. They were followed by the British instrumental combo, "Sounds Incorporated".

Although Jimmie Nicol appeared calm on the outside as he laughed with The Beatles backstage, inside he was on edge because he didn't really know, nor could he control, his day-to-day life; and Nicol needed full control of his life to be comfortable. He relates his feelings, "I never knew from one day to the next whether I would be going on to these different countries. I was very much a freelancer. If Ringo had gotten well after Holland, I wouldn't have made Denmark. And if he had come back in Hong Kong, I wouldn't have made Australia."[22] The demands of performing with the biggest band in the world and not knowing your future from one day to the next was stressful and taking its toll. *Was it possible he was playing so well to impress The Beatles to make a permanent personnel change?* They certainly were all hitting it off socially. *Or should he focus on getting back to London with his own band and TV appearances?* All of these possible opportunities were racing through his mind. Nicol's nerves were starting to fray as he recalls:

> I really wasn't thinking how nice it is to go to Hong Kong or Australia. If one is told that you are going to do something, then you have the security you know. If they keep you hanging on… well maybe, maybe; it puts a lot of pressure on you because you don't really know. You are uneasy and you cannot relax. Or at that particular time, I could not relax.[23]

Epstein's fear of failure had fallen onto Nicol's shoulders, and Jimmie was beginning to feel the pressure. In London, press officer Tony Barrow was constantly checking in with Derek Taylor on tour to find out how Nicol's efforts were working to maintain The Beatles' reputation on tour. "Derek Taylor called me from most stops along the route of the tour," says Barrow. "To everyone's immense surprise and relief, he was able to assure me that the substitution made absolutely no difference to The Beatles' reception at any point during the tour, and there was no apparent deterioration in the music they made on stage."[24] Though Barrow's words are somewhat of a backhanded compliment to Jimmie, they do confirm that Nicol was doing his job, both in public and behind the drum kit, to preserve The Beatles' popularity.

Nicol was feeling increasing anxiety as they reached Hong Kong. Paul, George, and John were perhaps the only individuals who could comprehend the stress Jimmie was feeling, and they were sympathetic and appreciative of his efforts. Starting in Holland and Denmark and following through the tour, John and Paul would regularly ask Jimmie after each show or press conference, "How's it going Jimmie?" Nicol's brief reply was always, "It's getting better" a phrase that would stick in the back of Paul McCartney's mind and prove useful in the future. Though the pressure must have been extreme for Nicol, he did not let it affect his playing onstage. Brief newsreel footage from the Hong Kong show demonstrates a confident Nicol comfortably playing, smiling, and swaying his head back and forth to the music. John Lennon is also seen happily playing his rhythm parts.

The concert set list for the show was by now familiar to Nicol. According to Hong Kong DJ Ray Cordeiro the set list included the following songs:

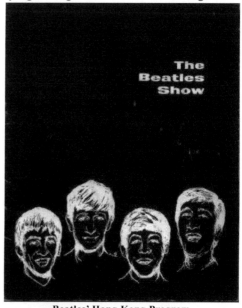

Beatles' Hong Kong Program.
Photo Credit: Anonymous collector

> *I Saw Her Standing There*
> *I Want To Hold Your Hand*
> *You Can't Do That*
> *All My Loving*
> *She Loves You*
> *Till There Was You*
> *Roll Over Beethoven*
> *Can't Buy Me Love*
> *This Boy*
> *Long Tall Sally*

Like most concerts of this era, these shows were very noisy and difficult to hear. The local newspapers chose to critique the audience's behavior rather than the show itself. One paper commented that the "incessant shrieking of fans was mental torture to those in the audience who came to appreciate the music." In Paul McCartney's recollection, "Hong Kong was different – it was all army personnel, which was very funny. We had expected Asian people in Hong Kong, but the army must have got the tickets first, or must have known about us. As for the show, it was a slightly flat performance in a smallish place. They behaved themselves, and it looked like a Khaki audience. He continues, "We played, but I don't think we enjoyed the shows too much – although at least we could be heard."[25]

Meanwhile, back home in London, Jimmie Nicol's every move was documented in the papers and on the six o'clock nightly news. The Beatles were the number one story for a week. According to Johnny Harris, "Oh God, it was ridiculous, He had entered the Kingdom of whatever… The Beatles you know… [Imitating the news anchor] '*And now the fifth Beatle is walking over there. There he is. Jimmie Nicol the fifth Beatle, blah blah blah….*'"[26]

June 10, 1964, Hong Kong to Darwin to Sydney

The Beatles slept in the next day, recovering from travel, press conferences, and two concerts - with a bit of late night partying thrown in. It was a well-needed rest before heading onto the next leg of the tour that would take the band Down Under to Australia. Jimmie was informed that Ringo was not yet out of the woods and that "Mr. Nicol's services" were still needed in Australia. So the young drummer kept his emotions in check and soldiered on.

On the afternoon of June 10, The Beatles arrived at the airport to fly from Hong Kong to Sydney, then the biggest city in Australia. The Beatles were looking forward to the beautiful hot sun that Australia is famous for. Roughly 500 fans showed up to bid them farewell. At the airport, DJ Bob Rodgers recorded some interviews with The Beatles as they waited for their flight. On the interviews, John and George can be heard singing a bit of *Waltzing Matilda* and *Tie Me Kangaroo Down Sport* in anticipation of their pending visit to the land of Oz. McCartney discusses his Hong Kong purchases, but stops short when asked if he needs a boomerang in Australia.[27]

Meanwhile, Jimmie Nicol sat quietly contemplating the next leg of his extraordinary journey. Many thoughts were on his mind. *Would Ringo be coming back soon? Or will he remain longer in the hospital? Can the receptions in Australia possibly top The Netherlands and Hong Kong? Who will be in my band (the Shubdubs) back home if and when I return to London? What songs should the Shubdubs play on TV and in concert?* As he contemplated his future, Jimmie and The Beatles boarded their flight to Sydney, waiving at the fans as they walked up the stairs of their plane. Little did Jimmie Nicol realize that more surprises were in store for the Aussie leg of his whirlwind Beatles' world tour. Even a small controversy was brewing Down Under regarding his deputizing for Ringo Starr.

Chapter Twelve

Beatle Jimmy Nicol: Sydney, Australia

June 11, 1964, Darwin & Sydney, Australia

The Beatles took off from Hong Kong's Tai Tak airport on the evening of June 10. During the flight, Aussie Disc Jockey, Bob Rodgers, asked John Lennon whether The Beatles could expect to get out and see any of Australia during the visit. Lennon remarked, "We don't expect to get out of our rooms. If we do, we'll be lucky. But it won't last all of our lives like this."[1] Nicol's impression was that, "Going to these places may sound very magical to people… Oh The Beatles went to Holland, Denmark and toured the world. But really, the life is hotels, cars, and airplanes. So therefore, your whole world is a series of boxes."[2] From Nicol's perspective, being a member of The Beatles was great in some respects; however, being locked up in the "boxes" of a Beatles tour was not to his liking.   He had already snuck out of his "box" at each city they had visited, and he planned to do the same when the group touched down in Sydney.

The plane made a brief layover stop in Darwin en route to their first major Australian destination of Sydney. The flight landed at 2:30 in the morning. Unbeknownst to The Beatles, media announcements revealing this information went out over the radio the prior evening at 11:00 p.m. Estimates of over 400 fans showed up to greet the band on their layover in the middle of the night. Surprised by the fan reception, Paul McCartney remarked, "I didn't expect anyone to be here!"[3] One has to wonder how many of these teenagers simply crawled out of their bedroom windows, without parental authorization, to catch a glimpse of the band in the middle of the night.

During the long haul from Hong Kong to Sydney, Nicol and Lennon continued to talk. They seemed to share the same sense of humor and enjoyed talking about music and the amazing fan reaction that followed them around the world. Nicol started to wonder if his friendship with the band's founder and leader might create the slightest possibility of his replacing Ringo Starr as The Beatles' drummer at some point. However, even if the spontaneous Lennon had considered the possibility, he would have had a difficult time convincing George Harrison who was fiercely loyal to Ringo Starr.

One musician had a different opinion of The Beatles' deputy drummer. "On board, I noticed that Jimmie did not really reach out to me," recalls Sounds Incorporated drummer, Tony Newman. Sounds Incorporated, another Epstein band, had joined the tour in Hong Kong as a warm-up band for The Beatles' world tour. "As a fellow drummer I thought we might talk. I tried to hook up with him, but he really didn't seem interested. The other Beatles and our band were all good friends. We would chat on the planes."[4]

Along the way, Jimmie also sat down for a one-on-one interview with DJ Bob Rodgers. At this point, Rodgers surprised Nicol, telling him his radio station had tracked down Jimmie's cousins in Sydney. Nicol, surprised by the revelation, elatedly responded: "Oh! That's marvelous!"[5] What followed was a humorous dialogue about the places Jimmie would like to visit while in Australia and the story behind his recent, unique souvenir purchase:

> Rodgers: "What would you like especially to do while   you're in Australia?"
>
> Nicol: "Well, em… This outback… I've heard of this word…"
>
> Rodgers: "… Big open spaces."
>
> Nicol: "I'd fancy going there."

Next Rodgers asks about Jimmie's recent and strange souvenir purchase.

> Nicol: "(Laughing) I bought a camel seat in Bangkok, yes. And I want some of those boomerangs in Australia and some spears and things."
>
> Rodgers: "I hope like a boomerang you will come back to me (in Australia) Jimmie."
>
> Nicol: "Oh so do I."[6]

According to one report, some twenty thousand fans were expected to swarm Sydney's airport when The Beatles arrived. Security was in place with a plan for The Beatles to board an open vehicle and drive around a barrier for fans to wave. According to airport manager, George Inglis, "We have no set blueprints as we would have with Royalty. Flexibility is the keynote with an operation of this size."[7]

As the plane made its way from Darwin to Sydney, it was lashed with heavy winds, turbulence and rain. Plans were underway to possibly divert the plane from Sydney to Brisbane. Many of the early fans at Sydney's Mascot International Airport were forced outside to wait all night, when the airport terminal closed. It was miserable, cold, windy, rain-lashing weather; yet more and more fans kept arriving throughout the night.

Finally, over an hour late on arrival, The Beatles' plane landed in Sydney at 7:43 a.m. The B.O.A.C. flight landed smack in the middle of a gale storm. As the plane moved into its final place on the tarmac, the immigration officials boarded the plane to take care of paperwork to expedite matters. The group was offered the opportunity to bypass the trip on an open-bed truck for viewing by the fans, but chose to bravely soldier on. In a bit of corporate showmanship, an official of rival airline TAA hustled logo umbrellas up to The Beatles as they made their way down to the flat bed truck, much to the chagrin of napping B.O.A.C. officials. This gave TAA free advertising as photos of the group hanging on to TAA umbrellas went around the world in one day, seen by millions of newspaper readers and newsreel watchers.

The trip around the airport for fans to wave at The Beatles and for "the boys" to wave back, was Beatlemania at its most farcical. John, Paul and George were wearing capes and Jimmie had on his raincoat. News coverage was extensive, as one commentator described the scene, "After a long trip over from Hong Kong, battered by the rain and the wind, The Beatles are caged up like circus animals in a rain-drenched parade."[8] The *Daily Mirror* in England described the scene as "Squeals for rain-lashed Beatles", as "Two thousand drenched fans screeched and squealed a welcome to The Beatles when they landed in Sydney, Australia early today after flying from Hong Kong."[9]

Greeting fans at Sydney's airport. Photo Credit: Topham/© TopFoto/The Image Works.

As the drenched Beatles made their way around the tarmac, laughing and holding their over-sized TAA umbrellas which acted as spinnaker sails, George suddenly lost his umbrella. Laughing at his misfortune, George is given a hat to protect himself. Harrison dons the hat and does a little tap dance and doffs his cap, mocking the absurdity of this exercise. Lennon and Nicol are seen huddled together, laughing as they get drenched and battered by wind gusts.

In advance of The Beatles' arrival in Sydney, the Hong Kong police chief had sent along a confidential missive to the Sydney police with a less than flattering description of what to expect from the coming storm that accompanied the group. "The Beatles themselves are an amiable if cring-ing group who hole up in their rooms and whimper like children while their supporters besiege the hotel demanding to see them. You must maintain the most stringent vigilance against small girl in-filtrators in pink, blue and white party dresses, aged from ten to twenty-four; they are more ruthless than our Tong killers," the chief explained with dripping sarcasm. "In our experience you can rely upon The Beatles to co-operate with you in the preservation of law and order – so long as they lose no box office takings, by public-spirited collaboration with the police. Apart from their performances they lay dazed in their suites."[10]

The Beatles headed to their hotel, The Sheraton at King's Cross, to dry off, with the only problem being that the group beat their luggage to the hotel. The band was ensconced on an upper floor of the hotel which had been reserved for them, along with a gold carpet, cocktail bar, a televi-sion, and a sun balcony (with no sun) that boasted of a panoramic view of the harbor. The group would have about seven hours to recuperate in their rooms before facing the media. There would be no concert scheduled on this date, only a press conference, interviews, and some hotel rest and re-laxation, followed by another trip the next day to Adelaide.

Jimmie Nicol viewed his arrival in Sydney with mixed emotions. He was thrilled that he might have an opportunity to visit his cousins; however, he was greeted with a minor controversy. It seems that Sydney DJ, David Ford, took umbrage with the presence of Jimmie Nicol substituting with The Beatles for the ailing Ringo Starr. In a bizarre protest, the publicity-seeking DJ railed against unsuspecting Jimmie Nicol on air and in the newspapers. His beef was that hiring Nicol was a slight to Australian drummers who should have been chosen; never mind that Nicol had been carefully selected for his skills, experience, diplomacy, and even his early Beatles' haircut. Ford stated, "I see no need for them to bring Nicol. In Sydney, just about every instrumental group, which has cashed in on the Beatle plague craze has a drummer complete with a Beatle wig. So why not give one of these mimic artists a chance."[11] Needless to say, Nicol and The Beatles refused to comment on this absurd proposition, and the hullabaloo quickly dissipated.

By late morning, Jimmie was back in dry clothes, escorted from the hotel by Beatles' roadie Mal Evans, to a waiting station wagon containing his second cousin, Gladys Richardson. Newsreel footage showed the car drive away so utterly covered with swarming girls, it resembled bees on honey. The newsreel commentator describes the moment as, "Ringo's 'ring-in' Jimmie Nicol left the hotel almost incognito to visit his cousins."[12]

Nicol spent the day unmolested with cousins and found time for a bit of shopping and sightseeing. Meanwhile, The Beatles were once again confined to their hotel room "box", occasionally waving to screaming fans (with George dressed in towel on the balcony) and wondering where was the warm Australian sun. The Fab 3 decided to take naps until the afternoon press circus began. Nicol was able to pick up boomerangs and a toy Koala bear for his son Howie. However, upon his return in the afternoon, Nicol was stopped by security entering the hotel, despite telling them, "But I'm a Beatle!" After someone was sent upstairs to retrieve his identification, Nicol was allowed upstairs in time to join the boys for the forthcoming press conference. The irony of the stand-in Beatle - being asked to play drums with The Beatles, yet being barred from entering the hotel to join his fellow Beatles - was not lost on Jimmie Nicol.

At around 4:30 p.m. press officer, Derek Taylor led the group into the hotel conference room for yet another round of media rugby, complete with pushing, shoving, and news types all creating the same sort of chaos as the teen fans stuck outside. Taylor formally introduced the group to the media as a mock prologue to royalty, "Ladies and gentlemen, I would like to introduce The Beatles." As usual, scores of photo journalists let off a hundred bursts of flash bulbs as John, Jimmie, Paul and George smiled, joked, and smoked cigarettes. This was followed by the TV photographers who filmed the press conference as the questions began to fly, each one swatted away like flies by the nimble wit of Lennon & Company.

Q: "What did you think of your wet welcome today?"

John: "Very good. I thought they were very nice coming out in all that rain."

Q: "Paul, what do you expect to find here in Australia?"

John (intercepting Paul's question)): "Australians" (laughter)

Q: "Have you been practicing up your Australian accents?"
John: "No, cobber, not at all." (laughter)

Q: "Well, what do you think made the difference that suddenly pushed you up above the other groups?"

George: "We got a record contract."

Finally, after the usual silly questions, the reporters remember Jimmie Nicol is in the room. It was time, once again, to ask him what he thought of his experience.

> Q: "How about you, Jimmie? You haven't said any-
> thing. How do you feel, Jimmie, being in with The
> Beatles – a new talent – standing in for Ringo?"
>
> Jimmie:"It's a good experience, man."
> Q: "How is Ringo?"
>
> Jimmie: "Umm, he's much better. He joins them on
> Sunday."
> Q: "What do you do then?"
> Jimmie: "Umm, I go back to London and they're
> fixing up a band for me, and I do some television."
>
> John: "And he's away."
>
> Q: "You're progressing pretty well with your Bea-
> tle-haircut."
>
> Jimmie: "Yeah, well I've been growing it for about
> three months."

Getting back to questions for all of The Beatles, George takes the opportunity to use a pun to make a subtle point that *he* is ready for Ringo's return…

> Q: "Is there anything special you want to see, apart
> from some sunshine?"
>
> Paul: "Kangaroos and all that, Dingoes and all
> those."
>
> George: "Dingo!? He's coming on Sunday."
> (laughter).

Paul and John tell reporters they will not be going out tonight, but Jimmie Nicol stays mum, thinking he will want to explore Sydney's nightlife. Lennon deflects a potentially troublesome ques-tion directed at Paul about taking his unmarried girlfriend on holiday, implying via a gay reference that it would be better than two gentlemen going out on a trip. The resulting laughter helps change the subject back to the more typical questions about John's book and their records.

Eventually, the inquisitors come back around to Jimmie Nicol for another brief flurry of ques-tions.

> Q: "Have you got an agreement that Jimmie
> mustn't speak?"
>
> George: "Ask him a question."
>
> Jimmie: (Referencing the fact that most of the ques-
> tions are directed to particular Beatles, he explains
> to the clueless media) "I can't answer questions

that, umm, I don't know anything about."

Q: "What's the group you play with in England, Jimmie?"

Jimmie: "Well, I've played with a lot of groups in England. Just before I left, I was playing with a rhythm and blues band…"

Q: "You were in the Blue Flames for a while weren't you?"

Jimmie: "Yeah, that's right… well, only for a matter of days. I played on Friday, I didn't even know what I was doing just on Wednesday, you know."

Q: "Does Brian Epstein manage you?"

Jimmie: (Pausing to think before he speaks) "… nobody… No, he doesn't"

Beatles: (All laugh at the response)

John: (To Jimmie) "You'd know if it he did!" (laughter)

The reporters next inquire how Jimmie felt when he played his first concert with The Beatles.

Q: "Pretty frightening?"

Jimmie: "The first show was very frightening, yeah. But, uh, they reassured me."

Paul: "He did grand."

John: "He did a grand job."

After another five minutes of questions inquiring whether the other Beatles still got nervous before concerts and how they felt about their fame, the press conference wrapped up. Swarms of media came forward for autographs and a few last questions and photos, as Derek Taylor led the boys back upstairs to their suite. Jimmie filled the others in on his travels around Sydney and the visit with his cousins. Once again, John, Paul and George would be trapped up in their hotel room, prisoners of their fame, waiting for the next gig or public obligation. Fortunately, they could rest their vocal chords on this night in the hotel room because no concerts were scheduled. Out came the drinks and food, and visits from a selected pool of female fans, launching another night of "party in a box".[13]

The party in the hotel room suites was legendary, but not just for its extracurricular activities. All of the James Bond novels that the Beatles had been reading came to life briefly at this bash. "In Sydney, we had quite a 'famous party'," says Sounds drummer, Tony Newman. During the party, Derek Taylor had discovered a man who had brought along a miniature Minox camera that was hidden behind his tie, "James Bond style". He was surreptitiously taking potentially incriminating photos of The Beatles enjoying their drinks and female companions. "Derek came to me to ask for help in trying to pull the film out of the Minox," says Newman. "So we fiddled with it for a while and finally got the film out." The man was unceremoniously ejected from the party. "Derek had a funny way of announcing things. He went and popped a balloon which got everyone's attention," recalls Newman. "Then he announced, 'We have a spy among us' (laughing)"[14] Another potential PR crisis was averted.

Tony Newman also noticed the frequent absence of Jimmie Nicol at these legendary evening parties. "We would pop up to The Beatles' suite and it seemed like many times, Jimmie was not at the parties and had gone somewhere."[15]

For the less recognizable Jimmie Nicol, in the evenings when The Beatles' party got going, he could sneak out and taste the night life in another foreign city. On this night, along with roadie Mal Evans, the two ventured forth in search of a Sydney night club. The two men set out for Sydney's popular nighttime strip on Goulburn Street. They had many choices there, including the

Chequers in Sydney, Australia.
Photo Credit: © 2011 Jim Berkenstadt

notorious Goulburn Club – a major casino of its day; the Mandarin Club and Chequers. Nicol opted to go to Chequers in hopes of seeing some live music. Little did he know he would become part of the entertainment before the night was over.

In 1964, Chequers was at the top of its game as perhaps Australia's best loved cabaret nightclub. Opened in the late 1950s, the club was owned by Keith and Dennis Wong, whose family came from a long line of entertainment, restaurant, nightclub and racing circles.[16] Chequers' brilliant reputation reflected in part the owners' willingness to import the most popular nightclub entertainers from around the world, sparing no expense, to pack their house of 550 patrons. In June of 1964, the Wongs had paid £5000 per week to snag US recording artist, singer, songwriter, and actress Frances Faye.

Faye was a raspy-voiced singer who had created a dazzling, yet controversial, night club act since the 1950s. At a time when topics of alternative sexual lifestyles were kept out of the public eye, Faye would celebrate her bisexuality openly onstage. It was clearly her energetic live appearances in nightclubs that earned her the best reviews of a long and respected career. In 1964, Faye was at her height - both artistically and commercially - when Mal Evans and Jimmie Nicol strolled into the Chequers club for a night of entertainment. Unbeknownst to Nicol, Faye was a huge early fan of The Beatles, likely having seen them perform in New York on the Ed Sullivan TV show earlier in the year.

Jimmie recalls the evening vividly, "I went down to, you know, enjoy myself. Well, as soon as I walked through the door she was just finishing the latter part of her [first] act. And she said, 'The Beatles are coming!' be-

Frances Faye jams with Jimmie Nicol
at Chequers in Sydney.

cause everyone turned 'round."[17] After finishing one more song in her first set, Faye invited Beatle Jimmie Nicol backstage to her dressing room. They talked about Faye's career and Nicol shared his experience touring with The Beatles. At this point, Faye asked Jimmie if he would care to sit in with her band as the drummer. Nicol - who never turned down a chance to play live or jam - jumped at the opportunity. "And then the second show, I did the whole lot," recalls Nicol; "Her whole second performance at the club."[18] Nicol loved the chance to branch out and play more free form Jazz style drumming with Faye. When asked if it was difficult to come up onstage and sit in with a strange band, Nicol casually explained, "If you've got soul, you can do it."[19] The crowd was on its feet to cheer The Beatle sitting in with Frances Faye. Head waiter Andre proudly proclaimed, "This is wonderful, we have a million pound act for nothing."[20]

The gig went well for both performers. Faye promised to send Jimmie all of her albums as a thank you gift, along with a sweater for making her night. An enthusiastic Nicol was excited to be invited back to play with Faye again upon his next return to Sydney. "So there might be a chance of um, of working with her for a little while, and obviously, her being an American will give me an opportunity to go over to the States to work with her and study playing... which I think is important."[21] Nicol had made another important musical contact in his quest to play and learn from as many different artists as possible. The night ended late for Nicol and Evans who made their way back to the hotel for the next day's adventure.

That same night, Paul McCartney made one attempt to sneak out of the hotel around 11:30 p.m., "looking for Sydney", he says. However, "I couldn't find him." Admitting he was a tourist at heart, Paul reluctantly conceded that he had to turn back because he had been surrounded by too many fans outside the hotel.[22]

Meanwhile, as Nicol and The Beatles headed for bed, half-a-world away, Ringo Starr was just being released from his hospital bed. He had gone home to pack and rejoin the band in Australia. Ringo expressed his frustration to one TV news reporter, stating how restless he had been, "...sitting in hospital watching the boys when they arrived there in Holland. It's funny as well, you know," said Starr, "wondering what you're doing away from them." He explains that he is "Fine, fit and everything," (humming a bit to prove it), yet he admits he won't be able to "yell away with the rest of them for a week."[23] Starr expresses his appreciation to Jimmie Nicol, stating, "I would like to thank Jimmy [sic] for stepping into the fray. He is a great drummer and a friend.[24] The last time I saw him was about eighteen months ago—before it all happened really—and I remember he's a great drummer."[25]

Nicol was unaware that this was the beginning of the end. On a night when he felt on top of the world thanks to his Beatle celebrity, it was rapidly drawing to a close. He was also unaware that his friends at Pye Records were already exploiting Jimmy Nicol & the Shubdubs with a new single he had recorded earlier in the year. The *Daily Mirror* reported in Patrick Doncaster's daily Discs column, "Beatles stand in drummer, Jimmy [sic] Nicol stars on 'Husky' (Pye) which could beat its way to Pop Thirty."

The next day's adventure would include a morning flight to Adelaide and a reception that would dwarf anything Nicol and The Beatles had ever seen.

Chapter Thirteen

Beatle Jimmy Nicol:
Adelaide, Melbourne & The End

June 12, 1964, Adelaide

The Beatles set off from Sydney to Adelaide early in the morning. Their Ansett ANA plane carried the group and their inner circle first class, while the economy class was crammed full of the ever increasing press corps. Along the way, there was a bit of turbulence, but things settled down to enable newsreel photographers to take some irrelevant mid-flight footage of The Beatles looking out the window, taking photos, and eating fruit. As John Lennon sat writing out the Adelaide concert set lists and quizzing nearby DJs about which Beatles' songs were the most popular, DJ Ernie Sigley sat with Nicol to see if he would let down his guard and discuss his opinion of Ringo Starr's drumming. Jimmie had come a long way since June 3 when George Martin had called him to replace Ringo Starr. He had grown comfortable in his role playing live with the group, socializing with them and just being a part of the inner circle. Nicol became quietly candid and, while briefly outside the earshot of the others, he revealed, "I don't think that he can play in time."[1]

When the group disembarked in Adelaide on a beautiful sunny day, they were surprised to find not one single fan nearby to greet them. However, they need not have worried. The local police had kept all of the fans off official airport grounds. Despite the lack of fans to wave to, The Beatles and Jimmie stood at the top of the steps waving happily for the film and news photographers on the tarmac (and to their non-existent fans). Then the boys all piled into an open convertible vehicle to start their trip to Adelaide. Once their fleet of cars exited the airport, the group was amazed to find thousands of their fans lining both sides of the 8 mile stretch all the way into Adelaide. "It was amazing," says DJ, Bob Francis. "It was a 12.5 km journey all the way to the centre of Adelaide, and people 10-deep were throwing rose petals out on the roadway to see them arriving."[2]

As the group neared the Town Hall in the center of Adelaide, their eyeballs grew larger in disbelief. Was it possible that the biggest crowd of all time had gathered just to wave and scream at The Beatles? Estimates of 300,000 people of all ages came out to greet The Beatles as their motorcade attempted to inch slowly toward the Town Hall. The reception had turned into a massive ticker tape parade, the type typically reserved for returning war veterans, the Queen, or a victorious soccer team. To John, Paul, and George, who had become used to Beatlemania, this reception was beyond anything even *they* had ever witnessed, and it had happened on the other side of the world from their homes.

For Jimmie Nicol, who sat up on top of the front seat above the others waving, this was clearly what it looked like to be on top of the entertainment world. He was not only part of the most popular musical quartet in the world at this moment, he was now permanently a part of history. The iconic photo of Jimmie Nicol giving a hearty thumbs-up to an adoring crowd throwing confetti is forever a fixture in Beatlemania. From newsreel accounts, the fans were clearly screaming for Jimmie as if he were a permanent member of the band. There is no doubt at this point that Nicol did not want this gig to end! Jimmie Nicol, a newly minted "public figure", could easily imagine a full-time position with the group.

Beatles arrive in Adelaide with no fans at the airport. Photo Credit: © Mark Hayward Archive.

"I am sure he wanted to stay with The Beatles permanently. Who wouldn't?" says Sounds Incorporated drummer, Tony Newman. "When we arrived in Adelaide, The Beatles were in this open car and they got a reception bigger than the Queen," he recounts. "And there was Jimmie sitting up on top of the seat waving. But he looked separate. He was in my opinion odd man out. There were the three Beatles and then there was Jimmie. The Beatles seemed to be accepting of him and yet it was, 'you have your temporary drummer here, but not bonding."[3] All four Beatles had enthusiastic responses to the sea of fandom that had shut down a major Australian city. Paul McCartney recalls his reaction to the reception in Adelaide, "That was like a hero's welcome, that was. That was the kind of thing where we'd go to the Town Hall and they'd all be in the center [of the city]. I think we quite enjoyed all that stuff. It could get a bit wearing, but that [Adelaide] certainly wasn't.

The Adelaide Crowds at the Town Hall.
Photo Credit: © Mark Hayward Archives.

When there was that many people, you know, you were just flabbergasted."[4] Nicol enthusiastically told one reporter, who asked about the reception, "Oh! This is the best I've seen anywhere in the world."[5] George Harrison summed the day up, "Yea. Shocked and Stunned. Just happy that it was, 'Oh, we're still popular down here too." Continuing the description with his acerbic wit, he says, "I just remember everybody saying, 'There's more people here than came to see the Queen.'

I should think so, she didn't have any hit records!"[6]   Last, but not least, bandleader John Lennon was even impressed by what the band had accomplished thus far, and the massive outpouring of love and support they encountered at this reception. "You know it was funny. I think there was more people trying to see us there than anywhere [in the world]. I think the whole of Australia was there."[7]

Once the group finally made its way safely inside the Lord Mayor's Town Hall for a reception, the crowds were chanting and screaming and definitely not leaving. At this point, The Beatles' erstwhile public relations man, Derek Taylor, suggested that the band go up to the balcony for another wave to the crowd before heading to the Lord Mayor's function. Taylor says, "I made great demands on them which they met. Balcony waving… 'C'mon guys one more wave. Let's get out there.'"[8] On this day they happily obliged.

Out on the balcony, the sound of 300,000 people was deafening, like a jet engine on steroids. The atmosphere was electric. Newsreel footage provides the perspective of The Beatles on the balcony waving, showing us what they see: a massive, swaying sea of people all squeezed together, as far as the eye could see; not an inch of sidewalk or street is visible. Even the trees - each major branch - held teenagers clinging and waving. Police and other adult volunteers are attempting to help fainting girls, but there is just no way to carry them out of the crowd. George took photos of this ocean of adulation, as Paul waved. Lennon and pal Jimmie Nicol huddled together talking, laughing, and waving incredulously at the manic mob below.

Local DJ, Bob Francis, approached the microphones on the balcony and addressed all of Adelaide, "Can we have a little quiet please? Would you like the boys to talk to you? And say a few words, if it's possible?" At this point, the screams are so deafening that they have easily defeated the pesky public address system, to say nothing of ignoring the DJ's plea. Francis continues, "What do you think of the reception, George?" Harrison tries to yell his response, unsure if anyone on the street below can hear him, "It's marvelous. Hello! Hello! It's fabulous, it's the best reception ever, best reception ever."[9]

From the balcony of the Town Hall, it was time for the boys to retreat inside for a reception with Adelaide's Lord Mayor and his friends and family. Once again there would be no escaping the media which filmed every moment of the visit. Each Beatle happily signed autographs and received stuffed bears and other gifts. Nicol signed bundles of autographs without realizing his hair was still full of confetti. Then the formal photo op was created with the Lord Mayor between *his* Beatles. Lennon made sure to put his arm around Jimmie to pull him in for the photo shoot.

As The Beatles grew weary of the meet-and-greet, it was time for them to make a sneaky retreat to prepare for the next event at their hotel - yet another press conference. They snuck out through the back entrance of the Land Titles Office to a waiting car that would take them to their South Australian Hotel on North Terrace. This deception gave the group a twenty minute head start on the enormous crowd that remained out front of the Town Hall, waiting in vain for a last wave from The Beatles.[10]

Some of the more clever teenage fans had already booked rooms in the South Australian, thinking they would have complete and full access to waltz up to The Beatles' suite and knock on their doors. The Beatles were quickly whisked up to their suite, with less than an hour to recover before being thrown to the lions again in the form of print, photo, radio and newsreel media. When the teenage girls and hotel guests attempted to reach the band, they were foiled. According to one newspaper report, "They made it as far as the Beatles' door on the floor below theirs, but guards and hotel employees sent them back to their rooms. The girls said they paid nearly £9 each to be sure of seeing the Beatles, but they had seen even less than the thousands of teenagers waiting in the streets."[11]

At Derek Taylor's bidding, it was time once again to go downstairs to address the press. The questions covered a number of issues, including: The Beatles' reaction to the amazing city reception; meeting the Lord Mayor, and more. Nicol showed up a minute late to a rousing welcome.

> Lennon: "Come here, Jim!"
>
> McCartney: "There he is! Jimmy!"
>
> Announcer: "There's Jimmy Nicol—drummer for Ringo Starr."

This was followed by a big round of applause from Lennon, McCartney, and Harrison. A bit later in the conference, Nicol is asked a question that was very likely on his own mind…

> Q: "Jimmie, do you think that Brian Epstein is going to wave his magic wand at you sometime and include you as a fifth Beatle? Or a stand-in drummer for Ringo permanently?"
>
> Nicol: "That I don't know."

Though awkwardly worded, the question directly asks whether Nicol would or could be permanently replacing Ringo Starr. Nicol had not seen or spoken to Epstein since the initial meeting back in London when he was hired. Yet so much had happened to Jimmie in such a short space of time. He clearly felt a good vibe playing with this band. He had figured out the music very quickly, had kept the tour rolling along without a hitch, and had befriended the group as they experienced the same things together on this tour. What *did* the future hold for Jimmie Nicol?

Inquiring further of Nicol, the reporters ask about his late night jamming with Frances Faye back in Sydney and all of the other bands he had played with.

> Q: "Jimmie, having played with all these bands—what's it like being suddenly thrust in with The Beatles?"

Nicol: (laughs) "It's the 'end', you know!" [This was slang at the time, meaning that something was the best].

Q: "Do you have any trouble getting the same beat as Ringo?"

Nicol: (modestly replies) "Well, I do my best."

Lennon: (comically) "Awwww!"

More questions continue for the others about publicity stunts, exciting moments, the length of tonight's concert, performing comedy sketches in their Christmas Show, and the fans' welcome. John quips about the difference between this greeting and those in England, "Well, I've never seen

The Adelaide Press Conference. Photo Credit: © Mark Hayward Archives.

so many grandmas at once." A final question about why The Beatles don't play the Cavern anymore seems to irritate Lennon, who says they wouldn't be able to visit places like America and Australia if they always played the Cavern. He explains that choices have to be made as to where they will go. With that, the band gets up and leaves. Another press conference is in the history books.

Back up in the hotel suite, Derek Taylor suggests yet another balcony wave to the fans that have now surrounded the hotel. The chanting was constant as the fans yelled, "We want The Beatles... We want The Beatles." By this time, the group was growing weary of "the balcony wave". After a busy day that included flying in from Sydney; waving from the plane, the car and the Town Hall balcony; the Lord Mayor's reception; and the press conference, they still faced two concerts in the evening. Somehow Taylor got the boys out to the balcony for a wave to the fans. Camera men followed as Jimmie went out onto the balcony, smiling broadly and giving thumbs up to the camera and fans. An emotion similar to intoxication plays across Nicol's face at the response from fans. In contrast, a newspaper photo from Adelaide's *Sunday Mail* shows Lennon and McCartney looking down at the masses, appearing weary and unsmiling. At one point, McCartney playfully pretends to climb over the balcony and jump down to the fans, who scream their approval. The day already seemed to be a week long, a "hard day's night" indeed.

Meanwhile, outside, one girl got so emotional seeing Paul that she bursts past police and hotel employees and raced, screaming for McCartney, through the saloon bar, into the main foyer, and up the staircase. She is finally stopped, trying to force her way through press and TV personnel camped outside The Beatles' suite. This gives police and hotel employees time to grab her and carry her back to the street as she tearfully explains, "Please let me see him once — just once – please, please, please!"[12] Unfortunately, the balcony appearances failed to achieve the desired effect of dissipating and quieting the crowed. In Adelaide, it only served to fuel the passionate fire of the teenage girls who *had* to get to The Beatles.

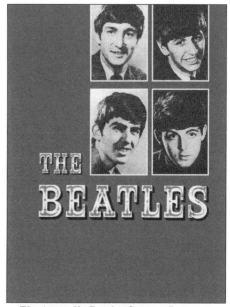

Word had officially arrived that Ringo Starr was on his way to meet the group in Melbourne, accompanied by manager Brian Epstein. At the same time, four thousand fans continued to stand vigil outside the hotel while The Beatles hosted a small reception for their Australian Fan Club organizers before the show. It would include the usual chat, autographs, photo ops, and the offering up of gifts from the Fan Club; all good PR to keep The Beatles in good stead with their huge fan base of Australian subscribers.

Australia was about to get its first experience of The Beatles in concert on this night, not once, but twice. DJ Bob Francis was able to convince his radio station to pay a hefty fee to Epstein's NEMS Corporation for the honor of taping and broadcasting the first evening show at 6:00 p.m. As a result, one of Jimmie Nicol's last efforts on drums with The Beatles would be forever preserved for posterity. Francis also had the honor of introducing the band at Centennial Hall. Some 50,000 requests had

The Australia Beatles Concert Program.
Photo Credit: Courtesy of Author.

been received for the 12,000 available seats. The show was cleverly titled, "The Beatles Show", and was sponsored by Surf Detergent.[13] Francis recalls one humorous clause found in the contract hiring The Beatles. "It says, 'Every effort must be made to ensure stomping by patrons is not tolerated.'"[14] Obviously, this clause would not be enforced.

At 6:00 p.m., the first of the warm-up bands trotted onstage. Leading off was The Phantoms, an Australian Rock group that played an instrumental blend of music reminiscent of England's Shadows and America's Ventures. The Phantoms remained on-

The Australia Beatles Concert ticket stub.
Photo Credit: Courtesy of Author.

stage to back up singer, Johnny Devlin, who sang a frenzied set of 1950's Rock hits. Next up was another Johnny. This time Johnny Chester came onstage to sing a slightly calmer set of songs, but wowed the crowd with his own special lighting that flooded over him during the most passionate parts of his love songs. At this point, the crowd of mostly young women was literally falling out of their chairs having to wait for The Beatles. Wait they must, as one more group was up to bat before The Beatles, another member of Brian Epstein's stable. The wildly syncopated Sounds Incorporated took the stage by storm, performing its mostly instrumental rockers. Though quite vibrant in its tightly rehearsed performance, Sounds Incorporated did not seem to garner the same reaction as the hometown Aussies that preceded them.

The moment all of Australia had been waiting for was finally about to happen, a Beatles concert on Australian soil. At five minutes past 7:00 p.m., DJ Bob Francis takes the stage. 3,000

As The Beatles bow, Nicol plays on. Photo Credit: © Mark Hayward Archive.

teenagers at Centennial Hall crash through the human sound barrier. "STOP STOP… Scream after the numbers… Please let's hear them sing," pleads Francis (who is engineering the recording of the concert and wants his radio listeners to hear something of The Beatles on the subsequent broadcast).

He continues, "What can you say… [Met by a wall of screams]… Wait, Wait… I want complete silence… You can't say anything else, but ladies and gentlemen… [Pausing for effect]… THE BEATLES, THE BEATLES!" At this point, complete pandemonium breaks out, both sonically and physically, as the release of energy causes the screaming teenage girls to lose complete control. Johnny Devlin observes, "I saw girls in Adelaide lying on the floor, beating their heads into the seats until they bled."[15]

Beatles and Nicol rocking hard in Adelaide. Photo Credit: © Newspix/Photo.

The Beatles set list contained the following songs:

I Saw Her Standing There
I Want To Hold Your Hand
All My Loving
She Loves You
Till There Was You
Roll Over Beethoven
Can't Buy Me Love
Boy

As Paul kicks off *I Saw Her Standing There* with his famous count-in of "1, 2, 3, 4…" Nicol starts in on drums as the guitars all begin churning the intro in perfect sync. Nicol is locked in with

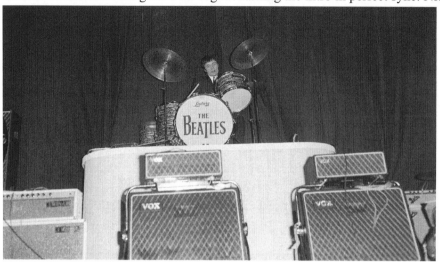

Nicol drumming up on the riser- Adelaide. Photo Credit: © Mark Hayward Archives.

the band. The songs now seem like *his* songs. The band is in great live form, except for one John and Paul lyrical miscue in the middle of the song that could not be heard by the 3,000 crazy fans. As the song ends, Jimmie decides to do a signature Big Band post-ending drum

roll on the snare as they all take their bows. "A lot of drummer fans were disappointed, I'm sure, because they wanted to see Ringo," says Nicol. "I think I was accepted by most of the fans 'cause I fit in. I wore the suit and the hair and tried to play like Ringo in his nonchalant fashion. I also bowed when the rest of them did and it went over big."[16]

After *I Want To Hold Your Hand*, Paul thanks "everybody for the marvelous welcome we've had to Adelaide" which only brings more uncontrollable screaming from the fans. Once again, at the end of the last chord, Nicol decides to add a big post-song cymbal crash. He is truly having a blast-visibly worked up into a great emotional state, with contorted facial expressions as he bangs away on the skins. Jimmie is clearly giving Australia a reason to remember *this* Beatles drummer! Paul, George, and John look comfortable up front, enjoying the amazing reaction of the fans.

They scream, yell, shriek, wave, cry, shout, and chant "yeah, yeah, yeah", falling out of their seats onto the floor. And yes, they break the "no stomping" rule. Some girls simply swoon and faint out of sheer ecstasy at being in the same room with The Beatles singing. Jimmie taps out a quiet rhythm on his snare rim to accompany McCartney singing the romantic ballad, *Till There Was You* to yet more fainting damsels. George

In concert at Adelaide.
Photo Credit: © Mark Hayward Archives.

Harrison riles them up again with his enthusiastic rendition of *Roll Over Beethoven*. At the end of *Roll Over Beethoven*, Nicol plays another song-ending solo for about 10 seconds, helping to milk the applause. The *Sunday Mail* described the amazing transformation of the fans. "Girls who had demurely taken their seats at the opening of the concert were transformed when The Beatles were on stage. Crying, clenching their fists and pounding the floor, they were in a faraway world of their own creation."[17]

As The Beatles play on, one Centennial Hall employee observing the "seething mass of young humanity" comments, "They are behaving beautifully. So far they have smashed only three chairs."[18] Newsreels accounts show Nicol bashing away, mouth wide-open, right hand injuring Ringo's crash cymbal and left hand pounding on the snare, while alternating with jabs to the defenseless ride cymbal, all in perfect rhythm with the high energy show. Jimmie has two extra sets of sticks on stage, as he pulverizes every beat of every song. One almost gets the sense from his ferocious, yet controlled, playing, that Nicol is fighting to hold onto his precious job and good fortune in these, his last two Beatles performances.

Finally, Paul incites the crowd to clap, scream and stomp, "since it's not our building anyway," as the group gallops into their rousing closer of *Long Tall Sally*. Nicol is comfortable bashing away on the crash cymbal as McCartney shreds his voice. With one last crash, The Beatles jump to the front of the stage to bow and then take off backstage. DJ Francis is hoarse yelling, "Let's hear it for them… MAW!!" The PA system plays "God Save The Queen", which quiets the crowd momentarily out of respect. However, once it concludes, the screams grow louder again.

Sounds Incorporated drummer, Tony Newman, watched from the wings as Jimmie Nicol sat in for Ringo Starr and recalls, "I was not very much impressed. To me - someone who would go all out drumming - he [Nicol] came across as a dull person with not much energy. He did okay reproducing Ringo's parts. But they were pretty simple. I don't want to put him down, but he was adequate."[19] Newman's assessment of Nicol's drumming may have been colored by his long-established friendship with Ringo Starr and The Beatles. The photo and video evidence of Nicol in action during this concert do not show a "dull" or "adequate" drummer lacking in energy. Warm up singer, Johnny Chester, had a different take on Nicol's drumming, "I thought he was terrific and he was! I remember making a comment about Jimmie's playing to one of the members of Sounds Incorporated who had worked with The Beatles many times, and whoever it was, said, 'Yeah he's good, but wait 'til you hear Ringo, he REALLY rocks.'"[20]

Not wanting to run the gauntlet of fans back to their hotel between shows, The Beatles chose to remain securely backstage, toweling off and relaxing. During this free time they discussed how much fun the first show had been, did some more paperback reading of their latest James Bond books, and even entertained a few lucky guests.[21] Jimmie Nicol was deep in thought, realizing that his next two shows in Adelaide the next night were sure to be his last as a Beatle. No doubt he had mixed emotions about the benefits of continuing on, versus getting back home to some normalcy; reforming his own band, the Shubdubs; or playing a bit more with Frances Faye back in Sydney. In the end, Nicol's fate was already sealed by two men flying toward Melbourne, Ringo Starr and Brian Epstein. Johnny Chester ate and socialized with The Beatles and other musicians backstage between shows. "My impression was that Nicol was a bit overwhelmed by the attention that we all received, myself included."[22]

The second show started promptly at 8:00 p.m., with the same set of warm-up acts. A number of reporters remained for the second show, despite impending deadlines and risk of severe ear damage from the screams. DJ Ernie Sigley recalls the second show with Jimmie Nicol pounding out a perfect beat as The Beatles stormed the stage at Centennial Hall. "I was just in love with them," he declares. As for the rabid fans, he was incredulous that, "The place stank because the floors and seats were full of piss. Half the little girls were so excited they wet their pants."[23]

The noise from the second show was reported to be even more thunderous than the first for The Beatles' portion of the show. Police had to form a barrier in front of the stage to protect the group and their instruments. The cops ordered the kids back to their seats if they wanted to see the show go on. According to an eyewitness report from Gillian Smart writing for *Disc Weekly*, "Moments later, they erupted in a frenzy as the band opened with *I Saw Her Standing There*. The loudest screams came when George and Paul sang together, and another major explosion happened when John climbed on top of a piano."[24] The police were ready and in position as a rush of fans approached the stage after the last bow of The Beatles, but they were held back until the group had safely left the hall. The Beatles returned to their hotel, sneaked in a side entrance, and raced all the way up the stairs to their suite undetected. Let the celebrations begin…

That night The Beatles had been invited to a society soiree held in their honor in the Adelaide Hills. The band members, however, had a different type of party on their minds - one that involved social intercourse with their beloved fans who had been after them all day. At last, some of the female fans were finally going to get the opportunity to get up-close and personal with their beloved idols.

The evening began with food and drink, with The Beatles in the living room area of the suite mingling with the DJs and reporters they had allowed in on regular occasions. By midnight, however, the band grew weary of being stared at and asked the same questions; So they retired to their rooms for some Olympic feats of a different nature.

Tour manager Ravenscroft delicately explains, "They had girls in their room, yes. That was in the hands of Mal Evans, who was very good at picking the right girls. It was very discreet and well organized. When they were getting involved in that sort of thing, I kept right out of the way."[25] Journalist Jim Oram is a bit more forthcoming in his hotel accounts of the evening's festivities: "John and Paul, particularly 'rooted' themselves silly," he said; "A seemingly endless and inexhaustible stream of Australian girls passed through their beds; the very young, the very experienced, the beautiful and the plain. In fact, I can vividly remember one spoilt virgin in Adelaide who proudly took her bloodstained sheet home with her in the morning."[26] Nicol recalls, "To begin with, Paul was not the clean [innocent] chap he wanted the world to see. His loves of blonde women… are not told. John was into sex as well as partying all night with the rest of us. But I did as they did. To sit here and list each and every little thing we did in such a short time, well, I just can't do it; The Beatles living life to the fullest."[27]

DJ Bob Francis observed a homesick George trying desperately to reach his girlfriend, Pattie Boyd, on the phone with the time difference problems. He told Francis he was overcome by the Adelaide welcome and was desperate to go home. But for John and Paul at least, there were the usual diversions to ward off homesickness. "They let the girls they wanted get to them," says Francis, "Top models and other choice pieces."[28]

The system for this bacchanal involved Mal Evans rounding up the gals and bringing them upstairs to a holding area in the suite. From this "reservoir", the minders would allocate a continuing supply of carnal pleasure to any Beatle or other tour member who subscribed to the service. Certain reporters would also help themselves to this female "inventory", promising access to the Beatles as a reward. One reporter, who asked to go nameless, was "getting busy" with one of the fans when Derek Taylor walked into the room and casually asked, "Would anyone like to meet John Lennon?" The reporter recalls with a wink, "The girl slipped out from under me so quickly that I was left doing push-ups on the bed."[29]

DJ Rodgers summed it all up humorously, "There was no [birth control] pill in 1964 and with the amount of Beatle screwing that went on I just can't believe that there wasn't an explosion of little Beatles all over Australia in 1965. Maybe there was."[30] Meanwhile, hundreds of autograph books piled up at the hotel and were sent up to the suite to be signed by Neil Aspinall, Mal Evans and Derek Taylor, who grew quite adept at reproducing the lads' signatures, while the band *played* on…

June 13, 1964, Adelaide, Australia

At midday, The Beatles awoke well rested from their evening of merriment. After a lunch time meal, it was time to get back to work pleasing the fans. This meant yet another trip out to the balcony to wave to the fans who never seemed to go home. With this chore out of the way, the band retired back into the suite for yet more radio interviews with DJ Bob Rodgers. Paul McCartney joked that he had seen "three or four people" waving back to them below the balcony. Lennon put the estimate closer to "four million."[31]

Rodgers then sat down with Jimmie Nicol for a penultimate one-on-one interview to inquire about his future plans.

DJ: "I want to talk to Jimmie."

McCartney: "Ahhhhhhhh" (screaming like the teen girls outside for Jimmie).

DJ: "Jimmie, you've got your final performances tonight and then Ringo arrives tomorrow."

Nicol: "Yeah, that's right. I'm looking forward to meeting him."

DJ: "And then it's all over for you. What's going to happen? I hear you may not be going back to England?

Nicol: "Not for a little while no. I fancy going back to Sydney."[32]

The finality of this amazing journey had been spoken, yet it was still hard to believe for Nicol. He was still wearing The Beatles' clothes; still in the hotel suite with The Beatles; the fans were still outside screaming; and he was still planning to play two more concerts as The Beatles' drummer in Adelaide that night. With mixed emotions, Jimmie Nicol was trying to comprehend the end. "Until Ringo joined us in Melbourne, Australia, I was praying he would get well - at the same time I was hoping he would not want to come back. I was having a ball, truly."[33] Nicol thought to himself, if these were to be his last shows, he was going to go all-out and make sure Australians remembered his thrilling drumming as a Beatle.

Meanwhile, half-a-world away in San Francisco, California, Ringo Starr and Brian Epstein were slowly but surely making their way towards a reunion with Jimmie and The Beatles. Starr briefly spoke with reporters at the airport before boarding another flight. As 300 fans screamed in the background, a jaded TV reporter talked to his audience. "We have been here before greeting Madame Nhu, accused murderers coming back from extradition, and now…Ringo Starr." Ringo tells the reporter, he hopes the airport officials will allow him to greet the fans.[34] After his brief layover, Starr and Epstein boarded a Qantas plane that would carry them, via refueling stops, to Honolulu, Fiji, Sydney, and onto their final destination, Melbourne.

That night, Jimmie Nicol played his last two shows as a Beatle to another combined 6,000 crazy, screaming, crying, stomping fans at Adelaide's Centennial Hall. Towards the end of the second show, Paul McCartney graciously thanked Jimmie for his services as their drummer, and indicated that Ringo Starr would be returning to the tour soon. Nicol got a huge applause, but he realized that much of the cheering was for the announcement of Ringo's imminent return.[35]

Jimmie Nicol was proud of his services rendered, and he knew he had successfully fulfilled his obligations in keeping the biggest band in the world rolling along on its do-or-die first world tour. It was a bittersweet moment for the young drummer who had literally saved the band from breaches of contract, financial ruin and all sorts of bad publicity, had they not been able to pull off the first leg of their world tour sans Ringo Starr. He had done his job and done it well. After the concerts, it was back to the hotel for another night of ribald celebration.

June 14, 1964, Starr Turn

Perhaps the busiest day of The Beatles' tour Down Under began very early with Ringo Starr's 7 a.m. arrival at Sydney's Mascot Airport. Upon his disembarking to board yet another flight, Starr is cornered by journalist, Garvin Rutherford. Ringo has to put his Scotch and Coke down to discuss his various rings. Starr states he is not bothered at all about the loss of privacy and enjoys the fans' attention. Ringo claims, "I think at least half of the crowd can hear what we are playing. I mean, I can't hear what the boys are playing, but I know what I'm playing." In answer to another query about the loud screams drowning out the music in concert, Ringo jokes, "I think if they stopped and listened to us, we'd be finished (laughing)." Starr comments that the doctor told him not to sing for a couple of days, though Starr doesn't know how he will be able to hold off, once they start playing. He is clearly anxious to regain his drum kit from Jimmie Nicol and take over driving The Beatles' rhythm section again.[36]

In his the next interview with TV, Ringo explains that, he is resting his voice, but regarding his drums, he can "Still bash 'em." Starr informs the TV news crew that he cannot wait to rejoin The Beatles this afternoon and admits "...it's a bit funny [being] on your own." Manager Epstein is asked whether he has any trouble keeping The Beatles under control on tour. Brian replies, "Oh no—no no no no no." Starr chimes in, "Never! Never!", and both start laughing. With the required media questions answered it is time for Starr and Epstein to get ready for their next leg - bound for Melbourne.[37]

Meanwhile, due west across the continent in Adelaide, The Beatles make their way back to the Adelaide Airport for the journey to reunite with Ringo Starr in Melbourne. Once again, TV news cameras follow The Beatles' motorcade from the hotel all the way up the steps of the Ansett plane at around 1 p.m., set to carry them onto their next destination. Jimmie Nicol is seen in his white London overcoat, walking alongside John, Paul and George, carrying a stuffed Kola; and waving to the fans. McCartney admits to one DJ as they are leaving Adelaide, "I nearly cried in the car. Nothing like this has ever happened to us before."[38] Posing and waving on the steps of their plane, it does not seem as if the reality of "the end" has yet to set in. Jimmie continues to relish and enjoy the adulation as if it will continue forever.

Ringo Starr and Brian Epstein are the first to arrive in Melbourne this afternoon. They are immediately put into a closed car where newsreel footage presents Ringo giving his fans a hearty thumbs-up, as girls lining the fence barriers scream and throw confetti. A play-by-play radio announcer explains the closed car is due to Ringo's recent illness. Although the arrival goes smoothly, the plan for getting Ringo into the luxurious Southern Cross Hotel was non-existent.

Some 3000 screaming fans are waiting outside the hotel when they recognize Starr and his manager pull up at the front entrance. According to hotel PR manager John Williams, "When the crowd recognized him, they pounced like a flock of starving locusts. We rushed to the door and police helped us drag him inside. He [Ringo] was shaking like a leaf, so I took him up to Pete's office and poured him a large Scotch."[39] As Starr gulps down a second Scotch, Williams notices that fans have pulled out clumps of his hair. He concludes this is the reason The Beatles have such

All 5 Beatles together in Melbourne on the Southern Cross Hotel balcony. Photo Caption: ©Newspix/Photo File

long hair. As Ringo calms down, he starts up a conversation with Williams.

> Starr: "Rough town you've got here, mate."
> Williams: "Tell me about it, mate – I'm from Liver-pool."
>
> Starr: (Surprised and grinning) "Well, you'd feel right at home here then."[40]

Ringo is then escorted up to his room to rest, recover, and re-grow his hair. A few hours later, it was now John, Paul, George and Jimmie's turn to run the gauntlet from the airport to the Southern Cross Hotel. A TV announcer gives his viewers a running commentary on the plane as it approaches the runway and taxis in, building up the excitement of the biggest arrival in perhaps the whole history of the continent. An explosion of screams erupt as The Beatles deplane, only to climb another set of steps onto another flat bed truck for yet another circus-like tour on the tarmac - another offering of the idols for their 5000 fans who scream and wave banners in near freezing weather. Their truck looks to be a 1950s flat bed with sponsors' names taped to the side like a hastily-made school homecoming float. Jimmie stands in his white London Fog coat, in stark symbolic contrast and set apart from his fellow Beatles, John, Paul, and George who are attired in their black Hong Kong capes. The Beatles are waving and smiling enthusiastically. Jimmie waves, but his smiling face seems to belie a realization that the end is near.

As The Beatles board their transport to the hotel, a TV camera perched up very high catches the fans racing between parked cars in the lot - like rats in a maze - trying to catch up to the speeding getaway car. As The Beatles approach the Southern Cross Hotel, the police have decided to create a diversion to enable the group to safely enter the hotel. TV cameras show an ocean of swaying fans packed tightly together as a motorcade inches toward the front of the hotel. However, the police are driving a group of cars with no Beatles inside. Upon discovery of the ruse, a TV announcer states, rather perturbed, "This is not The Beatles! This is a diversionary measure. This is a police escort without The Beatles. They have fooled the fans. The Beatles aren't here; they have gone in the back of the hotel. The crowds have gone mad and are screaming... AND THERE IS HYSTERIA!"[41] The scene appears much more dangerous than in Adelaide, where the crowds were more relaxed.

Reports ranging from 80,000-250,000 fanatic, frenzied, fighting fans surrounding the Southern Cross hotel do not appear to be exaggerated. The police, who had received reports from Adelaide's welcome, call out soldiers, sailors, and even civilians to help them with crowd control. Barriers are flattened, girls are trampled, and police are being knocked off their motorcycles trying to control the crowd. One reporter described the frightening scene: "Girls and women fainted and were passed over the heads of the crowd to mounted police. They put them across their saddles and forced their horses to ambulances."[42] One TV newscaster reports, "You cannot see an inch of space in the crowd; only a sea of heads."[43] Hundreds were ultimately hurt in the melee.

"When the boys actually arrived, no one knew," says Epstein, "As it was necessary [and how!] for them to be smuggled in at the rear of the building."[44] They were quickly whisked upstairs for a joyous, yet brief, reunion with Ringo. At this point, Jimmie Nicol and Ringo shook hands. It was the official changing of the guard. The Beatles'

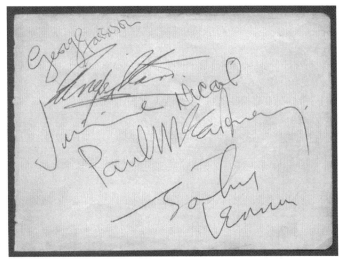

A rare set of Beatles autographs featuring 5 Beatles
signed at the Melbourne press conference.
Photo Credit: Courtesy of Anonymous Collector.

drummer had returned to take back his rightful place in the group and Jimmie Nicol was now, officially, the odd man out. "When they joined us in the suite, they seemed in particularly good form. They told us in delighted terms of the fantastic welcome they'd had in Adelaide, and we argued, comparing receptions in Melbourne and Adelaide," enthused Epstein.[45]

Downstairs, crowd control had reached serious proportions. Girls are smuggling their way into the hotel in laundry bags. Still others desperate for a touch, scale the roofs of adjacent buildings to get to the mezzanine floor of the hotel. Radio stations are whipping the fans up into a crazed frenzy outside the hotel. The real danger is that hundreds of girls are now pressing hard on the hotel's large plate-glass picture windows which are just barely holding up under the pressure. Serious injuries were now a real possibility. Fans, angry at being deceived by the police, begin pushing and shoving in all directions. Television coverage shows total panic spread across the faces of teens that are being carried, pushed, and trampled.

The chanting begins – "We Want The Beatles, We Want The Beatles" - from the teeming masses who are whipped into a frenzy. The news footage shows a very dangerous, uncomfortable crowd, shoving and hanging from trees, rooftops and flagpoles, ready to explode after being fooled by the police diversion.

Thinking quickly, hotel PR director Williams makes up signs, and with the help of others, presses them up to the glass, trying to hold back the dangerous surge. The signs tell the fans "Beatles on Balcony". Williams recalls, "For a moment I thought it was too late, but as we held the notices against the windows, magically the crowd pulled away and the air of panic began to subside."[46]

Finally, 5 Beatles, John Lennon, Paul McCartney, George Harrison, Jimmie Nicol, and Ringo Starr walk out onto the Southern Cross Hotel balcony to see and be seen by the rabid throngs. As they make their way toward the three microphones at the balcony's edge, Nicol and Starr are seen walking, talking, and smiling together no doubt discussing Jimmie's recent drumming experience with the group. George looks to be in shock upon seeing the gathering of fans. Jimmie has a big toothy grin; looking up and across to a rooftop of fans, he gives a thumbs-up.

Paul approaches the PA system and addresses the crowd, "Hello everybody, how are you?" The screams increase. Ringo takes a turn, "Hello! Hey!" He shakes his famous hair and the others crack up as fan volume increases to jet engine decibel levels. Jimmie waves along with the others, but he looks hesitant to use the microphone now that Ringo has spoken. He realizes his redundancy has begun.

The rabid, packed crowds cause John and Paul to recall the old newsreels of Hitler addressing his Nazi youth rallies. Regrettably, John puts a finger up to his lip to recreate Hitler's mustache, while he and Paul give a few satirical "Sieg Heil" salutes to the crowd, mocking the ex-Fuhrer of Germany. Ringo adds his Hitler mock salute, while Jimmie and George smile and hesitate to follow suit, waving in normal fashion to the fans. The Beatles' Jewish manager, Brian Epstein, likely did not appreciate this bit of balcony mischief. Nicol heard Lennon yelling as a joke to the kids (who couldn't possibly hear him), "Ah stupid bastards, Schweinehund…" "Terribly, politically incorrect," says Nicol's friend, Johnny Harris. "Jimmie and I could do those German accents pretty well too. So Jimmie thought Lennon was quite amusing."[47]

Nicol spots a TV camera along the edge of the balcony and points it out to Ringo. Ringo smiles at the camera and then jokingly grabs at his deputy drummer's neck to strangle Jimmie. Jimmie returns the gag, ringing Ringo's neck at the same time for good measure. They both laugh at each other with mutual respect in their eyes as Jimmie pats Ringo on the back. Perhaps a psychologist could analyze this moment more deeply, but on the surface it appears that the changing of the guard has gone quite smoothly. After ten minutes of waving, Neil Aspinall herds the 5 Beatles back inside the hotel. Amazingly, the crowd is instantly subdued as The Beatles move inside. Satisfied that they have seen their heroes, many of the fans disperse and start to head home. For the loyal thousands remaining outside, The Beatles take turns waving out of their hotel windows.

Later that evening it was time for the one and only press conference featuring 5 Beatles. Taking place in the Southern Cross Hotel ballroom, Derek Taylor begins the proceedings, introducing each Beatle by name, and then sets forth the ground rules for this 21-minute public information exercise. As the newspaper photographers lead off, George Harrison makes sure to get Jimmie into the very unique group photo of The Beatles with two drummers. Ringo and John start up a friendly banter, clearly expressing their enjoyment at being reunited. Jimmie remains muted as he smiles for the camera.

The question and answer session begins with reporters wanting to know what The Beatles thought of their wild reception in Melbourne. Lennon explains that it was on a par with Adelaide and that they were both the wildest they have ever seen. In the middle of questioning, five men show up behind The Beatles and interrupt to present each member with a didgeridoo instrument. While John is answering a question, one reporter asks Jimmie about his plans. Off-mike we can hear Jimmie state that he plans to stop in Sydney (most likely to talk further with Frances Faye about more drum work and perhaps a trip to the US). Jimmie is heard answering another question about forming a new band. "I don't know yet, until I get back," says Nicol. At this point, Ringo gets perturbed that Jimmie is talking over John. Derek Taylor is seen walking over to end Jimmie's side bar conversation. Clearly Jimmie is attempting to get his last bit of press attention, but he seems unconcerned that his discussions are on-mike, competing with the other Beatles. For the majority of the press conference Jimmie is cut out of the TV camera shot framing The Beatles.

Now that Ringo is back, few other reporters seem interested in questioning Nicol. Lennon makes a humorous observation stating, "There always seems to be about 800 people writing and asking questions and there are like two newspapers in each city. (Laughter) It's true!" Jimmie starts a drum roll with his hands on the table, restless from sitting and being ignored since no one has directed any questions toward him. The press conference concludes and The Beatles head back up to their suite. Jimmie Nicol has just completed his last public job as a Beatle.

If Jimmie Nicol ever felt outside The Beatles' inner circle during the tour, he was certainly feeling the cold shoulder now. With Ringo back in the fold, the four Beatles had quickly closed ranks. When Nicol returned to the suite, he was in for a scolding from Beatles' manager Epstein. According to Phantom's guitarist Dave Lincoln, who witnessed the encounter, Epstein was irritated with Nicol talking to the press on the side. Epstein told Nicol, in no uncertain terms, that he would not be returning to Sydney to play with Frances Faye and that, with his work complete, he was being flown one-way, directly back to London.[48] The two exchanged heated words, but Epstein would not budge. Nicol was not pleased with the manner in which this gig was ending, especially when Epstein firmly directed him back to his room to pack his suitcase for his trip home. This moment was very upsetting to the Nicol, the proud and independent professional, who had performed admirably in rescuing The Beatles tour from certain ruin. He viewed Epstein's attitude as a lack of respect. Jimmie felt discarded.

Reflecting later on this sad moment, Nicol was realistic, "They liked me. I think so. But after Ringo returned, they changed. It was like welcoming a close member of the family back. They treated me with nothing but respect as a musician. And I think they thought I was very good." But Nicol realized that being a great drummer was not the only important factor to being a Beatle. He learned that the close-knit brotherhood of the four Beatles was the most important factor. He continues, "John once told me I was better than Ringo, but that I just missed the ship."[49] Lennon told one newsman after the press conference that while Jimmie did an admirable job, he [Lennon] admitted they all felt a bit awkward not having Ringo around.[50] Yet despite the respect shown Jimmie Nicol by The Beatles and their entourage, he now felt he did not exist anymore. With Ringo's return, it was as if a brick wall had been built around The Fab Four that did not include Nicol. Jimmie had been closed out of the "inner circle" he had briefly inhabited.

That evening, the press was told that The Beatles were going to bed at midnight. Once all of the outsiders were sent away, the late-night party started up again - new city, new hotel, same party. Bringing in more "birds" for the boys had become a nightly tradition on tour; but it had been a nightmare for Devon Minchin who served as security director for The Beatles during their world tour. He says, "The band was girl-crazy. I lectured them good and proper," says the World War II veteran fighter pilot. "I told them they couldn't keep running around with good-looking female fans if they wanted to avoid trouble." The boys refused to listen. "They just kept on letting in the sexy birds into their suite."[51] When The Beatles finally left Australia, they presented their security director with a signed, humorous letter of thanks which read in part, "To the man who only allowed the finest birds and the best boomerang throwers into the suites, thank-you".[52] The letter was signed by John,

Paul, George, Ringo, Derek, and Neil Aspinall.

Jimmie Nicol wanted to make the most of his last night in Australia. So, at 2:30 a.m., he snuck out of the Southern Cross Hotel, borrowed a car, and made his way out into the Melbourne night. He intentionally chose to disobey Brian Epstein's curfew. Nicol continued to demonstrate his fierce independence on this tour from beginning to end. He found a bar and began to relax. "And within about 30 minutes, there was a screeching of brakes. It was terribly Hollywood dramatic," say Johnny Harris. "Mal Evans and Derek Taylor jumped out of the car and excitedly said to Jimmie, 'What are you doing? What are you doing?' Nicol replied, 'What do you mean, what am I doing? I'm having a drink.'"[53] The two Beatles' minders (who had no problem letting Nicol roam other cities on the tour while Epstein was away) had now turned 180 degrees on Nicol. They said, 'You can't come out here. You mustn't be out on the streets. You can't come into a bar.' Jimmie replied, 'What are you talking about, I'm not a Beatle anymore.' Taylor answered, 'You *are* a Beatle until we put you on the plane.' With that, Evans and Taylor grabbed Jimmie, paid for his drink, put him in the car, and took him back to the hotel."[54]   Nicol was livid and had had enough. He knew Brian Epstein was behind the incident. Epstein had his own hard and fast rules because there was an image of The Beatles that must be maintained. In Jimmie's mind, Epstein was out to get Nicol. More likely, Epstein was concerned that an inebriated Nicol might have talked to the media revealing confidential experiences as a Beatle. No matter what he might have said, Epstein would not have liked it.

June 15, 1964, End of the Line

The next morning, June 15 at 8:00 a.m., Jimmie Nicol and Brian Epstein slipped out of the hotel and drove to the airport. Nicol never got to say goodbye to the other Beatles. He says, "They were still asleep and I didn't think I ought to wake them up."[55]   The Beatles' late-night party had ended only a few hours earlier. Not wanting to disturb them, Nicol left with his suitcase, carry-on bag and some souvenirs.

While Epstein chatted with the concert promoter, Jimmie Nicol sat, waiting for his plane, all alone in the airport terminal and deep in thought. Another iconic photo shows Jimmie with legs crossed sitting alone in the airport, with nothing but empty rows of seats surrounding him. It is a stark contrast to the hundreds of thousands of fans whom, as recently as yesterday, had screamed just to be near him. He is seen, pensive and serious, possibly wondering: *what could have been, what just happened, and what the future might hold?* The photo reflects many emotions - sadness, loneliness, shock, despair, defeat, and depression. It is the single most powerful photograph ever taken of Jimmie Nicol, of a moment in time that would continue to resonate throughout his life. Reflecting on that moment, Nicol cryptically reveals, "Oh that's a beautiful photograph. Oh yes, lonely. That was meant to be. Well, if you look at that photograph, and you can see into the photograph, then you can learn a lot; with the odd man out. Just tie that photograph with the feeling you get from it and there's your answer about how I felt."[56]

One last TV reporter catches up with Jimmie at the airport. Nicol is smiling proudly. He relishes the chance to be interviewed all alone. It is a brief exchange and his last interview as a Beatle.

> Nicol: "…Seeing all these marvelous places and things and actually seeing all these things that are in the paper like the refugees and seeing the conditions they're living in. They still look happy though they are living in bad conditions, so…"
>
> Q: "Have the crowds been surprising?"
>
> Nicol: "Oh yes."

Jimmie Nicol's last interview as a Beatle. Photo Credit: © Newspix/ Photo File.

Q: "Do The Beatles get this kind of reception back in England?"

Nicol: "No. Not to the extent of here. I think the streets don't allow it. The streets are much bigger over here than over in London. Nevertheless, there is always a large crowd."

Q: "What do you feel you are taking back with you from Australia, apart from the experience?"

Nicol: "Oh dear, that's a hard question."

Q: "Money in the bank?"

Nicol: "Yeah, okay."

Q: "Do you have any change of plans in mind as a result of working with The Beatles?"

Nicol: "Well, I hope to do something that I want to do. Now there might be a possibility that I might be able to do something."

Q: "What do you mean by something you would want to do?"

Nicol: "Well, maybe earn enough money to study in America. That is what I want to do, is study drums in America and American music. And learn to arrange."

Q: "The Beatles manager Brian Epstein is here with you this morning to say farewell and I'd like to bring him on camera. Because I know he would like to say a few words before you leave."

Epstein: "I'd just like to say to you Jimmie that The Beatles and I are very very grateful for everything you have done. You carried out a fine job for us and we're very very pleased. We hope you have a great trip back to London and every success to you in the future."

Nicol: "Thank you very much Brian."[57]

Although Epstein and Nicol had not gotten along in private at the end of the tour, they both appear friendly for the camera. Here Epstein expresses his gratitude to his temporary drummer. Off camera, after the interview had ended, Epstein presented Jimmie Nicol with a gift of a gold watch. On the inside it was engraved, "To Jimmy, with appreciation and gratitude – Brian Epstein and The Beatles". The watch was somewhat of a joke, usually reserved for a "company man" who retires from a long career. Nicol would brood about Epstein and what the gold watch came to symbolize, in years to come. Epstein also handed Nicol a monetary payment of £500 for his days on tour. It is unclear if this was a bonus or his total fee. Though not as large a sum as Nicol has stated, it was still a huge amount of money at the time for a week and a half of work
. All that was left was the final walk onto the tarmac to his waiting plane. There would be no side trip to Sydney. This flight was destined for London. Silent newsreel footage captures Epstein and Nicol deep in conversation and smiling as Jimmie takes his final steps in public as a Beatle. It appears as if the manager and the stand-in drummer have made peace. Shaking hands, Nicol heads up the stairs, stops and turns around to give one last "Beatle" wave, a brave smile, and a last thumbs-up before disappearing into the plane.

As Jimmie Nicol entered the plane and the door closed, many believe he had turned away from the world's stage for what would be the last time. To some, Jimmie Nicol disappeared into obscurity. According to drummer, Tony Newman, "The day he left The Beatles tour, he dropped off the planet. And it was as if he didn't exist anymore. I was in London and when we got back, I never saw or heard of him again. Is he alive?"[58] This popular belief, that Jimmie Nicol disappeared into obscurity after The Beatles is a myth that has been perpetrated in music history books for decades. It is clearly wrong. Dave Lincoln of the Phantoms recalls, "He had big plans to become a big star, to cash in on his Beatle association."[59]

Nicol was emotionally spent. His days as a Beatle had been amazing, but stressful. As news cameras filmed his plane taking off, Jimmie felt a mixture of emotions: regret and bitterness for not becoming the new Beatles' drummer, yet also relief to get out from under the very strict guidelines imposed by Epstein and the "boxes" he built around his group. Nicol had tasted the ultimate in fame and glory. He was now flying back to a new reality. He pondered ways to use the momentum of his publicity to launch his own enterprise. Jimmie Nicol was not about to disappear into obscurity after being a Beatle. He was determined to create his own band and compete at the same level. Nicol aspired to be a successful bandleader, and felt he could achieve the same level of success as The Beatles. He was ready for his next career move.

As he settled in for the long flight back to London, Jimmie began to focus on these hopes and dreams.

Jimmie Nicol alone in his thoughts heading back to London, no longer a Beatle. Photo Credit: © Newspix/Photo File.

Chapter Fourteen

Jimmy Nicol & the Shubdubs

June 16, 1964, London

Jimmie returned to London, greeted by some fans and his family. He was clearly a changed man. His Beatles experience had caused a metamorphosis. Nicol no longer felt like an Everyman. He felt special. Nicol knew he would have to work hard to succeed with his new plan, but it would be on his own terms. He was certainly not the same drummer who dutifully went to recording sessions, played with Georgie Fame, and spent quiet time with his family. The new Jimmie Nicol had an air about him; he was glowing. He had been treated as one of the world's biggest superstars for thirteen long days and it had clearly created a change in his personality. "Yes. I was a Beatle for three weeks. The reality was there," says Nicol. "I was a Beatle."[1]

Derek Taylor tried to explain The Beatles' experience in Oz, "It was clear that many of the 11 million people in Australia viewed The Beatles in a messianic light. They were invited to lay their hands on cripples, to pose on balconies before almost the entire populations of many large cities, to watch ethnic dance displays and to attend mayoral receptions and meet with visiting heads of state."[2] How could Jimmie not be a completely changed person after such an extraordinary experience? Though he was high on his new-found fame, he also began what would become a life-long issue of harbored resentment. "After my part of The Beatles' tour ended, I went back to England on my own. None of The Beatles ever phoned me after that. No phone call."[3] Initially, however, Nicol concealed his negative emotions from friends and focused on conquering the world on his own terms.

When he returned to his home in Barnes on June 16, his singer friend, John Hodkinson was still living there. Jimmie returned the borrowed red suitcase to John. Later Hodkinson's brother Roy inherited the suitcase. Inside he found hotel registers of guests with room and phone numbers, including John, Paul, and George. He cleaned out the suitcase and threw away the materials.

John noticed the changes in Nicol and recalls that he was very optimistic about his career when he got back from The Beatles' tour. "He was full of it. He was recognized in the street and everything. I went down to the 'Talk of the Town' show in London with him. Shirley Bassey was on that night. And she actually made a remark that Jimmie was in the audience when she was there. So Jimmie stood up and took a bow."[4]

The next day, Nicol went down to Pye Studios. He walked into a recording session of Johnny Harris and producer, Tony Hatch. Harris recalls, "I was just in the middle of finishing a session with Tony. We were listening to a playback when Jimmie walked in. He looked amazing. He had a great outfit on, but something had changed."[5] Harris knew Jimmie Nicol very well. They had been roommates during many tours on the road together. He observed excitedly, "Jimmie seemed like he was elevated off the ground. It was an incredible experience. There he was with this marvelous big smile. He just looked different." The two old friends hugged, and Harris introduced Jimmie to Tony Hatch. "And so we went out to the pub to have a drink."[6]

At the pub, Harris said, "So tell me…." Jimmie replied, "How long have you got?" "So he told me the whole story, starting at the audition and through the whole tour."[7] In summing up the tour, Nicol admitted to Harris that eventually he could not take it any longer. "It was like living in a box, you move from compartment to compartment, plane, car, hotel, stage, back to hotel," said Nicol.[8] He continued his complaints about his restricted movements on tour, (though he "forgot" to mention he had moved about freely in several cities on tour before Epstein arrived in Melbourne). "You can't really go out anywhere. But, you don't really have to. They would come to you." Jimmie explained how they were given gifts at every stop, even furniture in Scandinavia. At the best hotels, the four of them would just walk in and snap their fingers and get anything they wanted. "That part was great," says Jimmie. But, says Harris, "He wasn't used to being a prisoner, which he essentially was."[9]

When it came time for Ringo to return and take over, Jimmie told Harris, "Epstein said, 'That's it. The Beatles had a good time with you. They enjoyed it.'"[10] And they sent him home. Now Harris was curious what "ex-Beatle" Jimmie Nicol was planning to do. Nicol replied, "I don't know John. I feel so different." Harris said, "Well you look different. There is actually an aura around you." "John," said Jimmie, "It's an unbelievable world that the guys [The Beatles] live in. But, you know, I couldn't take it after awhile with all the rules." Harris knew this about his friend. "He wasn't too good at that. He was a very free spirit."[11] Nicol and Harris agreed to get together again soon.

Immediately, Jimmie Nicol contemplated his next move. He had several options after The Beatles. He considered going back to Australia to play with Frances Faye in Sydney, hoping to latch on with her and travel back to the US. He could easily get back into London recording session work, having increased his visibility by playing with The Beatles. He also could rejoin Georgie Fame & the Blue Flames. Hodkinson recalls, "Georgie Fame thought he was going to come back after The Beatles and join up again. Thinking about it, he probably should have gone back to Georgie's group."[12] Fame was none too pleased, having loaned out Jimmie, and holding open his seat on drums for two weeks, only to have Nicol state he was not coming back. Fame remarked: "The [Beatles] tour went to his head."[13] However, Jimmie Nicol always wanted to move forward, never backward. In this case, moving forward meant forming [or reforming] his own touring and recording group, Jimmy Nicol & the Shubdubs. Unfortunately, Jimmie did not realize that he was burning some valuable bridges along the way.

Jimmy Nicol & the Shubdubs

While Nicol was still in Australia with The Beatles, Pye Records decided to capitalize on Nicol's tremendous worldwide publicity. They already had two songs in the can from Nicol's earlier Shubdubs' studio sessions. One executive at MarMar Records discovered that the Jimmie Nicol, touring with The Beatles, was the same artist who had released "Humpty Dumpty" a few months earlier on Pye. He quickly licensed the track and rushed the record into stores with a label credit that read, "Jimmy Nicol – Now with The Beatles". Ironically, by the time the 45 rpm record arrived in shops, Nicol had already left The Beatles and returned to England.

Although *Humpty Dumpty* had failed to chart, Pye was confidant the next single *Husky / Don't Come Back* would benefit from big sales, due to The Beatles' "aura" still hanging like a halo over Jimmie. Even *The Beatles Monthly* reported the new release in an article discussing both ex-Beatles drummers, Nicol and Pete Best. "Two former Beatles drummers – one more former than the other! – have singles issued this month. Will either ex-Beatle make the chart grade?"[14]

The Shubdubs' cover version of *Husky* was another example of Jimmie's musical influences coloring the band's song. *Husky* was the composition of noted Blues and swing pianist, Ray Bryant. The genius of Nicol's and Harris' arrangement of the song is best described as a collision of influences that shape the Shubdubs' take on Bryant's tune. One can certainly feel the presence of Ray Charles's 1959 hit, *What'd I Say,* with its up-tempo Latin Blues Rhythm, which underpins the foundation of the track. Another major influence, in the form of the instrumentation, is from the 1959 recording

**Husky by Jimmy Nicol & the Shubdubs.
Photo Credit: Courtesy of Author.**

of, *Topsy, Part Two*, by Jazz drummer Cozy Cole, who scored a huge Rock and Roll hit single with his release, after having been a featured sideman with Cab Calloway in the late 1930's.[15]

The first thing that attracts listeners to "Husky" today is the retro-chic sound that would fit perfectly in an "Austin Powers" film with its organ play and go-go flavored blend of Latin Rhythm and Soul. For Nicol, as a drummer, "Husky" is an opportunity to hear yet another tool in his skill set – the "Latin Beat" – and how this talented drummer serves it up, with the same conviction and groove as his Jazz, R & B, and Rock and Roll heart. The Shubdubs' clever blends of classic American Jazz, Latin, and Blues influences, and the excellent performance of the band on this song, make for another track that must have seemed perfect at this point in time.

Pye Records called Jimmie to discuss plans of forming a live touring band in order to support the new single. Nicol liked the idea and felt after The Beatles' experience that it was only fitting that he lead his own band to success. Jimmie Nicol began to think about whom he wanted in the touring version of the Shubdubs. "When I returned to England my name was made," says Nicol. "And the publicity I got was worth half a million [pounds]."[16]

Before the Shubdubs were even formed, one London newspaper was carrying the story, "Jim Plans To Rival Beatles"[17] The front page headline revealed exactly what Nicol's strategy was. He would show Brian Epstein what he could do on his own and perhaps make him wish he had made Nicol a permanent Beatle! On Wednesday, June 17, 1964, Richard Green of the *New Musical Express* interviewed Jimmie. The headline blared: "NME Exclusive: Jimmy Nicol tells about his fantastic BEATLES' CAPERS!" "It's marvelous to be back," gushed Nicol. "Everything has been so fantastic."[18]

Jimmie began the interview by complimenting his now former band members. "The Beatles are very nice people, all of them. They are individuals, of course, but they are friends and humorous. They accepted me right away and made me feel very comfortable."[19] After discussing his initial nervousness of playing in concert the first night, he goes on to describe his reaction to the recent crowds in Australia. "Everyone has a Rock and Roll heart there. The adults encourage their kids to go for Rock and Roll… What a scene!"[20]

When reporter Green asks Nicol if there were any bad moments, Jimmie is careful to avoid his issues with manager Epstein and instead, describes a close call in Adelaide. "When we were being driven back to the hotel from the theatre in Adelaide, the driver just pulled out on to a dual carriageway [street] in front of a car that was coming fast. We all put our hands over our eyes and held on. We all thought it was our lot [fate]."[21] There was no accident, just a very close call.

Perhaps the most interesting memory that Nicol recalled from the Australian visit concerned one man in the crowd. "There was a blind man who waved his stick as we passed by. Imagine that—a blind man. Someone must have told him as we got there. It was fantastic, man, just great!"[22] Nicol had given an important interview to England's biggest entertainment paper the day after his triumphant return. He now hoped to become a regular fixture in the papers as a solo act, as frequently as he had been for thirteen days with The Beatles.

Another Drummer in the Hospital

On only his second day home, June 18, tragedy struck another drummer in another top group. Dave Clark, drummer of the Dave Clark Five band, went into the hospital with a diagnosis of a duodenal ulcer. It was déjà vu all over again. Another drummer's illness giving Jimmie Nicol another career break. At the time, the Dave Clark Five had the No. 8 hit in the American Top 100 "Cash Box" charts, and the No. 13 hit in Britain's POP 30 with the song, *Can't You See That She's Mine.* The band was due to begin a summer engagement at the Winter Gardens in Blackpool in two days. Once again, the newspapers trumpeted the good fortune falling into Nicol's lap, with the headline: "Dave ill—so Jimmy is top of the CROCKS again!"[23]

Dave Clark's band did not want to lose the lucrative summer season altogether, so in stepped Jimmie Nicol to the rescue. Only this time, it was not to sub as the Dave Clark Five drummer. This time, they wanted Jimmy Nicol's band and he accepted. There was only one small problem; Nicol had not yet reformed the Shubdubs! He was in a panic. He had two days to reform the Shubdubs, rehearse, and get to Blackpool by Saturday in order to cover for Dave Clark. Newspapers showed the frantic Nicol with two phones up to both ears. Just as life had been *before* The Beatles, nothing was now easier *after* The Beatles. On the contrary, now the audiences were beginning to make demands on him.

Jimmie's first call went out to his old pal, Johnny Harris over at Pye. Harris had hung up his instrument to become a full time studio arranger and producer. Harris recounts Jimmie's call. "You know what John?" said Nicol, "I'm going to put a band together; The Shubdubs. I've got a gig." Harris relates, "We are to sub for Dave Clark Five's band in Blackpool." Jimmie continued his pitch. "I want you in it John. Would you do the arrangement for me? And can you get your trumpet out of mothballs?"[24] Harris complained that he hadn't played trumpet in a long time on a regular basis. "I've got no lip left." Nicol was desperate and insistent, saying, "You've got to John, because I need you. Please!" Harris agreed to put his career on hold and began helping Nicol get his band together.[25]

Jimmie Nicol & the Shubdubs.
Photo Credit: Courtesy of Dave Quincy.

It was not easy pulling everyone together because several of the band members were spread all over the place. "I've been on the phone all day trying to re-form the group," said Nicol to the papers. "The boys are all over the country. One is on holiday in Spain."[26] When this news story broke, amazing efforts were made to help Nicol get hold of his band members. The Automobile Association and the Royal Automobile Club set up road checks throughout England trying to get messages to the Shubdubs. Nicol was buzzed by his new gig, new band, and the continued flurry of media attention about his every move. "I just can't find the words to describe how I feel about taking Dave's place. One week you're drumming away with the biggest group in the world. Then you hear they want you to take over from the second biggest group."[27] A photo of Dave Clark showed him sitting in the Harley Street Clinic, lying in bed with shirt open, thermometer in mouth, and being attended to by a pretty nurse.

Nicol had his musical director and trumpet player in place; and Harris helped round up other players since he worked with so many as an arranger at Pye. Jimmie easily got his flat mate, John Hodkinson, into the group for the lead vocal duties; and then he picked up tenor sax player, Dave Quincy. "I was an original member," says Quincy. "The first gig was a three week season at the Winter Gardens in Blackpool beginning 20 June 1964. Jimmy Nicol & the Shubdubs went to the top of the bill!"[28] Harris chipped in by rounding up Hammond organ player, Roger Coulam, and Bob Garner on bass guitar. Hastily, Jimmy Nicol & the Shubdubs were in place and ready to start rehearsing for their three-week starring role in Blackpool.

Nicol had received at least £500 for his tour with The Beatles; "But," says Nicol, "for an engagement of three weeks in Blackpool [subbing for the Dave Clark Five] I received £350 per week."[29] However, now Jimmie had to become a businessman as well. As bandleader, he had to hire and rehearse his Shubdubs. In order to secure the constant services of the Shubdubs, Nicol decided to put them under a contract retainer and give each of them about £26 per week. This left £220 pounds per week for Jimmie. He also expected record royalties to flow in from record sales. However, Nicol did not take into consideration the change in pay scale at the end of the 3-week gig subbing for the second or third most popular group in the country. He failed to calculate that future gigs would not pay him at the same rate as the Dave Clark Five session. In addition, there were other costs such as transportation, stage outfits, food, and housing on tour. Though an optimist, Jimmie could not predict how his records would do in the store. One thing Jimmie Nicol *was* counting on was that his great headline-grabbing fame would continue as it had for The Beatles.

As the band came together for a brief rehearsal on Friday, the day before their 3-week top-of-the-bill at Winter Gardens, Jimmie got some great news. The New Musical Express featured a banner from Pye Records declaring...

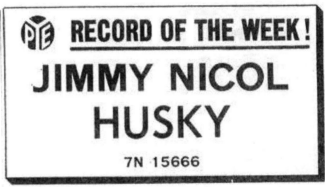

Husky: Record of the Week!

Husky's brash, hot Latin-Jazz-Rock number would serve as a perfect signature song for the new band in concert. Even America's *Billboard* magazine jumped on the bandwagon, proclaiming, "Pye has released an instrumental by drummer, Jimmy Nicol, 'Husky', who stood in for Ringo Starr during the Beatle's illness earlier this month."[30] The band rehearsed several songs for its upcoming series of shows, including *Humpty Dumpty, Night Train, Husky, Don't Come Back, Baby Please Don't Go*, and several songs Nicol had played in Georgie Fame's band. It did not take the group long to gel. They were veterans who had toured, recorded, and in some cases played together over the past 4-5 years. On Saturday morning, they set off for three weeks of concerts at Blackpool.

Winter Gardens, Blackpool, Top of the Bill

Winter Gardens is a large entertainment complex located in the center of the town Blackpool, Lancashire, England. The complex has several different entertainment venues, including a theater, ballroom, opera house, concert hall, and conference facilities. It officially opened in 1878, with the original intention to provide a place for all types of public entertainment.

Sax player, Dave Quincy, recalls the extended stay of the Shubdubs. "We went to the top of the bill. The show was of mixed variety with comedian Dick Emery and trumpeter Eddie Calvert, plus several other acts." Quincy recalls the reaction from the other acts to Jimmy Nicol's slotting on top after playing with The Beatles. "Most of the cast were bemused that we had come from nowhere to top of the bill, due to Jimmie's sudden leap to fame."[31]

Colin Green, Jimmie's old pal from Vince Eager's Quiet Three, was on the same bill supporting trumpet player, Eddie Calvert. He enjoyed the reunion with Jimmie, but indicated that other acts on the bill were not so bemused. "We did summer season in Blackpool. And Jimmie Nicol & the Shubdubs were brought in on the bill," recalls Green. "He was not very popular with some of the other musicians. There was a bit of an attitude thing from his having been with The Beatles. I'm not sure of everything that went on backstage, but there were a lot of bad feelings going on."[32] Green explained that it was unusual for a drummer to be a star headliner of his own band. Drummers typically sat quietly in the back of a band to provide support; but that was not Jimmie's style. Green continues, "There were questions like, 'What's he [a drummer] doing on the top of the bill on a variety show?' from the other acts. You get the picture. These guys had been working for years and years."[33] Of course, the same could be said for Jimmie Nicol.

Ready Steady Go!

From all accounts, the shows went down well with the fans who were excited to see a real live ex-Beatle performing during their summer vacation. One account read, "Report from Blackpool says Jimmy Nicol and Shubdubs proved most popular when they opened at the Winter Gardens on Saturday."[34] The demands from London continued as "Ex-Beatle" Jimmie was called back during the engagement to visit the ailing Dave Clark for a photo-op on June 25. The article described one drummer consoling another when Jimmie Nicol met Dave Clark in the Harley Street nursing home where he was resting his ulcer. Jimmie is pictured in his new, mod-sharp black suit and skinny tie. Dave is seen with white pajamas and still showing off his pecks with shirt open. The two are smiling with their Beatle haircuts as Jimmie poses with his arm around Dave. The report states, "Dave Clark, who collapsed last weekend suffering from a duodenal ulcer, expects to be out of the hospital at the end of next week. He will probably convalesce for a fortnight [2 weeks] before starting his summer season at Blackpool Winter Gardens. Meanwhile, Jimmy Nicol and the Shubdubs continue to deputize for the Dave Clark Five in Blackpool."[35]

That same day, Jimmie and his Shubdubs had been invited to appear on one of the most important musical television shows in England at the time, "Ready Steady Go!" Things were really looking up for the smartly dressed Mr. Nicol and his band. The show, which featured fashion as well as performances by the hottest bands of the day, had a popular following with the British sub culture referred to as the "Mods". The presenters for the show were Keith Fordyce and Cathy McGowan.

There was much chaos and commotion on the set as many bands readied themselves for the show. Top of the bill for this episode were The Rolling Stones, The Jynx, Millie Small, The Merseybeats, The McKinleys and, last but not least, Jimmie Nicol & the Shubdubs. Nicol walked around the studio, cool as a cucumber amid the chaos and preparations. This all seemed rather calm compared to what he had been through with The Beatles. However, now Jimmie Nicol was the center of attention. He felt and acted as if he had gained some sort of magic chalice from The Beatles that had forever sprinkled gold on him.

On set, Jimmie conducted an interview with Paul East of the *NME*, describing his reformed Shubdubs, which had a very forward-thinking, Jazz-Rock sound, far ahead of its time. "I like that kind of lineup," he said. Ever the humble one for an interview, Jimmie states, "I consider myself fortunate for being in a position where I can be a bandleader and put forward my own ideas. I have been influenced by Jazz players like Cannonball Adderley, and I'd like to study Jazz while playing it."[36] He then explains how he got the gig subbing for the Dave Clark Five in Blackpool. "I was just finishing lunch, around 3 pm, when the phone rang, and I was asked to go into town and talk about standing in for Dave Clark. Well, what can you say? I mean, it was great!"[37]

The interview is interrupted as Jimmie's song *Husky* starts to play over the loud speaker in the studio. This is a signal that it is soon time for his band to rehearse their lip sync version of the song for the show. Jimmie is surprised to hear his record and says, "I've not heard it properly yet. Let's go and hear it."[38] The reporter comments, "It seems that being a Beatle and a Dave Clark doesn't leave much time for anything else. Not even listening to your own records."[39] Jimmie was riding high and taking the media with him as he performed his song that night - taped - for broadcast the next day. Given his non-stop publicity and this TV show, he thought his dream of success, and even rivaling The Beatles, was coming true.

A Beatles Reunion (of sorts)

Another big surprise came in as the Shubdubs' Blackpool season was to end on July 11, 1964. Suddenly, Jimmie Nicol and his group were asked to appear on the same concert bill with The Beatles, the very next day. This news was welcomed by the band. According to singer John Hodkinson, "We got the gig of playing with The Beatles at Brighton because they promised that they would do one. I think it was a 'thank you' to Jimmie for helping them out."[40] Nicol says, "Brian put us on the same bill with The Beatles and the Fourmost one night at the Hippodrome Theatre in Brighton."[41] These statements from Nicol and his band mate seem to contradict the oft-debated argument that has persisted in Beatles books for years - stating Epstein did not like Nicol and tried to harm his solo career. Johnny Harris recalls, "I don't know how we got that Beatles show. We were in the first half and there were four acts

Concert Program for Beatles/ Shubdubs show.
Photo Credit: www.tracksimages.com.

in that. The Beatles, of course, closed out the second half of the show."[42] Most likely, the concert promoter was pleased with the idea to have the Shubdubs with Nicol playing on the same bill as The Beatles. Whether Epstein ever did try to blacklist Jimmie Nicol may never be known for sure, however, as time passed, Nicol himself came to believe it as reality.

The Beatles played an abbreviated summer seaside tour in 1964, performing at a small handful of resort venues. The first venue would be the Brighton show. From very early in the day when the musicians began to arrive for their soundchecks, the fans began to assemble in mass. News cameras captured the fans filling up the streets outside and around the venue. "That was amazing. They blocked up all the streets leading to the stage door because of all the fans and that."[43] Dave Quincy recalls, "The next gig after Blackpool was supporting The Beatles in Brighton 12 July 1964. Ringo did say hello to everyone in the Shubdubs when The Beatles arrived in the afternoon for the soundcheck." Quincy says, "After our soundcheck we went out of the stage door to find a pub. The crowd outside went crazy until they discovered we were not the 'Fab Four'!"[44]

The cameras of ITV News captured a dejected George Harrison arriving at the gig, unhappy because he had been involved in a small accident damaging his new Jaguar. Jimmie Nicol however, took notice of Harrison's car and reflected perhaps he too should own a Jaguar. After all, he was suddenly rolling in fame and money. Surely "Nicolmania" would continue and he could certainly afford to reward himself with a car commensurate with his new status.

Johnny Harris recalls watching The Beatles perform from the wings. "I went out to watch them perform because I had never seen them live."[45] He was surprised by the noise made by the fans:

> After the intermission, the MC stuck his head through the curtain to announce them and the fans just went crazy. With all the screaming, he just threw up his hands and said, 'And now, The Beatles.' All we heard was dun dun dun… They went into 'I Want To Hold Your Hand'. It was a complete utter waste of time.

There were 2000 in the theatre and about 10,000 outside who couldn't get in; all girls. And all they did was
scream all the way through the entire 35 minute set. I
never heard anything The Beatles said or sang. When
you've got 2000 girls screaming, and one takes a
breath, there are always others screaming. So there is
no stop. It is a complete, continuous jet engine.[46]

After the concert had concluded, The Beatles and all of the other artists were trapped for a
time, waiting for the fans to go home. Jimmie decided to take Johnny Harris over to The Beatles
dressing room and introduce his good friend to the Fab Four. "They're all four sitting there with
young ladies, sitting there with a portable TV set," recalls Harris. He asked each one to sign a book
for his wife's 15-year-old sister, which they gladly did. He continues, "I found George Harrison was
very responsive. Nice guy. John was watching TV. Paul and Ringo were quite nice."[47] Jimmie Nicol's
memory of the reunion was less than enthusiastic. "Backstage, we talked, but the winds had changed
since we last saw each other. They were pleasant."[48]

Harris watched in amazement that night as The Beatles dressed up as policemen and got inside a police car driving through the crowd of thousands. Meanwhile, a big limo was waiting out
front, standing there as a decoy. The plan worked for a few minutes until "some of the kids realized
it and they all started to scream and chase The Beatles in the police car."[49] Jimmie turned to Harris
and said, "Do you see that?" Harris had just witnessed the diversion for the protection and self-
preservation of the band. Nicol, continued, "That is the way it is everyday with them. It drove me
crazy. I couldn't live like that."[50] Left unspoken was that Nicol could not live without being the
center of attention either.

A Visit to Liverpool and a New Recording Session

After the Dave Clark Five gigs and The Beatles' show had ended, Nicol headed over to Liverpool to use his Beatles connection in their home town to push his single *Husky*. He began his publicity barrage in the editorial office of Bill Harry at the *Mersey Beat*. Harry described Jimmie as, "a
cheerful, good-natured drummer – who jumped into the headlines all over the world a very short
time ago."[51] Jimmie, who was in town to promote his current single, *Husky*, told the editor, "I last
visited Liverpool about five years ago, but that was with a Beat package show."[52]

Harry inquires as to what Jimmie thinks of all the publicity he has received since serving his
time on tour with The Beatles. Nicol replies, "It's great naturally. I don't think the publicity 'made'
me, but it certainly gave a push in the right direction. I tried to form a group before I temporarily
joined The Beatles and found it impossible to get work, but afterwards it was easy enough to form
a group. I have only two of the original Shubdubs with me now, however."[53] Nicol explains to the
Mersey Beat editor that his band would be heading back to London next week to record a new single.
"After that," said Jimmie, "we do a series of one night stands."[54]

Despite the publicity and record store promotions, Nicol's single, *Husky,* was not selling as
briskly as everyone had hoped, given the high profile publicity of TV's "Ready Steady Go!", subbing
for Dave Clark, and appearing alongside The Beatles. It was difficult to figure out the reason. People
were buying tickets to see Jimmie, and the newspapers still wanted to cover his weekly exploits.
One theory is the modern Jazz-Rock sounds of the Shubdubs were still a couple years ahead of their
time. Perhaps the fans of Jimmie Nicol expected to hear him performing simpler Rock songs; and
there was the fact that he was not the lead singer of his band. Regardless, Nicol was supremely optimistic and ready to try for another hit, this despite the fact of *Husky's* poor showing on the pop
charts.

Nicol was always curious to learn more about music and the business of making and selling
music. While back in London, he became more interested in the technical side of record making. "I

A ticket stub from The Shubdubs show at Torquay.
Photo Credit: Courtesy of Author.

want to go around the factories and see just how discs are manufactured," he said.[55]

A New Single

Given Nicol's continued publicity and notoriety, Pye Records suggested it was time for Jimmie and the Shubdubs to record another single. The group went down to Pye at Marble Arch and began work on two tracks during the week of July 20, 1964. All of the Shubdubs were present with the exception of tenor sax player, Dave Quincy. He says, "I left the band after The Beatles' gig as I had previously signed up to take a band on the Southampton-New York cruise run. I desperately wanted to get to New York for the music, and in those days you always had at least one free night in New York."[56]

The band found another sax player and proceeded to record two sides with Johnny Harris arranging. The songs were *Baby Please Don't Go* and a signature original b-side called *Shubdubery*. After three weeks of playing on stage together, the Shubdubs were musically tight. Bob Garner played bass, anchoring with Jimmie on drums. John Hodkinson handled the vocal duties, and Harris and Roger Coulam filled out the trumpet and organ parts respectively. *Baby Please Don't Go* was a Blues number that had first been recorded by Big Joe Williams in 1935. It was one of a group of songs that were considered part of the early black musical work ethic from the dawn of the twentieth century. Over the years it had become a Rock and Blues standard, because so many artists had chosen to record it over the years. More importantly, it needed to climb the pop charts for Jimmie Nicol & the Shubdubs to succeed. Pye Records had only signed Jimmie Nicol as a solo artist for a three-single (six-song) deal. In baseball parlance, it was 'three strikes and you're out'. *Husky* and *Humpty Dumpty* had not charted for Pye; so this single was a make-or-break. Nicol was supremely confident in the selection of the A-side; thinking, this new single would break through for them.

However, the young drummer-turned bandleader was unaware that another popular group was across town at rival Decca Records, recording the exact same song for a fall release. The deck was stacked in favor of a band called "Them". Them had a young vocalist named Van Morrison who could really sing the song with passion. Additionally, the flip side of Morrison's single was another soon-to-be popular song called, "Gloria". The ace-in-the-hole for Van Morrison was an unknown session guitar slinger playing on *Baby Please Don't Go* - Jimmy Page, who would go on to found Led Zeppelin.

At the beginning of August, Nicol & the Shubdubs went out for a series of one night stands. Sax player, Dave Quincy, was replaced

Jimmie Nicol at Liverpool's Cavern Club.

by tenor saxophone great Red Price. Price was a brilliant musician who had worked alongside Jimmie on the Larry Parnes' tour with Nicol and his 13-piece New Orleans Trad Rock group. He also had made a name for himself in the Ted Heath Big Band. The group kicked off its series of shows for The Royal Air Forces Association at the Town Hall in Torquay. The Shubdubs were headliners, supported by The Telstars and The Hunters. It wasn't a Beatles' gig, but it would help pay the bills. The band earned a handsome £150 on this night. On August 8, Nicol and his band were back in Liverpool to plug *Husky* at the Singers Record Salon at 1 p.m., followed by a headlining show at The Beatles' old stomping ground, The Cavern Club. These one-nighters were well received by the fans.

In late August, Nicol went out and bought himself a Jaguar. He still needed to earn £200-300 per week to really afford the car. However, his newfound public-figure status, rather than fiscal responsibility, dictated this purchase. He also had to continue paying his band under contract to keep them together. Fortunately, there were some one-nighters in and around London to pay the bills until the next single and the next big tour. Despite his steady work and optimism, things were not going well at home. Nicol and his wife were arguing frequently over issues such as: Jimmie's extended absences, extravagant spending on himself; and even the female admirers who now found Nicol to be quite extraordinary after his Beatles' gig. Pat was frustrated that Jimmie was home very little and not spending much time with his family. Nicol had clearly changed. He was a world-renowned drummer and now had a world-renowned ego to match. Jimmie had the additional stress of being a band-leader, which likened him to a small business owner. As such, he had the pressures of organizing and funding the band's activities which left little time for domestic duties. As a result, friction in the home continued to mount.

In September, Jimmie received 5,000 letters from mostly female admirers in Australia. Nicol was deeply moved by the continued support of the fans Down Under. Pat was likely unimpressed, feeling like she was in an impossible position to compete. The letters merely fed Nicol's ego that he was the "next big thing". Nicol phoned up Adelaide DJ, Bob Francis, to thank the many fans who had sent him the letters. He made a pledge to return to Australia in 1965. "I will possibly come sometime next year," he told Francis.[57] It was a promise he was confident of fulfilling.

Ultimately, the domestic bliss of pre-Beatles' days could not be repaired. Pat took their son, Howie, and divorce proceedings were filed with the court. Nicol moved out of his flat and back in with his mother. He was still exceedingly optimistic about his musical future, despite his domestic foibles. He had allowed his career ambitions to take precedent over his family life. Jimmie was still driven to succeed. However, he was beginning to realize achieving his goal - reaching the top of the musical world - would not be without sacrifice.

Though the pending divorce was kept out of the newspapers, Nicol could not keep the news of his erratic Jaguar driving a secret. In the September 2nd issue of the *Daily Mirror*, the headline read, "BEATLE NO 5 ACCUSED". The story explained that not one, not two, not three, but "Summonses alleging four motoring offenses [of excessive speeding] have been issued against drummer Jimmy Nicol of the Broadway, Barnes, Surrey, who took over in the Beatles when Ringo Starr was ill."[58] Nicol wore this notoriety like a badge of honor. It showed his rebellious, free-spirited character and told readers he was successful, driving his expensive sports car around town. What he failed to observe in the news story, was that he was no longer on the front pages. He had slipped to page 18.

Dave Quincy rejoined the band in September. He says, "The band settled into the one-night stand circuit in the UK and also looked forward to a short tour of Denmark in November 1964."[59] October looked promising for the Shubdubs as Larry Parnes and the George Cooper Organizations announced a major 35-night tour for that month. The Hollies, Millie, the Applejacks, Lulu and the Luvers were all to star along with Jimmie Nicol & the Shubdubs. The one-nighters were spread all throughout England, starting at the Finsbury Park Astoria on Saturday, October 17.[60]

Just in time for the UK tour, Pye released the brand new Jimmie Nicol & The Shubdubs single, *Baby Please Don't Go,* backed with *Shubdubery*. At the same time, rival Decca released its A-side, *Baby Please Don't Go* backed with *Gloria* as the new single by Van Morison's group, Them. The Shubdubs got two new songs to promote at its shows. Them got its first hit, reaching the Top 10 on the UK Singles Chart. Van Morrison summed up his band's winning formula. "What made our record, *[Baby] Please Don't Go*, was the plugging wasn't it? Somebody could record the most commercial pop record of all time, but if it didn't get the plugging, it never would make it. We were just lucky."[61] Jimmie Nicol was the unlucky one. The Shubdubs had been outgunned in the studio, on the radio, and in the "plugging" department. However, Nicol's group soldiered on with their live act.

Unfortunately for Nicol, Pye would drop him from their roster of signed artists by the end of the year.

Nicol autographed ticket from Club Dynamite.
Photo Credit: Courtesy of Jorgen Billing.

The Fifth Beatle's Return to Denmark

The tour of England was fairly uneventful for Jimmie & the Shubdubs; however, the forthcoming tour of Denmark would provide another significant and fateful encounter for Nicol. Many newspapers trumpeted the return of "The Fifth Beatle to Denmark". Fans wanted to see the man who had substituted for Ringo Starr a few months earlier with The Beatles. Now they could see Jimmie and his group in more intimate settings. The difference this time, however, was the Shubdubs were playing a different style of music from The Beatles, Jazz and Rhythm & Blues, instead of Rock and Roll.

Club Dynamite at the Hotel Stevns in Heddinge, Denmark, presented the first show of the Shubdubs on October 31, 1964. Club Dynamite was a private group of young people who worked together to bring new live music to their town. Securing Jimmie Nicol was a big coup for the youths. One news article previewed Jimmie Nicol as, "Famous Without The Beatles". Based upon its brief interview with Jimmie, the paper told its readers that *Husky* had "become one of the autumn's big sales numbers"; and pointed out that it had been recorded before The Beatles' temporary position and not, as many believe, after the fact. Nicol also volunteered that he was divorced with a 5-year old son and had a Jaguar, which the paper describes as: "The last, of the 4-wheeler category."[62] The warm up band was a local group called The Beatmakers. The Shubdubs were treated like royalty and very well-received for its performance.

From Heddinge, the group traveled to Copenhagen for a one-week stay. Kaj Paustian, the owner of a dance club called Le Caroussel in Atlantic Palace, had signed the band to play from November 1 - 6. The newspapers in Copenhagen trumpeted the arrival of "The Fifth Beatle to Denmark", and in reviewing the show, described Jimmy Nicol & the Shubdubs as a "very distinctive crew, among others, with saxophone, trumpet, organ and harmonica"[63] The shows were getting smaller in attendance. The big money that had been flowing in during the summer and autumn was not keeping up with the expenses of the band or Jimmie's domestic needs.

On October 6, 1964, a Swedish Rock ensemble came to Copenhagen to participate in a big musical event called "Pop I Top" (top of the pops) at the Falkonercenter. The Shubdubs would play along with Jerry Williams; The Violents; The Sharks; The Rocking Ghosts; The Black Devils; The Beethovens; Melvis & His Gentlemen; and The Defenders. It was to be a three-hour, rocking extravaganza. Backstage, Jimmie Nicol got the chance to chat with the clever instrumental beat group from Sweden. He became friends with guitarist, Bjorn Thelin. At the time, it seemed like just another backstage musician friendship, yet it was one that would ultimately have life-saving implications for Nicol. He would remember the band's name and its members would remember his. The group was called The Spotnicks.

The "Snobdubs" appear at the "Joker's Club" –Naestved, Denmark. Photo Credit: Jorgen Billing.

The Spotnicks took over for Jimmy Nicol & the Shubdubs in Le Caroussel on November 7, 1964. Jimmie had the opportunity to watch the mostly instrumental Rock band play, and it had the opportunity to watch the drummer who had recently played with the one and only Beatles. Nicol says of the fortuitous meeting, "On one of our last gigs we played in Copenhagen in 1964, which is where I met Bjorn Thelin from The Spotnicks. Bjorn and the others in the band thought I played good and we became good friends. I knew from the past who they were. The first time I heard them, they were on the radio with their "Orange Blossom Special" which was on the Top 30 in 1963"[64] Although, he could not possibly know it at the time, this new friendship would have far-reaching implications in the professional and personal life of Nicol in a future that posed many problems and issues ahead.

The tour of Denmark had stops in Naestved, Frederiksberg, Holte, Frederiksvaerk, and Ballerup, concluding on November 8. While in Naestved the band played a show at the "Joker's Club", located inside of the Hotel Axelhus. The ad promoting the show billed the group as, "The 5th Beatle Jimmy Nicol and the *Snobdubs* along with The Flames." The Shubdubs saw the unfortunate spelling error on the hotel advert promoting their show, but it was too late to change the poster. The next day, the group headed back to England for more one-night stands in December.

The End of the Shubdubs

"The one night stands in the UK continued into December, 1964", says Dave Quincy.[65] The shows were held in much smaller venues, such as the Plaza Dance & Social Club on Rookery Road in Handsworth, Birmingham; and the gigs were now few and far between. For Nicol and his group, the publicity of the "5th Beatle" in England had disappeared. Their new single *Baby Please Don't Go* failed to enter the pop charts, although their competitor, Them, had reached the Top 10 with its version of the song. The one-nighters were getting less frequent with smaller pay. Quincy recalls, "I think the band folded on December 26, 1964 after a gig in Modeford, Dorset."[66] Although he had lost his recording contract with Pye, Jimmie Nicol was hopeful that a new tour would materialize at the start of 1965, but trumpet player, Johnny Harris was not willing to wait around and lose his position as an up-and-coming arranger at Pye. He knew it was the end of the road for the Shubdubs:

> The Shubdubs' songs did not take off up the charts. Jimmie wasn't getting any work from it. The fans didn't breakthrough for him. He had been the Fifth Beatle, but so what.The gloss had worn off. Maybe they didn't like the music. I don't know. It just didn't work out. It was fine for me, but I was sorry for Jimmie. The Shubdubs disbanded. Jimmie said to me, 'If we can get a tour, we can go on the road.' I said, 'Jim, no. I got off the road many years ago. I can't do this anymore.' Jimmie said, 'I understand.' He could have gotten someone to replace me, but I don't think the band did anymore workafter that.[67]

For Nicol, the economics of keeping the Shubdubs together became an impossibility. He says, "In December, I played in bars for £10 per week, while by contract I had to pay my musicians, the Shubdubs £130 per week! I borrowed everywhere because I believed that one day there would be a turning point."[68] The time had come to retire his band that had started out with so much promise upon his return from Australia with The Beatles. Vocalist John Hodkinson says, "There were not many gigs for our band anymore. It was all crumbling really. Jimmie, the Shubdubs and I kind of all drifted apart really."[69] Nicol refused to fold; despite falling victim to his own delusions of grandeur. As the money ran out, his band

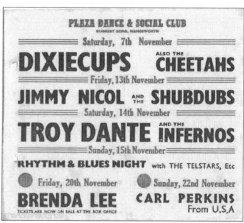

Handbill advertising one of the last Shubdubs' shows.
Photo Credit: Courtesy of Author.

members had to find paying gigs and they left him. Nicol felt betrayed and abandoned by his friends.

In his mind, Jimmie looked for someone to blame. He had seen Larry Parnes blacklist his friend Vince Eager in 1960. Now he believed that Beatles' manager Brian Epstein had blacklisted him and his band. They had clearly butted heads at the end of Nicol's tour with The Beatles. Now, Nicol's records had all stiffed and the publicity and gigs had all dried up. To Jimmie Nicol, there could be no other explanation. There seems to be little evidence to support his belief. In fact, long time Beatles' employee (at Epstein's NEMS Company and later The Beatles Apple Corps Ltd) Tony Bramwell disputes the possibility. "He [Brian] most certainly did not blacklist Nicol! Brian would not blacklist anyone. Why should he? Jimmie was a good lad! He had done a good job for The Beatles!"[70] But there was no changing Nicol's mind…

During December, The Spotnicks came to London for their tour of England. Nicol and the members of The Spotnicks got together again and began to form a long-distance friendship, one that would foreshadow better days ahead. Jimmie did not realize how good a friend he had made with Bjorn Thelin from The Spotnicks. Knowing that the Shubdubs were in demise, Nicol jokingly asked Bjorn whether the Spotnicks could get him a job in Sweden. Bjorn said he would see what he could do.

Though many believe Jimmie Nicol quit the music industry and vanished at this point in late 1964, nothing could be further from the truth. Nicol decided after the New Year he would mount yet another attempt at rivaling The Beatles and the other beat bands of the day. And, as always, he would do it on his own terms.

Chapter Fifteen

The Sound of Jimmy Nicol

January, 1965, London

Jimmie Nicol never imagined that thirteen days with The Beatles would change his life. But everything had changed. He had let his optimism and fame get the better of him. Now the fans and media had faded, his wife and son were estranged, and he had lost his record deal at Pye. Most all of the money earned with The Beatles and Dave Clark Five gigs had vanished like his fleeting fame, and now his band the Shubdubs had drifted away.

At this point, Nicol still could have resumed his role as reliable session musician, and he might have latched onto another group in need of a beat drummer, but he no longer wanted to record or play the musical ideas of others. He wanted to pursue his own music and his own recordings with a group of his own creation. He longed for the halo of celebrity that crowned him in the summer of 1964. Yet he wanted fame to come from *his* music, rather than his association as the "Fifth Beatle". He was still willing to risk everything to reach this goal. Even if he had to borrow money to achieve his dream, Jimmie Nicol believed he could make it to the top.

In January of 1965, Nicol was still represented by agents at The Roy Tempest Organisation Ltd. (R.T.O.) who were still attempting to book live shows for him. The organization, which was billed as "Europe's Largest Band Agency", introduced its "Top Twenty" groups for 1965 in the London music press. Jimmy Nicol and the Shubdubs on Pye Records was listed as the 7th best group on its roster. Apparently no one at Roy Tempest had received the memo that the Shubdubs had broken up and that Pye had dropped Nicol. Nevertheless, R.T.O. was ready and willing to help get Jimmie live shows once he got going again.

Nicol wanted to put another band together and make another attempt at fame on his own terms. He decided to hire a manager. He could not do it all and be a bandleader; drummer; PR "flack"; and manager at the same time. It was simply too difficult. He needed someone who knew the business side and had connections in the industry to get him a record deal, get him on the charts, get him in the papers again, and fill the concert halls. He settled on Tommy Sanderson, a former piano player turned music manager.

Tommy Sanderson was a popular pianist in the late 1950s and 1960s. He gained fame as a weekly guest on BBC Radio One's "Saturday Club - Light Programme". He often would appear with fellow session players under the moniker, "Tommy Sanderson and The Sandmen". Sanderson was among the elite London session players who could play Rock and Roll. "Tommy was a lovely man and a far better pianist and composer than he was given credit for," recalls Flamingo Club owner Jeffrey Kruger, MBE.[1]

In the early 1960s, Sanderson began expanding his career on radio and in the studios as a recording session pianist and composer. He began to sign up the cream of the musical crop that he met at BBC's "Saturday Club" and began to manage their careers. In the early 1960s he took on Lulu and The Hollies. Graham Nash of The Hollies recalls, "Tommy was very personable. When E.M.I. started our recording career, Ron Richards [a producer] knew that he had to get rid of our 'northern manager' to get control of the situation and the money end of the business… He introduced us to his friend Tommy Sanderson with whom, I believe, he had a prior relationship."[2] Continuing, Nash says that, "He obviously knew 'the business' and we definitely needed sage advice…"[3]

By early 1965, The Hollies had turned to another manager, and Sanderson was free to take on the "Fifth Beatle". Nicol was in great need of someone who knew "the business" and could take care of the "money end" of things. Strangely, Sanderson's first move was to have Jimmie get a haircut to announce their new partnership to the press. Dubbed the "seventy-two minute haircut", "the new manager of the boy who has become known as the fifth Beatle nodded towards the dark mane that straddled his new charge's shoulders and said, 'he'll have to have that off for a start.'"[4] The column commented that Jimmie's hair had grown out in "Rolling Stones" style for seven months, "But his fame didn't keep pace." Nicol explains that being a Beatle did not help other than to gain publicity, and it did nothing to help his Shubdubs crash the record charts.[5]

Tommy Sanderson was very encouraging, stating that, with the New Year, there would be great potential for Jimmie Nicol. Watching the lengthy haircut he exclaims, "I think this boy's got it."[6] With his tresses on the barber shop floor, and sporting a new "tulip-topped" cut, Jimmie and his new manager headed out to the rehearsal studios where a new band awaited to rehearse music for the New Year.

His manager suggested a formula designed for success. All Nicol had to do was to start his own band, rehearse, and invest his money in new equipment. Sanderson would do the rest. Jimmie followed his manager's direction. "I believed in my manager," says Nicol. "I started my own group, and felt completely confident that he would keep his promise and provide jobs for us. I signed a contract."[7] And Nicol began to dream of a place at the Top of the Pops.

While Tommy Sanderson tried to negotiate a new record deal for his "Fifth Beatle", Jimmie formed a new band. Only one Shubdub remained in this new band, John Hodkinson, who sang under the stage name of Tony Allen. "I moved out of Jimmie's house around the end of '64," says Hodkinson. "But I helped him out with his new band in early 1965."[8] This time, the new band would carry only the name of its star. The band was called, "The Sound of Jimmy Nicol".

The line up for The Sound of Jimmy Nicol included: Hodkinson (aka: Tony Allen) on guitar, vocals and percussion; Roger Cook on organ, piano and vibraphone; Roger Sutton on bass guitar; Bob Downes on tenor sax and flute; Grant Cross on tenor, alto sax, and flute; and of course, Jimmie on drums.

A New Record Deal

In mid-January, Jimmie's manager brought good news. Jimmie was signed to a new record deal with Decca Records. As an old established label, it boasted a historic roster of musical giants including Bing Crosby; Al Jolson; Louis Armstrong; Count Basie; The Andrew Sisters; Jimmy Dorsey; and many more. It was no small irony that the company had turned down The Beatles in 1962. Now, it was not taking any chances. Decca wanted to sign the drummer and bandleader, known in the news as the "Fifth Beatle".

The sessions were to be produced by Ken Jones, whose company Marquis Entertainment had a lease agreement with Decca to provide record production, engineering, mixing, management and publishing services. Jones recorded at Decca's West Hampstead, London studios. He had begun his career with numerous appearances on the BBC radio show "Saturday Club" in the late 1950s and early 60s as leader of the "Ken Jones Five". As a BBC regular, Jones was a long-time associate of Tommy Sanderson. It is likely that Jones talked to Decca to obtain a record deal for Sanderson's "Beatle". Unfortunately for Nicol, the deal was no longer for 3 singles. The Sound of Jimmy Nicol would have only one chance to make the charts in order to be offered an option to make more records.

Ken Jones had moved into record production in the early 1960s, when his own orchestra failed to chart. He had had great success producing hits for The Zombies in 1964, and he was one of the current "hot" Decca producers of the day. Jones used Gus Dudgeon as his engineer on the Nicol sessions. Gus had begun his career at Decca's Olympic Studios as a tea boy and tape jockey. He was eventually promoted to the position of sound engineer. He had several early pop recording successes engineering sessions for Bruce Channel and The Zombies, as well as auditioning Tom Jones and The Rolling Stones. With consolidation in the business, Dudgeon moved over to the West Hempstead Decca studios to work with Jones.

Nicol borrowed money from everyone he knew to finance and outfit his new group with the proper equipment. He also sold some of his older equipment to help with finances. His optimism again outweighed any fiscal considerations. The group would musically mirror that of Georgie Fame & the Blue Flames in taste and style. Sanderson put Jimmie's buying spree in the newspaper. The column stated that Nicol "could tell Economic Minister George Brown a few things about rising prices."[9] On January 17, The Sound of Jimmy Nicol began recording its new music. The paper reports, "And with the return to popularity of saxophones and the organ, it has cost him over £3,000 to equip the seven-man line up."[10] In today's money, this was the equivalent of spending £12,000 (or $19,500). It was an extraordinary amount of risk, but nevertheless, an amount Nicol was willing to gamble on his career. Jimmie cavalierly quips to the newspapers, "I nearly settled for a hydrodaktulopsycharmonica. [An old music hall instrument; drinking glasses played like a xylophone]"[11]

The band entered the studio with high expectations. Nicol surmised, if Ken Jones could place The Zombies high in the charts with a hit, certainly he could do the same for The Sound of Jimmy Nicol. The first song was *Sweet Clementine*, a traditional song that many children sing with the familiar chorus of "Oh my darling, Oh my darling, Oh my darling Clementine." Only this version would be arranged by Nicol and his pal, Roger Coulam, to sound more sophisticated and jazzy with a new melody. *Sweet Clementine* features an opening riff with cool 1960s-era organ played by Roger Cook and a repetitive heavy swinging tom-tom beat by Nicol. The vocals find Tony Allen crooning, "Oh my darling/ Oh my darling/ Oh my darling Clementine/ She's lost and gone forever/ Dreadful sorry my Clementine." At this point, cymbals crash to usher in the combined saxophone and organ solo. The song climaxes with all of the instruments and vocals blaring, but it just doesn't have the magic of a Top Ten hit. Ironically, it was chosen as the A-side of the forthcoming single.

The Sound of Jimmy Nicol's single "Clementine".
Photo Credit: Courtesy of Author.

Producer Jones focused on creating a distinctive, catchy master that was pleasing to the ears - with the potential of becoming a radio hit. He and his engineer were fast-paced with their production. Jones liked to add additional drum parts to thicken the sound, something that Nicol no doubt appreciated, as his performance was highlighted up front in the mix.

Dudgeon engineered the three-hour session. All three songs were to be completed in this time frame. "I only did four-track sessions at Decca," says Gus. "What I was used to, was committing to a balance at that particular point, and once that balance was done you were buggered on the mix, if you hadn't got the majority of it right in the first place. You had the whole rhythm section on one track, the vocal on another, and whatever solos on the other tracks."[12]

Bim Bam was the next song to be recorded. It is a rollicking little number with a driving R & B feel that draws on the energy of Little Richard and Booker T & the MGs. The rocking song is full of swagger in the band's tight delivery. However, it fails to deliver on the thin lyrical content, sung by vocalist Tony Allen who has nothing really sexy to work with. Perhaps its biggest failing was the lack of any real sexual innuendo at a time when Rock and Roll was intriguing its teen audiences with some not-so-subtle, risqué lyrics.[13] *Bim Bam* was destined to be a B-side. Decca described it to the press as, "A solid rocker, with plenty of drum pyrotechnics from Jimmy, vocal by Tony Allen."[14]

On the third song, *Roaring Blue* (an alternate b-side composed by producer Ken Jones), Dudgeon's sound balance levels were perfect. Every instrument is clear, and Jimmie's drumming is right up front on the mix. The track is a down and dirty soul instrumental, with some roadhouse-tested R&B riffs and a lyrical call-and-response melody with a down-home gospel vibe. The song features an "Amen" cadence that sounds like it was dictated by Jimmie at the song's finale. There is rawness to this recording that suggests it was part of a multi-take session. There may have been tighter tracks, but none with the spirit and emotion of this one. The track should have been chosen as the A-side because it has "hit" written all over it, but alas, Decca and Nicol preferred his lilting arrangement of *Sweet Clementine*.

Jones and Dudgeon spent about an hour recording each song. Dudgeon explains, "There was a mixing stage, but you'd probably only spend half an hour or so mixing the four-track down."[15] In no time at all, the songs were finished and ready for a trip to the pressing plant, and hopefully a quick climb up the record charts for The Sound of Jimmy Nicol.

In February, The Sound of Jimmy Nicol set out on a series of one-night stands around the United Kingdom, set up by The Roy Tempest Organisation Ltd. The shows were still billed as Jimmy Nicol & the Shubdubs, despite the signing at Decca under a new band name. The band appeared at small venues such as The Assembly Rooms, a new venue for modern dancing that was located in Buckie, Bannffshire, Scotland. It was a long way to travel on February 4, 1965, to play another small club, but Jimmie felt good about his new band and its forthcoming single. This time, he thought, he couldn't miss.

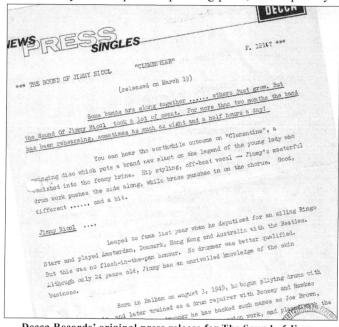

Decca Records' original press release for The Sound of Jimmy Nicol's new single "Clementine". Photo Credit: Courtesy of Author.

The New Single Is Released

The day had finally come for the big new release. The Decca Press Release trumpeted The Sound of Jimmy Nicol to the newspapers: "Some bands are slung together….. Others just grow. But The Sound of Jimmy Nicol took a lot of sweat. For more than two months the band has been rehearsing, sometimes as much as eight and a half hours a day!"[16]

The press release raves about the new track *Clementine,* in hopes the journalists will print the description verbatim: "You can hear the worthwhile outcome on 'Clementine', a swinging disc which puts a brand new slant on the legend of the young lady who vanished into the foamy brine. Hip styling, off-beat vocal – Jimmy's masterful drum work pushes the side along, while brass punches in on the chorus. Good, different….And a hit."[17]

The *Daily Mirror* announced the news, "Drumming ex-Beatle Jimmy Nicol swings in with an updated version of 'Clementine' for his Decca debut. Tony Allen supplies the voice for this outfit that is now known as The Sound of Jimmy Nicol."[18] The next day in the *New Musical Express,*

Nicol's new song was duly announced along with new singles by Billie Davis, the Applejacks, Bobby Rydell, The Crickets and Helen Shapiro.[19] Surely there was room high up on the charts - with this competition - for Nicol to finally break through. He didn't have to compete with The Beatles, The Rolling Stones, The Zombies, The Kinks, or any of the other big names during this particular week.

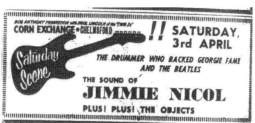
The Sound of Jimmy Nicol appears at the Corn Exchange.

Tommy Sanderson set about helping to plan more one-night stands. He also needed to get them some big national radio exposure. He would speak to his old buddies at the BBC's "Saturday Club" to arrange an appearance for the new group to showcase its debut single.

On April 2, the *Essex Chronicle* heralded the arrival of "The Drummer Who Backed Georgie Fame and The Beatles, The Sound of Jimmie Nicol, Plus! Plus! The Objects." The show took place at the Corn Exchange in Chelmsford on April 3. The band played its three new songs - *Sweet Clementine*; *Roaring Blue*; and *Bim Bam*, as well as several of the old Shubdubs songs including *Humpty Dumpty*, *Night Train* and others. The small, but enthusiastic crowd, appreciated the show at its Saturday scene. Though the club had an agricultural name, it was anything but a corny venue. It was a very important concert venue. Georgie Fame had preceded Nicol there the previous month, and Spencer Davis and the Yardbirds would play the following month. Though the crowd enjoyed the show, Nicol could not help but be disappointed that the press did not interview him or review the show.

During one of the performances in April, George Harrison came in with a friend to watch The Sound of Jimmy Nicol. In a gesture of goodwill and friendship, Harrison sent a drink over to Nicol onstage between sets. "He sent the waiter up with a drink, but I declined the offer," says Nicol.[20] Unfortunately, Jimmie misconstrued this gesture in a negative light. He explained his position, "I do have my self respect. I will not be bought by anyone. Of course, he [George] was trying to make up for how things turned out…We all know what happened, and he… you see, no words have to be spoken."[21] Although he did not use the words, Nicol again, seemed to be referring to his theory of "blacklisting" at the hands of Brian Epstein, and his belief that he should have permanently taken the place of Beatles' drummer Ringo Starr.

Sanderson came through on his promise to deliver The Sound of Jimmy Nicol to a national audience to promote the new single. His old friends at BBC's "Saturday Club" would provide the stage. Nicol and his band traveled to the BBC's Studio One at Aeolian Hall in London to record a live, in-the-studio version of their single, *Sweet Clementine*.

"Saturday Club" was familiar to Nicol, having performed on the show in his early days with the Oscar Rabin Band. The show had helped The Beatles spread their reputation from Liverpool to the rest of England. Nicol surmised that it was now his turn to reach a much larger audience with his swinging sound. Brian Matthew served as the show's host for Episode No. 340 that would air on Saturday April 10, 1965. The show had an impressive lineup of guests including Adam Faith; Freddie & The Dreamers; Martha & The Vandellas; The Animals; The Roulettes; The Silkie (a Brian Epstein group); The Sound of Jimmy Nicol; and Nicol's manager, Tommy Sanderson & His Orchestra. Unfortunately, no tapes of this show exist and the master tape was wiped. As soon as *Clementine* aired and floated through listeners' radio speakers, it was gone, along with any hope for big sales and a chart-topping hit.

Hitting Rock Bottom

All of Sanderson's managerial moves - designed to make Jimmie a star and a hit on the charts - ultimately failed. In the end, the arbiters of 1965 contemporary taste, the fans, decided to reject the single. Only a handful of people bought the disc; and once again, Nicol's song failed to chart at all. By the end of April, Decca Records dropped The Sound of Jimmy Nicol from their artist roster. Rock and Roll music may have been changing faster than Jimmie could keep up by 1965, but not for lack of trying or having genuine talent. His drumming and his band never sounded better.

With no gigs planned, no more singles, and no money coming in, The Sound of Jimmy Nicol and its manager, Tommy Sanderson, broke up and went away, leaving Jimmie to himself. To Nicol, it was déjà vu… again.

Neither Jimmie nor his manager understood that, as time passed, people would forget Ringo Starr had ever been sick and had a deputy. As people forgot Jimmie was the "Fifth Beatle", the audiences grew smaller and the breaks between jobs got longer. In total, he had invested up to £4,000

Jimmie Nicol living with his mom – bankrupt, divorced, and unemployed.
Photo Credit: Jimmy Nicol, Image #00164958 © Mirrorpix.

in new equipment and band expenses. It was all the money he had and had borrowed. Wages that should have been used to pay his band evaporated, and money that could have been used to feed and clothe his family, was gone. The characteristically optimistic drummer was finally ready to admit failure at last.

He had almost become a star, but he had just missed the target. He had made Beatles-sized wages, but now he was broke. He had made Beatle-sized headlines, but now he was forgotten. Instead of blaming himself for the failure, Jimmie placed the blame on the life-changing moment when Brian Epstein and The Beatles had hired him. "Standing in for Ringo was the worst thing that ever happened to me. Up to then I was feeling quite happy turning over 30 to 40 pounds a week. I didn't realize that it would change my whole life."[22] He had believed what people in the industry told him: "Everyone in show business said, I couldn't miss. I was the hottest name there was." But after the headlines died, he said, "I began dying too. No one wanted to know me anymore."[23]

Unfortunately, the London headlines had one final news story to report for Jimmie Nicol on April 30, 1965: "The Rise And The Fall Of The Fifth Beatle." It reported that, "Nicol's trail for stardom ended –at London Bankruptcy Court. His debts have spiraled to £4,066 pounds. And Jimmy has only 50 pounds to meet them."[24] Finally, Jimmie had admitted his financial crash as he stated,

"The only honest way out was to go bankrupt and admit I failed."[25] When asked about his future plans, a dejected Nicol shook his head and replied, "The future? Nothing; there's nothing for me now."[26] When asked for his reaction, a shocked Ringo Starr replied, "I didn't think he could fail. No one did."[27]

For Nicol, "facing the music" meant getting away from music and re-evaluating his life. Meanwhile, his contemporaries were doing quite well for themselves. Georgie Fame and the Blue Flames were appearing on Britain's "Top Gear" TV show and off to the US for TV appearances on "Shindig" and "Hullabaloo". As Nicol closed out his bankruptcy, The Beatles were perched atop the *NME* Top Thirty charts with the Number One song, *Ticket To Ride*; a song that likely reminded Jimmie of his brief ride with The Beatles only one year earlier. How could 10 months make such a difference? Back in June of 1964, he was on top of the world. Jimmie had family, friends and money.

Nicol felt like a semi-conscious boxer, lying dazed on the mat with the referee counting out, "7, 8, 9…" He had won – and relished – the heavy-weight title for thirteen glorious days as a bona fide Beatle, but he had not protected it; and now he was nearly down for the count, reeling from the punches of betrayal, unemployment, bankruptcy, divorce, and Epstein's alleged blacklisting. He wondered to himself if he could ever again rise up off the canvas, regain his stature, and reverse this brutal run of misfortune.

Peter & Gordon

On May 5, 1965 the papers announced, "The Fifth Beatle – Job Hunting". Paul McCartney turned to page 5 of the *Daily Mirror* that day to read that, Jimmy Nicol, the Fifth Beatle had "signed on at the labour exchange". This was Britain's government workforce program intended to help the unemployed find work. Nicol reported, "I was offered a job with the Bournemouth Symphony Orchestra, but I refused – it was a bit much."[28] The press had caught up to him at another court house where his ex-wife had cited him for being £30 in maintenance arrears. McCartney felt badly about Jimmie's situation and decided to help out, although in an anonymous fashion.

As it happened, another group was rising up the charts - Peter & Gordon, entering at Number Nine with their cover of Buddy Holly's, *True Love Ways*. The duo was about to tour England for a brief run of one-nighters. At the time, Paul McCartney was dating Jane Asher. Her brother Peter Asher was one-half of the famous duo, Peter & Gordon. Behind the scenes, Paul called up Peter and asked if they might need a drummer for their upcoming shows around London. Asher readily agreed to hire Nicol. The late Gordon Waller recalled, "It was 1965 that Jimmie Nicol did a tour in England with us. We first got to hear of him through Paul McCartney who told us he was great so we tried him."[29] Old friend and vocalist, John Hodkinson recounts, "He got a short gig with Peter & Gordon. He'd always get little gigs here and there. I sort of lost track of what Jimmie was doing after that. He sort of drifted away."[30]

Many referred to the duo of Peter & Gordon as "the Everly Brothers" of Britain. They were great harmonizers and strummed acoustic guitars while recording a string of chart-topping hits in the middle 1960s. Peter's friendship with his sister's boyfriend, Paul McCartney, led to a musical relationship that benefited the duo. Lennon and McCartney penned several hits for the two artists including *World Without Love; Nobody I Know; I Don't Want To See You Again;* and *Woman* (which is credited to Bernard Web, aka Paul McCartney under a pseudonym)

Thus, in the middle of May, 1965, Jimmie Nicol found himself back in the music business, hired to play drums for Peter & Gordon on tour. The set list closely resembled their back catalog. In addition to the aforementioned hits, they also played their newest hit, *True Love Ways,* and some covers and B-sides. It was easy work for Nicol to keep time along with the simple strumming of this famous duo.

One night, Peter & Gordon and Jimmie pulled into The Rialto Club in Derby on Nightingale Road. It was a club 100 miles north of London that featured both local and nationally famous acts. The Rialto had old stairs that gave Jimmie a hard time as he carried each piece of his drum kit upstairs into the club. That night, Gordon Waller's car got covered in lipstick messages from his female teenage fans, and they stole his windshield wipers. He was understandably upset with this situation, although from Nicol's point of view, at least Peter & Gordon fans had cared enough to mess up his car. It was good to get back up on stage and play music again, despite all that had occurred. However, no one ever told Jimmie that his life-saving gig had been arranged by a guardian angel; a person in the band who Nicol had come to blame for his woes: Paul McCartney and The Beatles.

After the Peter & Gordon tour ended, Jimmie was back on the dole again. As the summer stretched into fall, old friend Georgie Fame (perhaps at the behest of his friend McCartney?) reached out to help. It was a magnanimous gesture, considering Fame had loaned Jimmie to The Beatles, but was then subsequently spurned by him upon Nicol's return to London. Fame had a semi-regular engagement at a small nightclub in Leeds, and he hired Jimmie to accompany him at these shows. It was not big money, but it was certainly a job.

In the coming fall, Jimmie would receive two opportunities out of the blue and on the same day. One would be a regular, paying, dependable, local London job; and the other would be a journey with a band that did not speak much English. It came from a new friend, offering an opportunity to travel the world and explore new music, both live and in recording studios around the globe. Jimmie Nicol was about to make another fateful move in his career and his life. Would he choose the safe route this time, after all of the ups and downs of the past year? Or would he opt for an unconventional adventure based in a foreign country? Where would his drums lead him next?

Chapter Sixteen

From Oblivion To Outer Space

September, 1965, London

By the fall of 1965, Jimmie Nicol was isolated and alone. It seemed to Jimmie as if his friends had betrayed him, and he was estranged from his ex-wife and son. No longer was he hounded by fans or the media. Nicol's friends did not know where he was. He was not showing up at the recording studios or at the usual clubs. They had simply lost track of him. This was likely by design, as Nicol was certainly feeling embarrassed about his divorce, his lost earnings and his two failed attempts as bandleader. Filing for bankruptcy had not solved the problem of making money; it had only disposed of the old debts from his two failed bands. As money ran low, Nicol sold off some of his equipment and was forced to stretch every pound. What a difference one year had made: he had traveled the world with the royalty of pop music, yet he had also morphed from prince to pauper.

Nearly penniless, the drummer accepted the infrequent "charitable gig" from Georgie Fame to make ends meet. Jimmie had been without regular employment for several months, wondering what he should do next. He pondered his lack of success as a bandleader and the role he believed Epstein had played in sabotaging his solo career. He had dreams of traveling the world, and especially to the United States, to learn more about drumming and studying musical theory; hoping to latch on with Frances Faye and perhaps record with her in the States. That idea (which had been blocked by Epstein in Melbourne) no longer seemed possible.

Meanwhile, unbeknownst to Jimmie, another drummer in a far away foreign land was quitting his successful band. Derek Skinner was getting married, and his wife-to-be would not allow him to go on tour any longer. Skinner's hasty exit spelled potential disaster for a Swedish band called, "The Spotnicks". The band was only one month away from launching a major world tour and worried about finding a suitable drummer who could continue to drive their successful instrumental music forward. It was a familiar story, not unlike The Beatles' problem some fifteen months earlier.

The Spotnicks were formed by Bosse (nicknamed "Bo") Winberg in the late 1950s in Gothenburg, Sweden. Their original name had been "The Frazers", before it evolved into the Spotnicks in 1961.[1] Winberg recalls the origination of the name, "From the first launches of Soviet Sputniks, we thought of a similar name, and after a few tries, we arrived at The Spotnicks."[2] The space-aged name led to futuristic, outer space stage costumes and themes for the band, when manager Roland Ferneborg became the group's manager after seeing their 1961 concert in Stockholm.[3]

Winberg, a tall, lanky blonde, had learned to play guitar as a young man thanks to his interest in all things electrical. The Spotnicks' other core members included Bob Starander (later to be known as Lander) on rhythm guitar and vocals, Bjorn Thelin on bass and, a revolving door of drummers. Ferneborg got the band a recording contract early in its career and encouraged the band members to broaden their touring outside of their home country. By 1962, The Spotnicks had launched their sound with a tour of England, where they began an ingenious career-long marketing plan to record thematic albums based upon, and named after, the many cities and countries they would visit. Their first album was recorded in London and aptly named, "Spotnicks In London Out-A-Space". The successful experiment resulted in the band hitting the pop charts in England.[4]

From 1963 to 1965, The Spotnicks continued to tour foreign countries, including Spain, England, and France. Several TV and radio performances followed, along with musical videos. More albums named after cities continued. One single reached number one in Australia and was a big hit in England. It was a song that Jimmie Nicol heard on the radio and would remember; *Orange Blossom Special.* At the time, many in England were comparing the band to their own popular instrumental group, "The Shadows". In America, The Spotnicks were compared to another rocking instrumental outfit called "The Ventures".

In the summer of 1963, Derek Skinner took over on drums. In May of 1965, The Spotnicks' lineup changed again. With the core of Bo on lead guitar; Bob Lander on rhythm guitar; Bjorn Theilin on bass; and Derek Skinner on drums; they added newcomer, Peter Winsnes, on keyboards.

By late September of 1965, the group was in a bind with the sudden exit of Skinner. The tour was imminent and would take the band to the USA, Mexico, and Japan. Bjorn recalled The Spotnicks had watched drummer, Jimmie Nicol, & the Shubdubs perform in Copenhagen the previous year and were quite impressed. The Spotnicks were unaware of Nicol's financial situation, losing his record deals and unable to pay his floundering bands at the time. As fate would have it, Bjorn Theilin recalled his conversation with Nicol from December, 1964, when Jimmie asked about moving to Sweden to play drums. Thelin asked Spotnicks' manager, Roland Ferneborg, if they could offer the British drummer a chance to join their band.

The Spotnicks were all in favor of hiring Nicol to replace their departing drummer. "Jimmie was a very, very talented drummer," says Spotnicks founder, Bo Winberg.[5] Bo, who was always looking to improve the fortunes of his band, knew Nicol could propel The Spotnicks to greater success with his abilities, showmanship, and professionalism. It also didn't hurt The Spotnicks to bring on a drummer who had played with The Beatles. "He could play anything from Jazz to Country and Rock and Roll. And also he was a very humble guy."[6]

Spotnicks manager, Ferneborg, called Nicol in late September. He explained the now familiar situation to Jimmie of an upcoming tour and the urgent need to fill the drummer's stool. It was more déjà vu. Only this time, Nicol would not be a temporary fill-in as he had been with The Beatles and the Dave Clark Five. Nor would he need to perform a tryout. The Spotnicks had seen him play and were enamored with his rhythmic skills; moreover, they had already become friends. This was a generous offer of a permanent gig with a band on the rise. However, taking the job would mean leaving his son, his country and moving to Sweden where Nicol did not know the language or customs. Nicol asked for some time to mull it over. It was a big decision. "I had an event at a nightclub in Leeds and some other gigs with Georgie Fame," says Jimmie. "That's why I hesitated a bit when I got the offer from The Spotnicks."[7] Reluctantly, Ferneborg hung up the phone without getting his drummer, but he would not give up.

Meanwhile, on the same day, Nicol received yet another job offer. "It was marvelous. I received two telephone calls in one day. One to do *West Side Story* [as the orchestra pit drummer at London's West End] and the other one… to come with Spotnicks," says Nicol.[8] Jimmie gave strong consideration to staying in London. *West Side Story* would be a lengthy, steady gig that would pay well. It was the safe, easy, reasonable choice, versus traveling to Sweden and ultimately around the world with a band that knew a handful of English words. But Jimmie never shied away from a risky or challenging endeavor.

The Spotnicks' manager was persistent. He called back again the next day. "Roland Ferneborg didn't give up easily," says Nicol.[9] According to Spotnicks' keyboardist, Peter Winsnes, "Our manager gave him an offer he could not refuse."[10] Ferneborg pushed all of the right buttons with Jimmie, flattering his playing; sharing the hopes of his friends, The Spotnicks; and, best of all, telling him about the forthcoming tour that would take Nicol and the band on a trip through the United States, Mexico, and Japan. "Our manager made Jimmie a full, equal member of the band and offered to pay him the same as the other members," says guitarist Bob Lander.[11] This was taken as a significant sign of respect to Nicol. He would have equal pay and an equal say in the band's creative endeavors. "So," says Jimmie, "I decided to come with Spotnicks. I had progressed as far as I could go as a studio musician in England."[12] In reality, Nicol had very few professional options left in Lon-

Early Spotnicks promo photo with newest member Jimmie Nicol.

don at the time. He had burned more than a few bridges, when he became the leader of his own bands, forsaking Georgie Fame and the calls of Charlie ("the fixer") to attend lucrative recording sessions. Nicol then admitted the *real* reason for leaving his homeland. "And I wanted to *get away*. I wanted to see the world and Spotnicks offered that opportunity."[13] For Nicol, The Spotnicks represented a clean break from his problems of the past year. It was a fresh start and a new challenging opportunity.

Nicol accepted the job and moved himself and his rhythmic gear to Gothenburg, Sweden in only one

week's time. There were no goodbyes to friends and no mentions in the musical press that had already forgotten the "Fifth Beatle". Jimmie simply walked out his door and disappeared altogether from London's radar screen; a drummer in exile.

"Jimmie arrived at the Gothenburg airport Torslanda on October 7, 1965. It was a very dramatic landing and a great day for our band," says Winsnes.[14] Bjorn's family invited Jimmie to stay in their home to live with them before the start of The Spotnicks' world tour.

The media in Sweden heard the news and was anxious to ask the ex-Beatles drummer a few questions. Nicol was only too happy to share his new-found joy with The Spotnicks. Would Jimmie

become a Swedish citizen, they asked? "I am as yet undecided," he proclaimed in his diplomatic response. Evading the question, Nicol explains, "Right now I'm neither English nor Swedish – just one… Spotnick."[15] It was the perfect sound bite – clever and witty and a great start to a new life in which Jimmie Nicol could escape from the hardships and failures left behind in London. For many of Nicol's musician friends in London, the fall of 1965 was the last time they would ever see him again. To them, he had indeed vanished without a trace.

Jimmie Nicol with his broken cymbal.

The Spotnicks Introducing Jimmie Nicol

After Jimmie moved in and got settled, the first order of business was to rehearse with The Spotnicks for an upcoming show in Oslo, Norway. The band set up its rehearsal space with Jimmie's full drum kit in the living room of Bo Winberg's mother's house. As Jimmie was unpacking his gear to set up, the band noticed him pulling a broken cymbal from his luggage. The cymbal had a huge chunk missing, which comprised roughly 10% of the surface. Nicol was known as a big basher on the drum kit. The Spotnicks were unsure if Nicol had hit the cymbal too hard one too many times, or if it had merely broken in travel. It was clearly an attention-grabber that Jimmie brought along during his tour with The Spotnicks. Jimmie thought it had a unique sound with the chip missing, so the cymbal became part of the touring gear.[16]

The band ran through its repertoire of songs for an upcoming gig on October 8 in Norway, only two days after Jimmie's arrival. Nicol suggested a couple of songs that the band could rehearse to feature his drumming arrival with the band. The songs were his old *Husky* single from the Shub-dubs and a Bo Diddley-sounding song called, *Drum Diddley*. Peter Winsnes was quite impressed with Nicol's drumming in the band; it elevated the band's performances. He described Nicol's sound as, "Driving, swinging and funky! Jimmie played much heavier than our previous drummer."[17] The rehearsal went well and The Spotnicks immediately bonded with their newest member.

Their first gig together took place the next evening in Oslo. Nicol's indoctrination with The Spotnicks was a baptism by fire, and he was energized. The band was well received. Jimmie was impressed as he watched his band members receive a record industry silver album award at the concert. Their song, *Blue Blue Day* had sold 35,000 copies in Norway. Nicol was thrilled for his new band mates. He looked on and realized that his own fortunes had changed for the better. He was a permanent drummer in a successful hit making band about to travel the world.

Nicol loved the band's sound. "Spotnicks' sound is very unusual," he explains. "The nearest thing is the Shadows, but there is a difference. Musically there is a tremendous difference. Bo has a sound that he created when he was very young. He's kept it. I am so glad today it hasn't changed."[18] The feeling was mutual as the other Spotnicks relished the opportunity to add Jimmie Nicol's unique rhythmic sound to their band.

To help draw attention to their new drummer and new harder-rocking sound, Winberg decided to record a single to introduce their newest band member. They set up their gear and recorded two songs in October.

The first song was *Husky*, a remake of Jimmie's Shubdubs single. This version differed from the Shubdubs with the cool organ breaks of Peter Winsnes and the Space Pop/Surf Rock guitar of Bo Winberg. The drum solo is a travelogue of Nicol's drumming influences as he takes center stage for what seems like half of the song, playing his swinging solo. It is a stream of consciousness effort, filled with a combination of Big Band-swing, and Rock and Roll attitude that seems to energize the band when they come back in to end the song. "He is such a slugger on drums," says Lander.[19]

The Spotnicks are clearly showing their respect for Nicol's notoriety by the amount of solo space they give him on this track; and Jimmie doesn't let his band down. The solo provides a musical vocabulary that engages a variety of moods, providing peaks and valleys of flash and vibrant technique, as well as more introspective melodic and hypnotic repetition in his phrasing. At one point, Nicol executes

Spotnicks Introducing Jimmie Nicol. Photo Credit: Cover photo © Roland Ferneborg, 45 sleeve courtesy of Author.

a press roll that gradually descends in volume as he moves into a rapid 8th note pulse on his bass drum, which he maintains while he plays sparse phrases with his sticks. Interestingly, this section of the solo pre-dates two very popular recordings that used the same idea, but which came later in the history of Rock and Roll. These solos were by Ron Bushy on the classic Iron Butterfly track, *In A*

Gadda Da Vida in 1968, and by Ringo Starr's iconic solo on The Beatles' *Golden Slumbers/Carry That Weight/ The End* medley, from the *Abbey Road* album in 1969.[20]

The solo would be extended even further in concert, giving the other band members literally time to get a cup of coffee. Clocking in at an incredible 4:58 – nearly 3 minutes longer than the original – this version of "Husky" is much loser and relaxed. Whereas the Shubdubs version had a much tighter Jazz/Latin feel, The Spotnicks' version takes on a slightly less sophisticated, space-aged approach. In both cases, we hear Jimmie singing out the one-word lyric to the song ("Husky!") along with other guttural noises on the solo.

The Spotnicks proceeded to record a flip side, *Drum Diddley*, that clocks in at just under 2:00 minutes. *Drum Diddley* is a sharp, fun, driving, ball-of-fire from start to finish that illustrates – even better than *Husky* – what you get when your band hires a seasoned drummer with a high dose of energy, imagination, and swagger. The song draws upon the heavily African-influenced, trademark blues guitar, and drum rhythms of Rock and Roll pioneer, Bo Diddley, who had made this his signature beat for white American teens in the 1950s. Nicol and his Spotnicks continue this tradition on their version with relentless fervor that is downright infectious and hypnotic.[21] According to drummer and rhythm historian, David Stanoch, "The best part of listening to this solo from a drummer's standpoint is that you can literally hear the excitement of Nicol as he channels the influence of the musicians he loves – Diddley, Krupa, Nelson and Cole into one cohesive statement. The love that must have driven him to years of dedicated practice is forever captured in 1:54 of joyful noise by an artist at the peak of his powers."[22]

Once the songs were in the can, they went to the pressing plant under the supervision of The Spotnicks' label Swe Disc. Meanwhile, the band members ventured out to Ramberget, a mountain on the island of Hidingen in Gothenburg to do a promotional photo shoot for the 45-rpm cover sleeve. The band was generously featuring their new famous drummer by placing him smack in the center of the photo. "We were so proud to have Jimmie in our band and we wanted everyone to know," says Winsnes.[23] Outtakes from the shoot show the band getting on famously as they keep laughing and cracking up for the poor photographer. Eventually, the band would stand still for one serious pose. We see half the Spotnicks facing Jimmie on the left and the other half on his right. They are profiled, while Jimmie stares straight at the camera. All five members look like they are about to burst with laughter at the "serious pose".

When the single was released in late October, it featured a press release of sorts, printed on the cover with the band's pose. Entitled, "The Spotnicks Introducing Jimmie Nicol", the record sleeve features each band member's impression of their newest member:

> "The Spotnicks about Jimmie"
> Bo: "A very inspiring musician"
> Bob: "He swings like mad"
> Bjorn: "Crazy"
> Peter: "He makes us all swing"

The local newspaper reviewed the new single and was clearly unsure if it liked the new sound of The Spotnicks. "The Spotnicks sound good, as usual… But it is the new addition, Jimmie Nicol, who has the opportunity to show us what he's got. Consequently, we don't get to hear much of The Spotnicks' driven instrumentals, but instead they have added a real 'metal worker' behind the drums. Even the Jazz drum solos (which are full of nuances and good ideas) are sometimes almost meaningless… Jimmie Nicol is very welcome here in Sweden, but next time we want to hear The Spotnicks, as usual, again."[24]

November 22, 1965 was a big day for The Spotnicks and Jimmie Nicol. It was both a debut and a farewell for the band in its home town of Gothenburg. The concert was memorable for the debut of the two newest members, Peter Winsnes and Jimmie Nicol; and it also served to introduce the new single and to say farewell before the start of The Spotnicks' four-month long world tour.[25]

The Spotnicks gave their hometown fans a one-hour show that focused mostly on their hometown album, "Spotnicks at Home in Gothenburg". The songs performed included *I'm Coming Home*, and *Walk Right In*. But the true highlight of the show was the introduction of Jimmie Nicol, drummer extraordinaire. "Jimmy Nichol [sic] got his chance during a six minute drum solo in *Husky* – six minutes in which it was only Jimmy [sic] and his drums onstage. Six minutes which completely captivated the enthusiastic audience," according the local music reviewer.[26] The pop event was very well received, and the perfect promotion for the band and its new star, Jimmie Nicol. Peter Winsnes recalls the night, "He was a real 'showman' on stage. He had the gimmick of taking off his jacket while playing very fast on his bass drum during his solo. It was very exciting to watch. The audience loved him. He kept that steady, heavy British beat of the Sixties."[27]

The band was bonding quickly. "We really had a great time together," says Lander.[28] And conquering their home town musically before embarking on a world tour gave them great confidence for the good things to come. In anticipation of taking publicity photos and going on tour, a new bass drum head was painted by Winberg especially for Jimmie. It featured the band's name top-center, along with "Jimmie Nicol" split up, with an animated space man in between his first and last name. "Bo was very creative with his art," says Winsnes.[29] All that was left for the band was to pack their suitcases for a new adventure.

The Spotnicks in Disney Land.
Photo Credit: © Roland Ferneborg.

The World Tour – New York City and Los Angeles, USA

On Wednesday, November 24, 1965, The Spotnicks left Gothenburg en-route to their first stop, New York City. The 'round-the-world trip would take the band to New York, Los Angeles, Mexico City, Honolulu, Tokyo, Hong Kong, Manila, Bangkok, Beirut, Rome, Berlin, Copenhagen, and finally back home to Gothenburg. The plan for the US was to perform on TV, record an album, play some live shows, and meet with Chuck Berry and Chet Atkins. It all sounded like a dream-come-true for Nicol, who had wanted to visit the USA forever as a musician. Although it had not worked out with Frances Faye, he realized that fate had found a different way for this dream to come true - with a band in which he was a permanent and welcome member.

Of course, plans are merely hopes, and reality sometimes crashes down like a powerful hit on Nicol's cymbals. The band did make it to New York. However, they found that America was very protective of its own artists and required foreign artists to obtain a work permit before they could perform on TV, record or play concerts. The problem was that work permits were only given to foreigners who were already somehow established in the US. Peter Winsnes says, "To get a work permit in the USA it's best to be on the American hit music list. To get on the American hit music list, you should perform on TV. To be allowed to perform on TV you have to have a work permit."[30] The band got caught in the musician union's "Catch 22" and learned it would be unable to perform at all in the US. If that wasn't bad enough, their lead guitarist, Bo Winberg got blood poisoning in his finger and had his arm in a sling. Even with a work permit, The Spotnicks were still on the bench with a disabled player.

The band did not let this temporary setback get them down. They toured New York City, taking in the sites, including the nightlife in Time Square. After a week in New York City, the "tour", which had become a scenic tour, moved onto Los Angeles. A trip to Disney Land commenced on

THE SPOTNIKS.

exclusivo
polydor

The Spotnicks in their Tuxedos. Photo Credit: © Roland Ferneborg.

November 28, which included more promotional photos. In one picture, the band poses with the iconic Mickey Mouse in front of the Magic Kingdom. Another photo features the band sitting on a park bench, with Jimmie wearing a souvenir Indian headdress and laughing while the band is serenaded by saxophone-playing Keystone Cops. All in all, the US trip had been an opportunity to relax, have fun, and sight see. Now it was time to move on to Mexico for a lengthy stay that would mean extended work for the band, and would foreshadow Nicol's future life still two years away

The World Tour – Mexico City, Mexico

The Spotnicks playing in Mexico City. Photo Credit: From the personal archive of Manuel Martinez Pelaez, Courtesy of Gustavo Zamora

On December 1, The Spotnicks landed in Mexico City for an extended stay that would last for two months. They had been booked into the Alameda Hotel, Mexico's biggest, swankiest and tallest hotel. The Spotnicks would serve as the nightly house band entertainment for their entire stay. American singing star, Connie Francis, performed at the same time in one of the hotel's three other night clubs. The clientele was clearly upscale, with the men wearing trendy suits and the women in their swingin' Sixties dresses. These nightly performances featured the band rocking hard to an appreciative audience of dancing hipsters.

Early in their stay, the President of RCA Victor Mexicana, showed up at the new hotel's inauguration and to check out the band. He came away clearly impressed with the drumming skill and professional poise of Nicol. The two met briefly. It was a fortuitous meeting that would again have future implications for Nicol. The President, Louis Couttolenc, took an interest in Nicol's background, his Beatles' stint, and how he had come to join a Swedish band. A relationship was formed that would, offer Nicol new opportunities down the road.

The Spotnicks on vacation in Acapulco. Photo Credit: © Roland Ferneborg.

The band chose cool new tuxedos for most of their nightly gigs to better relate to their fashionable clientele. On one evening, the band was playing hard when an earthquake suddenly shook the hotel and the entire city. As the band played on, the chandeliers were rocking back in forth in rhythm with the music. Even as the swimming pool's water began to overflow and run down the stairs, Spotnicks manager Roland Ferneborg, who had a keen sense of marketing and promotion, yelled at the group, "Keep Playing!"[31] The result was a newspaper story commending the band the following day, which naturally led to even greater popularity. They regaled their readers, "Yup, there was an earthquake, the most powerful in Mexico City this year. The chandeliers in The Spotnicks' room on the 17th floor were swinging and clanking, and even the Mexican teeth were chattering. But The Spotnicks, from Sweden, pretended that nothing was happening. They were swinging as well and are now the idols at the hotel."[32]

The Spotnicks worked hard to earn a packed-house-following each night. The local music paper, *Audiomusica*, raved about the show and described the band in action. "The exciting Swedish group The Spotnicks (Polydor) captivated the audience with the overwhelming force of its rhythms and their original new sound that they produce."[33] Even as he fought to recover from his blood poisoning, Bo Winberg bravely played on by wrapping his guitar pick to his thumb.[34]

The trip to Mexico was not all work, as manager Roland carved out time for the band to take a break and vacation in Acapulco. The trip was a perfect opportunity for the band to relax and enrich their growing friendship. The group went deep sea fishing, swimming, tree climbing for coconuts and, as always, posing for yet more promotional photos. In almost every photo, Jimmie is seen spontaneously laughing and smiling. He was clearly enjoying being in a band that he could feel a part of, and his Swedish buddies seemed to share the same humor and mutual admiration. Nicol exuded a calm and experienced leadership that made him the focal point of their existence for a time. The others had great respect for Nicol, which is why they fea-

The Spotnicks stop in Hawaii. Photo Credit: © Roland Ferneborg.

tured him prominently in photographs and in their live shows. Nicol returned the same respect to his new-found friends. He had found a home.

Back in Mexico City, the band rang in the New Year with more sizzling shows of musical excellence. Nicol was charged up from vacation and provided the audiences with his showmanship, a cross between rhythm and vaudeville. His experiences with Vince Eager and the Quiet Three were paying off, as Jimmie would amaze the fans with his prolific drumming and stage antics. At this point, another one of Nicol's goals had been reached, namely competing with The Beatles, albeit in Sweden. The January 15, 1966 issue of *Billboard* announced the Swedish Disk Top List. The chart reflected the top ten most popular artists based upon records sales and success on the Norwegian Charts. The top spot, of course, belonged to The Beatles, but not far behind at Number 9 were The Spotnicks.[35] Although Jimmie had not been able to compete against The Beatles with his own bands,

he had finally found a way to do it as a member of an established band, and he was pleased.

By February 1, 1966, it was time for the band to move on. After a brief stopover in Honolulu, The Spotnicks headed to Japan for an extended stay of five weeks. The rest and relaxation in Acapulco would soon be a distant memory. A big surprise awaited the group upon their arrival in Japan; one that would almost seem like a flashback to Jimmie.

The Spotnicks performing a perfect bow to Japan.
Photo Credit: © Roland Ferneborg.

The World Tour – Tokyo, Japan

While the Spotnicks had been working hard in Mexico, not one, but two singles were battling each other up the Japanese record charts. The irony was that both singles were exactly the same recording under two different names. One song was called, *Karelia*, by The Spotnicks and the other was called, *Ajomies*, by the Feenades. The Feenades was the name of Bo Winberg's solo recordings. Both song titles (but one song) were recorded by Bo. "As a matter of fact," says keyboardist Peter Winsnes, "I played drums on the studio version of *Karelia*. Jimmie didn't play on it."[36] According to Bo, he and Peter are the only musicians on *Karelia*. "It was recorded in my mum's living room in 1964," says Bo.[37] Somehow the Feenades version had flopped in Finland, so Phillips Record Company sent it to Japan where it caught fire. Meanwhile, The Spotnicks' Polydor label had released the identical record-

The Spotnicks backstage in Tokyo at the Nitchigachi Theater.
Photo credit: © Roland Ferneborg.

141

The Spotnicks live on stage in Tokyo. Photo Credit: © Roland Ferneborg.

ing as *Karelia* under the band's name in Japan. The result was a wildly successful single that would greet the band headed to Japan for their tour.[38] "It was the same version on both recordings on the Japan charts," laughs Winsnes.[39] *Billboard* magazine reported that, "Sweden's Spotnicks, *beat aggregation*, are sending Japanese aficionados into orbit with their latest release 'Karelia,' which has sold 300,000 copies."[40]

As the Spotnicks' plane made its way from Hawaii to Japan on February 6, they did not realize the fans' welcome that their hit song would garner. "When we landed in Japan and looked out the window at all of the people with banners and signs we said to each other that there must be some real bigwigs on this plane," says Bob Lander. "But it was The Spotnicks they were waiting for. The record company had gone out on TV and announced that The Spotnicks were landing."[41] Throngs of Japanese fans were at the airport, carrying banners that read, "The Spotnicks Fan Club" and "Welcome The Spotnicks". To Jimmie Nicol, it must have seemed like déjà vu from his Beatles' tour.

Before leaving the plane, Spotnicks manager, Roland Ferneborg, insisted the band members change into their trademark astronaut costumes. They protested, but to no avail. The Spotnicks - dressed as astronauts - walked down the steps of their plane; and the cheering and screaming of female fans reached a fevered pitch. "At customs, the employees' jaws dropped when they saw us," says Lander.[42] The band was led to a VIP room where it was greeted by the media, and female fans

Jimmie, Peter and The Spotnicks recording in Japan. Photo Credit: © Roland Ferneborg.

bearing flowers. The Spotnicks sat down for a brief press conference. Jimmie looked like an old pro as the band fielded questions from reporters. His confidence and expression demonstrated his experience at the media game. He was pleased to be back in the limelight again, making money, and playing music with friends – and this time in a permanent band. In another flashback reminiscent of The Beatles with beauty queens in Hong Kong, Jimmie and The Spotnicks were asked to pose for pictures with Japanese Geisha girls holding flowers.

The next day, The Spotnicks were back to work with a full itinerary starting at 1:00 p.m. First up were magazine interviews with "Teen-Beat" and "Seven Aces" at the hotel. Jimmie and his band mates handled the questions with confidence and humor. With the Q & A out of the way, the band sat down with their manager to discuss the busy schedule that lay ahead for the next month in the Land of the Rising Sun. After dinner, The Spotnicks headed off to a rehearsal studio to perform a soundcheck run-through and tune up their instruments for the upcoming concerts.

On February 8, the band finally began its tour of more than 35 live shows in one month. During the tour, The Spotnicks traveled to cities all around Japan. Every minute of every day was tightly scheduled, filled with interviews, TV shows, travel to new cities, and live performances.

In concert, The Spotnicks were years ahead with their technical sound and their stage set up. Live video footage shows the band in their astronaut outfits being flown in from above on wires, down to the stage below. Behind the band was a rocket ship with the name "Spotnicks" painted on the fuselage. The set list usually contained about sixteen songs that could be performed in an hour. Jimmie noted that The Spotnicks nearly doubled their time on stage versus The Beatles. He liked this, since it afforded him a lengthy drum solo or two under the spotlight at each show.

The show begins after The Spotnicks land on the stage as "astronauts". The normally reserved Japanese fans excitedly anticipate the coming performance as The Spotnicks kick off their *Spotnicks Theme*. The moment the band kicks in, Nicol immediately takes over as the commander-in-chief with his rhythmic force, filling every row and aisle with sound while pouring forth his inexhaustible warehouse of beat ideas. "The audience loved him," says Winsnes. "He kept that steady, heavy British beat of the Sixties. I will say he helped to make our stage show really exciting!"[43] The Spotnicks' version of *When The Saints Go Marching In* also featured some amazing organ playing by Peter, which surely sounds like a precursor to Ray Manzarek's style a year later with The Doors. During the tour, The Spotnicks' record company paid to professionally record some of the concerts for a possible future live album.

The set list included many popular songs of the day, certain Spotnicks' standards, and, of course, their current hit:

Spotnicks Theme
Last Space Train
Johnny Guitar
Happy Silence
When The Saints Go Marching In
Crying In The Storm
Karelia
Hey Good Looking
Memory of Summer
Wabash Cannon Ball
What'd I Say
Have Nagila
Look Up To The Evening Star

The concerts were selling out in most cities; thanks to the hit record, *Karelia* on the charts and the many TV shows and interviews the band was doing. Most of the audience was filled with teenage girls. At one point, The Spotnicks even played alongside a symphony orchestra in Sapporo. Although most adults in Japan were against long-haired teen pop stars, such as Herman's Hermits who had recently visited, they seemed to accept the cleaner cut Spotnicks and their slightly milder pop music.[44]

At one point, The Spotnicks held a recording session in a Japanese recording studio. During the session, The Spotnicks recorded: *Moscow*; *Mood of Asia*; *Subject in Orbit*; and *Sentimental Guitar* (aka *Vostok 6*). In the studio, Jimmie looked on intently with one hand under his chin, smiling as he focused on the playback. One can sense the excitement Nicol feels to be recording with a band he truly feels a part of.

Between concerts, TV shows, and travel, Nicol and his band took time out to visit Japanese record stores, as well as sacred temples and local cultural sites. The band also met with the Japanese director of their Polydor label. He would present the group with a record award for sales of *Karelia* reaching 1,000,000 in Japan, a feat that clearly rivaled Nicol's "old band", The Beatles. Jimmie and his Spotnicks had conquered Japan.

On March 3, 1966, The Spotnicks said farewell to Japan and continued on with their world tour that would take them to brief stops in Hong Kong, Manila, Bangkok, Beirut, Rome, Berlin, and Copenhagen, before returning home to Gothenburg. The tour had been wildly successful. Jimmie was highly impressed with the organization of the tour as well as the professional level of playing with his band mates. Things were looking up for the British drummer living in Sweden. The coming year would be filled with concerts, TV, recording sessions, recognition, and more than a few surprises for Mr. Nicol and his Swedish comrades. Yet, as 1966 dawned, Jimmie Nicol would face a growing restlessness, an increase in "extracurricular habits", and a desire to change his scenery.

Chapter Seventeen

The Spotnicks

Back Home in Gothenburg

After their arrival back home on March 13, 1966, The Spotnicks were pleasantly surprised to find a brand new Mercedes Benz tour bus awaiting them. It would transport the band to its regional gigs in luxury and cost a whopping 50,000 Swedish Kronors (approximately $7,500 USD).[1] Re-

Jimmie Nicol driving the new Spotnicks tour bus.
Photo Credit: © Peter Winsnes.

flecting on the tour and arriving back home, Spotnicks' leader Bo commented, "It is nice to play at home again after four months out in the world. The best was Japan. There, we were really popular."[2]

A few days later the band would try out its new tour bus with a concert in Trollhattan, Sweden, some 46 miles away from Gothenburg. The band members enjoyed their new ride as they approached their triumphant 1966 Swedish premier. The show was very well received, and Jimmie Nicol was clearly the star of the evening according to observers.

For the finale, each band member came out wearing clothing from the five parts of the world they had just visited and played songs from these foreign lands.[3] The band clearly appreciated the different cultures of the world, and in turn, reflected the varied cultures in their musical repertoire. Nicol was energized by the variety of the music they were playing. It kept things interesting and challenging for his restless nature.

During late March and early April, The Spotnicks set up to record again. They began to track a new album which would be Jimmie Nicol's debut with The Spotnicks on a long play record. The band listened to a live recording of its concert in Japan and selected a few songs to record in the studio, including *Look Up To The Evening Star; Crying In The Storm; Happy Silence;* and *Ode to Dawn.* They also came up with several more tracks to add into the recording mix, including *Autumn in Japan;* the currently popular James Bond song, *From Russia With Love;* plus the two songs from Nicol's debut Spotnicks single. The band benefited from Nicol's studio experience as a professional session player and arranger; and in some cases, Jimmie also acted as the producer on the sessions.

On April 6, 1966, The Spotnicks were visited at the studio by the Swedish Radio Show,

"Teenage Evening". The band members were interviewed and talked about their recent world tour and their current studio work. The Spotnicks played back some of their latest studio and live recordings on the show, featuring the songs *The Old Love Letters; I've Lost You; Happy Silence* (live); a live version of their hit *Karelia*, with Jimmie on drums; *Drum Diddley;* and *Piercing the Unknown*. During the interview, Nicol sat quietly in his black turtleneck, calmly smoking a cigarette and watching band leader Bo fielding most of the interviewer's questions in his native Swedish tongue. The band members drank beers, smiled for candid photos, and answered questions for their teenage fans. Nicol marveled at the well-organized efficiency of the group as it smoothly transitioned from a world tour, to a local show, to recording and meeting the press. He could not help but reflect on the stark contrast between the well-oiled machine of The Spotnicks' organization and his own two post-Beatles bands that had been more chaotic and inconsistent with their schedules.

Big news continued to pour in from Japan, as *Billboard* announced that the Spotnicks were "No 1 in Japan".[4] Jimmie felt at ease knowing that he no longer had to run the band, make the plans, hustle, finance everything and play each night. Now he could just sit back and enjoy being an artist in a successful band. He was content… for the time being.

Jimmie's First Spotnicks Album

At the end of April, The Spotnicks released their first album with Jimmie Nicol on board. The title was a tribute to their recent huge success in the Far East. It was aptly titled, *The Spotnicks in Tokyo*. The cover featured the five Spotnicks in front of a Japanese building giving a respectful, traditional bow, bookended by two pretty Geisha girls.

The tracks on the album included the following songs:

Look Up To The Evening Star
Drum Diddley
The Old Love Letters
Piercing The Unknown
Playboy's Bunny Hop
Crying In A Storm
From Russia With Love
Happy Silence
Ode To Dawn
The Lonesome Port
Husky

The sound quality of the recording and the separation of each instrument is years ahead of its time with a sound that measures up to today's standards. On the song, *Crying In A Storm*, Jimmie employs the drum beat made popular by Jerry Allison of Buddy Holly's Crickets on *Peggy Sue*. The driving beat serves the band well as it focuses the listener to feel the thunder of a storm; Bo and Peter trade off dramatic phrases on guitar and organ respectively to demonstrate one of Mother Nature's worst days. *Happy Silence* is another interesting track. It strays from the usual Spotnick space pop into a 1960s era Jazz bop, featuring Jimmie Nicol's clever jazzy playing on the rim of his snare. Many times before recording a track, Nicol says, "I would sit with Peter, Bob, Bear and Bo and play Jazz for a few hours to warm up before recording."[5] *Happy Silence* clearly emerges from this Jazz jamming. Clerwall begins his review with an apology to all of the longhaired pop groups. "[Please] excuse me, but the most interesting record release in a long time comes from the shorthaired The Spotnicks. All of the songs are instrumental. The technical genius and solo guitarist Bosse Winberg, after some experimentation has once again found the famous space sound."[6] He describes the songs as both sad and enjoyable. Then Clerwall takes the time to reflect on the band's addition of its newest member. "For the English drummer Jimmie Nicol, who famously made an appearance last year in

The Beatles as a replacement for Ringo Starr, this album is his LP debut. He demonstrates, without a doubt, what an asset he has become for the group."[7]

The reviewer continues to make his case for the export of The Spotnicks' international songs, describing how the band recently played a performance for the world's only female astronaut, Russian Valentina Teresjkova, the past week in Stockholm. The title of the song, "Vostock 6", is the name of Valentina's spacecraft. "Valentina was deeply moved and gave each member of The Spotnicks a pin with the Russian space emblem. She promised to try to arrange a performance for The Spotnicks in the Soviet Union."[8] Ever the diplomats, The Spotnicks were scoring points around the world with their music.

The Spotnicks Record a Christmas Album

After a short break, the band dove into yet another recording session in the heat of summer, 1966. It seemed strange to be recording an album of Christmas favorites in the warmth of summer, but it was necessary to get it ready for the Yuletide season. According to one report, the band argued a bit during these sessions. The discussion did not center on which songs to record, but rather, which country they wanted to live in. One of the issues was that Sweden's taxes were very high, cutting into the band's earnings. There were discussions of different countries, but after all of the members had their say, Bo voted for Gothenburg and Sweden.[9]

Despite very warm weather, the band forged ahead with its holiday album, to be titled *The Spotnicks in Winterland*. Winberg recounts the process, "We recorded that one during a heat wave down here in Gothenburg. It was 95 degrees [Fahrenheit] and we were playing songs like *Jingle Bells*!"[10] The band would take regular breaks to go swimming in hopes the next day's recording session would provide cooler weather. As a result, Bo says, "We ended up being delayed with the album…"[11]

Ultimately, Nicol and his Spotnick buddies laid down twelve holiday-pop (mostly) instrumental tracks:

> *Sleigh Ride*
> *Winter Wonderland*
> *Here Comes Santa Claus*
> *Rudolf The Red-Nosed Reindeer*
> *Frosty The Snowman*
> *Silent Night*
> *White Christmas*
> *Jingle Bells*
> *Winterland*
> *Parade of Wooden Soldiers*
> *I Saw Mommy Kissing Santa Claus*
> *Auld Land Syne*

The drumming on this album was quite basic for Jimmie as he mostly kept time on his snare, waiting to add a special fill or cymbal crash at the song's turn-around. However, he did step in to arrange The Spotnicks' rendition of *Silent Night*. The sentimental arrangement features a subtle military snare funereal beat to slowly propel the guitar-led melody along. At some point during the sessions, heat stroke must have struck The Spotnicks while recording the song, *I Saw Mommy Kissing Santa Claus*. The chorus style vocals were purposely pitched-up to give the song a silly "Chipmunks" vocal styling. Although Alvin & The Chipmunks had released a holiday album in 1961 entitled, *Christmas with the Chipmunks*, they had not recorded this song on their album. The Spotnicks were all about having a good time, and this humorous tribute to the cartoon-singing rodents was yet another example.

With the Christmas album finished, The Spotnicks set out on a summer tour of seventy Swedish amusement parks, a perfect way to reach its core audience of young people. The band played an abbreviated set of 10 songs at each show. Jimmie felt happy to be accepted on his own talent, and not just as a former Beatle. According to one media account at the time, "No wonder he feels he has finally come home. On his business card, he can write Jimmie Nicol or Spotnicks. It does not matter which. Now the two concepts mean the same for him."[12]

Upon their return to Gothenburg, The Spotnicks polished up their "live Japan" tapes for yet another album release, and they immediately began to record an album of new songs. Since the band planned to launch another world tour in the fall, they decided to create an album that would contain musical flavors from around the globe. It was aptly titled, *The Spotnicks Around The World*. One of the first tracks they laid down was, *Uska Dara*. It is a fascinating Turkish instrumental folk song, featuring Jimmie playing a repetitive galloping beat with his sticks on the rim of his snare, while the band uses a Turkish ensahl, a stringed instrument with a bow, to drive the melody. The counterpoint of the song is handled by Bo basically playing an off-beat, two-chord riff on his electric guitar. The result is a very realistic recording of this intriguing Turkish track.

Appropriately, the band gave a star turn to its drummer on a song about Hong Kong, a place where Nicol had played with The Beatles. However, this track contains a surprise twist; not only does Jimmie play drums, but we also get to hear his first solo vocal performance on record. Nicol double tracks his vocals as he sings the lyrics to this 1939 Hoagie Carmichael classic. His phrasing is relaxed and calm as he tries to elicit the oriental mood of the song about "The story of an unfortunate colored man/ Who Got Arrested Down In Old Hong Kong/ He got twenty years privilege taken away from him/ When he kicked old Buddha's gong."[13] Coincidentally, Nicol's recording of *Hong Kong Blues* would pre-date his one-time Beatles band mate, George Harrison, who would record the identical song some 15 years later on his solo album, *Somewhere In England*. The album finishes with a Hawaiian song called, *Steel Guitar Rag,* featuring a 16-string Hawaiian guitar, and a Swedish song named after a pancake mold, called, *Plattlaggen*. When the 14-song album of international songs was completed the tracks included:

Casting My Spell
Geisha Girl
Green Eyes
Hong Kong Blues
Mood of Asia
Plittlaggen
Recado
Sentimental Guitar
Steel Guitar Rag
Subject in Orbit
Turista
Uska Dara
What Now My Love
Worrying Kind

The Debut of "James George"

With three new albums ready for release, Bo suggested to his label Swe Disc that they also record another single to highlight their ex-Beatles drummer. Given the green light, The Spotnicks recorded two songs backing their rhythm maker: *C'mon Everybody* (an Eddie Cochran song), and *Stagger Lee*. The 45 rpm single was credited to James George (aka Jimmie Nicol & The Spotnicks). George being Nicol's middle name.

Jimmie was no stranger to taking center stage, ever since his drum solos with Colin Hicks and his stage antics with Vince Eager. He knew how to have a good time and how to incite audiences. Nicol recalled watching Eddie Cochran kidnap his audience every night with *C'mon Everybody* back in the spring of 1960 on his tour with Vince Eager, and he knew just how to record this rollicking romp. Although not blessed with a great set of pipes, his conviction and energy speak volumes on these two rockers. As the master of ceremonies, Jimmie's vocal delivery is infectious. The groove on *C'mon Everybody* is more buoyant than *Stagger Lee*. Nicol's parched, but highly spirited vocal delivery really rocks the track.

The band is well-rehearsed on both songs, although the music seems more fitting for a small local pub at closing time than as a hit record in 1966. It was clear that these songs fit more with swinging England than Sweden. Therefore, it made sense to leave The Spotnicks' name off the record and to exclude the tracks from their international pop albums. It was, however, a way for The Spotnicks to thank and highlight their famous drummer for his services rendered.

Another Spotnicks World Tour

In the fall of 1966, Nicol and his Spotnicks set out on the first leg of their next world tour. This trip took the prolific band to Germany, Holland, Belgium, Switzerland, and Austria for three weeks in October. As the band moved around Europe, their albums were reaching more

The Spotnicks second world tour with Nicol, on a ferry to Germany. Photo Credit: © Peter Winsnes.

countries. In Japan, they were approaching one million albums sold, and their records were now for sale in 80 different countries. This success would continue as their new albums were released to the public in late 1966.

While the tour rolled along, the familiar sameness of moving from city to city, hotel to hotel, and stage to stage, began to take its toll on Nicol. He always looked for something new to challenge him. He began to feel stale from the repetition and grew anxious again; concerned that his career

The Spotnicks in party mode. Photo Credit: © Peter Winsnes.

was not moving forward fast enough. Part of the problem was that The Spotnicks' music was not very challenging to Jimmie as a drummer. Most of the songs they recorded together and played in concert entailed very basic 4/4 time signature drumming - patterns Nicol could play in his sleep. Winsnes, who roomed with Nicol on the tour, could tell Nicol was starting to feel bored musically. Nicol's style of music (as evident on his two Swe Disc singles) leaned toward Big Band Jazz and much harder Rock and Roll than the clean cut Spotnicks were playing at the time.

The Spotnicks in Paris filming short music videos.
Credit: © Roland Ferneborg.

As the tour's tedium set in for Nicol, he turned to more frequent use of marijuana for "relief" and entertainment. At first, Nicol kept his use of the "evil weed" out of sight of his band mates and manager. However, one night in Cologne, Germany, the band was off duty and Jimmie decided to introduce his smoking pastime to his roommate. Nicol and Winsnes were planning to go see Bill Haley and his Comets play later that evening at a night club near their hotel. Winsnes explains, "Jimmie opened the window and lit up his joint, sucked on it, held the smoke deep down and blew it out the window. Then he handed it over to me. He told me to hold the smoke deep down in my lungs for as long as I could. It was the first time for me, but the effect came immediately. When we finally made it to Bill Haley's show, I had the greatest, happiest experience of swinging Rock and Roll!"[14] It was an epiphany moment for the newly initiated Spotnick, one that would change him and his band. "In a way, you could say that Jimmie Nicol introduced cannabis to the band via me," says Winsnes, who became a "weed-prophet" to the band.[15] Nicol began to smoke regularly to numb the sense that his life was stuck in neutral. He could play his shows while stoned, and his life during the days of travel seemed more interesting when high.

For many years, The Spotnicks had been unable to tour France, despite their popularity there. The problem centered on a contractual dispute with their French record label. While on tour in Europe, the issues were resolved, and the French label launched a big Spotnicks promotion. Therefore, at the start of November, 1966, The Spotnicks headed to Paris to perform a series of live shows, recordings, press conferences, and two TV programs.[16] Never one to miss a promotional opportunity, famed fashion icon, Pierre Cardin, decided to launch his new space-aged men's clothing line with the help of The Spotnicks. Cardin & Company created an entirely new line of onstage costumes for the band to wear, as well as everyday clothes. The Spotnicks' high fashion acted as a billboard ad for Cardin throughout Europe. In return, the band got to keep all of their new, cutting edge duds. Sporting one of Cardin's inspirations, The Spotnicks performed and recorded a popular French song called *La Pachava*. It was a fun dance song of the day that featured a tricky 5/4 time signature rhythm that appealed to Jimmie.[17]

In mid-November, The Spotnicks went into Presidents Recording Studio in Paris. The purpose of the session was to record a theme song, *Suspicion,* to be used in a French TV crime drama.[18] In addition to his full drum kit, producer Frank Poursel brought in two timpani drums for Nicol to use. In the studio, Nicol was the consummate pro in the group. He could play with a burning cigarette dangling from his mouth as he followed the Producer's direction; and he wore his sunglasses - even inside the studio - to hide the telltale red-eyes that resulted from smoking pot. The shades became a daily accessory for the red-eyed drummer.

In late November, the group returned to Sweden before heading out on the next leg of its world tour. On November 26, The Spotnicks released their Christmas collection, *The Spotnicks in Winterland*. The Swe Disc label chose Jimmie's arrangement of "Silent Night" to go out to radio as the single. However, the song was immediately met with controversy. The Swedish public radio service, Sveriges Radio, blacklisted the song from its airwaves. What reason was given by the radio service for banning *Silent Night*? The official response: "The song, 'Silent Night' should not be per-

The Spotnicks back in Mexico. Photo Credit: © Roland Ferneborg.

formed on a guitar."[19] It was a short-sighted move by radio station. Nicol was slightly miffed, as it denied airplay to the song he had arranged. Nonetheless, the album continued to sell well, partly due to the controversy.

Around the same time, Jimmie's single, *James George,* came out. It did moderately well and received decent airplay. Nicol and his band mates were pleased. The Spotnicks played one more show in Karlsborg, Sweden as a warm up for their coming world tour. The concert was another full stage show of dance music and classics performed for their fans. The group was ready to mount yet another round-the-world tour to cement its success that had been aided by their recording popular international music stylings, such as, *Karelia* for Japan; *Turista* for Hong Kong; *Comme Ci Comme Ca* for France; and *Hava Nagila* in the Middle East. For The Spotnicks' drummer, however, a restless tedium had begun to settle in. Jimmie was itching for something or someplace new. Little did he know he would soon find what he was looking for out on tour.

December, 1966, World Tour, Mexico and Beyond

As the year 1966 drew to a close, Jimmie and his Spotnicks found themselves in Mexico City at the El Senor Real playing an extended gig. The club was situated some distance from the city center. Nicol explored the city on his own, to discover its cultural and underground resources. He began skipping some of the activities and rehearsals of The Spotnicks. Meanwhile, The Spotnicks had to carry on their social life and band rehearsals without their drummer in attendance. Jimmie's long absences began to annoy the band, along with some of his other social habits. Winsnes relates the change that came over his drummer-buddy, "There were really no problems in the band with Jimmie until our second visit to Mexico in December 1966. Jimmie began using heavy drugs together with some others. He was only showing up at the gigs."[20] Nicol's restlessness had caused him to search for something more powerful than his frequent use of marijuana. Bob and Björn even strayed into the city to purchase handguns. "It would be a bit dangerous late at night after the gig, when we had shared a gallon of Smirnoff and the boys started to play with their guns," relates Winsnes.[21]

Jimmie's drug use and long absences began to take their toll on his band mates. "It got worse," says Winsnes. "One night Jimmie was so stoned that he fell off his drum seat. Our manager had to call to Sweden for a new drummer." Manager Roland Ferneborg was unwilling to accept a heavy drug user in his group, a band that was now perhaps the most popular non-English band in the world. Starander explains, "Jimmie met some other musicians in Mexico who had a bad influence on his

Nicol would soon leave The Spotnicks.
Photo Credit: From the personal archive of Manuel Martinez Pelaez, Courtesy of Gustavo Zamora.

life."[22] Nicol had become unreliable and would have to be replaced. "So we got the best pop drummer in Sweden at that time. His name was Tommy Tausis," says Winsnes.[23] Tausis was reluctant to uproot himself from Sweden to fly down to Mexico. However, Roland Ferneborg would not take no for an answer. Roland said to Tausis, "Go to Bracke [a very cold place] and play there instead. We're sitting here by the pool enjoying the sunshine."[24] His plan worked and Tommy Tausis got on a plane for Mexico to join The Spotnicks.

Founder Bo Winberg was resigned to fate, when the end came for Jimmie. "He was a very humble guy and he had become a very good personal friend of mine," say Winberg. "I really missed him when he jumped off the Spotnicks in Mexico. Well, that's life."[25]

Jimmie Nicol had vanished, yet again. It was time to move on. Nicol felt the itch to try something new. He wanted to live in Mexico and immerse himself in its culture. He wanted to branch out on his own again and to look for new challenges. Perhaps the timing and circumstances were right for another attempt at running his own show again. Winsnes says, "Jimmie's experience as a studio musician, arranger and drummer really helped The Spotnicks. But, in the end, I don't think The Spotnicks played Jimmie's favorite kind of music."[26]

With the new year of 1967 about to begin, Nicol needed a new start in his life. He was sure of himself and he thought starting up his musical career in another foreign land would provide the happiness and success that he continually searched for, as always, on his own terms. The Spotnicks bemoaned the loss of their amazing friend and drummer, but Winsnes says, "Jimmie Nicol just disappeared into the Mexican night!"[27]

Chapter 18

Mexico

In January of 1967, Jimmie Nicol vanished once again. There were no farewells to his friends in The Spotnicks who had helped him find a way out of London and bankruptcy. He left no trail and no forwarding address. He wanted to construct a new life in yet another foreign country. No one in England or Sweden knew for sure where Jimmie Nicol had relocated. He had shared his love of Bossa Nova with members of The Spotnicks. Since this musical genre originated in Brazil, rumors circulated that Jimmie had perhaps moved to South America - and Brazil specifically - to study Bossa Nova. However, Nicol chose to live and work in Mexico City where he had jumped off The Spotnicks' tour. He was anxious to learn a new language and immerse himself in a new culture.

The drummer fell in love with his new home. Mexico City in 1967 was an immense and modern city with its share of issues as it strained to contain its growing youth population. The city, a collection of skyscrapers along with miles of brightly painted wood and mud brick dwellings, strained to hold it's populous. Outside of the urban areas, were vast expanses of mountains with long stretches of plains, steep ravines, and steamy jungles.

The hot weather was a staple that went hand in hand with siestas. To Nicol, the daily hot sunshine was in stark contrast to London's weather. It helped him to relax and clear away any doubts or dark thoughts that might have crept in at the start of his new life. Nicol was enthralled with his new surroundings. He relates, "I get many vibrations from Mexico. I can't explain it, it's like a magical land, you can do anything here that you want to if you have a will to do it."[1] Nicol's statement would prove to be prophetic for he would soon begin to plan many new, creative projects.

At first Nicol was interested in blending into the local music scene in Mexico City. Rock and Roll had first developed in Mexico in the mid-1950s. According to Mexican music historian, Federico Rubli Kaiser, "In contrast to their development in the United States, the origin of Jazz and Rock and Roll in Mexico could be described as symbiotic: the two styles had the same source, and they nourished one another through this association."[2] As a drummer of many genres, Nicol was fascinated by this amalgamation of Jazz and Rock, and even more, he craved the Latin rhythms of Mexico and South America. Though he was only 27 years old, Nicol had traveled the world several times over and had played with the best of the pop world, yet he was still eager to learn more about his craft and to create his own music.

To accomplish his goal, Jimmie decided to visit the clubs to jam with local bands. To his surprise, he found that musicians were not altogether a welcome group in late 1960s Mexico. The clubs were called "Cafes Cantantes" or Singing Coffee Houses. At the time, no alcohol was permitted, only coffee and soda. In a way, Nicol must have felt like he was flashing back to his early roots, sitting in with various bands at the 2 I's Coffee Bar in London.

Gustavo Diaz Ordaz's Mexican government did not approve of the Rock scene, nor did Mexico City's Regent (Mayor) Ernesto Uruchurto. The Regent instructed police to shut down many of the music clubs, that is, when the police were not extorting money from the club owners to stay open. Uruchurto's goal was to eliminate the city's nightlife completely. Some of these clubs heroically stayed open, despite abuses suffered by the musicians at the hands of police who did not approve of their lifestyles.[3]

One of the Cafes Cantantes that remained open, booking Rock bands, was the Champaign A-Go-Go. It was at this club where Jimmie Nicol began a regular gig. Some referred to the place as gaudy, but the journeyman drummer called it home for a time. The illuminated marquee outside the club, announced the famous drummer, "Jimmie Nicol! El Quinto Beatle!" Despite the lingering ill will toward Brian Epstein, Nicol was not averse to using his Beatles fame as the "Fifth Beatle" to attract a crowd. Due to Mexico's crack-down on live music, the term, "black hole of Mexican Rock", arose to describe the scene. It meant that bands would only play covers of American and British hits. Original Rock compositions were almost non-existent in 1967 Mexico. Mexican radio favored foreign hits and traditional Mexican music over home grown Rock and Roll. Once again, Nicol was playing drums on familiar hits of the day, not unlike the old days of 1964, when he recorded pop covers in support of the Top Six label. For the time being, Nicol was satisfied with a return to his roots.

At the cafes, Jimmie formed an international trio with a Canadian on bass guitar and a Frenchman on lead and rhythm guitar. Nicol, of course, played drums and he began contributing to the vocals regularly. The other band members' names are long ago lost in the sands of time. It was a beginning for Nicol, but he had much greater ambitions.

A Spotnicks Farewell

In March of 1967, the last of Jimmie Nicol's Spotnicks' albums was released on Swe Disc. It was aptly titled, "The Spotnicks in Acapulco", to reflect The Spotnicks' recent tour of Mexico and vacation in Acapulco. Unlike the previous albums, this one would be a two-drummer effort. Five of the songs were recorded while Jimmie was still in the band. They included the following:

Suspicion (recorded in Paris, 1966)
La Pachava (recorded in Paris, 1966)
El Toro Bravo (recorded in Paris, 1966)
Moscow (recorded in Tokyo, 1966)
Wham (recorded in Gothenburg, 1966)

The other tracks were recorded by Nicol's replacement, Tommy Tausis. The album was a varied collection of songs that again reflected a multi-cultural theme. However, the title and album cover were clearly aimed at the Mexican market where the band had recently served a lengthy residency. The Swe Disc press release touted the "unique album cover with 17 colorful photos to look at."[4] The photos were all taken of the band at play in Acapulco.

Local Gothenburg record reviewer, Lennart Clerwall, provided a sneak peak of the new album. He described it as, "Quite simply, amazing, without a doubt, The Spotnicks' best LP."[5] Clerwall fails to explain why this album is the best ever, other than to say it is the most varied. However, he takes the opportunity to take a mild swipe at Nicol, whom he knows has left under a cloud. "I mean no offense to Jimmie Nicol or any of the previous drummers for The Spotnicks, but Tommy Tausis is the solution to all the drummer problems The Spotnicks have had over the years."[6] Despite his hometown leanings, Clerwall apparently was unaware that Nicol had played on five of the songs he had raved about on the album. All of this

Nicol in Mexico with The Spotnicks. Photo Credit: © Roland Ferneborg.

was moot, however, as *Billboard* revealed, "The sales action is nil for *The Spotnicks in Acapulco* LP pressed in Mexico."[7]

To Jimmie Nicol, this was old music in his rear view mirror. He was forging ahead, looking to create a new original Rock sound in Mexico to fill the country's "black hole". He was looking for new musical collaborations to battle the Mexican bias against its own organic Rock and Roll generation. Nicol would soon find it and strive towards his goal in a place "where you can do anything... if you have a will to do it."[8]

The Beatles Pay Tribute

Meanwhile, halfway around the world, The Beatles - or at least Paul McCartney - had not forgotten about their deputy drummer who had performed so well under pressure during the 1964 world tour. McCartney was walking his dog Martha, on a beautiful spring day near his home in St. John's Wood in London. He recalled the hectic days after Ringo fell ill and the band had to begin its tour with session drummer, Jimmie Nicol. Jimmie's reply to Paul and John, when they asked him how he was handling the drumming and Beatlemania chores, had stuck in Paul's head. Nicol would always give them the same thumbs-up answer, "It's getting better." According to McCartney, that was all he'd ever say – "It's getting better, it's getting better."[9] It was Jimmie's consistent, optimistic mantra that suddenly gave McCartney the inspiration to write a new song.

"I just remember writing it," says McCartney. "Ideas are ideas, you don't always remember where you had them, but what you do remember is writing them."[10] McCartney originally wrote the music for the song on the Binder, Edwards, and Vaughan piano in his music room. The image of Jimmie Nicol keeping such a positive tone on their tour with all of the pressures of playing Ringo Starr's parts, and his role as a Beatle at press conferences and parades, gave McCartney a buoyant theme to work with in writing the song. "It's an optimistic song," Paul relates. "I often try to get to optimistic subjects in an effort to cheer myself up, and also realizing other people are going to hear this, to cheer them up too."[11] Of course, the song had a dark side as well, which allowed McCartney and his songwriting partner John Lennon to vent their frustrations with teachers who were not cool and made their lives generally miserable. Lennon even added the now famous counterpoint lyric to Paul's "It's getting better all the time," with his own laconic line, "It can't get no worse."[12]

The song would be recorded in late spring of 1967, destined for *Sgt. Pepper's Lonely Hearts Club Band*, an album that would define the 1960s as *the* iconic record of the decade. *Sgt. Pepper's* transformed Rock and Roll into an art form musically with its thematic approach - as well as its unconventional cover featuring many of the most interesting personalities of the twentieth century. Despite this brief tribute to their temporary drummer, Nicol was likely unaware of this "shout-out" by McCartney upon the album's release in June of 1967. However, he was aware that British and American pop music was blending with the underground youth culture and its accompanying experimentation with hallucinogenic drugs. Nicol (who was no stranger to the Mexican underground) sensed a new musical phase coming, an era of psychedelic music with more introspective lyrics and interesting rhythms that appealed to him. He felt it would also appeal to an audience of Mexican young adults and teenagers.

RCA Victor Mexicana

In his enthusiasm to jump-start his career by creating original music in Mexico, Nicol sought out a connection he had made one year earlier in Mexico City with The Spotnicks. The contact was Louis Couttolenc, President of RCA Victor Mexicana. Couttolenc had come to see The Spotnicks at the Señorial Hotel and was quite taken with the drummer. They had talked about the state of music around the world. The label executive was impressed with Nicol's maturity, confidence, ability, and worldly musical knowledge. Jimmie Nicol was a name that he remembered.

The year 1967 was a turning point for major label record companies in Mexico. They realized that, to increase sales, they would need to change their image from staid business stalwarts to hip modern trend-makers. The reality was that the largest segment of Mexico's record buying population at the time was teens and young adults. These youths had different preferences for their music. Having been exposed to American and British Rock for the past few years, they were no longer content to buy the traditional Mexican music of their parents' generation. RCA Victor Mexicana, CBS, and Capitol de Mexico were entering a new era of fierce competition for the 15-30 year old record market. Armando de Llano, President of CBS, admitted, "The principal problem today is that we haven't been giving the teen-age market the music it wants. But we are seeking the new Mexican soundmaker, the idol. There is no one now. But one of us is going to find him."[13]

Once again, Jimmie Nicol's timing was perfect. He needed to restart his career, and RCA Victor Mexicana needed of an experienced, youthful music man to guide them to the teenager's disposable income. Couttolenc was thrilled that Nicol, who already had made a name in the music industry, had decided to settle in Mexico. His competitors at the other labels would be jealous. He hired the "Fifth Beatle" to become his A & R man to help discover the next big "idol" in Mexico's pop music. Nicol was thrilled with his new responsibilities, which were largely undefined at first. He told the press that he had left The Spotnicks to work for RCA Victor Mexicana, to "do whatever I want at RCA."[14] The RCA president happily proclaimed, "We are behind Nicol 100 percent. We know he'll help us find the new music we are seeking."[15] It is ironic that a Mexican record company would turn to a British musician to increase its share of the Mexican pop music market. Although Nicol had not set any sales records with his own bands, he did know how the British music industry worked; and he could lend his experience to the Mexican label that trailed the UK and US markets by a few years.

Nicol got to work right away at the RCA Mexicana offices. As a young record executive, he had a number of ideas he wanted to propose. One of his first suggestions was to send people into the go-go cafes, Rock clubs, and neighborhoods dressed in modern clothing, to catch the live music, talk to the kids, mine their preferences, and analyze the data. RCA also began to open up additional sales offices throughout Mexico.[16] As Nicol stirred up the dust at RCA, Couttolenc told the press, "The word here is aggressive. We know how big the teen market is and we're going after it as never before."[17]

Jimmie Nicol had not given up on the idea of recording more of his own music. With the carte blanche RCA had presented to him, Nicol came up with an idea that might mutually benefit the label's goal as well as his own. Fate would provide Nicol with a musical partner when he toured RCA's Mexico City studio one day in June, 1966. Louis Couttolenc was proud of his newly refurbished, state-of-the-art Dynagroove studio, and he wanted his newest executive Nicol to use it as his own laboratory. He wanted Jimmie to have every advantage to discover and record the next big-selling "idol" for the teen market.

Earlier in the year, Couttolenc had spent $75,000 to add the latest Dynagroove equipment and recording processes to his studio.[18] Dynagroove was a 1963 RCA initiative to enhance the LP record-making process. RCA heralded the process as "adding brilliance and clarity, realistic presence, full-bodied tone and virtually eliminating surface noise and inner groove distortion."[19] Nicol was anxious to record his own music when he saw all of this shiny new hi-tech equipment.

Los Nicolquinn

During the summer of '67, Nicol met a young musician named Eddie Quinn. Quinn was a youth of only 20 at the time, young, handsome, and seemingly perfect for the teen market they were targeting. After a bit of jamming together, Nicol decided to ask RCA to sign up Quinn and himself with the idea that they would form a musical group together. RCA agreed and the group, "Los Nicolquinn", was born. Nicol described Quinn as follows: "My partner is a cat of 20 years, of Hungarian, Mexican, and Jewish decent. He is a composer, singer, guitarist, pop-economist, co-producer, and speaks great American. He is the youth in fact of Mexico!"[20] The two set to work composing nine of the ten tracks on their forthcoming album. Billboard magazine announced the big news of Mexico City, "Jimmy Nicol and Eddie Quinn (RCA Victor Mexicana) have formed a group they call

Nicolquinn to present shows throughout Mexico and in Southern states in the US."[21]

Forming Los Nicolquinn accomplished several goals for Nicol. He believed he had found the next big musical "idol" for RCA and Mexico; and he would be able to control, play and record his own music by combining forces with Eddie Quinn. In essence, Jimmie Nicol could, in fact, become the "next big thing" in the Mexican musical world, or at least the Svengali behind the "next big thing".

The two partners set about writing songs together. Some of the song lyrics seemed to reflect Nicol's emotions at the time. He felt like he had been exiled from England or at least from the music business there. Jimmie continued to blame Brian Epstein, when in fact much of Nicol's fate had been determined by his own miscalculations. Nevertheless, Nicol felt adrift in the world when he co-wrote the album track, *I'm Lost*. The lyrics appear to reflect his pessimistic feelings as he tries to establish his roots in yet another foreign land. He sings:

> "I am badly beaten up/ And as the years go passing by/
> I'm lost/ I'm lost/ I'm lost/ I'm lost/
> And as I go on like this/ I ask myself why should I live/
> I'm lost/ I'm lost/ I'm lost/ I'm lost/
> Now I know I won't go back/ And if I do, I'll break my back/
> I'm lost/ I'm lost/ I'm lost/ I'm lost."[22]

In addition to writing about exile, he also appears ready to find a new love interest in the song, *Whims and Fancies*. Nicol complains in the song that:

> "I can't seem to find the one for me/ though I try very hard/
> Little chick with your whims and fancies/ tell me where you are/
> I will wait for you till ever/ whims and fancies/
> whims and fancies/ whims and fancies."[23]

"*Whims and Fancies* is deliciously British Camp, and not to be taken seriously," says rhythm historian David Stanoch. "It is the musing in song of a worldly playboy, all delivered in an upbeat pop/ear candy confection over a couple of repeating upbeat riffs that don't really even add up to a complete song in the traditional sense - but maybe that wasn't the point?"[24] The tongue-in-cheek Nicol vocal was not out of place with some of the lighter music produced in the psychedelic go-go era; and, although he did not know it at the time - as with many of the happenstances in Nicol's life - his song's wish would come true, and he would find his "little chick" quite soon.

Unknown, another Nicol & Quinn original, is a rather dark but imaginative work, and quite original in its arrangement. Stanoch likens the song's intro to a familiar riff from Detroit's classic R&B era. "The first four bars, with its syncopated bass line, Motown drumbeat and piano might lead you to believe you're headed for a jaunty romp like *Baby Love*, by Diana Ross and the Supremes, until it all comes screeching to a halt with the arrival of the spooky Vox organ and Nicol's wooden robot-like spoken word vocals - punctuated by a cyclical and insistent crash on a Chinese cymbal throughout the song, which all conjure up visions of a 50s Sci-Fi 'B' movie."[25]

Minor key intervals throughout the track create a suspenseful and foreboding mood. It seems to be a story describing the grim journey from life to death. The use of British-style police sirens in the chorus offers an interesting effect as well. It may well have been a commentary on the student protests and harsh police reactions beginning to surface in Mexico. The song, which could certainly *give* someone on LSD a "bad trip", was clearly not hit radio material in Mexico or anywhere else in the world, but it was a brave attempt at audio aesthetics.

When it came time to record their songs, Nicol set about hiring additional musicians on brass and strings and worked with them on the arrangements. He set up the studio and produced most of the sessions. Nicol and Quinn shared some of the keyboard duties. Additionally, Quinn handled the guitar and bass, while Nicol held down the drums and extra percussion. Photos from the album's back cover show the duo recording their tracks, interacting, and laughing in the studio.

Eddie Quinn seemed to be working well with his new creative partner. He described his collaborator during this period in a sort of hip, beatnik narrative. "He is famous, he is the fifth Beatle, plays drums in a very special way, sings, dances, composes, arranges, directs, and invents wild things; he is publicist, photographer, English and 27 years past."[26]

Los Nicolquinn recorded one cover version of a song called *Something Stupid*. The song had originally been written by C. Carlson Parks in 1966. Just prior to Nicol & Company entering the studio, the track had been covered by Frank and Nancy Sinatra in March of 1967. Their version had become the best known version and placed the Sinatras No. 1 on *Billboard's* chart for four weeks.

Los Nicolquinn's version was mostly instrumental with strings, organ, bells, and drums. It was a jazzy, cocktail lounge arrangement that served as a relaxing closer to an otherwise pedestrian album of attempted psychedelic music.

Once the recording and mixing was wrapped up, the tapes went off to RCA for pressing. Jimmie designed the back cover of the album with a photo collection of "band" at work photos. RCA hired a Mexican artist named Navarro to design the graphic illustration of Nicol and Quinn for the colorful and mod front cover. Nicol clearly did not want it left up to fate regarding *who* were the hip, new original Rock artists of Mexico. He invented Los Nicolquinn in his own image to be the "next big thing", and he would describe to Mexican record buyers exactly what this meant:

Los Nicolquinn album cover – the "next big thing" in Mexico.
Photo Credit: Courtesy of Author.

Essentially, 'Los Nicolquinn', which is the integration of both names, is a new musical expression and stands for: Clothes, music, thoughts, plans, ideas, a band, an act, it is pop music, jazz, movies, institutional, creative, and spectacular. It Drinks Gallons of coffee, is elegant, wild, international, new, new, Made in Mexico. 'Los Nicolquinn', is truth, peace, art, commercialism, what people dig, entertainment, opinions, a drama, a great performance in every track. But essentially 'Los Nicolquinn' means a huge reality, reality that moved the enthusiasm of an artistic director, sound engineers, acoustic technicians, and in true fact all of RCA Victor Mexicana to achieve this album, which gives it the qualification of 100 marks out of 100, concerning technique, talent and quality.[27]

This certainly was a grandiose description by Jimmie Nicol of an album which clearly could not possibly be all things to all people. This self-written vanity piece attempted to place himself at the center of Mexico's creative universe. In essence, Nicol declared this album to be perfect ("100 marks out of 100") and one that would set every trend in music, fashion, film, and all walks of life. Even The Beatles' *Sgt. Pepper's Lonely Hearts Club Band* would have a difficult time living up to this description, although it did seem a more realistic fit at the time, than Los Nicolquinn's album. Jimmie's optimism, ego, and "gallons of coffee" were way over the top in his attempt to manufacture in himself and Eddie Quinn as Mexico's first major pop stars. Unfortunately, words alone could not create the buzz necessary to catapult his latest recording effort. The music would have to stand on its own merits and strike a nerve with the Mexican youth culture. It failed. The *Los Nicolquinn* album would go the way of the Shubdubs and The Sound of Jimmy Nicol recordings. It would not break any sales records or cross over to other countries. In short, it was a commercial flop.

According to *Billboard*, Los Nicolquinn toured a few cities in Mexico and a couple of southern American states briefly that summer. Music history has failed to preserve any evidence of these shows by way of posters, handbills, ticket stubs, or newspaper reviews. Just as The Beatles would not have been able to adequately reproduce *Sgt. Pepper's* live in 1967 due to limitations in technology, the same could be said for *Los Nicolquinn*. Whether such a tour took place is moot, for nothing seemed to work to sell the album which stands very much as an audio period-piece from Mexico's Summer of Love. It was a record that attempted, but ultimately failed, to capture an era of free love, free sex, drug experimentation, mind expansion, and psychedelia.

Clearly the collaboration with Quinn seemed to usher in a new phase in Jimmie Nicol's career in which he strived to create momentum and differentiate his art from his past Beatles link. He was now making music simply for fun and his own creative interest. These tracks are such rarities, known only to the few hundred Mexican youth who happened to pick up a copy in the summer of '67; and the collaboration with Quinn was too short-lived to know what might have been.

Before the year was out, RCA would find its next big original pop star. His name was Armando Manzanero and he was hailed as a "writing talent and performing artist." It would not be Jimmie Nicol's discovery, nor would it be Los Nicolquinn. RCA's A&R ace, Ruben Fuentes, discovered Manzanero's music and his first recording started buzzing through the Mexican pop world even before the album was released. This new idol was a true Mexican and had worked his way up the ladder, for years backing and writing songs for others until he was discovered. Nicol was disappointed his "discovery" had not been the "next big thing"; and despite his best efforts with Eddie Quinn, Los Nicolquinn's impact failed to ignite any type of cultural revolution as Jimmie had predicted. It would be difficult to blame Brian Epstein for this failure, given that he had recently passed away. Ever the optimist, Nicol pressed onward and upward.

Jimmie Nicol – Composer of Film Soundtracks

Yet another unanticipated project came his way, when RCA asked Nicol to compose music for film soundtracks. In the autumn of 1967, RCA's connections paid off when Nicol secured a job as co-composer of a film score. The film was going into production in the Mexican city of Cuernavaca, some sixty miles outside of Mexico City. *"El Mes Más Cruel"* (translation: *The Cruelest Month*) was filmed entirely in black and white. At times the film aspires to be a Mexican version of the French New Wave cinema. Written and directed by Argentinean Carlos Lozano Dana, *El Mes Más Cruel* is beautifully photographed and captures the lush 1960s Cuernavaca in its cosmopolitan period.

The film deals with the complexities of developing and deteriorating relationships and the supposed intellectual sophistication of the "Swinging Sixties" set.[28]

No soundtrack album of the music, written and produced by Nicol and his co-composer Eduardo Salas, was ever released. The film was ultimately screened in Mexico on September 25, 1969; but it met with a tepid response and was pulled from theaters after only a one week run. Although the film failed commercially, it did receive a second-place finish in the Mexican Independent Film Festival in the late 1960s. Renewed interest in the film brought one more screening in 2006 by "Cineteca Nacional" (The National Film Archives Institution of Mexico).

In the meantime, Jimmie Nicol's trio continued to play in Mexico City's cafes. But Nicol had an ambitious new idea to promote himself. He wanted to mount a major stage show extravaganza that would tour Mexico. Once again, Jimmie would utilize his "Fifth Beatle" fame and create a Larry Parnes-styled musical variety show centered on the music of The Beatles. He knew he needed help mounting such an ambitious endeavor in his new home country. He would need someone in the entertainment field who could assist with the language barrier and knew how to stage live concerts in Mexico. He asked one of his friends, an American, if she knew of anyone who could assist him. She knew just the right person, and this person would play a significant role in both Nicol's personal life and his career in Mexico.

Chapter Nineteen

Julia and the Aesthetics of Revolt

Growing up as a little girl in Mexico City, Julia Villaseñor aspired to be a dancer performing onstage for an audience. "I started at six years old and took lessons at the National Institute of Bellas Artes [Fine Arts]," says Villaseñor.[1] Bellas Artes is the cultural agency of the Mexican government and the premier institution in Mexico for stimulating artistic production of all arts and arts education throughout the country.

The industrious dancer realized her dream early in life, and by the time she was in her twenties, she had danced throughout Mexico and other countries. Sometime in late 1965, Villaseñor was offered the opportunity to live in Sweden as part of a traveling dance troupe and to teach dance there as well. I went to Sweden on a tour of the country with a Jazz group featuring Osten Warnerbring," says Villaseñor. "Warnerbring was a well-known Swedish singer, composer and musician."[2] He had begun his career as a Jazz musician, but eventually mastered many musical genres in popular music.

Professional dancer Julia Villaseñor.
Photo Credit: Courtesy of Julia Villaseñor.

In an amazing coincidence, Julia reveals that she stayed with the manager of The Spotnicks, who had just recruited drummer Jimmie Nicol. "When I went to Sweden, I lived with Roland Ferneborg and his wife."[3] While there, Julia never got the opportunity to meet any of The Spotnicks because the band and her dance troupe were always touring in different cities. "When I lived with Roland and his wife, I only met Jimmie by seeing him on a Spotnicks poster on the wall in Roland's office. It is *really* a coincidence that I saw him in a photo there," she relates. "But I didn't know Jimmie until I met him here in Mexico and I never saw Jimmie play with The Spotnicks in Mexico City."[4] In the late summer of 1967, Villaseñor returned from Sweden to her home in Mexico City.

At this time, Nicol was searching for someone to help him launch his ambitious Beatles traveling musical variety show. Jimmie would be the star, but he knew that choreography and interpretation of the music would be of great visual importance. "An American girl who was a friend of Jimmie's contacted me," says Villaseñor. "I went to a hotel to meet him and I did not know he was a 'Fifth Beatle' or anything at the time. We became very good friends and I started talking to him about his show idea."[5] As Jimmie and Julia met almost daily for production discussions, Villaseñor had to convince Nicol to create a more realistic concept in which to achieve his goal. She told him, "In Mexico you cannot realize a large show production. There is not enough money in Mexico's entertainment industry to produce the kind of big show you're thinking about."[6] There also was not a consumer economy in Mexico at the time that could have supported the ticket price and sales to mount such a large scale production.

Jimmie Nicol in the British Royal Guard uniform.

Jimmie appreciated her advice and agreed to scale down his expectations. "So," says Julia, "I created a smaller show production for him. We had his trio for the music. I was interpreting the music in dance and I chose the Beatles songs and created a medley."[7] Villaseñor even designed and made the costume "uniforms" for the show. The performers all wore British Royal Guard uniforms that Julia had created down to the last perfect detail of the buttons. Jimmie not only performed on drums, but he also sang The Beatles songs and spoke to the audience during the show. Julia also created a large screen slide show of visual images to accompany some of the music in the show.

Jimmie began to share some, but not all, of his past life and career with Julia, omitting mention of his former marriage. However, when he mentioned that he had recently toured with The Spotnicks, Villaseñor was surprised and shared her story with him. "When I met Jimmie and he told me about leaving The Spotnicks, I was able to talk to him about our common acquaintance Roland and all about my dancing in Sweden. It was such an amazing coincidence."[8]

The "Beatles" variety show played well in Mexico City and the surrounding areas. The seats were filled and the reviews were quite favorable. As a collaborator, Villaseñor had more than earned Nicol's respect, and now the couple began dating as well as working together. Their creative and romantic relationship blossomed along with the show's success. "The show was very well received and Jimmie and I got very famous from this show," says Julia. "The Mexico City TV station tried to hire us at this time to perform our variety show on TV, but we did not accept because they did not want to pay us anything and they wanted us to be exclusive to them for five years."[9] The show ran through the end of 1967. "Then after the show finished, Jimmie and I got married," says Julia.[10]

Nicol had lived in Mexico for one year. He had achieved some of his creative goals and failed in others. He had found the love he had searched for in his song, *Whims and Fancies*. However, one goal still eluded him. Ever since The Beatles, Nicol had been looking for mass acceptance of his creative work on a large scale.

Newlyweds Jimmie and Julia in Mexico City.
Photo credit: Courtesy of Julia Villaseñor.

He always felt the fans in Australia had truly appreciated his talents when he toured with The Beatles. After all, he had been accepted as a celebrity in his own right while sitting in at the Chequers Club with Frances Faye; and he had impressed fans with his drumming in Adelaide. In addition, the Australian fans had sent thousands of fan letters to his home in the fall of 1964. In his mind, Nicol could be the "King Beatle" of Australia if he could only get back there.

In December, 1967 Jimmie energetically lobbied his bride to move to Sydney, Australia. Julia recalls, "He liked Sydney a lot and he wanted me to go with him." Nicol said, "Julia, we are going to Sydney. It is a great place to live." Julia, a strong, independent young woman replied, "No, I don't want to go to Australia. I am never going to Sydney. It is too far. I don't want to leave my family here."[11] Nicol did not consider that Villaseñor might say "no" to his requested move. He had already told people in Sydney that he would likely be moving there in 1968. This news was leaked to *Billboard* which promptly published as fact that, "Jimmy Nichol [sic] the drummer who filled in for Ringo Starr when The Beatles toured Australia, is reported to be coming back here to live...."[12] However, in the end, the power of love won out over Jimmie's Australia plans; and the new Mr. and Mrs. Nicol settled into a creative and domestic life together in Mexico. There, they would live in the house of Julia's parents.

Mexico City, 1968

Jimmie Nicol's love for Julia helped him to better appreciate life in Mexico. He optimistically summed-up the first year in his new home country. "I have lived here a year or so and I can't get away from it, this country has something I haven't found in a third of the world. I call it feeling. Mexicans talk with anybody. If they don't like something somebody says, they don't like it. If they like it they go mad about it. It is an exotic country."[13]

The newlyweds continued to perform a scaled-down version of their live Beatles presentation. "I was able to speak a little English," say Julia. "And Jimmie learned to speak a little Spanish. So we could communicate. But he had a very funny accent when he spoke Spanish (laughing)."[14] Julia describes Jimmie as very "phlegmatic", a person who is calm, serene, never alarmed, and almost never gets angry. He was enjoying his new life with his bride and appreciating the Mexican art scene to which Julia had helped him gain entree. Julia reveals a pastime they used during their free time to relax and have fun together. "We used to play chess together. I taught him to play. And he'd always lose (laughing). I would call him a grasshopper when he would lose. Oh, Jimmie, you are a grasshopper. He would get a little annoyed... he didn't like to lose. But it was just a game."[15]

The year of 1968 would not be all peace, love, and psychedelia like the preceding year. Things were changing in Mexico and all over the world. The turmoil caused by the difficult conditions of poverty and harsh government rule in Mexico brought student protesters in large numbers who began to clash with the military. At the same time, Rock music in Mexico became inextricably connected to political protest. The government believed that Rock music caused chaos and therefore must be quashed in order to keep order. As a result of government crackdowns on student protesters, more clubs were closed down. In a reaction to this oppression, artists and their performances began to take place as impromptu Public Street displays.

The street performances in Mexico City grew more frequent and larger in terms of audience participation. Julia says, "It was a time of change. I told Jimmie, we should play for the people in the streets. So we began to play the 'Happenings' that were starting at the time for young people."[16] "Happenings" were live events or performances meant as public art. Although some of the main elements of the Happenings were planned, they contained a large degree of improvisation. The idea was to eliminate the boundary between the artist and his audience; and the interaction between the audience and the artwork allowed the audience, in a sense, to become part of the art.

"We played many Happenings in a very beautiful area of Mexico City called Zona Rosa," says Julia.[17] Zona Rosa, a neighborhood in Mexico City, had been populated by artists and intellectuals since the 1950s. The locality contained galleries, book stores, cafes, bars, restaurants, and beautiful gardens. Many painters, writers, musicians, and political activists made this part of the city their home. It was therefore a natural destination for the Happenings of the era. Jimmie and his trio would play their repertoire at the Happenings, and Julia would interpret their music in dance for the young bohemians.

Occasionally, Nicol was asked to sit in with a popular local band called Los Checkmates, a name coincidentally linking Jimmie, the newly initiated chess player, to his new favorite pastime. Although formed in Mexico, Los Checkmates was an international amalgam of players hailing from Canada, the United States, Holland, and Mexico. The band was a popular staple in Mexico City, playing local clubs and universities. In 1967, Los Checkmates recorded its only album of US and British cover songs sung in English. The album was popular for its well-played, garage pop versions of the Turtles *Happy Together*, Spencer Davis Group's *Gimme Some Lovin*, and even The Beatles', *I'm Down*. Roughly 500 copies were sold in Mexico City. In 1968, the band's membership began to shift. At one point during the summer of '68, they brought on Nicol for some live shows in Mexico City.[18] Jimmie was no stranger to the hits covered by Los Checkmates, and he was a perfect drummer for the Rock outfit. Unfortunately, the group never recorded any tracks with Nicol during his brief tenure. Significantly, Jimmie's friendship with Los Checkmates created more musical alliances which would play a role in his future.

The spectre of The Beatles continued to haunt Jimmie Nicol's mind. He shared his perceived ill treatment at the hands of manager, Brian Epstein, with his wife. "Jimmie did not like the way he was treated by Epstein," she remarks. "Epstein gave him a gold watch with an inscription from The Beatles on the inside, giving thanks to him." One day, Julia recalls Jimmie getting very upset. She recalls, "He took off The Beatles watch and smashed it into a drawer. I just picked up the pieces and put them on the table. Jimmie felt as though Brian had finished his career in England."[19] Nicol told his wife, "Brian didn't want to have to compete with a 5th Beatle! He blacklisted me so I couldn't work with other artists. He stopped it all."[20]

Whether Brian Epstein damaged Jimmie Nicol's career or not is debatable. However, in Nicol's mind, it was clear as day that his career had intentionally been derailed by Epstein. To Jimmie, it was a déjà vu of Larry Parnes blacklisting Vince Eager. "Jimmie was damaged emotionally and financially by The Beatles experience," says Villaseñor. "He was a great drummer, better than Ringo," she asserts.[21]

To demonstrate her case, Julia relates a story of a concert the two attended on September 28, 1968 at the Palacio de Bellas Artes to see Duke Ellington and his Orchestra. "Ellington had heard about Jimmie living in Mexico City and he auditioned Jimmie while he was here."[22] After learning the drum parts from *West Side Story*, Nicol played an Ellington rehearsal. The result was an immediate job offer from the Duke. "He offered Jimmie an opportunity to come to the United States and be in his Orchestra," says Julia. "But Jimmie didn't want to leave; because we were just married and he didn't want to go off traveling and touring at that time."[23] Although the example is persuasive regarding Nicol's diverse rhythmic abilities, it fails to account for Ringo Starr's already close-knit relationship with the other Beatles, and Starr's unique talent as an innovative Rock and Roll drummer in his own right. Regardless of the relative merits of the Starr vs. Nicol debate, it was now history. Jimmie had steered his *own* course for the past four years, through the Shubdubs, The Sound of Jimmy Nicol, The Spotnicks, Los Nicolquinn, and his many creative endeavors in Mexico.

Rock and Revolt

In the late summer of 1968, the turbulent decade hit a crescendo of social change and unrest. It was a time of experimentation with drugs, sexual mores, politics, the arts, and protest. In Mexico, a vocal and united student movement formed to challenge the ideals, policies, and power structure of the Mexican government. According to Mexican music historian, Federico Rubli, "We considered ourselves the new order, armed with flowers, peace and love symbols - and Rock music. With new sensorial and sound experiences, as well as attitudes, we wanted to cultivate the aesthetic of revolt."[24]

Students were out in the streets - at the Happenings, on buses, in the public plazas - trying to reach out to all people. Although they lacked any central leadership, they coalesced around the common themes of peace, love, and music. The revolt was non-violent and driven by optimism, conviction and experimentation. On August 1, 1966, the National Autonomous University of Mexico (UNAM) led 50,000 students in a peaceful protest against the repressive actions of the government and violations of university autonomy. More protests followed. According to Villaseñor, "We were always protesting the government here."[25]

As the 1968 Summer Olympics approached, student demonstrators emphasized in a press release that they had no interest in protesting or disrupting the Olympic Games. Despite this public statement, the Mexican government was determined to stop any further demonstrations that might cause the host country to be seen unfavorably in the court of world opinion. In September, the army was ordered in to occupy the UNAM campus. Scores of students were beaten and arrested on trumped-up charges. On October 2, 1968, nearly 10,000 high school and college students gathered at the Plaza de las Tres Culturas to protest the latest actions of the Government and to listen to speeches in a peaceful gathering. The Mexican government assaulted, the gathering, slaughtering hundreds of the protestors, passersby, and journalists in the process.

Jimmie and Julia witnessed the terrible events leading up to the Olympic Games. Villaseñor recalls, "We had many problems in our city before the Olympic Games. We had terrible problems with politics, and many students were killed. Jimmie and I were together and we saw many of the students killed simply because they were protesting."[26] Fortunately, the newlyweds escaped injury. But it was not an easy time for the young artists. "Jimmie did not like politics," says Julia. "He had no interest in it."[27] The scene was both peaceful and surreal at their Happenings, a powerful contrast to the bloodshed of the recent Plaza de las Tres Culturas slaughter. The juxtaposition was quite glaring and did not go unacknowledged by the couple; it clearly had a major emotional impact.

The year had been filled with a new marriage, creative partnerships, street Happenings, and protest. Jimmie and Julia kept very busy with their live performances on stage and in the streets. However, towards the end of the year, their domestic bliss began to wane, although the creative partnership continued. They had been in love, but now their relationship had become fraught with misunderstandings and conflicting imperatives. Their cultural differences were apparent, and Jimmie displayed occasional angry outbursts. Where there had once been fiery love, now there were only embers; and that was not enough. "We were only married for about one year," recalls Julia. "After we got a divorce, Jimmie went to my house and asked my father if he could stay and he stayed in our house with my parents and me. We were separated but still friends."[28]

The Beatles *Get Back*

On Thursday, January 2, 1969, The Beatles began a series of filmed rehearsals at Twickenham Film Studios in London. The plan at the start of the rehearsals was somewhat vague; however, film director Michael Lindsay-Hogg discussed an idea for filming a live performance by The Beatles once they developed a well-rehearsed set list of songs. This would be a special and unique event because The Beatles had stopped playing live concerts back in 1966. Lindsay-Hogg filmed every breathing minute of the rehearsals, including tuning, jamming, playing, talking, and even The Beatles ordering out for lunch.

That same day, while the group took a break from playing, Lindsay-Hogg raised the question of where to play the live concert performance in a filmed discussion with Paul McCartney. The film director steered the discussion toward his favored idea of playing in Tunisia, North Africa. "… because the whole thing I could see torch lit; with 2,000 Arabs and friends around. I thought the venue was perfect."[29]

At the time, there was disharmony within the group about the band's general direction. Ringo Starr was not interested in traveling outside of England for any reason at the time. Sensing the divergent opinions within the quartet, Paul McCartney quipped to his director, "You know, I think you'll find we're not going abroad, 'cause Ringo just said he doesn't want to go abroad. He put his foot down. So, us and Jimmie Nicol might go abroad (laughing)."[30] Little did McCartney realize that Jimmie Nicol was now living abroad himself in Mexico City. Once again, the memory of Jimmie Nicol subbing with The Beatles in 1964 came to McCartney's mind, although in jest. Jimmie was long gone from The Beatles, yet neither he nor The Beatles had forgotten each other.

Anticlimax

In March of 1969, Jimmie moved out of Julia's family home to live with her friend, Gelsen Gas. "He was a producer and director. He had a beautiful house up on the mountain where many artists would go and visit."[31] Gas was creating a new film called *Anticlimax*. It would be an experimental film, typical of the era, surrealistic and abstract. "So, Gas hired me and Jimmie to help out on the film. I remember, I had three Swedish girls that came from Sweden and I created the choreography for them in the film. Very interesting because it was so abstract."[32] The experimental film was filled with improvisation at every turn, from the acting and visuals to the choreography and audio soundtrack. Every day was something different. "There was a lot of experimenting in those days partly because our generation was experimenting with drugs", says Villaseñor."[33]

Anticlimax uses a series of vignettes to explore the modern life of a young man named Domino. Some of the vignettes are humorous, some surreal, some artistic, and some just plain bizarre. Domino is a young engineer who appears disturbed by his boredom with everyday conformity to modern life. These events are illustrated by his encounters moving around a surreal Mexico City landscape. Most intriguing is that these moments are all tied together by an experimental musical soundtrack and sound effects that Nicol composed along with Gelsen Gas.

As the opening credits roll over a visual image of a bubbly wake left behind by a speed boat, we hear a single bass guitar line noodling. Jimmie plays a lonely set of bongos behind the action as two hands are shown digging in the sand, like an archeologist, to find a canister that is dusted off to reveal the word "film". As Domino dresses and leaves his home for another mundane day, he asks a befuddled police officer for directions. Here Nicol uses bubbles blown into water to represent the cop's inconsequential instructions. Domino chooses to go in the complete opposite direction suggested by the police officer, underscoring the rebellious nature of the 1960s generation, especially in light of recent violence by the authorities against student protesters.

Jimmie and Julia on TV Musical Ossart. Photo Credit: Courtesy of Julia Villaseñor.

Domino boards a public bus as Nicol stirs up the sexual tension among the passengers with a Bossa Nova big band tune. We see men leering at women's legs and women fixing their stockings onboard the bus as the music crescendos. One reviewer describes the ride as a "sexually charged symphony of thighs, rumps and glances."[34] As Domino roams the city, a friend driving by calls out and picks him up. A rapid-fire drum solo on Nicol's snare, accompanied by space-aged noises and a fuzz box guitar playing chunky chords, represents the two bachelors having fun driving fast in their car. We see the speeding action of the car leaving behind another wake - this time via road pavement patterns - as the music morphs into an instrumental Rock tune that suggests a version of *Wild Thing* the hit song popularized by the Troggs in England in 1966. There are also bells and flutes in the mix, along with the sounds of screeching tires - all adding to the trippy scene.

Julia playing on Jimmie's drums.
Photo Credit: Courtesy of Julia Villaseñor.

At one point, Domino is at home dreaming. We hear some hand-made rhythmic sounds that are not familiar at first. Julia describes the scene, "I watched Jimmie create some of the experimental music for the film. I cannot explain exactly what that was like (laughing)." In the dream sequence, Villaseñor says, "He played drums, but he used his hands and played rhythms on a big girl. She weighed about 300 pounds and she was naked while he played with his hands drumming on her."[35] The film shows a brief clip of Nicol's hands playing "buttock bongos" on the Rubinesque woman. At other times, Nicol plays a melodic little piano instrument that he blew into while playing the keys. Julia also played on the film soundtrack with a Kalinka stringed instrument.

A visit to the supermarket by Domino becomes a statement about crass commercialism, as he randomly pulls hundreds of cans off the shelves to the sound of Nicol playing a military style march on his snare drum. Nicol again uses his drum kit to represent the repetitive life of Domino, going back and forth between home and office, with a solo tom tom repeating the same phrase to underscore life's recurring madness.

Rapid bongo rhythms represent the speed with which Domino falls in love with a woman and marries (not unlike the relationship of Nicol and Villaseñor). After a scene representing death, the viewer realizes that Domino's life is nothing more than a film being watched by an audience. Villaseñor sums up the project. "It was not a commercial movie; just an experiment."[36] Though an experiment, it was yet another way for Nicol to satisfy his creative vocation and continue his keen interest in music composition.

After *Anticlimax* wrapped up, Jimmie and Julia began to appear on a Mexico City variety TV show. The program was named "TV Musical Ossart", and each show was one hour long. Julia relates, "We appeared on 20 or 30 programs and our part of the show was musical. We had a piano player, bass, guitar, drums and me. When we were on, we would perform three cover versions of the most current popular songs."[37] Despite being on TV, the pay was meager. The couple grew tired of performing pop covers and became more interested in pursuing live shows featuring Samba mixed with Jazz stylings.

Bossa Jazz and Adios

Jimmie Nicol Show on the Psychedelic Go-Go album.
Photo Credit: Courtesy of Author.

Julia and Jimmie began yet another new band. "We still worked on creative projects together," says Villaseñor. "I put together a band this time. It was to play Bossa Jazz and Jimmie played drums."[38] Bossa Jazz was a popular musical sub-genre at the time, which derived from Brazilian Samba and strong American Jazz influences. One of the keys to Bossa Jazz was to value the pauses and silence between the notes. The enchanting upbeat rhythms reflected the optimism of the singers and composers of this style of music.

Julia assembled the band with players characteristic of Bossa Jazz: classical guitar, piano, bass, percussion, and drums. Jimmie fell instantly in love with this new form of music. "He was very passionate about this music and he started to study and learn Bossa," says Julia.[39] She named the band "Abraxas". She even made some of the percussion instruments by hand. At first, Jimmie took on the lead vocal duties, although it was a style more familiar to Villaseñor. One night, Nicol lost his voice and Julia had to take over. "I had to sing the show that night. And from that night on, I took over the vocals."[40]

Abraxas played its initial gigs around Mexico City. Musically, the band was getting quite good and working well together. However, there was an undercurrent of ill will running below the surface of the group. Tensions developed between Nicol and the piano player. Julia had recently turned her romantic attentions to the piano player, and this was causing a problem for Nicol. "He decided not to go on tour with me and the band because he got very jealous at this time. I was going with the piano player in the band," she explains, "and Jimmie could not stand this."[41] Abraxas would continue on without Nicol.

Nicol's jealousy of his ex-wife was too much for him to take. It was the final straw that would end their creative partnership forever. One day, Julia came home to find a handwritten note of farewell from Nicol on her table. Jimmie wrote, "Julia, I admire you a lot. I am very proud of your singing and leading the band. I wish you all the success. Love, Jimmie."[42] Around this time, Nicol moved out of the house of Gelsen Gas, and according to Julia, "He disappeared. It is like he just vanished! And I never saw him again in my life; from that day until now... gone!"[43]

Jimmie Nicol Show

Jimmie Nicol untied the bonds to his ex-wife and principal collaborator, setting himself adrift in Mexico once more. He had become a musical nomad. Nicol found a new house to live in that enabled him to move forward into several new endeavors; and, once again, he turned to playing and recording music. Orfeón Record Company approached Jimmie to record a Rolling Stones cover song for an album they planned to create, exploiting the psychedelic go-go era in Mexico. Founded in 1958, Orfeón was one of the first Mexican record companies to acquire multi-track equipment and create its own studios.

Nicol was pleased with the new studio work, thinking it might lead to a new record deal. He found himself in Orfeón's studio located in Naucalpan de Juarez, Mexico. Jimmie assembled some of his musical colleagues to form a one-off band for the recording, calling them the, "Jimmie Nicol Show", to record a cover of The Rolling Stones' 1968 monster hit, *Jumpin' Jack Flash*. The song begins with Nicol's drumming, which now seemed somewhat sloppy and looser than his recordings of previous years. We hear Jimmie at the start, yelling out Mick Jagger's famous opening line, "Watch it!" in English. What follows is a fairly pedestrian cover version featuring a nameless, Mexican, double-tracked vocalist singing the entire song in Spanish. Though true to the original hit, this version contains very little of the passion and emotion of its original. The song was placed in the honored first-track position on the album which was released on vinyl in Mexico in 1969 under the title, *Era Psicodelica Del Go Go* (*The Psychedelic Go Go Era*). Sales were decent in Mexico for Orfeón's exploitation of the psychedelic era, but not good enough, however, for Orfeón to sign Nicol to his own recording deal.

Jimmie Nicol – Jack of all Trades

As a new decade dawned, Jimmie thought of new fresh ideas for his career – some of which he had never attempted in the past - deciding to finally become an entrepreneur. He also resolved to diversify his business activities in order to better sustain himself financially.

Nicol's first project was to build a small recording studio in his house with two tracks for stereo recording. He enjoyed using his own hands to craft the studio. Working in construction had always been a favored hobby for the drummer. He would record his own music and charge others to record at the studio of the "Fifth Beatle". Jimmie continued to pursue his love of playing Bossa Jazz, and hanging out and partying with Los Checkmates. He filled in on drums whenever there was a call, simultaneously integrating himself into the local Rock and Jazz scenes.

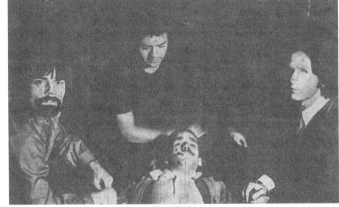
Blue Rain.

One of the bands that Jimmie befriended was called the "Flying Karpets". Although the Karpets was utterly lacking in talent, this bunch of (alleged) US draft-dodgers enjoyed drinking and smoking together. Nicol had met some of the Flying Karpets through his friendship with Claude Henri of Los Checkmates. It was a small community of musicians, and they all enjoyed each other's company and "party supplies". The Flying Karpets had put out one album of mostly psychedelic cover songs a year earlier. One critic described their vinyl debut this way, "This is a pretty terrible album. The band can't play particularly well, the lead vocalist is even worse and that puts the harmony vocals at some exponential kind of vile growth."[44] Though Nicol was not enamored with the Karpets' playing, he still enjoyed "flying" with them and offering his advice.

Interested in sharing his music industry knowledge and experiences in a new arena, Jimmie was hired as an independent consultant to contribute educational musical programming to radio and TV on XHIPN Channel 11. Channel 11 was Mexico's flagship station for educational and cultural television. Nicol also began to prepare course curriculum for students to learn about music business and history at the National Polytechnic Institute. Founded in 1936, the Polytechnic Institute is the most important, public, technical, higher education center in Mexico. History fails to record Nicol's reputation as a teacher in Mexico, but given his passion for the subject and his past fame, it is likely the students enjoyed his many stories and lessons about the music industry.

Perhaps the most unusual vocation started by Nicol, the entrepreneur, was the creation of a

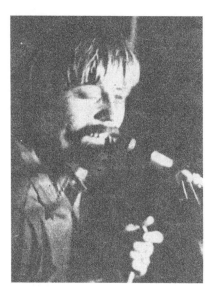

Nicol recording with Blue Rain
in his home studio in Mexico.

button factory. In the late 1960's, buttons were all the rage and provided students and protesters with a visible form of expressing their politics, their beliefs and their love of music. Chris Riggs of the Flying Karpets described Nicol's enterprise. "These are buttons that Jimmie makes in his small button factory in two or three shifts. They are crazy with lots of colors and others are made of The Beatles in Yellow Submarine and stuff."[45] Jimmie busied himself employing workers to manufacture the buttons, while he went out and paid sales calls directly to retail stores, taking orders and making deliveries. For a time, the button factory was a successful and lucrative endeavor.

Blue Rain

Despite all of the business and educational activities keeping him busy throughout 1970, Jimmie still yearned for the camaraderie of playing in a Rock band. Always the optimist, Nicol wanted to start another group, create original Rock music, and hopefully get another record deal. In November, he started inviting some of Los Checkmates and Flying Karpets over to party at his home. The group included: Remy Bastien, a bass player; Chris Riggs, a guitarist, piano player and organist (both ex-Flying Karpets); Claude Henri, a vocalist and lyricist (an ex-Checkmate); and Nicol. It was likely no coincidence that the friends Nicol invited over each played a different instrument, such that their combination could create a new band. "The story is that soon after we got together, we got drunk at the place in which Jimmie lives," says Riggs.[46] Out of the happy haze of partying, the idea for starting up a new band emerged.

The band was an integrated group of American, Mexican, French, and British descent. Remy Bastien liked the fact that they all came from different nationalities. "We can incorporate more sounds into our music. And it is something like a League of Nations."[47] The group came up with a name for itself…"Blue Rain". Chris Riggs says the origin of the name came simply from, "… a sense of sadness or the blues. I believe Blue is good rain. That it can have many meanings, mainly it means the blues. But we don't call it Blues Rain, just Blue Rain."[48]

The plan called for the cocktail-fueled pop group to write several original songs to sing in English and create international appeal. It was ambitious, and the project would begin in Nicol's home studio. Blue Rain began jamming, along with talking, smoking, and partying. That was the plan. "We improvise, but we don't worry about creating equal parts. We simply leave it natural," Nicol explains.[49] To Jimmie it was all about communal connection. "We are connecting mentally. We feel good when playing because we are communicating."[50] Riggs tried to keep the new band focused on the task of making of an album. He believed that Nicol's experience and connections combined with the band's friendship would ensure success. "Everything that we are doing, we are preparing it to do an LP," says Riggs, "that surely we will record in the studio here or perhaps we will go to a record company."[51]

Blue Rain was managed by a mutual friend Simon, who had helped them create their band name and had tried to provide moral support to the fledgling band. The strongest connection within Blue Rain, however, was their love of partying; and playing music seemed to take a back seat. Unlike his previous bands, this time Nicol was more realistic and even voiced some creeping doubt regarding the band he had assembled. "Musically we are not connected. Musically even, the group is not very good, but mentally yes. We are mentally connected. Simon, I believe, is the most important for the group working together." As if to rationalize the band's lack of ability, he adds, "And musically isn't that what we are looking for?"[52]

Despite the best efforts of Simon and Jimmie, Blue Rain floundered for half a year without ever creating an album's worth of decent recordings to pitch to a record label in Mexico. It was a ever creating an album's worth of decent recordings to pitch to a record label in Mexico. It was a great social and communal experiment with "mental connection", yet one that would never take flight. No album was released by Blue Rain and no recordings from Nicol's private studio have ever surfaced. The only record of Blue Rain's existence is a *Mexico Canta* fan magazine that, ironically, combines its cover story "Blue Rain has an Ex-Beatle", with a photo of Paul McCartney talking about his frustration in The Beatles. Nearly seven years after his brief tenure with the group, Nicol was still being linked to The Beatles - a blessing on some days, but a curse on others.

The break-up of Blue Rain in 1971 represented a significant turning point in Nicol's life and career. For a few more years, he continued his studio hobby at home, along with teaching, radio programming and running his button factory. However, for all intents and purposes, Jimmie Nicol was throwing in the towel. He was finished as a drummer, band leader, singer, arranger, composer, and producer. His professional music career had taken him from drum repair shop and small coffee house trios to the Top of the Pops and The Beatles. It had sustained him and allowed him to live and travel throughout the world. The money had come and gone and come and gone. Professionally, however, it was time for Jimmie Nicol to hang up his drum sticks for good... and once again, become an escape artist and vanish. The only questions pending in Nicol's mind were w*here would he land next* and *what would he do in his new life after music?*

Chapter Twenty

Lost and Found

Jimmie Nicol was ready again for a new life, and ready to return to his homeland. His drumming days were over, and he was ready to try something new and different. None of his friends or his ex-wife, Julia, knew exactly when Jimmie left Mexico City in the middle 1970s. In his last interview in Mexico, Nicol was cryptic about how long he would remain with Blue Rain. "I don't know, time will tell." And in answer to why he had lived in Mexico so long, he replied, "Because this is where I am most happy."[1] By 1975, this feeling had obviously changed. His motives for leaving Mexico remain shrouded in mystery; perhaps it was the failure of Blue Rain to coalesce musically or to get a record deal. Perhaps the profits from his button factory shrank as the student protests began to wane. Or perhaps Nicol simply missed his home country after a self-exile of nearly ten years. He had missed out on seeing his young son, Howard, grow up during his decade away. Nicol felt certain he could now return to London and begin a new life without being haunted by the Beatles' connection and his old British music career.

Jimmie's ex-wife, Julia, who would never see him again, chalks it all up to his Zodiac sign of Leo. "He was much more talented than people knew. He was a very proud person. He was a Leo."[2] Although many dismiss astrology and the traits ascribed to each sign of the Zodiac, it is hard to ignore Nicol's former wife, when she ascribes some of the so-called attributes of a Leo to Jimmie Nicol's life and career.

One significant "trait" of a Leo is his love of being on center stage and making an impression on people. Nicol had spent his entire career, from the late 1950s through the early 1970s, on stage as a music performer, even joining in with dramatic and comic flair in Vince Eager's stage show. Photos of his time with The Beatles on stage and at civic receptions show his entranced look of bliss as the adulation of the fans washed over him. Even Nicol's autograph was always front-and-center, larger than his band mates.

People born under the sign of Leo usually exhibit an extremely independent streak and detest control or being dictated to. These characteristics were clearly apparent in Nicol's rebellion against Brian Epstein's strict rules while on tour. Nicol usually disobeyed these rules and went out on his own to explore night clubs and cities in direct violation of Epstein's edict. It is also interesting to note that, upon his return from The Beatles' tour, Nicol immediately shed his job in Georgie Fame's band and working on studio sessions, to forge his own independently controlled bands – Jimmie Nicol & the Shubdubs, and The Sound of Jimmie Nicol. Once in Mexico, Nicol controlled his destiny in creating an image of himself (along with Eddie Quinn) as the next big Mexican original pop star, who is "…elegant, wild, new, Made in Mexico… truth, peace, art, and what people dig…."[3] Examples of Jimmie's independent spirit are plentiful throughout his career.

Of equal interest is the Leo's characteristic luck in money matters, often having resources appear randomly from unthought-of sources. Nicol must have been pleasantly surprised by his earnings as a session man from Johnny Harris' entree into the London recording scene. He was earning more in one full day than the average London factory worker made in a week! When The Beatles paid Jimmie for his brief tenure, the money from this short stint helped finance his own band The Shubdubs, new mod suits, and the extravagant Jaguar. Of course, the best example is the out-of-the-blue call from The Spotnicks offering Nicol a lucrative financial gig after he had filed for bankruptcy and was out of work.

The Leo's warmth, enthusiasm, and optimism are traits that seem to match Nicol's personality by most accounts. Jimmie never had a problem fitting into bands or making friends throughout his career. Even Paul McCartney was inspired by Nicol's "getting better" slogan of optimism years later. Jimmie was never short on this trait, as exemplified by his days as a leader of his own bands. He always believed his music was going to impact the youth culture; rise up the record charts, receive heavy airplay, and make him the star he thought he should be. His inability to come to grips with his career defeats or to acknowledge his musical misfires might also be ascribed to this type of personality. Blaming his time with The Beatles and the Epstein "blacklisting" was easier than admitting his own solo musical career miscues.

Regardless of one's belief in the accuracy of Zodiac signs, Jimmie Nicol was back in London. He had vanished from Mexico and was ready for a new career. He wanted to work with his hands and he wanted to be anonymous. Upon his return, Nicol made no effort to contact his old buddies, Vince Eager, Johnny Harris, Georgie Fame, John Hodkinson, and the rest. Indeed, most of his friends had read the *Billboard* story back in 1967 which stated that Nicol had moved to Sydney; and they erroneously believed that their old drummer and friend had permanently settled Down Under. This misdirection enabled Jimmie to return to London unseen, unnoticed and under the radar - just the way he wanted it.

He quietly set about creating an anonymous business in the building trade, specializing in the renovation and remodeling of London area homes. It is interesting to ponder the changes in Jimmie that caused him to retire abruptly from his many creative musical endeavors and to pursue a remodeling business. Regarding this point, the historical record is mostly silent. Nicol himself, only vaguely hints at the reasons. "When the fans forget, they forget forever," He reveals. "After The Beatles thing was over for me, I played around for a few years, and then I got away from the music scene. I mean, when you've played with the best, the rest is just, well, the rest."[4] It is interesting that Nicol only reveals part of the story of walking away from his music career. He never comments on his efforts to launch the Shubdubs and The Sound of Jimmie Nicol, or his failed album *Los Nicolquinn;* or the non-starter, Blue Rain. And he also omits the story of his exile years, moving from The Spotnicks to Mexico and back to London in the mid 1970s.

As he launched his remodeling business, Jimmie believed it would also be beneficial to study good business practices. Nothing was ever "half-way" with Mr. Nicol. He wanted to totally immerse himself into a new field and succeed. He had learned much from running his own button manufacturing business in Mexico; and now he was starting a business that provided a service. Yet he looked at the finished result of his labor as a product. "I had experience in business," he relates. "I have studied courses in public relations, marketing and advertising."[5] He carefully researched the types of components that best fit into the houses he would remodel. "I've studied products. And my company is a product... I have to analyze what advantages the product has and the disadvantages. What public sector is going to buy it?"[6]

In his remodeling career, Nicol recognized the importance of a good business plan to engage the customer and to deliver a quality finished product. He relates, "Planning is where you identify your market, identify the product, and state the product... what requirements it needs. What needs you will satisfy for the customer. What dream are you going to sell the public? How are you going to sell them the dream?"[7]

During the day, Jimmie Nicol was working to build his new business. However, on more than one occasion, his love of music would pull him into the North London pubs in the evening where bands were playing live music. One evening around 1978, Nicol spotted his old friend and fellow musician, John Hodkinson, the friend who had been living with him when he received "*the call"*. Nicol felt comfortable now in his new career and identity to approach his old friend. Hodkinson recalls: "One night Jimmie came up and slapped me on the back in my local pub."[8] It had been close to 13 years since the men had seen each other. It was a happy reunion and the two caught up on each other's lives since the days of The Shubdubs. "I turned around and I couldn't believe it," says Hodkinson.[9] Other than the occasional appearance at the local pub, like a UFO dropping out of the sky - Nicol mostly kept to himself and focused on his business.

Also in the late 1970s, he made one side trip to Stockholm to visit his friend, Bo Winberg, of The Spotnicks. This time the trip was purely social; however, it did reconnect Jimmie with his old band. This later helped The Spotnicks in the 1980s when making a TV documentary about the long history of the band. Nicol graciously agreed to appear on the program.

Perhaps the most significant event for Jimmie, in the 1970s, was to reconnect with his son, Howie. In the late 1960s, while Jimmie was traveling the world in search of musical success, young Howard and his mother had moved to the city of Rochdale. Rochdale is the second largest of ten metropolitan boroughs that make up Greater Manchester; and it was here that Howie attended Greenhill Upper School in the 1970s. He eventually moved to London to begin his apprenticeship at the BBC from 1980-1985, and he worked as a sound recordist in the TV and film industry.[10] Very little is known about this reunion of father and son during the dawn of the 1980s, but it is an interesting coincidence that Howie was beginning a career in the entertainment industry at nearly the same time his father had retired from entertainment to pursue the building trade.

A Spotnicks Reunion

As Jimmie and Howie began to reconnect with each other, an opportunity arose that brought back the retired drummer for one more encore with his old Swedish band, The Spotnicks. Hans Sidèn, an author and photographer, and Gosta Hanson decided to produce a TV documentary about the career of the band. Since Jimmie had played an important role in the band's history, he was asked to travel back to Gothenburg once more to film his thoughts and recollections of his time with Sweden's top instrumental pop band. Spotnicks keyboardist, Peter Winsnes, recalls the reunion of Nicol with his old band. "We should meet again in Gothenburg in December 1983 for a TV documentary called *The Spotnicks – A Quarter Century of Space Pop*."[11]

Nicol's role in the film included a brief interview. He had not made a public appearance anywhere in years. Jimmie was decked out in a grey tweed sport jacket, white shirt and black tie. He sported the identical "Beatle haircut" from the mid-1960s and his trademarked mustache from Mexico. The one noticeable thing about his appearance was the deterioration of his teeth, with several missing on the bottom row. He related why he had joined The Spotnicks and how pleased he was that Bo had not changed the band's signature sound over the years. The TV Guide in Gothenburg described the program on December 22 with a brief reference to Jimmie. "The Swedish Pop and Rock group Spotnicks did world tours since the 1960s, had their songs on the England record charts, got a drummer from the Beatles and became super popular in Japan and Germany and several other countries - but in Sweden they have never had their own TV show, until now."[12]   The TV

Jimmie Nicol back at the Dolen Hotel.
Photo Credit: © 1984 BEATLES UNLIMITED/ KOOP GEERSING.

175

program, which included a live performance in the studio (sans Nicol) was only aired in Sweden, which was fine with Jimmie who had happily returned to a quiet life in England.

The Beatles Convention

Jimmie returned to London and continued his work in remodeling. He also continued to stay in contact with his son, Howie, who was still working at the BBC. In the spring of 1984, the Dutch branch of "The Official Beatles Fan Club" tracked down Jimmie through his son, Howie. Founded in November of 1963, the Dutch Beatles Fan Club was officially sanctioned. Later they published *The Beatles Unlimited Magazine* to satisfy the demand of growing foreign interest in The Beatles

Nicol signs autographs for the fans.
Photo Credit: © Ton Van Draanen.

1984 Nicol Beatles autograph. Photo Credit: Author.

after their *British Fan Club* dissolved in 1971. *Beatles Unlimited* was both a magazine and a fan club. It was planning a Beatles convention in June, 1984, when staff reached out to Jimmie Nicol. Enough time had passed that Jimmie was comfortable with the idea of meeting Beatles' fans in Holland, when his son approached him with the offer. Howie acted as Jimmie's manager in negotiating the deal and organizing their trip over in June.

The Fan Club put Jimmie and Howie in the same "Beatles" room at the Doelen Hotel in Amsterdam. There he was met by Koop Geersing, a member of the Fan Club staff, a Dutch radio announcer and photographer. Geersing was struck by Nicol standing by the room's balcony, recalling the thousands of fans screaming and looking up to The Beatles' window twenty years earlier. Geersing recalls, "He didn't show any emotions. I did a photo shoot on the balcony. Jimmie was just smoking his pipe and was leaning over the balcony as if he was remembering Beatlemania all over again."[13] Koop recalls Jimmie and his son were very friendly and keen on how the city had progressed over the years. Nicol spent time site-seeing and taking pictures with his Zenith mirror-reflex camera.

After settling in, it was time for Jimmie and his son to head over to the convention where fans had waited twenty years to see and meet Jimmie Nicol and hear his adventures in The Netherlands as a Beatle. Koop recalls Nicol's arrival at the event, "It was his first time at a Beatles' convention and he really enjoyed himself. He was nice when asked for an autograph and took time when being photographed by fans."[14]

The most interesting part of the convention was Nicol's speech and the question and answer period that followed. Fans were obviously interested in every aspect of Jimmie's time in The Beatles' "inner circle"; yet Nicol had an ulterior motive as he realized the vast economic potential for his "secret" information. In his remarks, Nicol explained:

> I think when we played on that tour; the fans accepted me as a Beatle. But basically, the fans had no choice. They were already 3 Beatles. So the fans had a good deal to start with. They had Paul, George and John. Some fans said it couldn't be The Beatles without Ringo there, but that really isn't it. They should also realize what the other guy [Jimmie] is actually making possible; because it was either The Beatles with me or no Beatles at all. I mean nobody is indispensable. Ringo would have still been ill; he would have had to go into the hospital, so somebody else would have had to do it. I happened to be the right person, in the right place at the right time, with the right tools.[15]

The fans peppered Nicol with questions. "What happened to you after you finished your tour with The Beatles?" Nicol replied carefully and slightly annoyed, "I went back to England on my own. None of The Beatles ever phoned me after that. No phone call." Another fan asked, "What was it like being inside The Beatles? Did they accept you as one of them?" Again, he felt some irritation. Nicol thought to himself that the fans' questions reflected their lack of understanding of his situation. He measured his response to not reveal too many details. He

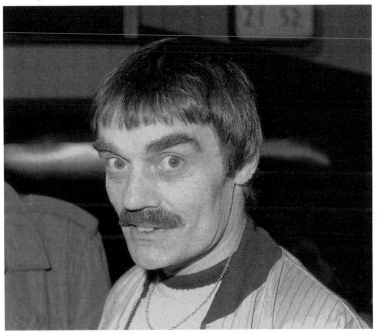

Nicol speaking at the convention.
Photo Credit: © 1984 BEATLES UNLIMITED/ KOOP GEERSING.

was holding back. "Being inside The Beatles' circus for a while, it was disappointing. The only comment that I can make at this stage is that it was disappointing. Not fascinating, because I had been used to it before. You see, when Rock and Roll first hit, I was used to screaming kids. I was used to touring. I had done it before. That was another reason The Beatles chose me; because I not only had the experience as a musician to play their tunes, or the right image, but also how I would deport myself… One had to be a diplomat."[16] Jimmie further explained that it was the intention of The Beatles to pass Nicol off as if he was Ringo Starr. He revealed, "They did not want to admit, even though it was black and white in the press, that there was anybody else playing drums except Ringo you know. In words, they wanted it to look that, 'no it's not Jimmie Nicol, Ringo isn't ill.'"[17] Nicol's remarks may well have seemed to be a direct shot at The Beatles. However, it was likely directed at his old, deceased nemesis, Brian Epstein, and the group's management. Certainly Nicol could not have forgotten Paul's and John's introductions of Jimmie to the fans, in concert as their drummer? Nor should he have forgotten his picture replacing Ringo's on the VARA-TV program.

As the questions from convention fans got more specific, Nicol began to hold back more information, clearly frustrating the purpose of the question and answer period. Geersing noticed the tension in the room. "He was clearly holding information behind, because – as he told the audience – he was writing a book about his time with The Beatles. According to Jimmie there were a lot of things happening that people didn't know about."[18] Nicol was focused on his *not* being asked to join The Beatles permanently; but he would not reveal any specific details.

Later, behind the scenes, Nicol disclosed his irritation with the question and answer session. "I think the interview [with fans] was not rehearsed and I think it was very badly arranged," he told organizers. "It should have been planned. The questions weren't planned. I think people asked questions without really thinking."[19] The convention organizers attempted to learn more about The Beatles' mysteries from the drummer in private, but Jimmie held firm. He reiterated, "You will read my suppositions. And they are only suppositions, which I intend to include in the book. I have my own personal viewpoints of why I didn't get to *stay on* with The Beatles; obviously, because I was very very close to the situation. In other words, I was part of the situation, the internal situation; the internal politics; and the internal movement. I had eyes and ears. At that particular time, I was still

Nicol revisits Treslong Studio. Photo Credit:
© 1984 BEATLES UNLIMITED/ KOOP GEERSING.

quite an intelligent person. So therefore, I saw many things; I heard many things, but I did not comment about them."[20] It is difficult to reconcile the fact that Nicol believed he should have been made a permanent member of The Beatles; especially in light of prior statements he had made about feeling like the "odd man out" while with The Beatles. Yet, cryptically, he repeated that "all would be revealed" in his book.

The autobiography of Jimmie Nicol, promised in 1984, would become yet another mystery. Although convention organizers were anxious to learn more about The Beatles' "inner circle", they also were interested in Nicol's current activities. On this topic, Jimmie was much more forthcoming. "Oh yes, I am currently composing my own music now and recording. It is just a hobby because I am mainly concentrating on my construction company. It is in the process of expanding."[21]

The Last Live Performance

After relaxing a bit, it was time for the signature event at every Beatles' convention – the performance by a Beatles' cover band; and this convention was no exception. The Clarks had been hired to provide a "Beatles experience". Hailing from The Hague, The Clarks for years had been billed as the most famous classic Rock cover band in The Netherlands, playing the hits of The Beatles, as well as Chuck Berry, Elvis Presley, and The Rolling Stones.

Jimmie and Howie went along to Treslong Studio in Hillegom to watch the proceedings and reminisce about The Beatles' interview and concert there some twenty years earlier. Micha Hasfeld of The Clarks was very excited to see Jimmie Nicol watching their show. He had a favor to ask of the "Fifth Beatle". "That day, I just went up to Jimmie

Jimmie Nicol's last public performance sitting in with The Clarks. Photo Credit:
© 1984 BEATLES UNLIMITED/ KOOP GEERSING.

178

Nicol playing with The Clarks.
Photo Credit: © 1984 BEATLES UNLIMITED/ KOOP GEERSING.

and said, 'This is such an honor for us. You must play at least one song with us.'"[22] Jimmie was pleasantly surprised by this request. He replied, "Which number would you like me to play on?" Hasfeld said, "What about 'I Saw Her Standing There'?" Surprisingly, Nicol answered that he did not know this song. "Would you play it for me please?" Hasfeld happily complied. "So I played and sung it for him behind the stage."[23] After hearing the song, Nicol was ready to once again ride the drummer's stool and play drums live to his fans. But first he had to look the part. The Clarks were dressed in 1964 period blue suits with black lapels. The drummer of The Clarks yielded the drum rostrum and sticks to Jimmie; and, in a momentary flashback to 20 years earlier, Jimmie donned the drummer's stage jacket for the occasion.

Nicol took care in adjusting the drum kit while slipping his sunglasses over the collar of his t-shirt. Hasfeld describes the moment, "I remember he adjusted the drums in a special way. He put his drum seat as high as possible, so he could hit the kick harder; which was typical for the old fashioned drummers because there was no amplifying for the drums, like we do now."[24]

When Nicol was ready, Hasfeld counted in the famous song, "Ah 1, 2, 3, 4ahhh", and the song blasted off to the roaring approval of the convention fans, with Nicol steady on the beat. "And we played the song and I will never forget it," says Hasfeld. "I think he was a pretty good drummer, playing steady, hitting hard and no fooling around."[25] As the song ended, the crowd went wild, seeing the former Beatle deputy playing live again. The look on Nicol's face was one of great elation. He stood up behind the kit, arms outstretched, to accept the love and adulation one more time, his eyes sparkling and his mouth open wide with a huge smile. It was all about the music. He had ripped through three Beatles songs in all, twenty years later with no rehearsal and the fans loved it! It had

Jimmie Nicol takes his last bow as a drummer. Photo Credit: The Clarks.

also been a long time since Nicol's son, Howie, had seen his dad play live. As the evening came to an end, there were handshakes and kudos all around for the jubilant Nicol. Yet no one in the room seemed to realize how special this performance was, for it sadly marked the last known public pe-

Jimmie steers the canal boat.
Photo Credit: ©1984 BEATLES UNLIMITED/ KOOP GEERSING.

Nicol waves to fans on the canal 20 years later.
Photo Credit: ©1984 BEATLES UNLIMITED/ KOOP GEERSING.

formance of Jimmie Nicol on drums.

The second day of the convention was more relaxing for Jimmie and Howie. Organizers took the Nicols on another nostalgic ride along the canals of Amsterdam, again reliving another Beatles' experience with Jimmie. Nicol enjoyed the trip down memory "canal". "I had him steer the ship while I took photographs of him," says Geersing.[26] It was a fitting end to an interesting weekend, one which stirred many memories and emotions for the London drummer-turned-builder. Geersing remembers Nicol fondly as a "warm personality", and his son Howie as quite "humorous".

Father and son traveled back to London where they would resume their largely separate lives. The trip had been a success and had provided some good times. However, there was some tension between Jimmie and Howie that had surfaced during the convention. During the post- question and answer discussion with the convention organizers, father and son had disagreed over one major point in discussing the proposed "tell-all" Nicol book.

"The thing that people are missing and making too much of a point of," said Howie, "is he's not a Beatle. So it cannot be."[27] Jimmie quickly snapped back in disagreement with his son's statement. "Yes! I was [a Beatle] for three weeks. The reality was there. Oh no, I was a Beatle!"[28] Choosing his words carefully, Howie responded that right now in the present Jimmie was not a Beatle. Howie suggested the book should be set in the present. Jimmie seemed irritated, that once again, others were trying to frame *his* story. Nicol continued to debate his son. "I mean the selling point is obviously The Beatles. Would you not agree Howard?"[29] Howie grudgingly gave some ground in his reply. "I'd say that is one of the strong points."[30] And so it continued. Father and son's disagreement over the book's focus, and whether Jimmie had indeed been a Beatle or not, were serious differences of opinion. These and other issues would ultimately contribute to an ongoing rift between father and son as they returned to England.

In 1986, Howie Nicol left the BBC and became a partner at Fabsound; a company that specializes in sound recording, sound post-production, DVD and video production in the London area. Nicol describes the start-up at the new company. "I began in pop promos [music videos] with help from many. I recorded some fabulous sounds on long-form documentary with Robert Palmer, Joe Cocker, Prince and the Freddy Mercury Tribute."[31] It was apparently no coincidence that the name of Howie's company, "Fabsound", obliquely referenced his dad's time in The Beatles, who were, of course, nicknamed the "Fab Four" in the 1960s.

Howie Nicol's reputation and rise in the film sector of the music industry coincided with an inverse direction for Jimmie Nicol's career as a builder. Likely due to an economic downturn, Nicol's building trade revenues began to fall off significantly. The former drummer had not moved forward with his book idea as the 1990s dawned. "After the money ran low," he says, "I thought of cashing in some way or other. But the timing wasn't right."[32]

Jimmie began to withdraw even more into himself. On a personal level, Nicol began an extended period of isolation. He was not actively employed in work or purpose, and he appeared to some observers as melancholy and despondent. None of his old musical friends were aware of Nicol's circumstances. Jimmie was very proud and would never have asked for assistance from friends or family. However, he seemed to grow more despondent as yet another career appeared to be fizzling out. In one of his last interviews, Nicol revealed, "It's hard to describe the feeling, but I can tell you it can go to your head. I see why so many famous people kill themselves."[33]

In the intervening years of 1984-1994, relations between Jimmie and his son Howie deteriorated. According to one source (who declined to be identified) there was very little, if any, father-son interaction. Neither Jimmie nor Howie have ever publicly expressed the reasons behind the estrangement.

The year of 1994 would mark the 30th anniversary of The Beatles' tour of The Netherlands. Once again, Beatles Unlimited editor and Fan Club Convention organizer, Renè Van Haarlem, thought it would be fitting to bring the now 49 year old Jimmie Nicol back to Amsterdam as his special guest. Perhaps, says Van Haarlem, "Nicol will have finished his book and be ready to share his story with The Beatles."[34] Van Haarlem had kept Howie Nicol's contact information. "The contact always went via Howard – never directly to Jimmie," relates Van Haarlem.[35] In August, 1994, Van Haarlem traveled from The Netherlands to London. His goal was to meet with Howie at his home in the South London neighborhood of Balham and make his pitch to secure Jimmie Nicol's return to Amsterdam and The Beatles convention. He was also keen to see if Nicol would be bringing his promised autobiography for the fans. René was completely unprepared, however, for Howie Nicol's response, when he rang the doorbell at his home....

Chapter Twenty-One

Wanted: Dead or Alive

Beatles Unlimited editor and Fan Club organizer, Renè Van Haarlem, was in utter shock. Howie Nicol had just informed him that his father, the one-time Beatles' drummer Jimmie Nicol, would be unable to attend the 30th Anniversary Beatles Convention in The Netherlands. The reason Howie gave put a lump in his throat.

After ringing the front doorbell, Howie came outside. "Hi Howie, nice to see you again," said Van Haarlem. "This year is the 30th Anniversary of Jimmie touring our country with The Beatles. We would like to know, if Jimmie would come to The Netherlands again for our convention?" Howie's response was shocking and abrupt. "René," he said. "Jimmie has died."[1]

Van Haarlem was stunned. The conversation was brief. According to Van Haarlem, "He did not tell me what had happened to Jimmie, nor when Jimmie had died – no cause of death given! He was very short with me. I could tell he wanted to get rid of me." Howie did create the impression that Jimmie had died, "some time ago."[2]

The words hit Van Haarlem like a ton of bricks. Just ten years earlier, Jimmie Nicol had attended his convention and had been showered with affection by appreciative fans of The Netherlands. Jimmie had happily relived his Beatles' experiences; signed autographs for fans; promised a book about his Beatle adventures; and even sat in playing drums with Beatles' cover band, The Clarks.

"I was astonished," recalls Van Haarlem. I wanted to know if the book Jimmie told us he was writing [back in 1984] was to be published after all." Howard tersely replied, "No." René offered his condolences to Howie and left. He did not push for any more answers. Not that any would have been forthcoming. He felt sorry and sad for what had happened.[3]

Now it was all over for Van Haarlem and the fans. The only thing left to do was to inform his friends of the sad news; and to look for another guest for his upcoming convention. In 1994, the Internet was in its infancy. There were no smart phones; no social networks such as Twitter, YouTube and Facebook; no blogs; no high-speed broadband; and most people did not even have computers in their homes. No mention of Nicol's death was made in subsequent publications of the Beatles Unlimited fan magazine. The only way people began to hear of Jimmie Nicol's death was by word-of-mouth. Curiously, none of the newspapers, TV, or radio stations thought the story was important enough to investigate in 1994.

Howie Nicol has steadfastly refused to discuss his conversation informing Van Haarlem of his father's death. No one knows the details of Jimmie's untimely death. After the statement, rumors and questions began to circulate throughout Europe regarding the possible cause of death. Was it cancer? Or had Jimmie had an accident or even committed suicide? However, no answers were forthcoming. Eventually, the rumor of "1988" surfaced as the year of Nicol's untimely, but mysterious death.

The Beatles Anthology

In 1994, Howie Nicol began working on The Beatles' multi-part documentary television series, *The Beatles Anthology*, as a sound recordist. It is no small irony that, just as The Beatles were gearing up to present their history and legacy on film and compact disc, one-time "Fifth Beatle", Jimmie Nicol, had passed away and his son began working for the band's film production. Howie Nicol relates, "Turned my attention to recording around 1995, worked on the incredible Beatles Anthology with Apple [Corps] and 'Bingo' [I win] a BAFTA."[4] BAFTA, short for the British Academy of Film and Television Arts, founded in 1947, is England's version of America's Academy Awards. Howie's work on *The Beatles Anthology* had earned him a BAFTA in the category of "Television – Best Sound (factual)" for 1995.

By the time Howie Nicol had begun work on *The Beatles Anthology*, rumors had spread back to London from The Netherlands that Jimmie Nicol had died of cancer. Many of Jimmie's old musician friends such as Johnny Harris, Colin Green, Vince Eager, and Tony Sheridan wondered if Nicol had passed away. They were all surprised to learn that he had even been living in London since 1975, without their knowledge.

A search of London's death records revealed that persons named James George Nicol had indeed died in 1988, 1990, and 1992. Of the four deceased Nicols sharing Jimmie's name, only one had been born in 1939. In searching further, the 1939 James George Nicol had not been born on the same month and day as Jimmie Nicol. Although he could have died abroad, things grew more mysterious concerning Jimmie's untimely death. These inconsistencies - combined with the lack of newspaper coverage on a "Beatle death" and Nicol's penchant for vanishing whenever he sought a change or to go deeper into a solitary life – only served to stir further rumor and conjecture. However, lurking behind Howie's proud moment and his bronze BAFTA trophy was a family secret, one of apparent, unraveling deception that was destined to be revealed and cause greater family issues.

During the making of *The Beatles Anthology*, Paul McCartney, who was actively involved in the production, became aware that Howie Nicol was the son of Jimmie Nicol. McCartney approached Howie during the recording of the television film. He told Howie "how much he would like to see Jimmie again."[5] McCartney suggested that Howie "Ask Jimmie if he would appear in the [Anthology] programme".[6] Howie quickly and simply replied to McCartney, "No."[7]

Did Howie's one-word reply reveal that his father was indeed dead? Or if Jimmie Nicol was alive, did Howie know his dad would never agree to participate in The Beatles' historical film, for the same reasons that had haunted him for decades?

In 1996, as *The Beatles Anthology* was being released on VHS video for home distribution, Britain's *The Mail On Sunday* decided to do a chronicle about "The Sad Story Of The Penniless & Forgotten Fifth Beatle" - Jimmie Nicol. Nicol's quotes appeared to be recycled from many years past. It did not seem the tabloid had newly interviewed the ex-drummer. However, the paper claimed to have located the living, breathing Jimmie Nicol! Reporter, Art McCulloch, described the ex-drummer in the present tense. "Now aged 57, with his thinning hair, stooped shoulders, missing teeth and scruffy clothes, there is nothing to remind you of the smiling young man with the tight suit and the moptop haircut."[8] Was this sufficient proof that Jimmie Nicol was alive? If so, why had the reporter been able to describe him, yet not interview him? In typical, cruel tabloid fashion, the writer - by contrasting the millions being raked in by *The Beatles Anthology* - had chosen to dump on "The Beatle" who did not make it to the top. The story related that Jimmie was eking out a living as a carpenter. Unfortunately for Jimmie Nicol, he could not escape being tied to The Beatles, even in the "Afterlife".

One day at a North London pub, a Beatles' tribute band was playing live. One of the band members named Dom noticed a man at the bar intently watching his group perform. He was dressed in a cardigan and had silvery hair and a very thick moustache. The man looked to be about 60 or so. Dom recalls, "God, that bloke looks familiar". After the set, the gentleman came over to the band as they were packing up. "He complimented our 'Ringo' - Neil on his drumming and said, 'I used to play drums many years ago,'" says Dom. The band was not paying too much attention to the gentleman, focused instead on getting some food. Neil, the drummer, continued a conversation with the man about drumming techniques. As Dom came over to Neil to tell him they all had to get into the van, he heard Neil ask the fellow, "So what's yer name?" The bloke replied, "Jimmie".[9]

On the way back to Liverpool, Dom kept thinking about the fellow they had met in the pub and why he seemed so familiar. "Then, it suddenly hit me," says Dom. "It must have been Jimmie Nicol. Today, I kick myself for being so bloody impatient and not realizing it and quizzing this bloke more on exactly who he used to play drums with 'many years ago."[10] Interestingly, the pub was within walking distance of Jimmie Nicol's last known apartment in the Kentish Town neighborhood of North London.

Jimmie Nicol and son Howie in better days.
Photo Credit: © 1984 BEATLES UNLIMITED/ KOOP GEERSING.

Obviously, not everyone reads the tabloids; and, as a result, the story of 1996 (which contained no present day quotes or photos of Jimmie Nicol) did not receive widespread coverage. The Internet was still not a household tool for widespread dissemination of news and information around the world. However, the mystery of Jimmie Nicol's "death" was actually solved. During the making of *The Beatles Anthology*, historian Mark Lewisohn (who has authored several significant historical tomes on The Beatles' history) was serving as historical consultant on the production. When asked if Jimmie Nicol was alive, Lewisohn was able to substantiate that he personally saw Jimmie Nicol alive at this time, during the time of this project. "As for Jimmie, I last saw him in 1995 and I know his son."[11] Most of the world was unaware that Mark Lewisohn had seen Jimmie Nicol alive; and his eye-witness account had not appeared in the news media. As a result, many people who had known Jimmie Nicol in the 1960s still believed the story that he had died in 1988. In a similar fashion, not unlike the "*Paul is Dead*" worldwide rumors of 1969, the "death of Jimmie Nicol" story had legs and refused to die.

The experience had no doubt been embarrassing for Howie Nicol who had apparently offered a deception to the Beatles Unlimited editor. Had Jimmie asked his son to lie for him to preserve his anonymity; to help him remain invisible to the public? Or, had Howie realized his dad would not want to participate in any more Beatles related events and merely told a "story" to the Fan Club editor to get rid of him? Either way, this story of his father's untimely "death" had raised many questions. Although Jimmie Nicol had not died in the physical sense, conceivably relations between father and son had

Howie Nicol's Anthology and Wingspan projects.
Photo Credit: Courtesy of Author.

deteriorated so badly, that to Howie, his dad was dead to him in a metaphorical sense. Perhaps it was just easier for Howie to tell Renè Van Haarlem his dad was "dead", than to reveal the genuine status of their relationship?

For Howie, whose prominence in the film industry grew after The Beatles' project, there was no easy solution to reconcile his statement of his dad's demise. One thing is for sure – fans and friends of Jimmie Nicol became more interested than ever, to know if he was dead or alive. For Jimmie Nicol, the experience only made him want to go further underground. He wanted to be completely alone. He never wanted to talk about The Beatles again. He was proud and he wanted to earn his living and be left in peace.

In 2001, Howie was employed on another high profile project as sound engineer for a new documentary. This time his work was acknowledged with a nomination by the US Cinema Audio Society for an award of "Outstanding Sound Mixing for Television – Variety or Music Series or Specials". His star was clearly on the rise. The name of the program was, "Wingspan", a musical history documentary about none other than Paul McCartney and his post-Beatles band Wings. Clearly, Paul McCartney appreciated the young Mr. Nicol's talents and took him under his "wings" for another project.

Nicol spotted in 2005-London.
Photo Credit: © Gavin Rodgers/ Pixel 07917221968.

In the years 2004 and 2005, there was renewed interest in The Beatles, and Jimmie Nicol's role in particular. In May of 2004, London reporter, Jonathan Este, was asked to track down Nicol for *The Australian* newspaper. The Australian fans had a continuing interest and love for Jimmie. Este located Howie Nicol first. According to the reporter, "His son wasn't interested in helping me find Jimmie. He said his dad, from whom he was estranged, wanted to be left alone and that was that."[12] Este later located Nicol's 90-year old mother, whom he found to be quite frail. Unfortunately, Nicol's mother could not recall anything from her son's heyday in the music industry. While there, however, Este was able to obtain Jimmie's phone number.[13]

Este called Jimmie's telephone number for days. Finally, Nicol picked up. When Este tried to engage Nicol in an interview, Nicol replied, "I really don't want to talk about it – I can't remember anything."[14] Este kept trying to engage Nicol by staking out his ground floor flat in Kentish Town, hidden in a back alley. It was to no avail. Nicol knew how to stay out of site. When Este visited nearby pubs, none of the regulars knew who Jimmie Nicol was. Once again, Nicol was able to lay low.

In 2005, London's *Daily Mail* came snooping around for the ex-Beatle. A book of Beatles photographs, *The Beatles Unseen*, had recently been released, including some pictures of The Beatles on tour of Australia. Of course, Nicol's appearance in many photos caused an editor to send another reporter out to get the "Where is he now?" story on Nicol. Reporter, Paul Harris, and Photographer, Gavin Rodgers, were assigned the story. Rodgers recalls the day. "His flat was tucked away and it was impossible to watch, but I got lucky when I saw the guy come out of the alley around the back and it was the bloke Jimmie." Rodgers and Harris stalked Nicol as he went out for a walk. First he visited a building society – likely checking the work boards. Then it was time for a bite to eat at the Continental Café, before returning silently to his London home. "We then spent several days trying to speak to him but he went underground," says Rodgers.[15] Rodgers had photographed Nicol's rare, brief foray into the neighborhood and back, mostly with a telephoto lens so he would not look conspicuous. Finally, there was physical, photographic proof that Jimmie Nicol was alive and well in 2005!

The two followed Nicol back to his flat from a distance. "At the flat you could see sheet music through one window, but no sign of any drums," says Harris.[16] Clearly, Nicol was still quietly composing music that no one would ever hear. He had once told a reporter in Holland, "My purpose in life, my quest in life, is to make music. That is what I am on the earth here for... to make music."[17] True to his word, Nicol continued to create music, but no longer for public consumption.

Harris rang the bell. Predictably, Nicol did not come to the door. "He never answered his doorbell," relates Rodgers. "He knew we were there."[18] Eventually, Harris was able to get Nicol on the telephone with the intent to ask him if he had seen the new book, *The Beatles Unseen*. The conversation was predictably brief. Jimmie replied, "I'm not interested in all that now. I don't want to know, man. I don't care about any book."[19] Later, photographer Rodgers felt badly about following

Nicol spotted in 2005.
Photo Credit: © Gavin Rodgers/ Pixel 07917221968.

someone who so obviously wanted to be left alone. "Clearly he did not want any publicity or fuss. I felt a bit guilty hosing him down [stalking and shooting his photo] but that was the job I was given."[20]

Harris later located Howie Nicol and told him he had made contact with his father. Howie replied, "You actually got to speak to him? That's a bit of a miracle in itself. He is in no way, shape, or form interested in talking to anybody about it." Howie tried to further explain his dad: "He doesn't live his life as other people do, and I respect that entirely." But, added Howie, "It is reassuring to know you've spoken to him. It's nice to know he's still out there."[21] Once again, Jimmie Nicol had been spotted, and then quickly disappeared again.

The *Daily Mail* article had renewed interest in the one-time Beatle. Copies of the article were flashed across the Internet, and Beatles fans around the world took notice again. He was alive! BBC radio pulled out the old Shubdubs track, *Night Train*, for one of its "Solid Gold Sunday" shows. Of course, the song followed The Beatles *Another Girl* in order for the DJ to explain its relevance. In Australia, Craig Jackson, a DJ on Radio Adelaide 101.5 FM, named his program "The Jimmy Nicol Show," in tribute.

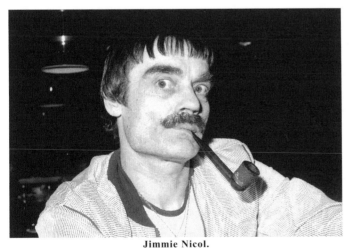

Jimmie Nicol.
Photo Credit: © 1984 BEATLES UNLIMITED/ KOOP GEERSING.

In Sydney, a Rock band named itself, "The Jimmy Nicols". They did so "in the spirit of the man who knew what it was to be great, but now eats dinner from a TV tray. The band was inspired by the fact that Jimmy Nicol knew what fame and adulation would have felt like," says the band's drummer, Rebecca Anderson. Admittedly, Anderson says, "He is underappreciated, which is sad."[22] This band clearly understood a bit of what Jimmie Nicol had been through, and they were proud to pay tribute to the great underappreciated drummer.

Jimmie had indeed headed down a lonely road. He appeared, to the few who observed him in 2005, to have become confused emotionally. Many issues had been festering over the years. When times were good and he was busy, he had apparently been able to compartmentalize these issues, so that he could pursue his music career and later the construction trade. When he was no longer in the limelight and his construction career began to fade, Nicol isolated himself completely from friends and family. Many of his life's issues came to the fore, such as financial problems; frustration with Epstein's perceived blacklisting; failed efforts to succeed with his own bands; failed marriages; bankruptcy, and now estrangement from his family. At first, Nicol checked out of the music industry, but later he checked out of engagement with people entirely. Many wondered if his loss of purpose may have created mental health issues.

Nicol's ex-wife Julia seemed to understand Nicol's condition. Though they had not seen each other in some thirty years, she had seen the changes in him as his musical career began to wind down in Mexico, and she knew how The Beatles' memories weighed heavily on his mind. "Jimmie was affected for his entire life because of his experience with The Beatles. He didn't get to stay with The Beatles. He thinks he failed because of that time with them. He was frustrated. So maybe his whole life had been frustrating from being the 'Fifth Beatle'. I think it affected his mental health."[23] Julia believes, being out of the limelight made her ex-husband feel isolated, lonely, and despondent.

Several of Nicol's old musician buddies commented on the mysterious vanishing drummer at this time. Georgie Fame laconically remarked, "The [Beatles] tour went to his head. Last time I heard of him, he was in Mexico playing psychedelic music. That was 1967."[24] Nicol's trumpet player and arranger friend, Johnny Harris, lamented, "After the Shubdubs, I tried to keep up with Jimmie over the years. I couldn't find him. I would love to talk to him. I couldn't find a telephone number. None of the musicians knew where he was. It was a shame the way things worked out."[25] Colin Green, who had played with Nicol in Vince Eager & The Quiet Three, says, "He is a bit of an enigma because after that whole Beatles escapade, he kind of disappeared. I know he did that whole Spotnicks thing. Then I heard of him being in Mexico City, however, I have never had that confirmed at all. I mean I am still on the music scene in London and I haven't heard anything of him in years…"[26] The Spotnicks' Bob Lander says, "Personally, I think he ended up in Brazil. I knew he had a taste for hot weather and pretty girls."[27]

Back to Mexico

In 2009, Julia Villaseñor went to an alternative medicine doctor in Cuernavaca outside Mexico City. "He uses little metal things like copper, iron and aluminum and puts them on parts of your body to heal you," she explains. "It is to heal or prevent many types of sickness."[28] The brother of Julia's doctor worked in the medical office to assist with administrative tasks. When she arrived for her appointment, the brother excitedly told her, "Julia, your ex-husband, The Beatle was up here."[29] Villaseñor was shocked and surprised at the news that her former husband had traveled back to Mexico, and that she had narrowly missed seeing him. They showed her pictures of Jimmie to prove he had been there. "So, now I knew he was alive," she says. "But I knew that he was ill or something. Of course the doctor and his brother would not reveal confidential information about another patient. I didn't know anymore because he didn't show up again or see me."[30] The doctor told Julia that Jimmie had flown in from London to see him and then flown immediately back to London. The Houdini of musicians had appeared in Mexico and quickly disappeared again.

The Beatle Who Vanished is an apt title for the life and career of Jimmie Nicol. It was as if he were an apparition who came and went as he pleased; touching people's lives and playing an assortment of great rhythms. As I related a summary of Nicol's life to my friend, Roy Tull, he suggested that I had to try and locate Jimmie and talk to him. I agreed with him. As an author and historian, I felt I owed it to myself and my readers to make the extra effort to locate Jimmie Nicol one last time. I hoped to tell him (if he was still alive) that someone had finally documented his life and career through the decades, and not just for the two weeks he served as a drummer in The Beatles. After years of research, interviews, and writing, the time had come to fly to London and Australia, in search of Jimmie Nicol, *The Beatle Who Vanished.*

Epilogue

In Search of Jimmie Nicol

After researching Jimmie Nicol's career for six years, I wanted to see if he would speak to me about his colorful and creative career. I wanted to fill in a few holes, especially in his early formative years. However, having discovered Nicol's famous vanishing act, I suspected Jimmie had successfully disappeared from the public eye forever. He did not want to be reminded of his Beatles connection that gave short-shrift to his entire career as a drummer, session man, producer, composer, and arranger. Given the difficulty other reporters had encountered, I knew it would not be easy to find Nicol and talk to him; however, I wanted to attempt to solve some of the mysteries and motives of his career path if at all possible.

I was also curious to see if he would talk to me once he knew that I was attempting to accurately document his entire musical legacy. My other goal was to take photographs of Jimmie Nicol's birth home in Battersea and many of his musical haunts around London, including the 2 I's Coffee Bar; the Flamingo club: and the Pye, Decca, and Abbey Road studio buildings. The results are illustrated herein.

In April, 2011, I booked the flight and hotel reservations for London and I made contact with Vince Eager. Vince wanted to come along to see Jimmie after all these years if he could make it. He first had to check where his May tour schedule would be taking him. Perhaps if one of Nicol's old friends came along, he might just open his door to us.

Before I left for London, I wrote a letter to Jimmie (at his last known address), explaining my forthcoming visit to see him; the reasons for writing the book; and my desire to meet with him. I sent along some excerpts so he could understand the book was about *all* of his musical accomplishments, not just his two weeks with The Beatles. I hoped that he would contact me before I left to invite me over. There was a lot of preparation ahead as I mapped out the many locations I wanted to visit and tried to figure out how to use yet another new digital camera and its many "intuitive" (hidden) buttons.

In a way, I worried that I was becoming a stalker or paparazzi. Here I was, armed to the teeth with all of this audio and video recording equipment - all to capture the words and movements of Jimmie Nicol, a man who had gone out of his way to avoid the public since he disappeared into Mexico some 40+ years ago. Was this the right thing to do to finish the story, or was this an invasion of privacy? I decided that only Jimmie Nicol could answer that question once we met... if we got to meet.

On the Saturday before the trip, I received a message from Vince Eager that he was having trouble receiving my email, but that we could talk on Sunday by phone. I was excited for Sunday to come so I could try to set up a time when Vince and I could venture into Northern London to knock on Nicol's door. For Vince, it would be a reunion of some 50 years in the making. I had sent Eager the chapter on Nicol's time as a member of Vince Eager & The Quiet Three. He had emailed back that the chapter was excellent and he had a few changes or additions. I was "eager" to hear about these as well.

The next day, I called Vince and we talked about the factual changes to the chapter on Vince Eager & The Quiet Three. Vince also informed me that he planned to record a new album of songs in July with Quiet Three alumni, Tex Makins and Colin Green. I suggested that it would be a complete reunion if we could ask Jimmie to play with Vince on drums. Eager thought this was a great idea. We agreed that I would call Vince when I landed in London to get together for a summit at Jimmie Nicol's last known address.

Arriving at the airport in Madison, at the beginning a long journey to London, I began to reflect on how far I had taken this one topic. It is a small part of pop music history that, at the outset did not seem to contain sufficient information to pursue for even a magazine article. In 2004 I had first started to wonder why Jimmie Nicol was chosen to replace Ringo Starr in The Beatles, and why we never heard anything about him before or after The Beatles? He is clearly absent from most general music histories covering British Rock and Roll music. I had to see if there was a real story lurking behind the headlines; and there was. However, I never realized there was an entire musician's biography and mystery wrapped up in one person!

As I began to research Nicol on the Internet, the mostly Beatles-related sites devoted the same few sentences to his "deputizing for Ringo". As I began to dig deeper, however, I found little clues and mentions of other bands Nicol may have played with. The first reference was to an obscure British band called, Colin Hicks & His Cabin Boys. Once I learned the band's line up, it was fairly easy to locate some of the musicians. I even found the kid who served as their roadie in Italy. He was now running an extremely kinky porn site in California. The web search that accidentally located him was entitled, "Colin Hicks + jail". I had heard a rumor from a former band member that Hicks was in prison. It turned out not to be true, but Max, the roadie, had spent a bit of time there on obscenity charges.

So it went… one artist would finish telling me his recollections and give me the email or telephone number of another person who had also played with Nicol. The pieces started falling into place. Along the way, I scoured the EBay sites in Italy, England, the USA, Australia, and Mexico, finding ultra rare news articles, videos, and recordings Nicol had made in his career – most of which people had never heard or seen. Jimmy's ex-wife, Julia, proved to be the most difficult person to locate and interview. I did not even know her name. However, after contacting a prominent Mexican Rock music historian, he led me right to her door.

Nicol's birthplace, 93 Silverthorne Road.
Photo Credit: © 2011 Jim Berkenstadt.

It was an interesting emersion into one artist's journey, one with big highs and big lows. Finally, it was a story with a mystery at the end: the "death of Jimmie Nicol". So, here I was, heading off to London to find out if Jimmie Nicol was still alive today. If he was, would he talk to me about his career? Did he want the world to believe he had died back in the late 1980s (or early 1990s)? Or was there something lost in the translation between his son Howie and the Holland Fan Club organizer? I had a long list of questions and hopefully, they would soon be answered.

London

On my first day in London, I thought it best to start at the beginning, namely Jimmie Nicol's birthplace home as listed on his birth certificate. So I took the Tube to Clapham Common and walked about two miles to 93 Silverthorne Road in Battersea. The row houses where Nicol grew up were still in very good condition, considering they dated back to the 1940s and 1950s. A new neighborhood has emerged with young mothers pushing their babies in prams. This is quite a change from the war torn, bombed-out city in the throes of rebuilding when Nicol came into the world. I found his home, took the photos and made my way back to the hotel through an amazing crush of commuters traveling home at the end of the week. Since no one has ever located and documented the birth place of Beatle, Jimmie Nicol, I felt proud marking the spot. This would be the *only* Beatles' birth

The 2 I's Coffee Bar. Photo Credit: © 2011 Jim Berkenstadt.

place located in London. The rest, including other rare Beatles such as Pete Best, Stuart Sutcliffe, and Chas Newby, all hailed from the greater Liverpool area.

On my second day, I decided to visit the places where Jimmie Nicol earned a living playing the drums. The first stop was the 2 I's Coffee Bar at 59 Old Compton Street. It was easy to find and was marked with a special plaque to honor Britain's "Birthplace of Rock And Roll". Looking into the vacant space and seeing the stairs leading down to the club helped me imagine the room crammed full of teens, hopped up on coffee and a new, wild form of music being played by the likes of Tommy Steele, Vince Eager, and a teenage drummer who would sit in with anybody… Jimmie Nicol.

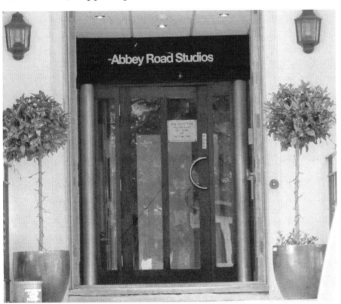

EMI Abbey Road Studios. Photo Credit: © 2011 Jim Berkenstadt.

Just down the road on Wardour Street was the old location for the Flamingo club, the place where Jimmie played with Georgie Fame & the Blue Flames before The Beatles came calling. Today, sadly the building is used as an inexpensive Chinese fast food restaurant. There are no plaques and no indications that this once proud building housed the hottest live rhythm & blues band in London's swingin' Sixties.

Back on the Tube, I found myself in St. John's Wood, an upscale neighborhood that houses EMI's Abbey Road Studios, the place made famous by The Beatles. Walking the magical zebra crosswalk that The Beatles used for the cover photo of their classic album, *Abbey Road*, I made my way over to this venerable old studio. It was easy to envision a very nervous, yet determined Jimmie Nicol striding up the stairs with his friend, John Hodkinson, in tow, moving through the throngs of newsmen into Studio 2 for his rehearsal/tryout with The Beatles. It was only a 20-minute session that would change his life forever. At the end of the audition, John Lennon had said to Nicol, "You're in." What happened before and after that momentous occasion was revealed in this book for the first time.

From one studio to another, I traveled to the site where Decca Studios was formerly located at 165 Broadhurst Gardens. This was the scene of The Beatles January, 1962 recording test at which

A & R man, Dick Rowe, famously turned down the group for a record contract. Later, this studio was where Brian Epstein brought his protégé, Tommy Quickly, to record *You Might As Well Forget Him*. It was here that Epstein also first met and observed Jimmie Nicol playing drums on the session, one of many recording dates Jimmie Nicol would play in the first half of 1964 before becoming a Beatle. Today the building looks every bit the same as it did in the 1960s, with one exception. Rock and Roll had died at this site and has been replaced by opera! The studio is long gone, but today the building serves as the location hous-

The former Pye Studios. Photo Credit: © 2011 Jim Berkenstadt.

ing the English National Opera. I concluded the building had to be haunted by the howling feedback of The Kinks! Oh well, I suppose this is what some call progress…

Pye Studios was the place where Jimmie Nicol had recorded all of the Beatles' cover songs, learning Ringo Starr's drum parts for the Top Six record label. He also recorded his Jimmie Nicol & the Shubdubs' singles at Pye and his Ska recordings with Cyril Stapleton and Chris Farlowe under the fictitious band name, The Beazers. Walking through London's famous Marble Arch to get there, I was not surprised to find Pye Studios gone. This is valuable upscale real estate located in the heart of London tourism. Pye has been turned into a huge, upscale Gentlemen's Casino that takes up an entire block on Bryanston Street.

The next day, I decided to visit Jimmie Nicol's neighborhood in Camden/ Kentish Town. Vince Eager was unable to meet me after all, so it was time to go it alone. Getting off the Tube, I

walked down Kentish Road, observing a very young population of 20 and 30-something inhabitants who had turned the area into their own version of Chicago's trendy Lincoln Park. Within a block of Jimmie's small street, I saw what was likely his regular pub. O'Reilly's was populated with 60-70 year old guys spending the afternoon drinking and talking together. This was a classic old London neighborhood pub; probably over 100 years old. I asked around to see if anyone knew Jimmie, but they honestly did not seem to know him. It was not surprising because his reputation had been that

Nicol's flat with strange shadows cast on the wall.
Photo Credit: © 2011 Jim Berkenstadt.

of a loner for so many years. After lunch and a Jack Daniels (liquid courage), I decided the time had come to knock on the door of Jimmie Nicol. I had secured his address from an Australian reporter who had come over to do a story in honor of The Beatles' 40th anniversary of touring Down Under. He indicated Jimmie lived on the first floor, based upon a search of London's Electoral Rolls.

I approached the street with some trepidation since it looked like a back alley. As I walked down the alley, I thought I had gone to the wrong place. Where are the flats? All I saw was one back door to a store and a fenced area for storing garbage. I kept walking until the alley turned sharp right. There I saw a big pile of dirt and a big wall with greens on the left. I walked down the alley that turned into a dead-end in 100 yards. As I did, I marveled at how Nicol had found a very quiet, impossibly hidden, end-of-the-world, dead-end in which to live. It was the perfect place to hide, in plain sight. After I took a digital photo of the alley and looked at it, I noticed a strange image created by the sun's rays falling upon the green vines hanging down on the wall at the end of the alley. The image was literally five feet from Nicol's front door. Was it me, the Jack Daniels, or was I seeing a shadow image of The Beatles' album cover, crossing **Abbey Road**? How strange was this image of The Beatles seemingly walking over to Jimmie's flat? Of course, some folks think they see an image of Jesus on their burnt toast…

Finally, at the end of the street on the right, I found the number. The moment of truth had arrived. I took a deep breath, knocked on the door, and waited. No answer. I knocked again. I wondered if Jimmie Nicol was sitting inside, ignoring my visit; waiting for me to go away. But, just then the door began to open slowly…. Admittedly, I was incredibly nervous. A man in his mid-20's came to the door with a young child. I asked if Jimmie Nicol lived in the flat. He said, "Not here, mate." He had no idea who Jimmie Nicol was; and he had lived there for a couple of years, renting from a real estate agent. Thanking him, I went on my way.

I was left with an empty feeling. Did Nicol move? Did he perhaps pass away for real this time? It was certainly possible. When I told my wife, Holly, she joked in an email back to me that Nicol had probably moved right after receiving my letter.

Deciding I needed to hire professional assistance, I contacted a London-based private detective. This was so crazy. I needed to know, first-hand, if Jimmie Nicol was at least alive and, if so, I needed to make an attempt to visit him in person. The first word back from the detective was that Jimmie Nicol no longer lived at the apartment I had tried. Now he wanted big bucks to find the new address. I attempted a bit of negotiation to lower his price, but he wouldn't budge, so I found another private eye.

London has a full supply of "Sherlock Holmes". I had come this far, so I determined to keep trying. I recalled Ringo Starr's lyrics, "Gotta pay your dues if you wanna sing the blues, and you know it don't come easy." This Sherlock got right on the case. Keith Walker of Blue Moon Investigations had heard of the famous "Fifth Beatle" Jimmie Nicol and wanted to help out. Time was the enemy, however. I needed an answer by Tuesday at noon so I still had time to make a trip to wherever Jimmie might be living. I was scheduled to fly back on Wednesday.

On Tuesday at noon, I received the news from Detective Walker and learned that Jimmie Nicol was more successful at vanishing than even Osama Bin Laden. In fact, the apartment I had visited in Camden/ Kentish Town was still in Jimmie Nicol's name under a 99-year lease. However, Nicol had sub-let the flat to its current tenant through an agency, which would explain why the tenant had no idea who Jimmie Nicol was.

Jimmie had moved out. The detective had not been able to locate him living anywhere in England, and his research indicated that Nicol had moved out of the country! We were able to determine that he *is* definitely alive because the Detective learned about various systematic, present-day financial transactions in Nicol's name. Walker also found other evidence of personal consumption by Nicol. As of May, 2011, Jimmie Nicol was alive somewhere in the world. I was playing a real life version of *Where In the World Is Carmen San Diego?* My trip to London came to an end without knowing what country Jimmie Nicol currently lived in. My guess was that Nicol likely went someplace he had visited or lived before, but was it The Netherlands, Sweden, Australia or Mexico? The world is a big place when you are searching for one person. I eliminated Sweden because the Spotnicks would have been in contact with Nicol. I also eliminated Mexico City, as I believed someone would have informed his ex-wife Julia.

On to Australia

In July of 2011, our family traveled to Australia to visit our daughter who currently resides there. My wife, Holly generously organized the trip so that I could further research Jimmie Nicol's experiences in Sydney, Adelaide, and Melbourne with The Beatles. Right before we left, my letter to Jimmie (in London) came back from the Royal Mail… marked "Return to Sender". I still wondered if I could find any more clues to Jimmie's whereabouts while traveling through Australia. Given that Nicol had expressed his desire to return to Sydney in the fall of 1964, and then again in 1967, I searched the Internet to see if perhaps Nicol had moved Down Under. The results were another dead end.

Chequers Sauna Spa Massage. Photo Credit: © 2011 Jim Berkenstadt.

In Sydney, we visited the Sydney Sheraton Hotel at King's Cross where Jimmie and The Beatles first stayed upon surviving the rain-drenched trip around the tarmac of Kingsford-Smith International Airport at Mascot after being paraded around with umbrellas in an open cart. Today the former hotel is a condominium. However, it is completely unchanged from June 11, 1964, when The Beatles went out onto the balcony at 9:30 a.m. to wave to fans. The new condo residents likely are unaware that their rod-ironed balcony railing is the exact one used by The Beatles to wave at fans below, some 47 years earlier.

From the hotel, it was time to venture over to the former Chequers club where Nicol had snuck out at night to jam with Frances Faye on drums. The long, curving stairway with its original club sign remains the same today; however, the Chequers club no longer features live music. It has been turned into an adult pleasure palace; renamed "Chequers Sauna Spa Massage".

In Adelaide, we paid a visit to the Lord Mayor's Town Hall, where an estimated 300,000 scream-

The former Sheraton Hotel at King's Cross.
Photo Credit: © 2011 Jim Berkenstadt.

ing fans greeted The Beatles who made their way into town in an open convertible. It was difficult to see how 300,000 people had fit into such a narrow area around the Town Hall. Yet it was easy to imagine the look on Jimmie's face as he sat atop the car seat, smiling and giving the appreciative crowd a thumbs-up for the overwhelming reception.

Next, I visited The Arts Centre of Melbourne, which housed the "Kenn Brodziak Australian Beatles Tour Collection Archives". I was permitted to look through boxes of documents, records and photographs donated to the Centre by Brodziak, who was the promoter who brought The Beatles to Australia. Very quickly it became evident how complex the tour had been to orchestrate. There were hundreds of written correspondences, in the files, to and from Brodziak's office and covering every detail of the tour. There were dozens of requests for The Beatles to attend a myriad of public and private functions, most of which were turned down due to the lack of time for such events. The correspondence contained documents covering private and public security details; radio station promotions; Chambers of Commerce; musical instrument rentals; air, car, and hotel arrangements; the printing of tickets and programs; press conferences; speaking engagements; backstage passes; interviews; barbeques; and hospital visits. The planning was overwhelming, yet very well organized for its time.

One of the more interesting letters from June 9, 1964 (before The Beatles arrival in Australia) questioned whether or not Ringo Starr would be coming to Australia, or whether Jimmie Nicol would continue on in his deputy role. The key point coming from Brian Epstein in England to Brodziak was, "If Jimmy Nicol comes to Australia, then accommodations and transportation will be required and *he **must** be treated as one of The Beatles*."[1] By June 10, 1964, it became clear that Ringo Starr would not be able to make the Adelaide leg of the tour. In a letter to his Adelaide promoter-partner, Brodziak advised him that, "Jimmie Nicol will go to Adelaide and perform in all concerts. Jimmie can replace Ringo in the motorcade."[2] The records clearly indicated that Nicol's tenure with The Beatles was on a day-by-day basis, dependent upon Ringo Starr's condition and his ability to travel to Australia. Most significantly, within the hundreds of documents I reviewed, there was no mention from Brian Epstein's office regarding the possibility of Jimmie Nicol permanently replacing Ringo Starr in The Beatles. Equally clear from the correspondence, was Epstein's insistence that Nicol always be treated as "one of The Beatles". While I was in Melbourne, I had the opportunity to interview a woman in her early 60s who had seen The Beatles at the Southern Cross Hotel in Melbourne. On this day, police and horses were called in to control the crowd and prevent the kids from smashing through the hotel's first floor picture windows. The woman (whom we will call Susan to protect her request for privacy) was 16 years old when The Beatles visited. It was a school day and Susan decided to play hooky from her private religious school to welcome The Beatles to their hotel. "I pretended to be my mother and called myself in sick to the school," she recalls with a mischievous smile.[3] Susan had heard about the event for weeks on the radio and had played her Beatles records nonstop.

Susan and some of her girlfriends made their way to the Southern Cross Hotel where reports on the crowd varied from 80,000 to 250,000 fans. As they waited for The Beatles to arrive on top of the hotel balcony, they could feel the sway of the crowd and felt the danger of the squeeze as they heard hysterical screaming in the crowd. Finally, a huge roar went up as John, Paul, George, Ringo, and Jimmie all appeared on the balcony. Susan recalls, "I could not hear what they were saying into the microphone. It was too loud. I saw The Beatles, but there were five guys up there. We thought the fifth guy was Brian Epstein or someone in the entourage. None of us knew who Jimmie Nicol was."[4]

Unfortunately for Susan, who had very white-blond hair, the live TV cameraman decided to pan from The Beatles down to the crowd below the balcony. He immediately focused on the pretty blond girl who stood out from all of the brunettes in the crowd. The camera moved all the way in so that Susan's face almost filled the screen. It was obvious to the nuns watching the news on TV back at her religious school that Susan was not home sick! Rather, she was suffering from a different sort of illness, one which the media coined...*Beatlemania*.

The next day, when Susan went to school, she was still beaming from getting to see The Beatles in person. However, the school was laying in wait for her. A full school assembly was called, although none of the students knew its purpose. Then the nuns asked Susan to come up on stage to address her classmates. Poor Susan was ambushed and forced to admit that she had lied to the nuns by calling herself in sick and that she had actually gone to see The Beatles. The Nuns went one step further, using the assembly for a bit of propaganda to influence their flock of young students. Susan was fed the following words to address her school from the stage: "The Beatles are low taste, commercial rubbish. I am sorry I lied and did the wrong thing. I have been caught up in crass commercialism and taken in by this low taste Rock and Roll of The Beatles. I am sorry."[5] Poor Susan had been caught and publically humiliated for taking one day off from school to see The Beatles. It was her bad luck to be singled out by the cameraman who had 200,000 kids to choose from. From the looks of the Southern Cross Hotel crowd, Susan's school must have been empty that day. Unfortunately, the blonde Susan had been caught. But looking back, it was worth it.

Finding a "Nicol" in a Haystack

The next day, I connected with one of Australia's premier historical authorities on The Beatles' visit to Australia, Vince Medina Sanna. Vince was interested in the Jimmie Nicol angle of my story. He graciously showed my son and me some of The Beatles' historical sites in Melbourne; including the Essendon Airport where Jimmie Nicol sat all alone waiting to fly back to England, looking shell-shocked, like a soldier leaving a war zone with post-traumatic stress syndrome. The seat where Jimmie had sat was gone, yet the airport seemed to have been frozen in time. Everything remained decorated in the same way as that day in 1964 when Brian Epstein walked Jimmie to the plane and Nicol made one final wave to the TV cameras from the stairs of his flight. During this poignant moment, I wondered if I would ever find a new lead on Jimmie Nicol's whereabouts. The "needle in a haystack" analogy came to mind.

As we were walking to the Melbourne Town Hall, Vince surprised me by putting me on the phone with another of Australia's Beatles historians, Brendan Pearse. We exchanged pleasantries and then Pearse said, "I hear from Vince that you are searching for Jimmie Nicol. And I wanted to let you know that he has just been spotted."[6] I was in shock. I had traveled to London, only to find that Jimmie had moved to another country. Now I was in Australia, hearing that Jimmie had been found. I assumed that he was now somewhere in Australia, but I was again surprised by the story Pearse related.

Brendan explained that he had an acquaintance (whom we will call Bob) he sees from time to time at record conventions. Both Brendan and Bob are big record collectors. Bob had just returned in early July, 2011 from Holland where he had attended the Amsterdam Record Convention at the Jaarbeurs Convention Center in Utrecht, Netherlands.

While there, Bob relates that he was walking from his hotel to the Convention Center. "On the way, I passed an industrial construction site. As I was walking by, this man walked out from the site. He looked tired and grey, but somehow familiar." Bob stared at the gentleman for a minute and then thought he knew who the man was. "I went up to the man and said, 'Are you Jimmie Nicol the drummer?'" The man broke into a small smile and nodded his head in resigned agreement, as if to say, "You got me." Bob quickly pulled out a pen and paper and asked Nicol, "Would you mind signing an autograph for me?" Jimmie smiled, and without saying a word, took the pen and signed "Jimmie Nicol". Bob thanked him and was about to ask Nicol some questions when Jimmie quickly turned away and headed back into the construction site. Gone, vanished again.[7]

When Brendan finished his story, I was speechless. Jimmie had not only apparently moved to Holland, but he had moved very close to the location of the annual International Beatles Convention organized by Beatles Unlimited and recently held at a Theater in Utrecht, Netherlands. Here was Jimmie Nicol, invisible, working and presumably living within miles of the convention he had attended in 1984. This was also the convention at which his son, Howie, had advised the organizer that his father had died. The irony was incredible.

After the trip to Australia, I contemplated hiring another private detective to track down Jimmie Nicol in The Netherlands, but decided the time had come to stop searching. I had found enough to write about his career and journey. There was no longer a need to bother him. He did not want to be found, yet it was good to know he was alive and working.

I thought about the words Julia Villaseñior expressed to me after we spent hours talking about her life with Jimmie in Mexico. "If he knew this book was about his whole life and career, I think he would accept and appreciate it. When I read this book, I am going to cry. Maybe I can give a copy to his doctor here and he can send it to Jimmie. Maybe he might come back and visit us again in Mexico City. The only thing missing in your book is to locate Jimmie and have a conversation with him."[8] If only Julia knew how much I had tried to make that happen. However, some things are not meant to be. Julia's final words to me were, "If you get Jimmie to talk to you, please tell him I send all my love to him."[9] This was a sentiment that I had heard from many of his friends over the years.

Today Jimmie Nicol lives his life pounding out the beats of a different rhythm. The drumsticks have long been retired in favor of the steady meter of his present tool - the hammer. It is an honorable trade for a proud and hardworking Everyman. A trade in which Nicol can use his mind and body to create something beautiful – not music – but functional living and work spaces for others. For decades, Jimmie Nicol was admired by fans, family and fellow musicians for his drumming, compositions, arrangements, and musical productions. He was a drummer's drummer. Today, he has created a space for himself, all alone and away from "The Beatles Story". Yet he never fully escaped the fate of having been the only musician to play onstage with The Beatles after they became the most famous group in music history.

Nicol is now part of an extinct era - the Rockin' Fifties and the Swinging Sixties -that lives on only in the memories of aging baby-boomers, in yellowed teen magazines, dusty old 45 records, and in the black and white flickering of old British Pathè newsreels. These relics and the memories of a select few survivors are the only remaining artifacts of a fascinating and creative, yet perplexing, musical career. Hopefully this book establishes for posterity Jimmie Nicol's many accomplishments in music so that he may always be remembered as much more than *The Beatle Who Vanished*.

It is only appropriate that the last words should belong to James George Nicol:

"All my life, I have been my own master. Even before The Beatles. Nothing that has ever happened in my life, including The Beatles, has ever been a disadvantage to me. And if it has, I have always turned it into an advantage."[10]

The last known photo of Beatle Jimmie Nicol. Photo Credit: © Gavin Rodgers/Pixel 07917221968.

ENDNOTES

Chapter One
The Call

[1] Brian Epstein, **Brain Epstein: Inside The Fifth Beatle** DVD (Passport Video 2004) Chapter 5

[2] Brian Epstein, **Arena: The Brian Epstein Story** DVD (BBC Arts 1998)

[3] Glenn A. Baker, **The Beatles Down Under: The 1964 Australian and New Zealand Tour** (Pierian Press 1985) 19

[4] Mark Hayward and Keith Badman, **The Beatles Unseen** (Barnes and Noble 2005) 106

[5] The Beatles, **The Beatles Anthology** DVD (Apple/Capitol 2003) chapter 3

[6] Ibid

[7] Ibid

[8] Ibid

[9] Mark Hayward and Keith Badman, **The Beatles Unseen** (Barnes and Noble 2005) 106

[10] Pete Best, Interview by email with Author (November 16, 2010)

[11] "Georgie Fame" by Paolo Hewitt, georgiefame.absoluteelsewhere.net/index. Html, 2004, 4

[12] John Hodkinson, Interview with author (November 9, 2005)

[13] Hayward and Badman, 106

[14] Hodkinson Interview

[15] Ibid

[16] Johnny Harris, Interview with author (September 2, 2005)

[17] Jimmie Nicol, Interview, Holland Beatles Convention, (June 10, 1984)

Chapter Two
The Early Years

[1] Honeywell Junior School, www.honeywelljuniorschool.com/beliefscultureethosprosp

[2] Lars Akerstrom, **The Spotnicks – The First 45 Years,** (Gothenburg: Amapola Productions 2004), 150

[3] "He Said What He Thought About The Beatles", *Vi Unge Magazine*, April 1, 1966, 1

[4] Lars Akerstrom, 150

[5] "Jimmie Nicol", http://www.pmouse.nl/nicol/

[6] Ibid

[7] *Beatles Tapes IV: Hong Kong,* 1964, liner notes by Gary Schumacher, Jerden CD, 1997

[8] "Jimmy Nicol 1987 Interview", by Austin Teutsch, Beatlefan, Issue #90, 1994, 15-18

[9] "He Said What He Thought About The Beatles", 2)

Chapter Three
Post War Britain and the 2 Is Coffee Club

[1] "British Rock and Pop History", by Gordon Thompson, Professor, Skidmore University Lecture, 2007, 2

[2] Max Wooldridge, **Rock 'N' Roll London**, (NYC: St. Martin's Griffin, 2002), 12

[3] "The Birth of the Coffee Bars", by Mathew Partington, www.uwic.ac.uk/ICRC/issue006/articles/02.htm 2005, 1

[4] Ian Samwell, "Move It", http://www.iansamwell.com/, 1998, 2

[5] Vince Eager, Interview with Author, (September 23, 2005)

[6] Ibid

[7] "He Said What He Thought About The Beatles", 2

[8] Alan Clayson, **Ringo Starr: Straight Man or Joker** (Tampa: Sanctuary, 1998), 21

[9] Brian Bennett, **Drums and Drumming Today**, "The Beat Drummer" (London: Boosey & Hawkes, LTD. 1964), 15

[10] Clayson, 21

[11] Rick Hardy, Interview with Author (August 26, 2005)

[12] Ibid

[13] Ibid

[14] "The Magician in the Wings: John Kennedy" by John Edwards, *The Daily Mail*, August 4, 2004

[15] John Kennedy, **Tommy Steele**, (London: Corgi Books, 1958), 14

[16] John Edwards

[17] Kennedy 16

[18] Tommy Steele, **Mr. Parnes Shillings and Pence**, Jo Lusting Ltd, Prod. Ch. 4 TV, UK, 1986

[19] "The Tommy Steele Story"

[20] Tommy Steele, **Mr. Parnes Shillings and Pence**

[21] Ibid

[22] Kennedy 18

[23] Tommy Steele, Mr. Parnes Shillings and Pence

[24] "The Tommy Steele Story", 4

[25] Tommy Steele, **Mr. Parnes Shillings and Pence**

[26] John Edwards, **Mr. Parnes Shillings and Pence**

[27] Georgie Fame, **Mr. Parnes Shillings and Pence**

Chapter Four
Colin Hicks & His Cabin Boys

[1] "Europa Di Notte" (Colin Hicks & His Cabin Boys In Italy, 45 rpm, B-106-EP, Broadway International liner notes, 1959)

[2] Rick Hardy, Interview with the Author (August 26, 2005)

[3] Mike O'Neil, Interview with the Author (September 26, 2005)

[4] www.forgottenbands.blogspot.com, 2010, 2

[5] Bob Hunter Interview with Author, February 22, 2008

[6] Ibid

[7] "Highland Archives, Northlands Rock: Rebels with a Cause", www.internet-promotions.co.uk/archives/northlands/north1.htm 2005, 1

[8] Ibid, 1

[9] Ibid, 1

[10] "From Pools Girls to Rock "n" Roll Stars" by David Charters, *Liverpool Daily Post*, http://icliverpool.ic-network.co.uk ,February 22, 2008, 4

[11] Ibid, 4

[12] "Alessandro Blasetti", www.mymovies.it , 2008, 1

[13] Ibid, 2

[14] **European Nights** ,Film Narrator, dir. Alessandro Blasetti, 1958,(Released: VHS, Something Weird Video 2002)

[15] Ibid, 2

[16] **European Nights** (Film Narrator)

[17] Winterberg, Ingo, **Trixon – The Story of the German Drum Company**, (Germany: www.trixondrums.de publishing, 2007) 76

Chapter Five
Touring Italy and Searching for Elvis

[1] *Europa Di Notte,* Colin Hicks & His Cabin Boys, EP, Broadway International, B-106-EP, Liner Notes, 1958

[2] Max Lobkowitz Interview with Author, (October 3, 2005)

[3] "Colin Hicks", *Melody Maker,* May 17, 1958, 20

[4] Lobkowitz Interview

[5] Mike O'Neil Interview with Author, (October 10, 2005)

[6] Ibid

[7] Ibid

[8] Herb Reed of The Platters Interview with Author, (April 26, 2008)

[9] O'Neil Interview

[10] Ibid

[11] Lobkowitz Interview
[12] Ibid
[13] Ibid
[14] Ibid
[15] Ibid
[16] Ibid
[17] *Colin Hicks Anthology 1957-1961*, liner notes, Rockin' Ghost Records, RGR-500-RA, 1994
[18] O'Neil Interview
[19] Ibid
[20] Ibid
[21] Ibid
[22] David Matalon Interview with Author (August 29, 2010)
[23] Ibid
[24] O'Neil Interview
[25] Lobkowitz Interview
[26] O'Neil Interview
[27] Ibid

Chapter Six
Vince Eager & The Quiet Three

[1] Ibid
[2] Ibid
[3] Ibid
[4] Ibid
[5] Eager Interview
[6] "Vince Eager", *Melody Maker*, April, 1959, 2
[7] Eager Interview
[8] Eager Interview
[9] "Tony Sheridan", by Peter Jones, *Record Mirror*, January 17, 1959, 5
[10] Tony Sheridan Interview with Author, (October 27, 2010)
[11] Ibid
[12] Ibid
[13] Eager Interview
[14] Ibid
[15] Colin Green Interview with Author, (Sept 20, 2005)
[16] Noel Wallis Interview with Author, (Nov 9, 2005)
[17] Ibid
[18] Eager Interview
[19] Green Interview
[20] Ibid
[21] Ibid
[22] Eager Interview
[23] Ibid
[24] Ibid
[25] Ibid.
[26] Wallis Interview
[27] Green Interview
[28] Ibid
[29] Ibid
[30] Spencer Leigh, **Things Do Go Wrong: Eddie, Gene and the UK Tour** (London: Finbarr International) 2007, 48
[31] Ibid, 68
[32] Wallis Interview
[33] Spencer Leigh, 73
[34] Eager Interview

[35] Green Interview
[36] Spencer Leigh, 99
[37] Eager Interview
[38] Ibid
[39] Ibid
[40] Ibid
[41] Ibid
[42] Johnny Gentle Interview with Author, (October 27, 2005)
[43] Johnny Gentle and Ian Forsyth, **Johnny Gentle and the Beatles: First Ever Tour - Scotland 1960** (Runcorn: Merseyrock Publications, 1988), 25
[44] Eager Interview
[45] Ibid
[46] Ibid
[47] Ibid
[48] Review, *New Musical Express*, July 29, 1970, 9
[49] Ibid
[50] Eager Interview
[51] Ibid
[52] Wallis Interview
[53] Eager Interview

Chapter Seven
The Big Band Years

[1] "Rock 'n Trad Spectacular – The New Noise of 1960", *New Musical Express*, August 19, 1960, 7
[2] "Tour", *Record Retailer*, September 22, 1960, 8
[3] Joe Brown Interview with Author (March 21, 2012)
[4] Ibid
[5] "Will Dixieland kill rock?" *New Musical Express*, September 30, 1960, 2
[6] Ibid
[7] Ibid
[8] "Billy Fury Biography", by Nalle Wesman & Chris Eley, www.nic.fi/~nallew/pages/bio
[9] Review, *Melody Maker*, by Chris Hayes, October 1, 1960, 4
[10] Ibid
[11] Oscar Rabin, *You Danced To These Bands*, Liner Notes by Tony Watts, Castle Pulse, 2005
[12] Ibid
[13] Ibid
[14] Eager Interview
[15] Green Interview
[16] Ron Prentice Interview with Author (October 6, 2005)
[17] Ibid
[18] Wallis Interview
[19] Albert Lee Interview with Author (January 17, 2011)
[20] Ibid
[21] Ibid
[22] Prentice Interview
[23] Cyril Stapleton, *You Danced To These Bands*, Liner Notes by Tony Watts, Castle Pulse, 2005
[24] Ibid
[25] Harris Interview
[26] Ibid
[27] Ibid
[28] Ingo Winterberg, **The Trixon Collection of Ingo Winterberg,** (www.trixondrums.de publishing 2010), 64
[29] Harris Interview

Chapter Eight
In The Studio

[1] Harris Interview

[2] Ibid

[3] Ibid (Harris quoting Bill Wellings)

[4] "Top Six", www.easyontheeye.net/albums/hothits/index.htm , 2006, 1-2

[5] Harris Interview

[6] "Top Six", 2

[7] Ibid, 2

[8] Harris Interview

[9] Ibid

[10] "Where Are They Now? From The Spotnicks & the Shubdubs drummer – Jimmy Nicol", *New Gandy Dancer*, Issue 73, 2004, 34

[11] Ibid, 34

[12] Harris Interview

[13] Hodkinson Interview

[14] "Top Six", *Daily Mirror*, By Don Short, January 21, 1964, 1

[15] "Top Six", 1

[16] Harris Interview

[17] "It's A Beatle Mania LP", *Disc weekly*, issue 307, February 8, 1964, 1

[18] "Jimmie Nicol", www.pmouse.nl/nicol

[19] "The Rise and Fall of the Fifth Beatles", *Daily Mirror*, By Don Short, April 30, 1965, 9

[20] Stanoch

[21] Ibid

[22] "Hot Pop", *Billboard*, May 23, 1964, 20

[23] Hodkinson Interview

[24] Ibid

[25] Harris Interview

[26] Ibid

[27] *Dig The Buzz*, Chris Farlowe, CD liner notes, RPM, 2001, 1

[28] "Discs", *Daily Mirror*, By Patrick Doncaster, January 30, 1964, 21

[29] *Dig The Buzz*, 1

[30] Brian Epstein, **A Cellarful of Noise** , (London: New English Library, 1965), 72

[31] Epstein, 72

[32] **Panorama**, BBC-TV, recorded March 24, 1964, broadcast March 30, 1964

[33] "Discs", by Patrick Doncaster, *Daily Mirror*, April 23, 1964, 21

[34] Ibid

Chapter Nine
Fame Leads to "Fame"

[1] "It's Tough at the Bottom", *Radio Luxemburg Annual*, 1965, 13

[2] Ibid, 14

[3] Mike O'Neil Interview with Author (October 10, 2005)

[4] "Georgie Fame", by Paolo Hewitt, *Caught By The River*, October 24, 2004, 2

[5] Jeffrey Kruger, MBE Interview with Author (January 26, 2011)

[6] "Pop Music: Fame at the Flamingo: golden years in Soho", by James Maycock, *The Independent*, January 16, 1998, 1

[7] Tex Makins Interview with Author (January 4, 2011)

[8] "It's Tough at the Bottom", 15

[9] Kruger Interview

[10] "Georgie Fame", 2

[11] Peter Coe Interview with Author (January 23, 2005)

[12] "In With The In Crowd", Mojo, 2008, 46

[13] Makins interview

[14] Harris Interview

[15] Makins Interview

[16] "The Rise and Fall of the Fifth Beatle", by Don Short, *The Daily Mirror*, April 30, 1965, 9

[17] Kruger, Interview

[18] Makins Interview

[19] Kruger Interview

[20] Sam Leach Interview with Author, (February 15, 2006)

[21] Raye Du-Val Interview with Author, (September 23, 2010)

[22] http://www.bobbygraham.co.uk/bobbygraham/career.htm, 1

[23] Bobby Graham Interview with Mark Lewisohn (March 18, 2005)

[24] Sir George Martin Interview via email with Author (February 6, 2008)

[25] "Georgie Fame", by Paolo Hewitt, 3

[26] Ibid, 4

[27] Nicol, Holland Interview

[28] Hodkinson Interview

[29] Nicol, Holland Interview

[30] Greg Tesser, Interview with Author (November 15, 2005)

[31] George Martin, *The Beatles Anthology* DVD

[32] Tesser Interview

[33] Ibid

[34] Andy Babiuk, **Beatles Gear**, (Milwaukee: Backbeat Books, 2001), 132

[35] British Pathè, newsreel footage, June 3, 1964

[36] Tesser Interview

[37] Ibid

[38] Mark Hayward and Keith Badman, **The Beatles Unseen**, (NYC: Barnes and Noble, 2005), 107

[39] Hodkinson Interview

[40] Hayward and Badman, 107

[41] Hodkinson Interview

[42] Nicol, Teutsch Interview

[43] Ibid

[44] Ibid

[45] "The Rise and Fall of the Fifth Beatle", 9

[46] Harris Interview

[47] Ibid

[48] Nicol, Teutsch Interview

[49] Hodkinson Interview

[50] Ringo Starr, *Beatles Anthology* DVD

[51] "Jimmy the Cockney stands in for Ringo", by Don Short, *Daily Mirror*, June 4, 1964, 3

Chapter Ten
Beatle Jimmy Nicol: Denmark & the Netherlands

[i] Nicol, Teutsch Interview

[ii] "He Said What He Thought About The Beatles", 2

[i2] "A wonderful, wonderful welcome in Copenhagen!", by Don Short, *Daily Mirror*, June 5, 1964, 10

3-missing

4-missing? or is it below

[i4?] Edited by Johnny Dean, **The Best of The Beatles Book**, (London: Beat publications Ltd 2005) , 85

[5] Email from Neil Aspinall to Author (April 5, 2006)

[6] Johnny Dean, 85

[7] Ibid, 85

[8] Torben Sardorf Interview with Author (January 31, 2006)

[9] Andy Babiuk, 132

[10] Sardorf Interview

[11] Ibid

[12] Ibid

[13] Ibid

[14] Ibid

[15] Ibid

[16] Ibid

[17] W. Fraser Sandercombe, **The Beatles: The Press Reports**, (Toronto: Collector's Guide Publishing, 2007) 65, (taken from *Disc Weekly*, June 13, 1864)

[18] Ibid, 65

[19] Bill Harry, **The Ultimate Beatles Encyclopedia**, (NYC: Hyperion, 1992), 484

[20] "*Welcome... those Dutch girls say it with kisses*", by Don Short, *Daily Mirror*, June 6, 1964, 9

[21] Azing Moltmaker, **The Beatles in Netherlands 1964-1993**, (Holland: Foundation Beatles Fan, 1999), 29

[22] Ibid, 29

[23] Ibid, 75

[24] VARA-TV, Treslong Hillegom, Netherlands, June 4, 1964

[25] Moltmaker, 128

[26] "John Lennon Interview", by Jann Wenner, *Rolling Stone,* RS74, January 21, 1971

[27] Nicol, Teutsch Interview

[28] Moltmaker, 49

[29] British Pathé Newsreel, (June, 1964)

[30] Moltmaker, 377

[31] "Oscar Rexhauser, Legend of the Indo-Rock – from Surabaya to Holland", by Walentina Waluyanti, www.storyofindorock.nl, 3/27/09, 2

[32] Newsreel, June, 1964

[33] Nicol, Teutsch Interview

[34] Stanoch

[35] Ibid

[36] Moltmaker, 127

[37] Ibid, 61

[38] Ibid, 369

[39] Nicol, Teutsch Interview

Chapter Eleven
Beatles Jimmy Nicol: Hong Kong

[1] "Hold That Jet! BOAC Wait For The Beatles", *Daily Mirror*, (June 8, 1964) 11

[2] Ibid, 11

[3] Glenn A. Baker, **The Beatles Downunder: The 1964 Australia and New Zealand Tour**, (Ypsilanti: Pierian Press, 1986), 21

[4] Tony Sheridan Interview with Author, (October 27, 2010)

[5] Baker, 21

[6] Ibid

[7] "Ray Cordeiro remembers The Beatles' First Asian concert", by Ray Cordeiro, *BC Magazine*, Issue 283, ww.bcmagazine.net/hk.bcmagazine.issues/bcmagazine_webissue283/02-uncle%20ray.html , August, 2009, 2

[8] Baker, 22

[9] "Jimmy in 'Pool", by Bill Harry, *Mersey Beat* No. 84, July 16, 1964, 2

[10] *The Beatles Tapes IV: Hong Kong* CD

[11] Ibid

[12] Ibid

[13] Ibid

[14] Ibid

[15] Ibid

[16] Ibid

[17] Ibid

[18] Ibid

[19] Ibid

[20] Ibid

[21] Cordeiro, 3

[22] Nicol, Holland Interview

[23] Ibid

[24] Tony barrow, **John, Paul George, Ringo & Me, The Real Beatles Story**, (NYC: Thunder's Mouth Press, New York, 2005), 132

[25] *The Beatles Anthology* DVD

[26] Harris Interview

[27] *Talk Downunder Vol. 1*, LP, Raven, 1984

Chapter Twelve
Beatle Jimmy Nicol: Sydney, Australia

[1] Talk Downunder Vol. 1 LP

[2] Nicol, Holland Convention Interview

[3] Talk Downunder Vol. 1 LP

[4] Tony Newman Interview with Author (May 11, 2011)

[5] Talk Downunder Vol. 1 LP

[6] Ibid

[7] W. Fraser Sandercombe, 64

[8] Australian TV Newsreel, June 11, 1964

[9] "Squeals for rain-lashed Beatles", *Daily Mirror*, June 11, 1964, 2.

[10] Baker, 24

[11] Ibid, 22

[12] National News, TV Newsreel, June 11, 1964

[13] Baker, 35

[14] Tony Newman Interview

[15] Ibid

[16] "Venues-Chequers", www.milesago.com/venues/chequers/htm, April 3, 2011, 1

[17] Beatles Adelaide Press Conference, June 12, 1964

[18] Ibid

[19] Talk Downunder LP Vol. 1

[20] Baker, 34

[21] Talk Downunder LP Vol. 1

[22] Beatles Adelaide Press Conference

[23] British Pathé Newsreel, June 11, 1964

[24] "Ringo's out – and off!", *Daily Mirror*, June 12, 1964, 5

[25] "Ringo's days in hospital are not over- he says", by Cordell Markes, *NME*, June 19, 1964, 2

[26] Discs Pop Thirty, *Daily Mirror*, June 11, 1964, 21

Chapter Thirteen
Beatle Jimmy Nicol: Adelaide, Melbourne & the End

[1] Baker, 39

[2] "Bound For South Australia" By Bob Francis, *In Time* , Australia Broadcasting Corporation, www.abc.net.au, 2005

[3] Newman Interview

[4] The Beatles Anthology DVD

[5] Beatles Adelaide Press Conference, June 12, 1964

[6] The Beatles Anthology DVD

[7] Ibid

[8] Ibid

[9] Australia TV Newsreel, June 12, 1964

[10] Baker, 44

[11] "Beatles and the girls", *Sunday Mail- Adelaide*, June 13, 1964, 7

[12] "Let Me See Him… Just Once!", *Sunday Mail- Adelaide*, (June 13, 1964) 1

[13] Mark Lewisohn, **The Complete Beatles Chronicle**, (London: Hamlyn, 2004), 163

[14] Baker, 90

[15] Ibid, 94

[16] Nicol, Teutsch Interview
[17] "Beatle Saturday", *Sunday Mail- Adelaide*, (June 13, 1964), 96
[18] Ibid, 96
[19] Newman Interview
[20] Johnny Chester Interview with Author, (May 27, 2011)
[21] Ibid
[22] Chester Interview
[23] Baker, 95
[24] Sandercombe, 66
[25] Baker, 35
[26] Ibid, 35
[27] Nicol, Teutsch Interview
[28] Baker, 45
[29] Baker, 36
[30] Baker, 36
[31] John C. Winn , **Way Beyond Compare, the Beatles' Recorded Legacy volume one 1957-1965**, Multi-plus Books, Sharon, VT, (2003) , 212
[32] Talk Downunder Vol. 1 LP
[33] Nicol, Teutsch Interview
[34] Winn, 21
[35] Sandercombe, 67
[36] "The Beatles' Interviews", by Gavin Rutherford, 2SM, Sydney, CD Newsound 2000, track 9, (June 14, 1964,)
[37] "Ringo Starr Interview", Mascot Airport Sydney, *Fab 4 CD & Book Set*, Master Tone Multimedia Ltd., 1997 (June 14, 1964)
[38] Baker, 50
[39] John Williams, **The Fortunate Life of a Vindicatrix Boy**, (Charleston: Booksurge Group, 2005) 68
[40] Ibid, 68
[41] Channel 7 TV News broadcast, Melbourne, June 14, 1964
[42] "450 Hurt in Biggest Beatle Riot", *Daily Mirror*, June 15, 1964, 12
[43] Channel 7 TV News broadcast
[44] "Beatles Will Never Forget This Scene", by Brian Epstein, *NME*, June 26, 1964, 3
[45] Ibid
[46] John Williams, 68
[47] Harris Interview
[48] Baker, 57
[49] Nicol, Teutsch Interview
[50] John C. Winn , 216
[51] "Why I Had To Blast The Beatles", by Devon Minchin, *Australia Daily Mail*, June 8, 2003
[52] Ibid
[53] Harris Interview
[54] Ibid
[55] Nicol, Holland Interview
[56] Ibid
[57] Melbourne Newsreel TV footage, June 15, 1964
[58] Newman Interview
[59] Baker, 58

Chapter Fourteen
Jimmy Nicol & the Shubdubs

[1] Nicol, Holland Interview
[2] "The Beatles", by Derek Taylor, *Los Angeles Times*, May 1967
[3] Nicol, Holland Interview
[4] Hodkinson Interview
[5] Harris Interview

[6] Ibid
[7] Ibid
[8] Ibid
[9] Ibid
[10] Ibid
[11] Ibid
[12] Hodkinson Interview
[13] "Fame", 3
[14] *Beatles Book Monthly*, No. 99, July, 1964, 12
[15] Stanoch
[16] "The Rise and Fall of the Fifth Beatle", by Don Short, *Daily Mail*, April 30, 1965, 9
[17] "Jim Plans To Rival Beatles", *Daily Mirror*, June 16, 1964, 1
[18] "NME Exclusive: Jimmy Nicol tells about his fantastic BEATLES' CAPERS!", by Richard Green, *NME*, June 19, 1964, 2
[19] Ibid, 2
[20] Ibid, 2
[21] Ibid, 2
[22] Ibid, 2
[23] "Dave ill-so Jimmy is top of the CROCKS again!", by Patrick Doncaster, *Daily Mirror*, June 19, 1964, 4
[24] Harris Interview
[25] Ibid
[26] "Dave ill…", 4
[27] Ibid
[28] Dave Quincy Interview with Author (November 3, 2005)
[29] "The Rise and Fall", 9
[30] "London News", *Billboard*, July 4, 1964, 43
[31] Quincy Interview
[32] Green Interview
[33] Ibid
[34] "Meet Jimmy's Shubdubs", by Paul East, *NME*, June 26, 1964, 16
[35] "Dave Clark", *NME*, June 26, 1964, 8
[36] "Meet Jimmy's Shubdubs", 16
[37] Ibid
[38] Ibid
[39] Ibid
[40] Hodkinson Interview
[41] Nicol, Teutsch Interview
[42] Harris Interview
[43] Hodkinson Interview
[44] Quincy Interview
[45] Harris Interview
[46] Ibid
[47] Ibid
[48] Nicol, Teutsch Interview
[49] Harris Interview
[50] Ibid
[51] "Jimmy in 'Pool", By Bill Harry, *Mersey Beat*, July 16, 1964, 2
[52] Ibid
[53] Ibid
[54] Ibid
[55] Ibid
[56] Quincy Interview
[57] Baker, 122
[58] "Beatles No 5 Accused", *Daily Mirror*, September 2, 1964, 18
[59] Quincy Interview
[60] "Hollies-Millie-Lulu Tour in the Autumn", *NME*, June 26, 1964, 8

[61] "It's Hello From Them", *Mojo*, Issue 219, February, 2012, 33, (Original publication February 5, 1965)
[62] "Famous Without The Beatles", *Aktuelt newspaper*, October 30, 1964
[63] "The Fifth Beatle to Denmark", *Aktuelt newspaper*, October 31, 1964
[64] Lars Akerstrom, 151
[65] Quincy Interview
[66] Ibid
[67] Harris Interview
[68] "The Rise And Fall…", 9
[69] Hodkinson Interview
[70] Tony Bramwell Interview with Author (March 5, 2012)

Chapter Fifteen
The Sound of Jimmy Nicol

[1] Kruger, Interview
[2] Graham Nash Interview with Author, (June 20, 2011)
[3] Ibid
[4] "The seventy-two minute haircut…", by Patrick Doncaster, Discs, *Daily Mirror*, January 7, 1965, 11
[5] ibid
[6] Ibid
[7] "He Said What He Thought about The Beatles", 3
[8] Hodkinson Interview
[9] "Jimmy Nicol", The Rex North Column, *Daily Mirror*, January 18, 1965, 11
[10] Ibid
[11] Ibid
[12] "High Dudgeon", by Sam Inglis, *Sound on Sound*, July, 2001, www.soundonsound.com/sos/Jul1/articles/gusd-udgeon
[13] Stanoch
[14] "Clementine", *Decca News Press Singles* PR sheet, F 12107, March 19, 1965, 2
[15] "High Dudgeon"
[16] "Clementine", 1
[17] Ibid
[18] "Disc Column", by Patrick Doncaster, *Daily Mirror*, March 18, 1965, 23
[19] "Singles", *NME*, No. 949, March 19, 1965, 4
[20] Nicol, Holland Interview
[21] Ibid
[22] "The Rise and Fall…", 9
[23] Ibid
[24] Ibid
[25] Ibid
[26] Ibid
[27] Ibid
[28] "The Fifth Beatles-Job Hunting", *Daily Mirror*, May 5, 1965, 9
[29] Gordon Waller Interview with Author, (March 29, 2004)
[30] Hodkinson Interview

Chapter Sixteen
From Oblivion To Outer Space

[1] "Spotnicks History", www.spotnicks.net , 1
[2] Bo Winberg Interview with Author (August 22, 2005)
[3] "Spotnicks History", 1
[4] "Discography", www.spotnicks.net , 1
[5] Winberg Interview
[6] Ibid
[7] Lars Akerstrom, 151
[8] "The Spotnicks – A Quarter Century of Space Pop", produced by Hans Siden, Swedish TV documentary

December, 1983

[9] Akerstrom, 151

[10] Peter Winsnes Interview with Author (February 24, 2011)

[11] Bob Starander Interview with Author (April 18, 2012)

[12] "The Spotnicks – A Quarter Century of Space Pop"

[13] Ibid

[14] Winsnes Interview

[15] "He Said What He Thought about The Beatles", 3

[16] Lars Akerstrom, 152

[17] Winsnes Interview

[18] "The Spotnicks – A Quarter Century of Space Pop"

[19] Starander Interview

[20] Stanoch

[21] Ibid

[22] Ibid

[23] Winsnes Interview

[24] Lars Akerstrom, 152

[25] Ibid, 153

[26] "Success For Spotnicks – Memorable Night at The Concert House", People in Motion Section, *Göteborgs-Posten*, November 23, 1965 , 1

[27] Winsnes Interview

[28] Starander Interview

[29] Winsnes Interview

[30] Lars Akerstrom, 156

[31] Ibid, 159

[32] "The Spotnicks Shaky?", *Mexico City Newspaper*, December 10, 1965, 2

[33] "Happy Inauguration of the New Señorial", *Audiomusica*, Dec. 15, 1965, 1

[34] Lars Akerstrom, 160

[35] "Swedish Disk Tops List", *Billboard*, January 15, 1966, 20

[36] Winsnes Interview

[37] Winberg Interview

[38] Winsnes Interview

[39] Ibid

[40] "International News Reports", *Billboard*, February 5, 1966, 36

[41] Lars Akerstrom, 164

[42] Ibid, 165

[43] Winsnes Interview

[44] Lars Akerstrom, 165

Chapter Seventeen
The Spotnicks

[1] Lars Akerstrom, 179

[2] Ibid, 179

[3] Ibid, 179

[4] "International News", *Billboard*, April 9, 1966, 52

[5] "He Said What he Thought about the Beatles", 3

[6] "Today's Pop Genius, His Pop Brought the Astronaut to Tears", by Lennart Clerwall, People in Motion Section, *Göteborgs-Posten*, April 27, 1966, 1

[7] Ibid

[8] Ibid

[9] Lars Akerstrom, 181

[10] Ibid

[11] Ibid

[12] "He Said What He Thought About The Beatles", 5

[13] *Hong Kong Blues*, Lyrics by Hoagy Carmichael, Hoagy Publishing Co., September 6, 1939

[14] Winsnes Interview

[15] Ibid

[16] Lars Akerstrom, 183

[17] Ibid

[18] Ibid

[19] Ibid, 187

[20] Winsnes Interview

[21] Ibid

[22] Starander Interview

[23] Winsnes Interview

[24] Lars Akerstrom, 188

[25] Winberg Interview

[26] Winsnes Interview

[27] Ibid

Chapter 18
Mexico

[1] Ibid

[2] "The Symbiotic Origin of Jazz and Rock in Mexico", by Federico Rubli Kaiser, Mexico, DF, 2007, 14

[3] "After Avandaro: the black hole of the Mexican Rock", by Manual Martinez, Pelaez, www.maph49.ga-leon.com, August 2, 2012, 1

[4] Swe Disc press release, (March, 1967) 1

[5] Ibid

[6] Ibid

[7] "Swe Disc is Hot in Mexico via Moonlighters", Mexico City, *Billboard*, December 23, 1967, 32

[8] Jeremy Sandford, 6

[9] Craig Cross, **The Beatles: Day-By-Day, Song-By-Song, Record-By-Record**, (iUniverse Inc., May 14, 2005), 352

[10] Barry Miles, **Paul McCartney: Many Years From Now**, (NYC: Holt Paperbacks, Oct, 15, 1998), 313

[11] Ibid

[12] *Getting Better*, lyrics by John Lennon & Paul McCartney, Sony/ATV Publishing, (© 1967)

[13] "Image Battle Shapes In Mexico As Firms Gear for 'Tomorrow'", by Kevin M. Kelleghan, *Billboard*, July 22,1967, 49

[14] Ibid

[15] Ibid

[16] Ibid, 50

[17] Ibid, 49

[18] "RCA International Firms Latin American Ties in Precedential Mexico Meet" by Otto Mayer-Serra, *Billboard*, January 29, 1966, 4

[19] "Dynagroove", www.tronola.com/html/dynagroove.html, December 5,2011, 1

[20] "Liner Notes", *Los NicolQuinn* LP, by Jimmie Nicol and Eddie Quinn, RCA Victor CAMS-276, (July, 1966)

[21] "Mexico City", *Billboard*, July 22, 1967, 52

[22] *I'm Lost*, lyrics by E. Quinn and J. Nicol, Los Nicolquinn, RCA Mexicana, (1967)

[23] *Whims and Fancies*, lyrics by E. Quinn and J. Nicol, Los Nicolquinn, RCA Mexicana, (1967)

[24] Stanoch

[25] Ibid

[26] "Liner Notes"

[27] Ibid

[28] Catherine Bloch, "Columnista Invitado: El Mes *Más* Cruel", rev. of **El Mes Màs Cruel**, dir. Carlos Lozano Dana, www.filmeweb.net/magazine, December 1, 2006, 1-2

Chapter Nineteen
Julia and the Aesthetics of Revolt

[1] Julia Villaseñor Interview with Author, (December 6, 2011)
[2] Ibid
[3] Ibid
[4] Ibid
[5] Ibid
[6] Ibid
[7] Ibid
[8] Ibid
[9] Ibid
[10] Ibid
[11] Ibid
[12] "Australia news", by Jock Veitch, *Billboard*, December 30, 1967, 31
[13] Jeremy Sandford, 6
[14] Villaseñor Interview
[15] Ibid
[16] Ibid
[17] Ibid
[18] "Biography Los Checkmates", www.last.fm/musci/Los+Checkmates/+wiki, November 17, 2011, 1
[19] Villaseñor Interview
[20] Ibid
[21] Ibid
[22] Ibid
[23] Ibid
[24] "The Rise and Fall of 'La Onda Chicana: Mexico's First Original Rock Movement", by Federico Rubli Kaiser, Presented to the **Latin American Studies Center**, University of Maryland, April 13, 2011, 1
[25] Villaseñor Interview
[26] Ibid
[27] Ibid
[28] Ibid
[29] **Get Back/ Let It Be**, Filmed Recording session tapes (unreleased), Camera Roll/ Nagra tape reel 6A, January 2, 1969
[30] Ibid
[31] Villaseñor Interview
[32] Ibid
[33] Ibid
[34] Zev Toledano, "Anticlimax", rev. of **Anticlimax**, dir. Gelsen Gas, www.thelastexit.net , January 5, 2011, 1
[35] Villaseñor Interview
[36] Ibid
[37] Ibid
[38] Ibid
[39] Ibid
[40] Ibid
[41] Ibid
[42] Ibid
[43] Ibid
[44] "Flying Karpets 1968", by Dr. Schluss, www.psychedelicobscurities.blogspot.com , 2009, 1
[45] "Cocktail Pop: Blue Rain Has An Ex-Beatle", *Mexico Canta*, Issue 523-322, April 23, 1971, 38
[46] Ibid, 37
[47] Ibid, 39
[48] Ibid, 37
[49] Ibid, 38
[50] Ibid
[51] Ibid
[52] Ibid

Chapter 20
Lost and Found

[1] "Cocktail Pop", 38

[2] Villaseñor Interview

[3] Liner Notes, *Los Nicolquinn* LP

[4] Nicol, Teutsch Interview

[5] Nicol, Holland Interview 1984

[6] Ibid

[7] Ibid

[8] Hodkinson Interview

[9] Ibid

[10] "Howie Nicol – Sound Recordist profile", www.fabsound.co.uk, August 15, 2005

[11] Winsnes Interview

[12] Lars Akerstrom, 264

[13] Koop Geersing Interview with Author, (August 11, 2005)

[14] Ibid

[15] Nicol, Holland Interview

[16] Ibid

[17] Ibid

[18] Geersing Interview

[19] Nicol, Holland Interview

[20] Ibid

[21] Ibid

[22] Micha Hasfeld of The Clarks, Interview with Author, (June 10, 2011)

[23] Ibid

[24] Ibid

[25] Ibid

[26] Geersing Interview

[27] Nicol, Holland Interview 1984

[28] Ibid

[29] Ibid

[30] Ibid

[31] "Howie Nicol – Sound Recordist profile"

[32] Nicol, Teutsch Interview

[33] "Life Moves to a slower beat for Beatles' forgotten drummer", by Jonathan Este in London, *The Australian*, May 29, 2004, 2

[34] René Van Haarlan Interview with Author (May 2, 2012)

[35] Ibid

Chapter Twenty-One
Wanted: Dead or Alive

[1] Van Haarlem Interview

[2] Ibid

[3] Ibid

[4] "Howie Nicol profile"

[5] "Nowhere Man as Fab Four's Anthology Rakes In Millions, The Sad Story Of The Penniless & Forgotten Fifth Beatle", by Art McCulloch, *The Mail On Sunday*, September 22, 1996, 1

[6] Ibid

[7] Ibid

[8] Ibid

[9] "Beatle Links Fab Forum", by Dom, http://www.beatlelinks.net/forums/index.php, September 7, 2005

[10] Ibid

[11] Mark Lewisohn Interview with Author, (September 5, 2005)

[12] Jonathan Este Interview with Author, (October 4, 2005)

[13] Ibid

[14] "Life Moves To A Slower Beat For Beatles' Forgotten Drummer", 2

[15] Gavin Rodgers Interview with Author (September 26, 2011)

[16] "John, Paul, George and … Jimmie!", by Paul Harris, *Daily Mail*, (October 1, 2005) 1

[17] Nicol, Holland Interview

[18] Rodgers Interview

[19] "John, Paul, George and… Jimmie!"

[20] Rodgers Interview

[21] "John, Paul, George and… Jimmie!"

[22] "The Jimmy Nicols", www.triplejunearthed.com/Artists/View.aspx?artistid=3639

[23] Villaseñor Interview

[24] "Fame", 3

[25] Harris Interview

[26] Green Interview

[27] Starander Interview

[28] Villaseñor Interview

[29] Ibid

[30] Ibid

Epilogue
In Search of Jimmie Nicol

[1] Letter #1990-039.398, **Kenn Brodziak Australian Beatles Tour Collection Archives**, (June 9, 1964)

[2] Letter #1990-039.399, **Kenn Brodziak Australian Beatles Tour Collection Archives**, (June 10, 1964)

[3] Beatles fan "Susan" Interview with Author, (July 10, 2011)

[4] Ibid

[5] Ibid

[6] Brendan Pearse Interview with Author (July 11, 2012)

[7] Ibid

[8] Villaseñor Interview

[9] Ibid

[10] Nicol, Holland Interview

SELECTED BIBLIOGRAPHY

Akerstrom, Lars, **The Spotnicks** Gothenburg: Amapola Production, 2004

Babiuk, Andy, **Beatles Gear**, Milwaukee: Backbeat Books, 2001

Baker, Glenn A., **The Beatles Downunder: The 1964 Australia and New Zealand Tour**, Ypsilanti: Pierian Press, 1986

Barrow, Tony, **John, Paul George, Ringo & Me, The Real Beatles Story**, NYC: Thunder's Mouth Press, 2005

Bennett, Brian, **Drums and Drumming Today**, "The Beat Drummer", London: Boosey & Hawkes, LTD., 1964

Berkenstadt, Jim and Belmo, **Black Market Beatles: The Story Behind The Lost Recordings**, Toronto: CG Publishing, 1995

Block, Catherine, "Columnista Invitado: El Mes Màs Cruel", rev. of **El Mes Màs Cruel**, dir. Carlos Lozano Dana, www.filmeweb.net/magazine , December 1, 2006

Clayson, Alan, **Ringo Starr: Straight Man or Joker**, Tampa: Sanctuary, 1998

"Cocktail Pop: Blue Rain Has An Ex-Beatle", **Mexico Canta**, Issue 523-322, April 23, 1971

Cross, Craig, **The Beatles: Day-By-Day, Song-By-Song, Record-By-Record**, iUniverse Inc., 2005

Dean, Johnny, Editor, **The Best of The Beatles Book**, London: Beat publications Ltd., 2005

Doncaster, Patrick, "Dave ill-so Jimmy is top of the CROCKS again!" **Daily Mirror**, June 19, 1964

Doncaster, Patrick, "The seventy-two minute haircut..." Discs, **Daily Mirror**, January 7, 1965

Epstein, Brian, **A Cellarful of Noise**, London: New English Library, 1965

Este, Jonathan, "Life Moves To A Slower Beat For Beatles' Forgotten Drummer", **The Australian**, May 29, 2004

"Famous Without The Beatles", **Aktuelt** newspaper, October 30, 1964

Frame, Pete, **Rock Family Trees**, Cape Town: Quick Fox, 1979

Gentle, Johnny and Forsyth, Ian, **Johnny Gentle and the Beatles: First Ever Tour - Scotland 1960**, Runcorn: Merseyrock Publications, 1988

Green, Richard, "NME Exclusive: Jimmy Nicol tells about his fantastic BEATLES' CAPERS!" **New Musical Express**, June 19, 1964

Harry, Bill, **The Ultimate Beatles Encyclopedia**, NYC: Hyperion, 1992

Hayward, Mark and Badman, Keith, **The Beatles Unseen** NYC: Barnes and Noble, 2005

"He Said What He Thought About The Beatles", **Vi Unge Magazine**, April 1, 1966

Hewitt, Paolo, "Georgie Fame", www.georgiefame.absoluteelsewhere.net/index.html , 2004

"It's Tough at the Bottom", **Radio Luxemburg Annual**, 1965

"Jim Plans To Rival The Beatles", **Daily Mirror**, June 16, 1964

Kelleghan, Kevin M., "Image Battle Shapes In Mexico As Firms Gear for 'Tomorrow'", **Billboard**, July 22, 1967

Kennedy, John, **Tommy Steele**, London: Corgi Books, 1958

Leigh, Spencer, **Things Do Go Wrong: Eddie, Gene and the UK Tour**, London: Finbarr International, 2007

"Let Me See Him… Just Once!", **Sunday Mail-Australia**, June 13, 1964

Lewisohn, Mark, **The Complete Beatles Chronicle**, London: Hamlyn, 2004

McCulloch, Art, "Nowhere Man as Fab Four's Anthology Rakes In Millions, The Sad Story Of The Penniless & Forgotten Fifth Beatle", **The Mail On Sunday**, September 22, 1996

Miles, Barry, **Paul McCartney: Many Years From Now**, NYC: Holt, 1993

Moltmaker, Azing, **The Beatles in Netherlands 1964-1993**, Holland: Foundation Beatles Fan, 1999

"Parnes and Kennedy's Latest Vocal Capture", **Record Mirror**, May 24, 1958

"Rock 'n Trad Spectacular – The New Noise of 1960", **New Musical Express**, August 19, 1960

Rubli Kaiser, Federico, "The Symbiotic Origin of Jazz and Rock in Mexico", Mexico, DF, 2007

Rubli Kaiser, Federico, "The Rise and Fall of 'La Onda Chicana: Mexico's First Original Rock Movement", **Latin American Studies Center** lecture, University of Maryland, April 13, 2011

Sandford, Jeremy, **In Search of the Magic Mushroom**, NYC: Clarkson N. Potter, Inc., 1973

Sandercombe, W. Fraser **The Beatles: The Press Reports**, Toronto: Collector's Guide Publishing, 2007

Short, Don, "The Rise and Fall of the Fifth Beatles", **Daily Mirror**, April 30, 1965

Southall, Brian, **A-Z Of Record Labels**, Tampa: Sanctuary Publishing, 2000

"The Fifth Beatles to Denmark", **Aktuelt** newspaper, October 31, 1964

"The Fifth Beatle-Job Hunting", **Daily Mirror**, May 5, 1965

Thompson, Gordon, "British Rock and Pop History", **Skidmore University Lecture**, 2007

Toledano, Zev, "Anticlimax", rev. of **Anticlimax**, dir. Gelsen Gas, www.thelastexit.net, January 5, 2011

Wenner, Jann, "John Lennon Interview", **Rolling Stone**, RS74, Jan 21, 1971

Williams, John, **The Fortunate Life of a Vindicatrix Boy**, Charleston: BookSurge Group, 2005

Winn, John C., **Way Beyond Compare: The Beatles' Recorded Legacy Volume One 1957-1965**, Sharon: Multiplus Books, 2003

Wooldridge, Max, **Rock 'N' Roll London**, NYC: St. Martin's/ Griffin, 2002

JIMMIE NICOL'S CAREER DISCOGRAPHY

Colin Hicks & The Cabin Boys

1958 UK TV
"Giddy-Up-A-Ding Dong"

<u>Films</u>
1959
Europa Di Notte (aka: Europe By Night)

"Baby I Love You"
"Twenty Flight Rock"
"Iea Iea"

<u>Euro Singles/ EPs</u>	Label
1957 45 rpm	
"Empty Arm Blues"	
"Wild Eyes and Tender Lips"	Pye 7N1514
1958 EP	
"Johnny B. Good"	
"Mean Woman Blues"	
"Tutti Frutti"	
"Whole Lotta Shaking Going On"	Broadway EPB 104
1958 45 rpm	
"Johnny B. Good"	
"Sexy Rock"	Broadway B 1028
1958 EP	
"Iea Iea"	
"Oh Boy"	
"Book Of Love"	
"20 Flight Rocks"	Broadway EPB 106
1958 45 rpm	
"Oh Boy"	
"Rock And Roll Shoes"	Broadway B 1023

Colin Hicks & The Cabin Boys
1994 CD
Colin Hicks Anthology 1957-1961
(1958)Tracks:
"Empty Arm Blues"
"Wild Eyes and Tender Lips"
"La Dee Dah"
"Wasteland"
"Jambalaya"
"Little Boy Blue"
"Johnny Be Good"
"Mean Woman Blues"
"Tutti Frutti"
"Iea Iea"
"Oh Boy"
"Book of Love"
"Twenty Flight Rock"
Records

1998
"Wild Eyes and Tender Lips"

	Label
"Twenty Flight Rock"	Rockin' Ghost
	RGR-500-RA
"Wild Eyes and Tender Lips"	Sequel NEMCD 985

Vince Eager & the Quiet Three
(No recordings made)

Jimmy Nicol and His 15 New Orleans Rockers
(No recordings made)

Oscar Rabin Big Band with David Ede

Radio Broadcasts
1960 "Go Man Go" BBC radio
1960 "Saturday Club" BBC radio
1961 "Go Man Go" BBC radio
1961 "Saturday Club" BBC radio
1962 "Go Man Go" BBC radio
1962 "Saturday Club" BBC radio

2 I's House Trio
(No recordings made)

Cyril Stapleton Big Band   **(No recordings made)**

TOP SIX RECORDS	Label
<u>Singles/ EPs</u>	**1964** EP:
"Glad All Over"	
"I'm The One"	
"Needles And Pins"	
"I Want To Hold Your Hand"	
"Twenty Four Hours From Tulsa"	
"Hippy Hippy Shake"	Top Six – Six1

1964 EP
"Bits And Pieces"
"Little Children"
"I'm The Lonely One"
"Anyone Who Had A Heart"
"5-4-3-2-1"
"Over You"   Top Six – Six2

1964 EP
"Can't Buy Me Love"
"Just One Look"
"Boys Cry"
"Tell Me When"
"Not Fade Away"
"I Believe"   Top Six – Six3

1964 EP
"Don't Throw Your Love Away"
"Hubble Bubble (Toil And Trouble)"
"World Without Love"
"Don't Let The Sun Catch You Crying"
"Everything's Al'Right"
"Don't Turn Around"   Top Six – Six4

<u>Singles/ EPs</u>
1964 EP *Beatle Mania Special*
"She Loves You"
"Twist and Shout"
"Please Please Me"
"I Wanna (sic) Hold Your Hand"
"From Me To You"
"Love Me Do"   Top Six – T6508

<u>LPs</u>
1964 LP

Beatlemania
"I Want To Hold Your Hand"

	Label
"Roll Over Beethoven"	
"From Me To You"	
"Till There Was You"	
"Please Mr. Postman"	
"Twist And Shout"	
"All My Loving"	
"She Loves You"	
"I Wanna Be Your Man"	
"Love Me Do"	
"Please Please Me"	
"Money"	Top Six – TSL1

Jimmy Nicol & the Shubdubs (Pre-Beatles)

Singles/EPs

1964 45 rpm
"Humpty Dumpty"
"Night Train"   Pye – 7N15623 (UK)

1964 45 rpm
"Humpty Dumpty"
"Night Train"   Mar-Mar 313 (US)

The Beazers
(Chris Farlowe, Jimmie Nicol, Tex Makins & the Cyril Stapleton Big Band)

Singles/ EPs
1964 45 rpm
"Blue Beat"
"I Wanna Shout"   Decca – F11827

2001 CD
Chris Farlowe &The Thunderbirds
Dig The Buzzzzzzz

Tracks:
"Blue Beat"
"I Wanna Shout"   Cherry Records
                                                 RPM 220

Tommy Quickly
1964 45 rpm
"You Might As Well Forget Him" (aka: "Walk The Streets")

                                                 Piccadilly – 7N35183

Film	**Label**
1964	
Brian Epstein – Panorama	
(Tommy Quickly recording session)	BBC Panorama
Georgie Fame & the Blue Flames	**(No recordings**
made)	
The Beatles (with Jimmie Nicol)	
(No official recordings made)	

Concerts

Date:	Location:

June 04, 1964: K.B. Hallen, Tivoli Gardens, Copenhagen, Denmark (2 shows)
June 05, 1964: Treslong, Hilversum, Holland, (recording TV show, VARA)
June 06, 1964: Auction Hall (Veilinghal), Blokker, Holland (2 shows)
June 09, 1964: Princess Theatre, Kowloon, Hong Kong (2 shows)
June 12, 1964: Centennial Hall, Adelaide, Australia (2 shows)
June 13, 1964: Centennial Hall, Adelaide, Australia (2 shows)

Film/ DVD

1964/2003 DVD

The Beatles Anthology 3 & 4	Apple/Capitol
	C9 7243 4 92977 9 1

1964 DVD

The Beatles Take Over Holland 1964 World Tour I (Volume 1)	Fake Apple/Capitol
The Beatles Down Under World Tour I (Volume 2) The Beatles In Australia	Fake Apple/Capitol
The Beatles A Long And Winding Road (Episode 4)	Passport DVD5524
Fun With The Fab Four	Goodtimes DVD 05-

81384

1964 CDs
Bootlegs

The Beatles and Jimmy Nicol	DP 1
Beatles: Danmark & Nederland June 1964	Why Not WN 3002
The Live Beatles – Australia 1964	Bulldog BGCD 156
The Beatles Adelaide Reaction	Purple Chick
	PC-163164

1964 LP **Bootleg**	Label
Euphoria In Australia	Document Records DR 018 LP

Singles
1964/1983 45 rpm
The Beatles In Holland   Beatle Fan Records
                                                         BFR 19781983

1964 45 rpm PD
Euphoria In Australia   Document Records
                                                         DR 1806

Interviews**:**

The Beatles Tapes III: The 1964 World Tour   Jerden JRCD 7041

The Beatles Tapes IV: Hong Kong 1964   Jerden JRCD 7042

The Beatles Talk Down Under Volume 1   Raven RVLP 1002

The Beatles Talk Down Under Volume 2   Raven RVLP 1013

The Beatles' Interviews 1 & 2   Newsound 2000

Los Trovadores Tropicales (Amsterdam 1964)
(No Recordings)

Frances Faye (Sydney 1964)
(No Recordings)

Jimmy Nicol & the Shubdubs (Post-Beatles)
Singles/EPs
1964 45 rpm
"Husky"
"Please Come Back"   Pye 7N15666

1964 45 rpm
"Baby Please Don't Go"
"Shubdubery"   Pye 7N15699

Jimmy Nicol & the Shubdubs (Post-Beatles)
CDs

1964/1994
Instrumental Diamonds Vol. 2
Tracks:
"Husky"   Sequel Mex CD 150

The Sound Of Jimmy Nicol

Singles
1965 45 rpm
"Sweet Clementine"
"Bim Bam"   Decca F 12107

1965 45 rpm
"Sweet Clementine"
"Roaring Blue"   Parrot Par 9752

CDs
1965/2009
Roaring Blue

Tracks:
"Roaring Blue"   Psychic Circle
                                                                    PCCD 7028

Peter & Gordon – (1965)
(Unknown recordings)

The Spotnicks (1965-1967)
45 rpm
1965
Spotnicks Introducing Jimmie Nicol

"Husky"
"Drum Diddley"   Swe Disc SWES 1111

LP/CD	Label

1966 LP
The Spotnicks in Tokyo

Tracks:
"Autumn in Japan"
"Memory of Summer"
"The Spotnicks in Tokyo"
"Look up to the Evening Star"
"Drum Diddley"
"The Old Love Letters"
"Piercing The Unknown"
"Playboy's Bunny Hop"
"Crying in a Storm"
"From Russia With Love"
"Happy Silence"
"Ode to Dawn"
"The Lonesome Port"
"Husky"
"Sentimental Guitar"
"Recado"
"Mood of Asia"   Swe Disc SWELP
C38

1966 45 rpm
"Sentimental Guitar"
"Piercing the Unknown"   Polydor DP-1477

1966 LP
Spotnicks Around The World

Tracks:
"Casting My Spell"
"Geisha Girl"
"Green Eyes"
"Hong Kong Blues"
"Mood of Asia"
"Plattlaggen"
"Recado"
"Sentimental Guitar"
"Steel Guitar Rag"
"Subject in Orbit"
"Turista", "Uska Dara"
"What Now My Love"
"Worrying Kind"
"Ach Du Lieber Agustin" (Outtake)   Swe Disc SWELP
C42

LP/CD	Label

1966 LP rpm
The Spotnicks in Winterland
Tracks:
"Auld Lang Syne"
"Frosty the Snowman"
"Here Comes Santa Claus"
"I Saw Mama Kissing Santa Claus"
"Jingle Bells"
"Parade of the Wooden Soldiers"
"Rudolph the Red-Nosed Reindeer"
"Silent Night"
"Sleigh Ride"
"White Christmas"
"Winter Wonderland"
"Winterland"   Swe Disc SWELP
C48

45 rpm
1966
 (Artist name: "James George" aka: Jimmie Nicol & the Spotnicks)
(Nicol on lead vocals – both tracks)

"C'mon Everybody"
"Stagger Lee"   Swe Disc SWES 1160

1966 LP
The Spotnicks Live In Japan

Tracks:
"Crying in a Storm"
"Happy Silence"
"Hava Nagila"
"Hey Good Looking"
"Johnny Guitar"
"Karelia"
"Last Space Train"
"Look Up to the Evening Star"
"Memory of Summer"
"Over and Over"
"The Spotnicks Theme"
"Wabash Cannon Ball"
"What Did I Say"
"When the Saints Go Marching In)"   Swe Disc SWELP
C53

1967 LP   <u>Label</u>
In Acapulco Mexico
(Nicol only played on five tracks)
Tracks:
"Suspicion"
"La Pachava"
"Wham"
"El Toro Bravo"
"Moscow"   Swe Disc SWELP
C60

Los Nicolquinn (Mexico 1967)
<u>LP</u>
1967
Los Nicolquinn
Tracks:
"Cuando El Sol Cae" (aka: "When The Sun Goes Down")
"Mas Alla De Mi Vida" (aka: "Beyond My Life")
"Estoy Perdido" (aka: "I'm Lost")
"La Misma Vieja Forma" (aka: "The Same Old Way")
"Sol Negro" (aka: "Black Sun")
"Antojos" (aka: "Whims and Fancies")
"Facil" (aka: "Easy")
"Estoy En Camino" (aka: "I'm On My Way")
"Desonocido" (aka: "Unknown")
"Algo Tonto" (aka: "Something Stupid")   RCA Victor Mexicana
CAMS-276

El Mes Màs Cruel
(Mexico) 1967/1969
Film Score (Unreleased)
By Jimmie Nicol and Eduardo Salas

The Jimmie Nicol Trio
(With Julia Villaseñor)
(Mexico) 1967-1968
(No known recordings)

Los Checkmates
(Mexico) 1968
(No known recordings)

Anticlimax
(Mexico) 1969
Film Score (Unreleased)
By Jimmie Nichol [sic] and Gelsen Gas

TV Musical Ossart band
(Mexico) 1969
(No known recordings)

Abraxas   <u>Label</u>

(Mexico) 1969
(No Known Recordings)

The Jimmy Nicol Show (Mexico)   <u>LP</u>

1969
Era Psicodelica Del A Go Go (aka: *The Psychedelic Go Go Era*)   Orfeón LP-E-12-623
Tracks:
"Jumpin' Jack Flash" (sung in Spanish)

Blue Rain
(Mexico) 1970-71
(No known recordings)

<u>LP</u>
1984
De Bietels Tussen De Bollen
"Radio-Verslag Schiphol 5 June 1964"
"AVRO's radio journal 5 June 1964"
"Polygoon Bioscoop journal met P. Bloemdal"
"Radio-verslag opname TV Show Treslong Hillegom 5 June 1964
VARA"
"TV interview Beatles met Jimmy Nicol"
"Vervolg TV interview 7, Radio-verslag Blokker
middagconcert KRO 6 June 1964"
"Impressies uit de zall avondconcert in Blokker,
6 June 1964: I Saw Her Standing There, I Want
To Hold Your Hand, All My Loving, She Loves
You (live met Jimmy Nicol)   Beatles Unlimited
BU1-1984

The Clarks (guest drummer, Holland 1984)
(No Known Recordings)

PERMISSIONS AND CREDITS

Photos

Layout Cover Photo (drum case): Brian Ebner, Optic Nerve LLC, ©2012 Jim Berkenstadt

Cover Photo - Jimmie Nicol with Beatles: © Mirrorpix: cover

Back Cover Photo - Jimmie Nicol with Beatles: © Newspix/ Photo File

Every effort has been made to acknowledge all those whose photographs and illustrations have been used in this volume, but if there have been any omissions in this respect, we apologize and will be pleased to make the appropriate acknowledgement in any future editions.

INDEX

LSD, 167

M

Mabellene, 36
Makins, Tex, 7, 40, 57, 61, 66, 67, 202
Martin, George, 7, 11, 13, 14, 62, 69-71, 101
Matalon, David, 7, 36
McCartney, Paul, 13, 45, 67, 69-73, 75, 76, 79, 81, 86, 90, 93, 100, 102, 110, 111, 114, 141, 142, 165, 175, 181, 184, 194, 196
Melbourne press conference, 113
Melotones, 29
Mersey Beat, 128
Mexican Rock, 164, 202
Mood of Asia, 153, 158
Moody's Mood, 67
Moscow, 153, 164

N

Needles And Pins, 57
Newman, Tony, 7, 93, 98, 99, 102, 109, 119
Nicol, Jimmie, 7-11, 13-17, 20-25, 27-30, 33, 35-43, 45-53, 55, 56, 59-63, 65, 67-83, 85-91, 94-97, 99-101, 103, 104, 106, 109-112, 114-119, 121-133, 135, 136, 139-148, 152, 154-158, 160, 162-167, 169-174, 176, 178, 179, 181, 183-191, 193-199, 201-210

O

O'Neil, Mike, 7, 27-29, 34, 36, 65
Old Compton Street, 19, 20, 23, 65, 203
Old Love Letters, 156
Olympic Games, 175
On My Way, 205
Orange Blossom Special, 132, 144

P

Pal Johnny Harris, 52, 72, 124
Parnes, Larry, 23, 24, 27, 38-40, 42, 44-47, 49, 50, 52, 56, 60, 65, 86, 129, 130, 133, 174
Peggy Sue, 156
Phantoms, The, 106, 119
Piercing the Unknown, 156
Platters, The, 7, 33-36
Plattlaggen, 158
Play Rock, 135
Playboy's Bunny Hop, 156
Please, Please Me, 12, 57, 58, 106, 156, 189
Preludins, 86
Princess Theatre, 89
Producer Jack Good, 47, 49
Psychedelic Go-Go album, 178

Q

Quincy, Dave, 7, 124, 125, 127, 129, 130, 132

R

Rabin, Oscar, 49-52, 139
RCA Victor Mexicana, 149, 165, 166, 168
Ready Steady Go, 126, 128
Reformed Shubdubs, 126
Rexhauser, Oscar, 7, 80, 81
Roaring Blue, 138, 139
Roll Over Beethoven, 57, 58, 79, 81, 90, 107, 108
Rolling Stones, The, 51, 67, 126, 137, 139, 179, 188

S

San Miguel, 41
Sardorf, Torben, 7, 74
Saturday Club, 50, 135, 136, 139
'Satyricon', 80
Scotch & Coke, 78
Sentimental Guitar, 153, 158
She Loves You, 12, 56-58, 71, 79, 81, 90, 107
Sheridan, Tony, 7, 40, 85, 86, 194
Shubdubery, 129, 130
Shubdubs, 7, 9, 59, 60, 88, 91, 100, 109, 121-133, 135, 136, 138, 139, 144, 146, 147, 169, 174, 183-185, 197, 198, 204
Silent Night, 157, 160
Silver Beatles, 45
Silverthorne Road, 15, 202
Sounds Incorporated, 7, 89, 93, 102, 106, 109
Southern Cross Hotel, 112-114, 117, 207
Spotnicks, The, 6, 7, 9, 131, 133, 143-153, 155-166, 171, 172, 174, 184, 185, 198, 206
Stagger Lee, 158, 159
Starander, Bob, 7, 143

ABOUT THE AUTHOR

Jim Berkenstadt Credit: © 2011 Narayan Mayhon

Jim Berkenstadt is the Rock And Roll Detective®. A true Sherlock Holmes, Berkenstadt uncovers the lost history and mysteries hidden within decades of popular music. An international authority on The Beatles, he has co-authored three other books: ***Black Market Beatles; The Beatles Digest; Nevermind Nirvana; and edited John, Paul & Me: Before The Beatles.*** Berkenstadt has consulted to The Beatles and the Estate of George Harrison on numerous projects. He lives in Wisconsin.

www.thebeatlewhovanished.com

www.rockandrolldetective.com

QUICK ORDER FORM

Email Orders: info@thebeatlewhovanished.com

Website Orders: www.thebeatlewhovanished.com or www.amazon.com

Postal Orders: Rock And Roll Detective Publishing, c/o Jim Berkenstadt,
4230 East Towne Blvd., No. 254, Madison, WI. 53704 USA. Telephone: 608-250-2627

Please send the following book: <u>The Beatle Who Vanished</u> by Jim Berkenstadt

Quantity_____ copies @ US $20.00 each

Please send more FREE information on:

_____ Speaking Engagements

_____ Consulting

_____ Mailing Lists

Name: _____

Address: _____

City: _____ State: _____ Zip: _____

Telephone: _____

Email Address: _____

<u>Sales Tax: Please add 5.5% for products shipped to Wisconsin addresses.</u>
Shipping
US: $5.00 for first book and $3.00 for each additional book.
International: $15.00 for first book and $6.00 for each additional book (estimate

Made in the USA
San Bernardino, CA
13 June 2013